ENTREPRENEURSHIP IN VIETNAM

The **Nordic Institute of Asian Studies** (NIAS) is funded by the governments of Denmark, Finland, Iceland, Norway and Sweden via the Nordic Council of Ministers, and works to encourage and support Asian studies in the Nordic countries. In so doing, NIAS has been publishing books for the last three decades, with more than one hundred titles produced in the last decade.

The **Institute of Southeast Asian Studies** (ISEAS) was established as an autonomous organization in 1968. It is a regional research centre for scholars and other specialists concerned with modern Southeast Asia, particularly the many-faceted issues and challenges of stability and security, economic development, and political and social change.

The Institute's research programmes are Regional Economic Studies (RES, including ASEAN and APEC), Regional Strategic and Political Studies (RSPS), and Regional Social and Cultural Studies (RSCS).

The Institute is governed by a twenty-two-member Board of Trustees comprising nominees from the Singapore Government, the National University of Singapore, the various Chambers of Commerce, and professional and civic organizations. An Executive Committee oversees day-to-day operations; it is chaired by the Director, the Institute's chief academic and administrative officer.

Entrepreneurship in Vietnam

Transformation and Dynamics

edited by

Per Ronnås and
Bhargavi Ramamurthy

NIAS NORDIC INSTITUTE OF ASIAN STUDIES

ISEAS INSTITUTE OF SOUTHEAST ASIAN STUDIES

First published in 2001 by NIAS Publishing
Nordic Institute of Asian Studies
Leifsgade 33, DK–2300 Copenhagen S, Denmark
tel: (+45) 3254 8844 • fax: (+45) 3296 2530
E–mail: books@nias.ku.dk • Website: http://nias.ku.dk/Books/

First published in 2001 in Singapore by
Institute of Southeast Asian Studies (ISEAS)
30 Heng Mui Keng Terrace, Pasir Panjang, Singapore 119614
E-mail: publish@iseas.edu.sg • Website: http://www.iseas.edu.sg/pub.html
for distribution by ISEAS in the ASEAN countries, Japan, Korea, Taiwan, Australia and New Zealand.

British Library Cataloguing in Publication Data
Entrepreneurship in Vietnam : transformation and dynamics
1. Entrepreneurship - Vietnam 2. Manufacturing industries - Vietnam 3. Vietnam - Economic conditions - 20th century
I. Ronnas, Per. II. Ramamurthy, Bhargavi III. Nordic Institute of Asian Studies
338'.04'09597

ISBN 87-87062-84-4 (NIAS cloth)
ISBN 87-87062-89-5 (NIAS paper)
ISBN 981-230-116-X (ISEAS paper)

Typesetting by the Nordic Institute of Asian Studies
Printed and bound in Singapore by Prime Packaging Industries Pte Ltd

Contents

Figures

Tables

Acknowledgements

The origin of the present study goes back to 1991 when the first major survey ever of the non-state manufacturing sector in Vietnam was undertaken as a collaborative effort between the Asian Regional Team for Employment Promotion of the International Labour Organisation (ILO-ARTEP), Institute of Labour Studies and Social Affairs (ILSSA) of the Ministry of Labour, Invalids and Social Affairs in Vietnam and the Department of International Economics and Geography at Stockholm School of Economics, with generous funding from the Swedish International Development Authority (Sida).[1]

Apart from providing a wealth of information on this sector, the survey also provided a benchmark against which subsequent development could be judged. In 1996, on the initiative of Sida, it was decided to repeat the survey undertaken in 1991. The new survey was designed and undertaken jointly by a team at ILSSA led by Dr Do Minh Cuong and by Dr Per Ronnås at Stockholm School of Economics, together with the other three contributors to this volume: Bhargavi Ramamurthy, a research assistant, and Maud Hemlin and Carmina Cortés, who were post-graduate students at the time. The new survey had two components: (i) a repeat survey of the same enterprises that had been covered by the 1991 survey, and (ii) a survey of a random sample of not previously surveyed enterprises in the same locations as in 1991, and using the same methodology and questionnaire.

A result of collaborative work, the present volume documents the survey data analysis undertaken by individual members of the research team and incorporates contributions from a wide range of people in varying, but equally vital capacities. The research team at the Institute of Labour Studies and Social Affairs in Hanoi had the main responsibility for the implementation of the survey. The high quality of the survey data is a testimony of the professionalism and dedication that characterised all aspects of their difficult work. The many discussions with individual members of this team in the course of the preparation for the survey and the editing of the data greatly contributed to our understanding of the nature of the private manufacturing sector in Vietnam. Equally important was the generous financial support provided by the Swedish International Development Authority (Sida) and the enthusiastic support of many of its staff members. The input from participants at the seminar in Hanoi in September 1998 also deserves special mention. Carin Blomkvist at Stockholm School of Economics extended a helping hand with the editing at a crucial point in time. Sandra Jones helped turning the manuscripts into proper English, while Leena Höskuldsson at NIAS gave the manuscript a final and valuable scrutiny and, together with Gerald Jackson, NIAS's editor-in-chief, skilfully guided the editors through the entire publication process. Carmina Cortés did the painstaking work of transforming the final text, including a huge number of tables, into a camera-ready manuscript. Without their assistance the manuscript would never have turned into a book. The editors alone bear the full responsibility for any remaining errors, omissions or other shortcomings.

Note

1. The survey results were published in Per Ronnås, *Employment Generation through Private Entrepreneurship in Vietnam* (New Delhi: Sida/ILO-ARTEP, 1992), subsequently also published in Vietnamese under the title *Doanh Nghiep Nho o Viet Nam* (Hanoi: Nha Xuat Ban Khoa Hoc Va Ky Thuat, 1993).

1

Introduction

Per Ronnås

Disenchantment with the Soviet-inspired development strategy, adopted after independence in 1954 and extended to the whole country after the liberation of the South in 1976, led in the second half of the 1980s to an increasing awareness within the political leadership in Vietnam of the need for economic reform and a redesign of the country's development strategy. This strategy, which aimed at modernisation and socio-economic development through furtherance of large-scale state-owned industry within the frame of a centrally planned economy, was clearly ill-suited for the capital-starved, but labour-abundant and largely agrarian economy of Vietnam. The rigid system of central planning was somewhat loosened through reforms in the 1980s as enterprises were encouraged to develop horizontal contacts and to act outside the plan.[1]

The shift to a more market-oriented economy took a major step forward through a land law passed in December 1987, which paved the way for a *de facto* collectivisation of agriculture and the transfer of long-term user rights to tillers.[2] At the same time, the regulations on state procurement of agricultural produce were changed in favour of the producers. Soon afterwards the non-agricultural private sector was brought out of the grey zone of semi-legality as its right to a legitimate place alongside the state sector was recognised through a resolution in 1988.[3]

However, it is the comprehensive reform package launched in early 1989 in response to the acute macro economic imbalances which generally is seen as the most decisive step towards addressing the economic malaise. It was also this reform which made *doi moi* – the wind of change – the catchword of the day and opened the eyes of the outside world to the economic transformation taking place in Vietnam.

The reform amounted to a bold attempt to apply a macro-economic shock therapy at a time when the concept had yet to be invented by Western advice-dispensers to former socialist countries.[4] The reform package included a sharp increase in real interest rates which made both borrowing and lending rates positive in real terms. Government expenditures were severely curtailed and the practice of covering the budget deficit through increases in the money supply was stopped. The credit squeeze affected state enterprises as well, as their budget constraints were, at least for the time being, hardened. On the external side, the dong was devalued from 425 to 4,500 dong per US dollar, which effectively wiped out the black market in foreign exchange. Foreign trade restrictions were substantially reduced at the same time as further liberalisation of the domestic economy was taking place.

The effects of the reforms were immediate and dramatic. The hyperinflation was brought to a halt, empty shop shelves were suddenly filled with a wide variety of goods, and open-air markets mushroomed. Seldom have the effects of economic reforms been more immediate and visible. The remarkable success of the reforms clearly had a psychological impact. It created a forward momentum, which was fuelled by the international community as the perception of Vietnam changed from that of an outcast to an attractive target for investments and assistance. In retrospect, it seems clear that the general euphoria also harboured dangerous seeds of complacency; a belief that the basis for sustained high growth had essentially been laid in one stroke and that fine-tuning rather than further fundamental and painful reform was all that was needed to keep Vietnam on the right track. Very high growth rates and an improvement in all the main macro-economic indicators underlined the impression that Vietnam had at long last broken out of stagnation and embarked on the same road to prosperity as much of the rest of the region.

This does not mean that the need for economic restructuring was not recognised by the Vietnamese leadership. The importance of small-scale enterprises and the private sector, not least as a source of employment and income, was explicitly recognised in key documents such as the Socio-Economic Strategy up to the Year 2000, which was adopted at the Seventh Party Congress.[5]

Employment creation was a main concern as Vietnam charted the course ahead in the new economic environment created by the reforms in 1989. The past provided little comfort. Despite concerted efforts to industrialise since the unification in 1976, the share of the industrial sector in the total labour force increased by less than one percentage point between 1980 and 1990; from 10.4 to 11.2 per cent, while the share of the labour force in agriculture increased from 70.7 to 71.6 per cent.[6] The state sector employed a mere 15 per cent of the labour force.[7] From the point of view of creating a socialist society, these achievements were clearly disappointing, while from an employment perspective they were quite alarming. Apart from the long-term impossibility of absorbing close to three-quarters of the 800,000 net annual labour force increase in agriculture – where the population pressure on land was already exceedingly high – the return of large numbers of migrant labour from Eastern Europe and the Soviet Union and the demobilisation of soldiers following the withdrawal from Cambodia gave a sense of urgency to the employment problem.

It was against this backdrop that the Institute for Labour Studies and Social Affairs (ILSSA) in Hanoi and the Asian Regional Team for Employment Promotion of the International Labour Organisation (ILO-ARTEP), with financial support from the Swedish International Development Authority (Sida), embarked on a large-scale survey of non-state, small-scale enterprises in 1991. It was the first survey of its kind to be carried out in Vietnam in modern times.

The 1991 Survey

The survey, which was undertaken in the summer of 1991, covered a total of 923 non-agricultural enterprises almost equally divided between the southern and northern parts of the country and between rural and urban areas.[8]

The urban survey was carried out in Hanoi (150 enterprises), Haiphong (101 enterprises) and Ho Chi Minh City (252 enterprises) (Table 1.1). For practical reasons, the survey was confined to four

Table 1.1: Size, ownership and regional structure of the 1991 survey sample.

	Total	Household	Private	Partnership	Co-operative	State
Urban areas	*503*	*117*	*124*	*117*	*94*	*51*
Hanoi	150	35	35	35	30	15
Haiphong	101	25	26	21	19	10
HCM City	252	57	63	61	45	26
Rural areas	*420*	*232*	*181*	*1*	*6*	*0*
Ha Son Binh	79	41	32	0	6	0
Vinh Phu	67	50	17	0	0	0
Quang Ninh	68	58	10	0	0	0
Long An	104	46	57	1	0	0
Cuu Long	102	37	65	0	0	0
All areas	*923*	*349*	*305*	*118*	*100*	*51*

quarters in Hanoi and Ho Chi Minh City, respectively, and to three quarters and a small town in Haiphong. The samples were drawn from a complete list of enterprises in the selected quarters. A stratified sampling procedure was used to ensure the inclusion of an adequate number of enterprises with different ownership forms in the sample. Altogether the urban sample included 117 household enterprises, 124 private enterprises, 117 partnership enterprises and 94 co-operative enterprises. In addition, 51 small state enterprises were selected for comparative purposes. An upper ceiling of 50 workers was imposed on the private, partnership and co-operative enterprises both in urban and rural areas. For the state enterprises the ceiling was initially set at 100 workers, but was subsequently raised to 200 workers to ensure a sufficiently large sample population. In the few cases where it was found after the enumeration that the enterprise exceeded the employment ceiling, the enterprise was still retained in the sample.

The rural survey was undertaken in the provinces of Ha Son Binh, Vinh Phu and Quang Ninh in the north and Long An and Cuu Long in the south. It included altogether 420 non-farm enterprises, comprising 232 household enterprises, 181 private enterprises, one partnership enterprise and six co-operative enterprises. In addition, 100 purely agricultural households were surveyed for comparative purposes. The small number of partnership and co-operative enterprises in the sample was due to the very small number of such enterprises in the selected survey areas. The selection and sample procedure in the rural areas was similar to that in the urban areas. Three districts with a high density of non-farm enterprises were selected in each of the provinces Ha Son Binh and Vinh Phu and two districts in Quang Ning. The district towns and some other small towns in the selected provinces were included in the sample area to ensure a sufficiently large sample population and because these towns have an agro-industrial base and for all practical purposes are part of the agricultural-dominated rural economy. The rural economy in the Mekong delta, where the two selected provinces in the south were located, is more diversified than in the north and there is a much larger number of non-agricultural enterprises. The survey in Long An province, which at the time had more than 1,200 non-agricultural enterprises, covered two districts. In Cuu Long province, the survey was confined to 99 non-agricultural enterprises in the districts of Long Ho and Vung Liem.

Table 1.2: Distribution of surveyed enterprises in 1991 by main types of activities. Percentages.

	A	B	C	D	E	F
Total urban (non-state)	*2.5*	*87.0*	*3.6*	*0.9*	*1.1*	*4.5*
Hanoi	3.1	90.1	2.3	0.0	1.5	3.1
Haiphong	1.1	78.7	6.7	4.5	3.4	3.4
Ho Chi Minh City	2.7	88.4	3.1	0.0	0.0	5.8
Total urban (state)	*3.9*	*72.5*	*3.9*	*3.9*	*2.0*	*13.8*
Total rural	*26.5*	*37.4*	*10.8*	*4.4*	*3.9*	*17.0*
Ha Son Binh	0.0	95.5	0.0	0.0	0.0	4.5
Quang Ninh	25.0	26.6	3.1	4.7	3.1	37.5
Vinh Phu	7.7	33.8	30.8	4.6	9.2	13.9
Long An	36.6	17.2	10.8	6.5	4.3	24.7
Cuu Long	48.5	27.3	10.1	5.1	3.0	6.1

Key: A: Agro-processing, **B:** Manufacturing, **C:** Repair shops, **D:** Trade and commerce, **E:** Restaurants and cafes, **F:** Other.

The focus of the survey was non-manufacturing enterprises (Table 1.2). Thus, 89.5 per cent of the surveyed non-state enterprises in the urban areas had manufacturing as their main activity. Of these, only 2.5 per cent were primarily engaged in the processing of agricultural produce. The distribution was more or less the same in the three cities. The focus on the manufacturing sector was reduced in the rural survey in view of the scarcity of genuine manufacturing enterprises in the countryside. Altogether 63.9 per cent of the surveyed rural enterprises had manufacturing as their primary activity; of these, 26.5 per cent were engaged in agro-processing. An additional 10.8 per cent were repair shops. Restaurants, cafes and other trading enterprises made up 8.3 per cent of the sample and various other and mixed categories 17.0 per cent.

The 1991 survey revealed that the average urban private enterprise provided employment for 13.6 persons and produced a total value added of US$12,600, or US$813 per worker.[9] Its total assets averaged slightly over US$30,000. The average urban household enterprise, which by definition is smaller, employed 4.8 persons, 3.7 of whom were unpaid household members, and generated a value added of US$3,600, or US$648 per capita. Partnership enterprises had roughly the same average size as private enterprises. Co-operatives tended to be considerably larger than private and partnership enterprises, particularly in terms of employment, but had lower labour productivity. Because of the skewed size distribution – with a small number of very large enterprises – the median size of the enterprise was much smaller than the average size. Thus, half of the private and partnership enterprises in the three main cities produced a total value added of less than US$5,400 and a value added per worker of less than US$500 in the 1991 survey. The majority of the household enterprises were very small. In the urban areas half of the household enterprises produced a total value added below US$1,610 in the 1991 survey and had less than US$2,590 in total assets. The capital/labour ratio and labour productivity in these enterprises at the bottom of the scale was very low. Half of the urban household enterprises had less than US$623 in total assets per worker in the 1991 survey and produced a value added of less than US$380 per worker. The differences in size and economic performance between the non-state enterprises in Ho Chi Minh City on the one hand and Hanoi and Haiphong on the other hand were very large. Value added per worker as well as total value added was on average 2.5 to 3 times larger in Ho Chi Minh City than in the two northern cities. Virtually all urban non-state enterprises used electricity and the vast majority also made use of power-operated machinery. Even among the urban household enterprises, two-thirds used some power-operated machinery and only 17 per cent relied on hand tools exclusively.

Rural non-state enterprises were much smaller and more under-capitalised compared to their urban counterparts, irrespective of the type of ownership. The average rural private enterprise employed 10.4 persons compared to 13.6 in the average urban private enterprise, but produced on average only half the value added of the urban enterprise. For the household enterprises the difference was even larger. The average capital base of the rural enterprises was only a fifth of their urban counterparts, while the difference in the average capital/labour ratio was of the order of one to three. This was also reflected in a much lower level of mechanisation in the rural areas. Almost half of the rural enterprises covered by the survey used only hand tools. The value added per worker in the rural household enterprises was only 55 per cent of that in the urban household enterprises. Almost half of the rural household enterprises produced a value added per worker of less than US$200 in the 1991 survey and less than a quarter of the enterprises produced a value added per worker in excess of US$500. Clearly, a large number of rural household enterprises were nothing more than 'distress industries', owing their existence to an absence of other sources of incomes and yielding an income much below the subsistence level.

Many urban enterprises had a history that went well beyond the introduction of *doi moi* and no less than 60.5 per cent were established before 1988. In rural areas the agrarian reforms in 1987 had acted as a catalyst for entrepreneurship and as a consequence most rural enterprises (58.6 per cent) were quite young, established after 1987.

The survey results showed that access to capital determined who became an entrepreneur and who did not. It also influenced, to a large extent, the scale of the enterprise. In household and private enterprises, own capital and interest-free loans from friends and relatives made up over 95 per cent of the total invested capital at the time of the establishment of the enterprise in the urban areas. For the rural enterprises the share was marginally lower. Bank loans and other forms of capital played a totally insignificant role as a source of capital. The average starting capital was very much determined by availability rather than need. Differences in access to capital also determined who set up a household enterprise and who could start a private enterprise.

Half of the private enterprises in the three largest cities started with more than US$6,380 in capital, while less than half of the household enterprises had a starting capital in excess of US$900. The more limited access to capital in rural areas was reflected in much smaller initial investments in enterprises. Half of the rural household enterprises started with less than US$300 and a similar proportion were established with less than US$1,000 in capital. In view of this, it comes as no surprise that the majority of the enterprise managers stated shortage of capital as the main constraint at the time of the establishment of the enterprise.

The enterprises continued to operate in a pronounced cash economy after their establishment. The vast majority of them had no debts whatsoever. At the time of the survey, a mere 8 per cent of the urban and 2 per cent of the rural enterprises had loans from banks and credit co-operatives. Transactions between enterprises were as a rule also on a cash basis and credit was seldom received or given. Lack of access to external sources of capital was also by far the most frequently cited constraint to growth. Two-thirds of the rural and 55 per cent of the urban enterprises claimed shortage of capital as the main constraint to the growth of the enterprise (Table 1.3).

Most of the urban enterprises were found to act primarily on the local market and to depend on a personalised and informal network of backward and forward linkages. The vast majority of them procured all their inputs locally and sold exclusively on the local market. Approximately a third of all inputs were procured from individual households, while the state sector and other non-state enterprises supplied 27 per cent each of the inputs. By and large the forward linkages resembled the backward ones in this regard. However, while the urban household enterprises depended primarily on individual households for their market, the private, partnership and co-operative enterprises had strong links with the state sector. Approximately a third of the production of the private enterprises was sold to the state sector. Enterprises producing intermediary goods for other enterprises often had a close

Table 1.3: Main constraints to the growth of enterprises. 1991 survey. Percentages.

Constraint	Urban	Rural
Shortage of capital	54.9	65.7
Cannot afford to hire wage labour	3.8	2.2
Lack of skilled workers	3.6	2.2
Lack of technical know-how	7.3	4.5
Limited demand for current products	23.1	23.6
Too much competition	16.0	13.2
Lack of marketing/transport facilities	27.8	19.2
Lack of raw material	14.0	4.2
Lack of energy	17.1	7.2
Interference by local government officials	0.7	3.7
Government policies uncertain	10.7	9.5

Note: The enterprise managers were requested to list a maximum of three main constraints.

relationship with the purchasing enterprise. Production on advance order and sub contracting arrangements were very common.

Rural enterprises could be divided into two broad categories: those selling primarily on the local market and those producing mainly for the market in the large cities. Altogether about two-thirds of all sales were local, while large cities accounted for slightly less than a fifth.

The poorly developed marketing and information channels and the fragmented and localised markets inevitably affected both the ease with which inputs were procured and the marketing of the enterprise's own produce. About a third of both urban and rural enterprises experienced difficulties with the supply of raw material, although relatively few claimed that these problems were a main constraint to the growth of the enterprise. The supply of electricity was a more serious problem, particularly in the south. In Ho Chi Minh City over 70 per cent of the urban enterprises suffered from an unreliable and inadequate supply of electricity. For enterprises in Hanoi and Haiphong this problem was much less acute. Rural enterprises were found to be severely disadvantaged *vis-à-vis* urban enterprises in terms of power supply. Only a third of the rural enterprises covered by the survey had the physical and/or economic possibility of using electricity, and of those who did, 42 per cent complained about inadequate or unreliable supply.

Second to shortage of capital, market constraints were the most frequently cited impediment to growth. These took two forms: (i) competition from other enterprises, and (ii) lack of distribution and marketing channels and of information, resulting in an inability to sell beyond the local area, and in turn a fragmentation of the economy into a large number of small local markets. The survey results clearly suggested that it was the second of these two forms of market constraints that posed the greatest problem for the non-state enterprises. Thus, 'limited demand for current products' and 'lack of marketing and transportation facilities' were more frequently cited constraints to the growth of the enterprise than 'too much competition'. The problems of poor marketing and distribution channels and market fragmentation were more severe in the north than in the south and much more severe in rural areas than in urban areas. They also affected small enterprises more than large enterprises.

The vast majority of the non-state enterprises covered by the survey provided full-time employment on a regular basis for their workforces. Broadly speaking, the first three or four workers were unpaid members of the owner household and all additional labour was wage labour. Thus the share of wage labour in the labour force was a function of the size of the enterprise; it was higher in urban than in rural areas and much higher in private than in household enterprises. However, even in rural areas casual and seasonal labour was rather insignificant. Approximately a third of the labour force was female in both urban and rural areas, although in rural areas female wage labour was relatively less common. The age structure of the enterprises mirrored their growth pattern over time. Household enterprises tended to have a comparably older labour force as enterprises were seldom founded by young people and as these enterprises employed little wage labour. The wage labour force in the non-state enterprises was quite young and concentrated in the 20–39 age bracket, reflecting the fact that most workers were recently recruited and that they tended to be recruited young. The type of development of the non-state enterprises obviously had considerable implications on the pattern of employment generation. Development of the non-state sector through growth of existing enterprises created wage employment opportunities for primarily young people. Development through proliferation of new enterprises resulted in self-employment for middle-aged workers in particular and their family members. The lack of a formal capital market reinforced this situation, as in the absence of external capital, few young people would have the resources required to establish their own enterprise.

The importance of the non-state enterprises as a source of employment of urban youth was underscored by the fact that their educational requirements tended to be less than those of the state enterprises. Thus, they were found to create job entries for youth with middle level education only, who in most instances would not meet the formal requirements for state employment.

Wage levels and patterns in the urban non-state enterprises were quite similar to those in the small state enterprises. Both mean and median wages were roughly the same as in the small state enterprises, despite the generally lower educational level of the workforce in the non-state enterprises. However, variations in wage levels between enterprises in the non-state sector were larger than for the state enterprises, no doubt because of a higher correlation between labour productivity and remuneration in the non-state enterprises. Wages were found to be closely related to labour productivity and the economic performance of the individual enterprise. Among urban enterprises, the correlation between the average value added per worker and the average wage ranged between 0.71 and 0.85. In the rural enterprises the correlation was weaker, 0.35 on average, but still significant. It would appear that in rural areas the levels of income in agriculture created a general wage floor. From the point of view of policy-making, this was an important observation as it indicated that an improvement in labour productivity and economic performance of the enterprises was likely to be directly translated into higher incomes.

The study concluded that active promotion of the private sector in both urban and rural areas would be a most efficient means of promoting employment and income generation. The capital labour ratio in this sector was very much lower than in the state enterprises and thus much more in tune with the relative scarcity of productive resources in Vietnam. Yet wages and incomes in the non-state enterprises were at par with those in the state enterprises. Furthermore, production factors were more efficiently and fully utilised in the non-state enterprises than in the state enterprises. There was little slack in the use of production factors in the non-state enterprises and production growth in these enterprises could safely be assumed to result in an immediate expansion in employment and incomes. The close relationship between value added per worker and wage rates also suggested that increases in labour productivity would be directly translated into higher incomes for the workforce.

Shortage of capital emerged as the most frequent and serious constraint to the development of the enterprises in the non-state sector. The financial system in Vietnam has traditionally been geared towards serving the needs of capital allocation within the frame of a centrally planned state economy and was in the 1991 survey still ill-equipped to meet the need for efficient intermediation of capital in a multi-sector economy. From the point of view of economic efficiency, it was clearly unsatisfactory that there were no mechanisms for channelling capital to those who needed it most and where it would have given the best returns. A number of factors led to the conclusion that no single measure would contribute more to increasing employment and income generation than the creation of a financial system serving the non-state enterprises with credits on a strictly commercial basis. Thus:

- Lack of capital exercised a severe constraint on the growth of enterprises as investments were governed by the availability of own capital rather than by market opportunities and profitability.
- Growth of existing enterprises could be expected to be highly beneficial to employment and income generation, not least by creating wage employment opportunities for young people who lacked the means of becoming entrepreneurs themselves. The survey results also showed that labour productivity increased with the size of the enterprise as well as with the capital/labour ratio. Therefore, externally funded growth and consolidation of existing enterprises would not only increase employment but also labour productivity and, as a result, wages. At the same time, there was hardly any indication that capital replaced labour.
- Capital shortage slows down technological development, with a detrimental effect not only on labour productivity and incomes, but also on competitiveness and the long-term viability of enterprises.

- There were indications that a lack of access to formal sources of credit had repercussions on employment practices. Thus, it had become common practice among urban enterprises to require workers to make a contribution in cash or kind to the enterprise at the time of recruitment. Such practices were likely to bar poor people from obtaining wage employment.

The provision of physical infrastructure, such as premises for enterprises and a secure power supply, was another area where government assistance was found to be needed (Table 1.4). Inadequate physical infrastructure was a particularly severe problem in the rural areas. A shortage of premises was a major constraint to the establishment of new enterprises in urban areas, particularly in Hanoi, while an inadequate supply of electric power was a major constraint to industrial development in Ho Chi Minh City and in rural areas in general.

The absence of an institutionalised labour market was found to be a less acute problem than the lack of a capital market. Yet it was concluded that a gradual development of adequate labour market institutions would nevertheless be required to prevent inefficient labour intermediation from becoming a hindrance to employment generation.

Poorly developed marketing and distribution channels and inadequate instruments for disseminating marketing information were found to hamper the growth of potentially successful enterprises while, at the same time, shielding inefficient enterprises from competition. To some extent these are teething problems of a nascent market economy and could be expected to abate as markets become more developed. However, the government could play an active role in reducing these problems by offering its services as an intermediary between customers and sellers. The frequent linkages between state enterprises and urban private enterprises implied that the fate of many private enterprises was linked to that of state enterprises and that the economic problems afflicting many state enterprises could have repercussions on many private enterprises.

Lastly, it was concluded that special attention needed to be paid to enterprises in rural areas. Rural non-agricultural enterprises were found to have an extremely important role to play as a means of diversifying the rural economy and labour market, providing an exit for surplus labour in agriculture, and contributing towards a reduction of rural–

Table 1.4: Main types of government assistance desired by enterprise managers. 1991 survey. Percentages.

Type of government assistance	Urban	Rural
Removal of bureaucratic obstacles	6.7	17.2
Provision of premises, power & other infrastructure	41.6	19.2
Provision of easy credit	32.9	24.4
Restriction of imports	16.7	2.7
A more liberal import policy	10.0	3.7
Distribution of raw material	6.9	5.7
Assistance with technical know-how	6.7	1.0
Provision of training facilities for workers	0.0	0.0
Assistance with marketing	9.6	0.5
Clarification of long-term policies	23.1	18.4
Improved macro-economic policies	13.1	5.7
Other	21.6	29.4

urban differences in incomes and standards of living. However, the rural enterprises were on the whole ill-equipped to take on this role. Compared to urban enterprises they were small, economically weak, technologically backward and hamstrung by poor physical infrastructure and remoteness from markets. It was concluded that there was a real risk that large numbers of rural enterprises would be forced out of business as markets opened up and as competition from enterprises outside the immediate locality increased. Consequently there was a risk that surviving businesses would be marginalised and become 'second-class' enterprises with antiquated production methods, low productivity and incomes. Government support to rural enterprises should in particular focus on the areas of capital, infrastructure, marketing and technology.

Developments in the 1990s

The success of the reforms initiated in the late 1980s has been most obviously manifested in a sharp increase in economic growth indicators. The gross domestic product increased by an average rate of 7.9 per cent between 1990 and 1996, reaching well over 9 per cent in 1995 and 1996.[10] At the same time, inflation was brought under control, as it declined from over 67 per cent per year in 1990 and 1991 to less than 5 per cent in 1996 and 1997.[11] However, the high rates of economic growth have not translated into any substantial increase in non-farm employment opportunities and have done little to address the country's fundamental employment predicament.

Despite a fall in the share of agriculture in total GDP from 39.2 per cent in 1991 to 32.5 per cent in 1996, the share of the labour force in agriculture changed only marginally from 72.3 per cent to 70.7 per cent over the same period. Put differently, while manufacturing has accounted for well over a third of the growth in the GDP between 1990 and 1996, it has absorbed a mere 9 per cent of the increase in the labour force (Table 1.5). In the same period agriculture, more or less by default, absorbed three-quarters of the increment in the labour force, although its contribution to the growth of the GDP was only 20 per cent. As a result, the gap in labour productivity between agriculture and manufacturing has widened.

The failure to translate economic growth into increased non-farm employment and income opportunities casts doubt on the sustainability of the present development pattern. Pressure on land is already very high in most parts of Vietnam and a continued reliance on agriculture as the main source of employment will inevitably result in depressed labour productivity and incomes in this sector and in a widening disparity in incomes between those fortunate enough to have a wage job and the vast majority of the population who continue to depend on agriculture for a living. With regard to the industrial sector, two tentative conclusions can be drawn from the above picture. First, the effect of the sharp increase in foreign direct investments (mainly in the form of joint ventures with state enterprises) on employment and income generation has been relatively small. Second, despite economic liberalisation, private small and medium-scale manufacturing does not seem to have emerged as a forceful vehicle for employment generation.

A closer look at the manufacturing sector suggests that its dual nature, with large state enterprises accounting for much of the industrial production but generating little employment on the one hand and small private firms which are much more important in terms of

Table 1.5: Structure of labour force and GDP by main economic sectors.

	1990	1991	1992	1993	1994	1995	1996
Labour force (000s)	*30,286*	*30,974*	*31,815*	*32,718*	*33,664*	*n.a.*	*36,098*
% agriculture	72.3	72.6	72.9	73.0	72.8	n.a.	70.7
% industry	11.2	11.0	10.8	10.8	10.7	n.a.	10.4
% other	16.5	16.5	16.2	16.2	16.5	n.a.	18.9
GDP	*n.a*	*31,286*	*33,991*	*36,735*	*39,982*	*43,797*	*47,888*
% agriculture	n.a	39.2	38.6	37.1	35.4	33.9	32.5
% industry	n.a	19.3	20.4	21.1	21.9	22.8	23.9
% other	n.a	41.5	41.0	41.7	42.6	43.3	43.6

Note: GDP in billion dong at 1989 prices. Labour force figures for 1996 are based on labour force survey and are not entirely compatible with earlier figures.
Sources: *Nien Giam Thong Ke 1995* [Statistical Yearbook 1995] (1996). Hanoi: Statistical Publishing House, 29, 59; *Nien Giam Thong Ke 1996* [Statistical Yearbook 1996] (1997). Hanoi: Statistical Publishing House, p. 15; *Truc trang Lao Dong – Viec Lam o Viet Nam 1996* [Status of Labour – Employment in Vietnam 1996] (1997). Hanoi Statistical Publishing House, p. 405.

employment than in terms of production on the other hand, has changed little in the 1990s.

While production in the state manufacturing sector almost doubled at constant prices between 1990 and 1995, employment actually declined by some 13 per cent in the same period (Table 1.6). This somewhat striking development may perhaps be seen as evidence of a successful restructuring of previously highly inefficient and over-staffed state enterprises and, as such, has not necessarily been a negative phenomenon. However, it also highlights the inability of the state enterprises to serve as a vehicle for employment generation at the same time as they are weaned of state support and subsidies and forced to operate under hard budget constraints. By contrast in the non-state sector, growth in production has been accompanied by a growth in employment, albeit at a slower rate. However, the magnitude of the development of the non-state manufacturing sector has barely been sufficient to offset the employment decline in the state sector and has proved inadequate to serve as a major vehicle for employment and income generation.

In terms of sheer numbers, the development of domestic private enterprises has been quite impressive. The number of household enter-

Table 1.6: Development of employment and production in manufacturing by ownership form.

	1990	1991	1992	1993	1994	1995	1996
Labour force (000s)	*3,392*	*3,394*	*3,450*	*3,522*	3,604	n.a.	*3,760*
State sector	807.3	696.2	683.3	702.7	724.0	745.4	774.7
Non-state	2,585	2,698	2,767	2,819	2,880	n.a.	2,985
Production, total	*6,631*	*7,228*	*8,242*	*9,324*	*10,631*	*12,114*	*n.a.*
State sector	4,111	4,590	5,333	6,126	6,931	8,007	n.a.
Non-state sector	2,520	2,638	2,909	3,198	3,700	4,106	n.a.

Note: Production in billion dong at 1989 prices. Manufacturing includes construction. Non-state sector calculated as residual between total employment and state employment.

Sources: *Nien Giam Thong Ke 1995* [Statistical Yearbook 1995] (1996). Hanoi: Statistical Publishing House, 29, 59; *Nien Giam Thong Ke 1996* [Statistical Yearbook 1996] (1997). Hanoi: Statistical Publishing House, p. 31; *Truc trang Lao Dong - Viec Lam o Viet Nam 1996* [Status of Labour – Employment in Vietnam, 1996] (1997). Hanoi Statistical Publishing House, p. 405.

prises more than doubled from 840,000 in 1990 to 2.2 million 1996, while the number of private enterprises increased from a very small base to 21,000. In the same period there was a net establishment of some 8,900 limited liability companies and 190 joint stock companies.[12] It would appear that the growth in non-state manufacturing has taken place primarily through an increase in the number of non-state enterprises rather than through a growth in the size of these enterprises. Thus, the average output per household enterprise in the manufacturing sector increased by a mere 22 per cent, from 8.3 to 10.1 million dong between 1990 and 1994. Among the 'individual & mixed' enterprises the increase appears to have been higher, viz. 37 per cent.[13]

Since the publication of the results of the 1991 survey, several studies of the non-state enterprise sector, using firm level data, have been undertaken. Three general survey-based studies focussing on small-scale manufacturing enterprises in Hanoi and Ho Chi Minh City were produced in mid-1995.[14] Other studies have focussed on specific aspects of the non-state sector. Haggard et al. studied trading relations and networking in 149 small non-state enterprises in Hanoi in the context of market imperfections and high transaction costs,[15] while ethnic Chinese entrepreneurs in Ho Chi Minh City were in the focus of another study.[16] A study undertaken in the late 1990s complements the present study by focussing on 95 larger non-state manufacturing enterprises.[17]

The 1997 Surveys

The crucial role of private entrepreneurship and enterprise development in the current phase of Vietnam's development has prompted a need for more in-depth knowledge of the development of this sector in the 1990s and of its economic and operational characteristics today. There is a recognition that a dynamic non-state manufacturing sector is a precondition for attaining the twin targets of (i) restructuring and slimming state enterprises, and (ii) expanding non-farm employment and income opportunities. In particular, the ability of small-scale enterprises to survive and grow is of crucial importance, not only to creating jobs, but also as a main component in a strategy for sustainable economic development and a more equal distribution of incomes. Although a number of studies in the 1990s cast light on Vietnamese small manufacturing enterprises, empirically based information available on the factors and conditions which determine whether or not new small-scale enterprises will survive and develop and on the pattern and characteristics of their development remained inadequate.

To address this need and with the possibility in mind of using the successful survey undertaken in 1991 as a baseline, it was decided in 1996 that the Institute of Labour Studies and Social Affairs together with the Stockholm School of Economics (with financial assistance from Sida) should undertake a new survey along the lines of the previous one undertaken in 1991. The high quality of the earlier survey, which was undertaken only a few years after the launching of *doi moi,* and the possibility of undertaking a repeat survey of the same enterprises under virtually identical conditions – using the same survey methodology, the same team of researchers and enumerators in the field etc. – provided a unique opportunity to generate crucial information on the nature and pattern of development of small-scale private manufacturing enterprises during the transition process as well as on their ability to generate employment and incomes, and on the factors which influence this ability. It was decided that the new survey should include a repeat survey of enterprises surveyed in 1991 as well as a survey of 'new', that is, not previously surveyed, enterprises, which were to be sampled and selected in the same manner as in 1991. Thus, the new survey would be able to address three core issues:

- What are the economic, operational and employment characteristics of private manufacturing enterprises today and how do they compare with those prevailing in the 1991 survey?
- What are the main factors determining the success or failure of small private manufacturing enterprises?
- What are the nature, pattern and employment implications of endogenous development of small private manufacturing enterprises?

The new survey was undertaken in the same three main cities as in 1991, that is Hanoi, Ho Chi Minh City and Haiphong, and in two of the rural areas also covered by the 1991 survey, namely Ha Tay (formerly Ha Son Binh) in the north, and Long An in the south. The survey had two components: (i) a repeat survey of enterprises surveyed in 1991, and (ii) a survey of randomly selected, other non state manufacturing enterprises in the same locations. For ease of under-standing, these are hereafter referred to as two individual surveys. Chapters 2 to 6 focus primarily on survey (ii) while Chapters 8 and 9 are based on survey (i). Chapter 7 draws on both the surveys for its analysis.

The repeat survey depended critically on the ability to identify the previously surveyed enterprises and match them with the same enterprises today. During the 1991 survey each surveyed enterprise was given a unique numeric code. This code was attached to the other information on the enterprise in all the data files containing the survey results, to make it possible to merge variables from different files case by case. However, the actual name and address of the enterprise were not included in the data files. Thus the questionnaires completed in the field by the enumerators were the only means of linking the numeric codes with the names and addresses of the enterprise. As at the time of the 1991 survey there had been no thought of a repeat survey, the questionnaires used had not been systematically preserved. After a fair amount of detective work almost 500 of the 713 questionnaires from the cities of Ho Chi Minh City, Hanoi, Haiphong, Ha Tay and Long An were retrieved. From two of the other three rural locations included in the survey in 1991, Cuu Long and Vinh Phu, only a small number of questionnaires could be recovered, while it was decided to exclude enterprises in Quang Ninh (which had been one of the five provinces covered by the 1991 survey) altogether as the enterprises covered by the survey in this province in 1991 had been largely in the tertiary sector. Field visits were made to identify the repeat enterprises and to exclude purely agricultural households in the rural repeat sample and state enterprises in the urban repeat sample, as well as some enterprises for which an absolutely certain match between the 1991 data and the present enterprise could not be made. In this way, the repeat sample was reduced to 356. In addition, some 15 state enterprises covered by the 1991 survey in the three main cities were also included in the repeat survey. Thus, in Hanoi, 58 of the 135 non-state enterprises covered by the 1991 survey were included in the repeat sample; in Ho Cho Minh City this proportion was 79 out of 226; in Haiphong 81 out of 91; in Ha Tay 72 out of 72; and in Long An 72 out of 100 (see Table 1.7). Approximately two-thirds of the surveyed repeat non-state enterprises (233 out of 356), were found to be still operating, while the remaining 123 enterprises had closed down for various reasons. Among the state enterprises covered by the survey, nine out of the 15 were still in operation.

In order to maximise the possibilities of comparison, 'same procedure as last time' was a guiding principle in all aspects related to the design and implementation of not only the repeat survey, but also the survey of 'new' enterprises. Thus, the questionnaire used for the repeat as well as the new survey was essentially the same as the one used in the 1991 survey, as were the definitions and concepts used to interpret the questionnaire. The sampling procedure, detailed below, was also identical with the one used in 1991, as was the mode of implementing the actual survey through personal visits and interviews. Most importantly, with a few exceptions the same enumerators who carried out the survey in 1991 also carried out the survey in 1997. This factor was considered crucial in ensuring that the 1997 survey was undertaken in the same manner as the 1991 survey. It also facilitated and enhanced the results of the repeat survey as the enumerators often could remember the whereabouts of the enterprises covered in the 1991 survey and could determine on the spot if the present enterprise was in

Table 1.7: Distribution of repeat enterprises by location and form of ownership in the 1991 survey.

	Total	Urban			Rural	
		Hanoi	Haiphong	HCM City	Ha Tay	Long An
Total	***371***	*60*	*87*	*80*	*72*	*72*
In operation	***242***	*42*	*50*	*62*	*46*	*42*
Household	**84**	5	17	16	30	16
Private	**88**	14	11	22	15	26
Partnership	**28**	10	8	9	1	-
Collective	**32**	11	8	13	-	-
State	**9**	2	6	1	-	-
Other	**1**	-	-	1	-	-
Closed down	***129***				*26*	*30*
Household	**48**	5	8	7	12	16
Private	**35**	3	9	3	7	13
Partnership	**17**	4	7	1	4	1
Collective	**22**	5	11	4	2	-
State	**6**	1	3	2	-	-
Other	**1**	-	-	-	1	-

Note: The number of resurveyed enterprises was 371, but data for computing value added were not available for 14 urban and one rural surviving units; hence the total number of enterprises came down to 356.

fact the same as the one surveyed in 1991.[18] Similarly, coding and data entry were essentially carried out by the same people as in 1991.

The greatest challenge to the methodology of undertaking a survey – which in all important respects was similar to the survey undertaken in 1991 – was the transformation of the whole private sector which took place in the 1990s as a result of the market-oriented reforms and overall development in the country. Thus new categories of private enterprises – share holding and limited liability firms – had appeared on the scene, while the nature of co-operatives had changed fundamentally. In 1991 co-operatives were still synonymous with socialist collective enterprises. By 1997 the nature of these enterprises had changed

Table 1.8: Main area of activity in the 1991 survey of enterprises covered by the repeat survey.

	Hanoi	Haiphong	HCM City	Ha Tay	Long An	All areas
In operation						
Agro-processing	1	1	1	0	13	16
Manufacturing	38	37	58	43	7	183
Other	3	11	3	1	19	37
Unknown	0	1	0	2	3	6
Total	*42*	*50*	*62*	*46*	*42*	*242*
Closed down						
Agro-processing	2	0	1	0	11	14
Manufacturing	15	33	13	22	3	86
Other	1	5	2	2	12	22
Unknown	0	0	1	2	4	7
Total	*18*	*38*	*17*	*26*	*30*	*129*

entirely. The old type of collective enterprises had all but disappeared through closure, privatisation or transformation into market-oriented genuine co-operatives. These and other changes had to be taken into account in the design of the 1997 survey to ensure accuracy in the results. Thus, a few changes were made in the design of the 1997 survey. The most important of these refers to the stratification of the sample (see Table 1.9 for stratification categories). In the 1991 survey, enterprises in the urban areas had been stratified into four ownership categories: household enterprises, private enterprises, partnership enterprises and co-operatives. In addition a sample of 50 small state enterprises was surveyed in the three cities. For the 1997 survey it was decided to change the stratification somewhat. While the household enterprises and private enterprises were retained as individual groups, partnerships were combined with co-operatives into one group.[19]

In the rural areas the overwhelming predominance of household and private enterprises and the near absence of other types of enterprises had made stratification difficult in 1991. Thus, the 1991 rural survey covered almost exclusively household and private enterprises. In 1997 household and private enterprises were retained as two separate ownership

Table 1.9: Stratification of enterprise sample in 1991 and 1997.

Year	Area	Stratified sample categories
1991 (excluding state enterprises)	*Urban* Hanoi Haiphong Ho Chi Minh City	Household enterprises Private enterprises Co-operatives Partnerships
	Rural Ha Son Binh Quang Ninh Vinh Phu Long An Cuu Long	Household enterprises Private enterprises Co-operatives Partnerships
1997	*Urban* Hanoi Haiphong Ho Chi Minh City	Household enterprises Private enterprises Shareholding and limited liability companies Co-operatives and partnerships
	Rural Ha Tay Long An	Household enterprises Private Co-operatives and partnerships

Note: Ha Son Binh in 1991 corresponds roughly to Ha Tay in 1997.

categories for the purpose of stratification, while partnership, co-operative and limited liability enterprises were lumped together in a third category. At the outset of the survey it was decided to have a sample of 120 enterprises in each of the two largest cities – Hanoi and Ho Chi Minh City – and a sample of 100 in Haiphong. It was also decided to aim to include at least 30 enterprises of each of the three main ownership categories in the sample in each of the cities. In the rural areas the total sample was set at 80 in each of the two provinces covered by the survey, with the provision that at least 30 household enterprises and 30 private and other forms of non-state enterprises should be included in the sample in each of the provinces. As can be seen from Table 1.10, these targets were by and large met. In Ho Chi Minh City the target of 30 household enterprises was not met, apparently because many small enterprises (which, judging by their small size and limited use of wage labour would normally be considered household enterprises) were registered as private enterprises. Other criteria for determining and delimiting the population of eligible enterprises for the survey were as follows:

- The enterprise should primarily be engaged in manufacturing or agro-processing. In the 1991 survey this rule was somewhat relaxed in the rural survey, owing to the lack of manufacturing units. However, this was not the case in the 1997 survey.
- The size ceiling was set at 100 employees, which coincided with the de facto ceiling applied in the 1991 survey. However, it was determined a priori to use this ceiling for sampling purposes only and not to disqualify enterprises if in the course of the survey it was subsequently found that the number of employees marginally exceeded 100.
- The enterprise should have at least one full-time permanent worker, whether paid or unpaid. This corresponds with the rule applied during the 1991 survey.
- The enterprise had to belong to the non-state sector. Thus, no state enterprises were included. In the 1991 survey some 50 state enterprises had been included for comparative purposes. This was not the case in the 1997 survey.
- Enterprises that provided only labour and no other inputs of their own were excluded.
- Only enterprises established prior to 1 January 1996, were included, as for most quantitative variables the reference in the survey was the calendar year of 1996.

Within each of the three urban areas and the two rural areas, the survey was carried out in the same urban quarters and rural districts as the 1991 survey.[20] Only in cases where the total number of eligible enterprises in the quarter/district proved to be insufficient was the survey extended into a neighbouring quarter/district. As in the previous survey, official lists of registered enterprises were used to obtain the population of enterprises. Since household enterprises register with the local quarter/district authorities, while all other types of enterprises have to register with the city/province authorities, the lists of enterprises had to be obtained from two different sources. After excluding the repeat enterprises already surveyed in 1991 from these lists, the revised lists were used as a basis for selecting the sample.

The sample was selected at random, while adhering to the principle that the stratification criteria should be met. In order to allow for discrep-

Table 1.10: Distribution of new enterprises by location and form of ownership in the 1997 survey.

	Hanoi	HCM City	Haiphong	Ha Tay	Long An	All areas
Household	41	24	33	47	49	194
Private	3	35	26	20	28	112
Partnership	16	11	13	13	1	54
Collective	25	12	20	2	3	62
Shareholding & LLC	34	35	9	1	2	81
All forms	*119*	*117*	*101*	*83*	*83*	*503*
Agro-processing	14	10	16	4	28	72
Manufacturing	105	107	85	79	55	431

ancies between the enterprise lists and reality, and for incidences of absence of the owner or manager of the enterprise or refusal to co-operate in the survey, the sample drawn was 30 per cent larger than the desired sample size. In the event approximately 25 per cent of the sampled enterprises could not be covered by the survey for various reasons. In about a third of the cases this was due to a refusal by the owner or manager to co-operate, while in the remaining two-thirds of the cases it was due to the absence of the owner or manager or because it was found that the enterprise did not actually belong to the survey population, for instance because it did not engage in manufacturing or agro-processing.

The survey was carried out in several steps. Following the design of the draft questionnaires and the survey methodology, a pilot survey of some 30 repeat enterprises was organised in Hanoi. The experiences of this pilot survey were analysed and discussed at an informal workshop in Hanoi in August 1997. On this occasion, minor revisions of the questionnaire and of the instructions to the enumerators were also made. A workshop was held and then the enumerators took part in a training course. This provided an occasion to identify, clarify and iron out remaining ambiguities and possible sources of misinterpretation. As the enumerators had considerable prior experience, the training course also took the form of a discussion and yielded much valuable feedback.

The actual survey was undertaken in two stages. During the first stage, the enumerators went to the survey areas to identify the repeat enterprises and to obtain the complete lists of enterprises from the local authorities. The identification of the repeat enterprises was an important and time-consuming task. In many cases the enterprises had undergone a change in location or owner since the survey in 1991 and determining whether the enterprises were still in existence and their whereabouts often involved considerable detective work. On the basis of these visits updated lists of the repeat enterprises were prepared and random samples of the new enterprises to be surveyed were drawn up. During the second stage the actual survey was undertaken. The survey was launched in October 1997, and was completed six weeks later. An initial checking and cleaning of the data was undertaken in the field. Following data entry, a second round of data cleaning was undertaken and the data files for the repeat enterprises were merged with the data files from the 1991 survey.

After the analysis was completed for both repeated and 'new' enterprises, the results were disseminated in a seminar in Hanoi, in September 1998. The present volume documents both sets of survey findings. Chapters 2–6 deal with various aspects of the 1997 survey of previously unsurveyed, 'new' enterprises. Chapter 7 is a two-pronged analysis, comparing the overall transformation of the private manufacturing sector by comparing (i) the enterprises surveyed in 1991 with the 'new' enterprises surveyed in 1997, and (ii) the same set of enterprises surveyed in 1991 and 1997. Chapters 8 and 9 analyse the performance of two specific categories of resurveyed enterprises: those that registered more than 10 per cent annual average growth of value added and those that were surveyed in 1991 but closed down in the period 1991–97. Chapter 10 brings together the various studies and their policy implications for the dynamic private manufacturing sector in Vietnam.

Notes

1. Adam Fforde and Stefan de Vylder (1988), *Vietnam: An Economy in Transition*. Stockholm: Sida.

2. Politburo resolution (No. 10/NQTU) on 'the renovation of economic policy in agriculture'.

3. Politburo resolution (No. 10/NQTU) on 'the renovation of economic policy in agriculture'.

4. Politburo resolution (No. 10/NQTU) on 'the renovation of economic policy in agriculture'.

5. *Communist Party of Vietnam 7th National Congress. Documents* (1991). Hanoi: Foreign Languages Publishing House. See also Per Ronnås and Örjan Sjöberg (eds.) (1991), *Socio-Economic Development in Vietnam: The Agenda for the 1990s*. Stockholm: Sida.

6. Per Ronnås (1992), *Employment Generation through Private Entrepreneurship in Vietnam*. New Delhi: ILO-ARTEP / Sida, p. 2.

7. Adam Fforde and Stefan de Vylder, *op. cit.*, p. 51.

8. For details on the survey and the survey results, see Per Ronnås (1992), *op. cit.*

9. The exchange rate used was 5,100 dong per US$ for data referring to the whole of 1990. For those referring to the time of the survey in 1991, an exchange rate of 8,850 dong per US$ was used.

10. Ari Kokko (1997), *Vietnam 1997: Managing the Transition to Free Trade – Vietnamese Trade Policy for the 21st Century*. Macroeconomic Report 1997. Stockholm: Sida, pp. 2–4.

11. *Ibid.*, p. 5.

12. Raymond Mallon (1997), *Mapping the Playing field: Options for Reducing Private Sector Disincentives in Vietnam*. Mimeo. The figures refer to all non-farm enterprises.

13. *Nien Giam Thong Ke 1995*, pp. 29, 59, 173–174. *Nien Giam Thong Ke 1996*, pp. 124–125. The source is not clear on exactly what 'individual and mixed economy' enterprises include.

14. Kristina Kurths (1995), *Private Small Scale Industries in Vietnam: Development Environment and Empirical Results*. Working Paper Series in Economics and Finance No. 57. Stockholm: Stockholm School of Economics. Appold *et al.* (1996), 'Entrepreneurship in a Restructuring Economy: Small Private Manufacturers in Hanoi', *Journal of Asian Business*. vol. 12, no. 4, pp. 1–29. Donald Freeman (1996), 'Doi Moi Policy and the Small-Enterprise Boom in Ho Chi Minh City', Vietnam. *The Geographical Review*. vol. 86, no. 2, pp. 178–197. See also Pham Ghia Hai *et al.* (eds.) (1996), *184 surveyed small and medium-sized enterprises of Vietnam: Evaluation and analysis report*. Hanoi: GTZ and VICOOPSME.

15. Stephen Haggard *et al.* (1996), 'Trust and Search in Vietnam's Emerging Private Sector'. Mimeo. John McMillan and Christopher Woodruff (1998), *Networks, Trust and Search in Vietnam's Emerging Private Sector*. Mimeo.

16. Lotte Thomsen and Jakob Lindahl (1998), *De oversøiske kinesere i Vietnam*. Copenhagen: Copenhagen University.

17. Leila Webster and Markus Taussig (1999), *Vietnam's Undersized Engine: A Survey of 95 Larger Private Manufacturers Private Sector*. Discussions No. 8. Hanoi: Mekong Project Development Facility.

18. Enterprises which had changed owner through inheritance, sale or privatisation of running firms were treated as enterprises still in operation. Similarly, enterprises which had changed their location but not their owner and line of business, were also treated as still in operation. However, those enterprises that (i) had changed owners while the enterprise was not operating or following bankruptcy, as well as (ii) those that had been closed down a year or more or which had been formally declared bankrupt after 1991, were treated as enterprises no longer in operation, irrespective of whether an enterprise was operating in the same location at the time of the 1997 survey or not.

19. In the subsequent analysis it was decided to analyse co-operatives and partnership enterprises in the urban areas separately as they were found to still display quite distinctive features.

20. For administrative purposes the three large cities are divided into quarters while the provinces are divided into districts.

2

General Characteristics

Maud Hemlin[1]

Size and Efficiency

The biggest firms in the 1997 survey (in terms of employment) of 'new' enterprises are found in Ho Chi Minh City, where each firm has on average 24 persons in the workforce, 22 of whom are wage workers (Table 2.1). This figure stands in sharp contrast to manufacturing enterprises in the rural areas. It also exceeds the figure for Hanoi, where the average workforce is 17 people, and for Haiphong, which has an average labour force of just12 people.

Small firms in Ho Chi Minh City are in fact quite distinct from other Vietnamese enterprises in this survey, regardless of the criterion used to measure size. In terms of total income, the average Ho Chi Minh City enterprise earned close to 2 billion dong, more than twice that of Hanoi, and at least five times that of Haiphong (Table 2.1). To illustrate the size differences, while only 25 and 10 per cent of the enterprises in Hanoi and Haiphong respectively have total incomes of at least 1 billion dong, almost half of the surveyed firms in Ho Chi Minh City had incomes in excess of this amount (Table 2.2). The average level of value added for enterprises in Haiphong (112 million dong) is half the average for Hanoi (225 million dong), which in turn is half that of Ho Chi Minh City (555 million dong).[2] More than half the enterprises surveyed in Haiphong and Hanoi have value added levels below 100

Table 2.1: Main economic characteristics in the 1997 survey by location.

	Urban			Rural	
	Hanoi	**Haiphong**	**HCM City**	**Ha Tay**	**Long An**
Total income	798,439	334,848	1,846,500	316,568	272,745
Value added	225,164	112,484	554,865	124,207	84,699
Wage cost	88,470	46,862	177,889	42,240	24,442
Profit	70,614	34,360	141,725	31,176	36,708
Taxes	24,455	9,465	101,086	3,590	9,371
Assets	749,947	468,794	979,455	330,714	175,882
Debts	58,747	24,204	63,301	31,592	1,392
Labour force	17.2	12.4	23.6	13.1	6.9
Full time	15.7	10.4	22.7	11.2	5.1
Wage workers	15.8	10.1	22.3	10.3	4.7
Full time	14.2	9.2	21.4	8.8	3.0
Value added/worker	11,664	8,330	23,368	7,814	12,259
Assets/worker	42,602	33,586	48,630	18,022	23,548
Value added/asset	402	463	833	592	911
Debt/asset	3.3	3.9	3.5	3.6	2.1
Wage cost/worker	5,447	4,241	8,323	4,344	5,704
% wage workers	80.1	72.2	92.9	42.3	54.6
% profit/own assets	13.9	18.6	21.9	20.7	49.9

Note: Five per cent trimmed mean figures. Monetary data are in thousand dong.

million dong, while this is true of only 10 per cent in Ho Chi Minh City. Also in terms of asset values, Ho Chi Minh City hosts the largest of the surveyed enterprises, approaching 1 billion dong on average.

Comparing the set of enterprises surveyed in 1991 with the 'new' enterprises surveyed in 1997 yields interesting results. Tables 2.1 and 2.3 show that changes of quite impressive magnitude have taken place in the inter-survey period in terms of the size of enterprises in Hanoi and Ho Chi Minh City. The average level of income in Hanoi was 238.5 million dong in the 1991 survey, with income growth exceeding 200 per cent between 1991–97; that of value added is slightly less than 190 per cent.

Table 2.2: Size structure of enterprises in the 1997 survey by location.

	Urban			Rural	
	Hanoi	Haiphong	HCM City	Ha Tay	Long An
Percentiles:					
Total income:					
25	122,950	67,500	416,250	17,181	56,000
50	248,400	160,000	1,091,615	62,290	151,000
75	1,210,000	593,750	2,561,515	423,068	300,000
90	3,200,000	1,296,970	6,429,355	1,570,000	1,132,520
Value added:					
25	50,000	29,036	179,558	9,461	26,800
50	94,800	70,078	354,000	31,052	55,440
75	351,927	152,532	726,530	129,716	122,000
90	801,349	439,040	1,659,180	536,021	273,408
Total assets:					
25	130,000	100,000	283,200	24,750	19,200
50	312,000	210,000	565,000	56,500	113,500
75	1,306,500	709,750	1,301,143	358,378	260,000
90	2,390,000	2,084,000	3,116,000	1,539,400	634,000

Note: All figures are in thousand dong.

The increase in income and assets in Ho Chi Minh City is somewhat less, about 140 per cent, but 155 per cent in terms of value added, up from 218 million. The average enterprise in Hanoi has grown from approximately 79 million dong to 225 million (185 per cent), when value added is used as reference. There has been some change in the use of labour as well, but not at the same rate as income or capital. The average labour force was 12.4 people in Hanoi in the 1991 survey and 17.2 in the 1997 survey, a growth rate of less than 40 per cent. Also in Ho Chi Minh City, there is a gap between the growth of labour and capital, although this is not as large as in Hanoi where the average labour force consisted of 13 people in the 1991 survey, and the 1997 survey level of 24 people implies a growth rate of 77 per cent. But while the enterprises are growing in Hanoi and Ho Chi Minh City, they seem to be shrinking in Haiphong. The average level of income in the 1991 survey was 356 million dong, compared with 335 million in the 1997 survey. Moreover, also the value of assets was higher in the 1991 survey, implying a standstill or a rate of decline of about 5 per cent over the six year period between the two surveys. The average labour force has been cut by five persons, or close to 30 per cent, since the survey in 1991.

Table 2.3: Main economic characteristics in the 1991 survey by location.

	Urban			Rural
	Hanoi	**Haiphong**	**HCM City**	**Ha Tay**
Total income	238,557	355,931	758,400	76,866
Value added	78,739	110,447	217,865	35,763
Assets	244,093	494,831	422,370	24,957
Labour force	12.4	17.3	13.3	9.5
Assets/worker	17,595	26,165	35,382	6,551
Value added/worker	6,968	6,443	16,274	3,946

Note: Five per cent trimmed mean figures in thousand dong, 1996 prices. To recalculate 1991 survey figures to 1996 prices, figures referring to monetary flow were inflated 3.85 times, while figures referring to end year stock were inflated 2.79 times.

Small enterprises in Ho Chi Minh City in the 1997 survey are relatively impressive not only in 'quantity', but in quality as well. Among the surveyed enterprises in Hanoi, for instance, each worker has, on average, 88 per cent of the assets of a worker in Ho Chi Minh City at his or her disposal (Table 2.1). Yet value added per worker in Hanoi is only 50 per cent of that of Ho Chi Minh City on average, while wages are about 65 per cent. The surveyed firms in Haiphong have less capital at their disposal on average, 33.6 million dong on a per worker basis, resulting in a value added of 8.3 million, or about 36 per cent of that in Ho Chi Minh City, while average wages in Haiphong amount to about 51 per cent.

If one compares the state of the small-scale enterprises on a per worker basis in the two surveys, it is obvious that the businesses in these urban areas differ in their state in the 1997 survey as well. In Hanoi average capital per worker was 48.6 million dong in the 1997 survey, representing a growth of two and a half times since 1991 (Tables 2.1 and 2.3). However, value added per worker has grown less than 70 per cent, from about seven million in the 1991 survey to 11.7 million dong in the 1997 survey. The establishments in Ho Chi Minh City show a more coherent development. Here, the average value of assets per worker was approximately 35 million dong in the 1991 survey, resulting in a value addition of 16 million dong on a per worker basis. Six years later, these indicators grew by 37 and 44 per cent on average, and the relative ranking has remained practically unaltered. The growth in value added per worker is, however, 29 per cent over the six-year span, which is relatively less impressive. This increase has also been accompanied by a growth in average assets per worker, up 28 per cent from 26 million dong in the 1991 survey.

The size of the labour force appears to differ quite a bit between the rural areas: on average seven in Long An and 13 in Ha Tay (Table 2.1). But on closer inspection, these figures reveal rather little about the true relative size of the rural enterprises in the survey. In Long An, not a single firm has a workforce of more than 40 people, while in Ha Tay the maximum is about 90. Still, in both areas half of the enterprises surveyed have five or fewer persons in the labour force. Also the number of wage workers as given in Table 2.1 is misleading. More than half of the firms in Ha Tay have only one person or less employed on a wage basis, actually less than in Long An, where half the businesses included in the survey have three wage workers or more.

This calls for a closer screening also of other indicators in Ha Tay. In Ha Tay, a few very large enterprises result in very high average labour force and average value added (considerably higher than in Long An). The spread in the size of enterprises is much larger in Ha Tay than in Long An. This comes out clearly when we look at the percentile distribution (Table 2.2). Thus the smallest quartile of enterprises in Ha Tay are considerably smaller than their counterparts in Long An (except for total assets), while the largest quartile of enterprises in Ha Tay are larger than their counterparts in Long An. The difference in average value added is almost 40 million dong (32 per cent), but median value added in Long An is 55 million dong, and only 31 million dong in Ha Tay. With reference to the apparently higher asset values in Ha Tay, account needs to be taken of the fact that in Long An, 50 per cent of the surveyed undertakings have assets worth at least 1 billion dong. In Ha Tay, only 15 per cent of the enterprises reported such high values. A comparison with the survey made six years ago is unfortunately useful only for Ha Tay,[3] but reveals a ten-fold growth in asset value (Tables 2.1 and 2.3). Total incomes of the average Ha Tay enterprises have grown by more than 300 per cent over these six years, up from 77 million dong, while value added has increased by almost 250 per cent. While digesting these findings, what has been said above about the wide range in the Ha Tay sample should be kept in mind.

When comparing the present state of the two rural areas on a per worker basis, it is the small enterprises in Long An that look more impressive. With 23.5 million dong in assets per worker on average, they produce a value added per worker of 12.3 million (Table 2.1). The workers in Ha Tay have on average 76 per cent as much capital per head, and get just as high a proportion of Long An wages, but produce on average 63 per cent, or 7.8 million of the value added. Long An workers have approximately 48 per cent of the assets of a Ho Chi Minh City worker, but produce 52 per cent of the latter's value added per worker. And, to be noted, they receive on average 69 per cent of the wages of Ho Chi Minh City workers.

As mentioned earlier, the Long An sample did not allow a comparison between the 1991 and 1997 surveys, but for Ha Tay, the contrast, on a per worker basis, reveals that efficiency has not managed to keep up with the earlier mentioned impressive changes. Each worker had, on average, 2.3 million dong worth of capital in the 1991 survey, resulting in 4 million dong as value added per worker (Table 2.3). Assets per worker in the 1997 survey were 18 million dong, enabling average value added levels per worker of 7.8 million dong (Table 2.1). Thus, while value added has at best doubled over the six-year span, each worker got, on average, 700 per cent worth of new equipment over the same time.

The same kind of enterprise, in terms of ownership, looks very different depending on whether it is situated in an urban or a rural area. Household enterprises in the rural areas have an average labour force of less than four people (Table 2.4), and more than half of the establishments do not have any employees at all. Household firms in the cities employ about six people, and only one-fifth of the establishments have no employees. The average proportion of wage workers in the labour force is also of quite different magnitudes between these forms of enterprises. The average level of income is 62 million dong for rural household enterprises, yet half of them barely reach 40 million dong (Table 2.5). Its urban counterpart, in terms of income, earns 209 million, and a third of the firms here exceed this level.

In terms of assets, household undertakings in urban areas are, on average, about three times as large as their rural counterparts (152 million as compared to 46 million), but these levels are reached by only 35 per cent within their respective areas. The average rural value added, 28 million dong, is fairly representative of its household industries, but 65 per cent of the urban household enterprises are below the urban average of 69 million dong.

The difference between rural and urban private enterprises is not of the same magnitude as household industries. About 22 persons, on average, work in the urban private enterprises and 17 in the rural ones, but in the former, a higher share (89 per cent), work for wages while the proportion is 77 per cent for the latter. Average income for the surveyed urban private firms is 1.2 billion dong, about 1.5 times that of rural private enterprises. The urban–rural difference is of a higher magnitude when value added is concerned: 216 million dong in rural areas compared to 428 million in urban, and half of the rural units fall below 115 million dong in value added. Comparing assets, rural private enterprises have approximately 40 per cent of the assets owned by urban private undertakings. Furthermore, about one half of rural private enterprises are worth less than 250 million dong, a level exceeded by 75 per cent of their urban counterparts.

Urban partnership enterprises fall somewhere between urban household and rural private enterprises in terms of size. The labour force is no more than 11 people, but the proportion of wage workers is rather high (92 per cent), even approaching the levels of the shareholding and limited liability companies. That is, however, the only aspect in which these two enterprise forms resemble each other. Partnership undertakings have incomes of 322 million dong on average, but a few large observations skew this indicator, and only 30 per cent have such high incomes. After costs, this results in an average value added of 126 million dong, still slightly non-representative of the sample. Co-operatives are also a rather dispersed lot, with a quarter having the lowest incomes (below 162 million dong), while a quarter have the highest incomes (over 1.5 billion dong) (Table 2.5). The average workforce comprises 26 people, but about half of the surveyed co-operatives employ 13 workers at the most.

Shareholding and limited liability companies are an even more scattered group in terms of size, with the smallest undertaking having five and the largest having 215 persons in the workforce. A third of the surveyed firms in this category earn more than the average of 2.7 billion dong, while half have incomes exceeding 1.5 billion dong. The average value added at 702 million dong is by far the highest for all ownership forms, but then again, the workforce has a total asset value of more than 2 billion on average to produce such results.

A quick comparison deserves to be made in terms of efficiency between the different ownership forms. Using urban private enterprises as a basis may yield the most useful results, since these are neither too small, like household firms, to be completely unable to attract capital from banks, nor too big, like limited liability companies and joint ventures, to constitute 'islands' that are not quite typical of the Vietnamese industrial structure. Urban household and partnership enterprises have half the assets per worker compared with urban private enterprises, but manage to produce about 63 per cent of the value added (Table 2.4). Shareholding and limited liability companies, on the other hand, have 138 per cent of the assets per worker of urban private firms, and the average value added per worker is 122 per cent. Rural household enterprise workers have 22 per cent of the urban private firm worker's assets at hand, but produce 44 per cent of the average worker's value added. Wages do not, however, follow value added per worker very strictly, at least not on average terms. Wages in urban household and partnership enterprises are 83 per cent and 71 per cent of that of urban private enterprises respectively. Shareholding and limited liability companies pay 95 per cent on average, while rural household enterprises give their workers slightly more than 70 per cent of what urban private firms pay.

Table 2.4: Main economic characteristics in the 1997 survey by ownership form.

	Urban					Rural		
	Household	Private	Partnership	Co-operative	Shareholding*	Household	Private	Other form
Total income	208,797	1,273,722	322,269	1,061,546	2,680,609	62,113	868,500	1,521,963
Value added	69,469	428,378	125,780	313,701	702,404	27,841	216,321	416,506
Wage cost	21,729	156,852	51,210	137,018	208,187	5,449	71,165	141,717
Profit	28,906	93,250	35,395	80,765	220,077	15,214	77,989	74,771
Taxes	6,733	65,325	17,527	40,473	108,750	929	16,998	31,158
Assets	152,143	1,091,977	322,687	741,351	2,104,457	45,933	433,697	1,479,978
Debts	899	72,533	556	76,661	220,071	404	26,875	136,162
Labour force	5.7	22.5	10.8	26.0	31.9	3.5	17.2	30.0
Full time	5.3	21.6	10.6	21.4	29.7	3.0	14.1	24.7
Wage workers	3.6	20.7	9.8	24.3	30.5	1.2	14.5	27.4
Full time	3.4	20.0	9.6	21.1	28.3	1.0	11.2	22.8
Value added/worker	10,982	17,455	10,934	12,006	21,322	7,699	13,656	14,545
Assets/worker	28,015	51,759	29,276	30,299	71,453	12,565	29,022	50,709
Value added/asset	608	577	707	541	442	1,024	608	377
Debt/asset	0.7	5.4	0.3	7.5	7.4	1.5	3.7	7.0
Wage cost/worker	6,027	7,253	5,165	4,837	6,875	5,136	5,250	5,091
% wage workers	53.6	88.8	91.5	95.5	94.6	25.7	76.7	87.4
% profit/own assets	32.3	16.9	17.1	13.1	13.7	65.6	26.8	9.2

Note: Five per cent trimmed mean figures. Monetary figures are in thousand dong. *Shareholding and LLC.

Table 2.5: Size structure of enterprises in the 1997 survey by ownership form.

		Urban					Rural		
	Percentiles	**Household**	**Private**	**Partnership**	**Co-operative**	**Shareholding***	**Household**	**Private**	**Other forms**
Total income:	25	67,825	346,200	152,880	162,000	567,893	20,800	158,500	323,463
	50	122,425	780,646	215,000	450,000	1,554,725	42,000	315,000	790,000
	75	333,500	2,024,025	375,022	1,560,575	3,386,250	91,000	1,156,875	1,657,763
	90	655,464	4,289,363	1,199,000	4,153,234	10,811,645	173,704	4,200,000	10,951,755
Value added:	25	21,071	117,105	63,733	75,889	192,638	10,000	76,058	120,435
	50	49,555	317,540	87,542	117,283	503,540	22,400	117,875	269,950
	75	111,635	666,678	198,829	533,275	911,139	41,024	302,067	533,375
	90	203,208	1,507,759	318,810	953,158	2,280,635	71,600	760,341	1,808,466
Total Assets:	25	48,300	281,250	90,600	196,790	495,500	12,700	133,400	334,000
	50	121,555	644,500	202,000	653,000	1,331,643	31,000	260,000	847,500
	75	230,375	1,520,642	493,350	1,122,000	2,688,389	64,000	640,000	2,050,000
	90	472,820	3,830,000	1,045,000	1,908,340	6,969,000	141,680	1,504,600	5,179,000

Note: All figures are in thousand dong. *Shareholding and LLC.

Further, 98 per cent of the owner families of household and private enterprises in Ho Chi Minh City derive most of their income from the enterprise (see Table 2.6). The share is about the same everywhere, fluctuating around 95 per cent in urban as well as rural areas, except for the somewhat lower 74 per cent in Hanoi. In general, private enterprises seem to provide the main source of income to a somewhat greater extent than household firms, in the cities as well as on the countryside (Table 2.7). About two members of the family are occupied full time in the business, slightly fewer in urban than in rural areas, and approaching three among rural private enterprises. Hardly any family member works on a part-time basis, irrespective of the type of enterprise or location.

Table 2.6: Relationship of enterprise to owner-households by location. Percentages.

	Urban			Rural	
	Hanoi	**Haiphong**	**HCM City**	**Ha Tay**	**Long An**
Household members working in enterprise:*					
Full time	1.7	1.6	1.9	2.2	2.0
Part time	0.4	0.3	0.1	0.6	0.2
***Enterprise as main income:* †**	74.4	96.5	98.3	92.2	96.1
Change in household income:					
Declined	27.9 (21.4)	1.8 (17.3)	5.1 (43.8)	12.5 (27.5)	19.7 (12.2)
No change	39.5 (34.3)	17.5 (38.5)	6.8 (19.0)	4.7 (13.0)	22.4 (22.4)
Increased upto 25%	7.0	28.1	61.0	31.3	25.0
Increased 26–50%	11.6	15.8	22.0	21.9	13.2
Increased 51–100%	7.0	22.8	3.4	9.4	14.5
Increased >100%	7.0	14.0	1.7	20.3	5.3

Key: * Averages † Enterprise is main source of income to the owner household.

Note: Figures in parentheses are 1991 survey data, which referred to income changes in the period 1989–90; the 1997 survey referred to income changes in the period 1990–96. Data include household and private enterprises only in both surveys.

Table 2.7: Relationship of enterprise to owner-households by ownership form. Percentages.

	Urban		Rural	
	Household	Private	Household	Private
Household members working enterprise:*				
Full time	1.8	1.8	1.8	2.7
Part time	0.4	0.1	0.4	0.2
Enterprise as main income:†	85.6	100.0	92.6	97.8
Change in household income:				
Declined 1990–96	15.5 (26.7)	1.6 (9.0)	18.9 (39.6)	11.1 (24.6)
No change 1990–96	28.9 (17.6)	4.8 (10.4)	13.7 (31.5)	15.6 (24.6)
Increased (25%	26.8	46.8	33.7	15.6
Increased 26–50%	11.3	25.8	14.7	22.2
Increased 51–100%	12.4	9.7	10.5	15.6
Increased >100%	5.2	11.3	8.4	20.0

Key: * Averages. † Enterprise is main source of income to the owner household.

Notes: Figures in parentheses refer to the 1991 survey data, which referred to income changes in the period 1989–90; the 1997 survey referred to income changes in the period 1990–96. Data include household and private enterprises only in both surveys.

In Hanoi, where the enterprise is the main income for fewer households than in other areas, as many as two-thirds of the owner families experienced a decline or standstill in income in the 1997 survey (Table 2.6). In Ho Chi Minh City these changes amount to 12 per cent, and some 60 per cent have seen household incomes grow up to 25 per cent. Haiphong has almost one-fifth with no change or a decline in income, but on the other hand more than half have experienced growth rates exceeding 25 per cent over the past six years, and more than one-third mention rates above 50 per cent. Since 42 per cent in Long An, but only 17 per cent in Ha Tay report incomes at the same level as, or even less than, in the 1991 survey, it is difficult to discern any patterns or trends for rural or urban, northern or southern areas. However, in terms of ownership, a higher share of household than private enterprise owner-households have seen their incomes decline or remain at the same level as it was in the 1991 survey, both in urban and rural areas (Table 2.7). Comparing this to the answers given in the 1991 survey, regarding changes in income from 1989–91, things are looking bright for most entrepreneurs. The exceptions are Hanoi and Long An, where somewhat growing numbers are experiencing declining or unchanged incomes (Table 2.6), but across ownership forms, the only negative tendency is the higher share among urban household enterprise owners for whom incomes have not grown (Table 2.7).

Operational Conditions and Equipment

The physical prerequisites for small-scale enterprises appear to have improved considerably in the 1990s, especially in rural areas. In every area covered by the survey, rural as well as urban, a majority of the enterprises are located in premises mainly devoted to non-residential use (Table 2.8). It is only when categorisation by ownership forms is done that 57 per cent of rural household industries are found to be in buildings which primarily serve as the owner's residence (Table 2.9). For Ho Chi Minh City, this is a rather significant change, compared to the survey six years ago. Then, close to 30 per cent of the small firms were still occupying a part of the owner's house, compared to 5 per cent in the 1997 survey (Table 2.8). Haiphong is, on the other hand, experiencing more of a standstill. A slightly higher share of the 1997 survey enterprises are located in their owners' residences, and fewer are located in only non-residential premises than was the case in 1991, but indeed the changes are very small. Viewed from the angle of ownership, the major shift has occurred among household firms, of which more than 70 per cent were located in the owner's home premises in 1991 but less than 50 per cent in 1997 (Table 2.9). Urban partnership enterprises are instead located 'at home' to a somewhat greater extent today than was the case six years ago.

As small-scale industries are moving out of the owners' houses, it is becoming more common to move into rented premises, but there are rather big differences between areas, as well as ownership forms. In Ho Chi Minh City, more than half of all enterprises are now located in rented space, and enterprises in Hanoi are heading the same way, although to a lesser degree (Table 2.8). Meanwhile, about twice as

Table 2.8: Premises and equipment by location. Percentages.

	Urban			Rural	
	Hanoi	**Haiphong**	**HCM City**	**Ha Tay**	**Long An**
Premises:					
Mainly residential	27.7 (37.6)	21.8 (20.0)	5.1 (28.3)	49.4 (-)	33.7 (-)
Mainly non-residential	40.3	33.7	38.5	18.3	53.0
Only non-residential	31.9	44.6	56.4	31.3	13.3
Premises, ownership					
Fully owned	58.8	65.3	37.6	74.7	80.7
Partly owned	15.1	22.8	6.8	13.3	4.8
Rented	26.1 (17.3)	11.9 (21.1)	53.8 (43.8)	10.8 (-)	14.5 (-)
Other	0.0	0.0	1.7	1.2	0.0
Facilities:					
Tap water	98.3 (90.2)	99.0 (76.7)	98.3 (90.2)	68.7 (14.1)	48.2 (0.0)
Electricity	100.0 (96.2)	100.0 (96.7)	100.0 (93.4)	98.8 (33.7)	98.8 (48.4)
Public grid	26.9	46.5	27.4	80.7	71.1
Public grid & 3 phase	67.2	46.5	39.3	4.8	16.9
Telephone	92.4 (24.8)	81.2 (20.0)	97.4 (44.7)	36.1 (0.0)	55.4 (1.6)
Fax	11.8	1.0	33.3	0.0	2.4
Mobile phone	21.8	6.9	38.5	6.0	1.2
Equipment:					
Hand tools	5.9 (13.8)	6.9 (13.6)	4.3 (4.9)	21.7 (43.8)	15.7 (53.6)
Manual machinery	10.9	2.0	2.6	2.4	10.8
Power-driven machinery	25.2	4.0	17.9	22.9	18.1
Manual & power-driven	58.0	87.1	75.2	53.0	55.4
Access to road*:	72.3	74.3	90.6	60.2	47.0

Key: * Here 'road' implies such quality that motor vehicles can use them.
Note: Figures in parentheses refer to the 1991 survey. Figures on premises were not specified for rural areas in the 1991 survey.

many of the Haiphong establishments in the 1991 survey used rented premises as in the 1997 survey.

When the results are analysed across ownership forms, it is only among shareholding and limited liability companies that rented premises constitute the most common mode of securing space. In fact, it has actually become less common within all forms of ownership, with the exception of partnership enterprises; even there the change is rather marginal (Table 2.9).

The signs are very encouraging in terms of infrastructural developments in that access to basic facilities has grown rather impressively. Almost every urban enterprise now has access to tap water, which in the 1991 survey was supplied to 90 per cent of the Hanoi and Ho Chi Minh City enterprises and 77 per cent of those in Haiphong (Table 2.8). And while only 14 per cent of the enterprises in the earlier survey had access to tap water in Ha Tay (Ha Son Binh), the share in 1997 is close to 70 per cent, even surpassing Long An in this regard. Those enterprises still waiting for such facilities are mostly rural households, but taking into consideration that 8 per cent of this category had tap water in 1991, remarkable progress has been achieved. The share of private rural firms with tap water is, in the 1997 survey, as high as it was among their urban equivalents six years ago.

The supply of electricity in the urban areas was very well developed already by the time of the 1991 survey, and at least nine out of ten firms in the cities had access to power. In the 1997 survey the figures are even more encouraging, as enterprises in rural areas show a remarkable catch-up, from one-third and one half in Ha Tay and Long An respectively in the earlier survey. Almost all household enterprises have also gained access to a power supply in that period. The extended access to electricity has, in none of the areas included in the survey, come as a result of investments by the enterprises in their own generators. In fact only a minor share have such equipment, and those that do are 'other' firms in rural areas (still less than 10 per cent) and also a few rural private enterprises (less than 5 per cent). The number of small businesses having access to their own generators is somewhat higher in Ha Tay than in Long An, but the proportions are still only 4 and 1 per cent respectively.

Along with a better power supply has come an extended use of power-driven machinery, mostly as a combination with manually operated equipment (Table 2.8). Ho Chi Minh City records the least use of hand

Table 2.9: Premises and equipment by ownership form. Percentages.

	Urban					Rural		
	Household	Private	Partnership	Co-operative	Shareholding*	Household	Private	Other form
Premises: Mainly residential	45.9	7.8	17.5	1.8	3.8	57.3	27.1	4.5
	(71.4)	(29.7)	(11.4)	(1.1)	(-)	(-)	(-)	(-)
Mainly non-residential	40.8	39.1	42.5	24.6	39.7	35.4	45.8	18.2
Only non-residential	13.3	53.1	40.0	73.7	56.4	7.3	27.1	77.3
Ownership: Fully owned	75.5	51.6	55.0	47.4	30.8	89.6	70.8	40.9
Partly owned	10.2	18.8	7.5	21.1	15.4	2.1	14.6	27.3
Rented	13.3	29.7	37.5	29.8	53.8	8.3	14.6	27.3
	(23.2)	(31.3)	(35.1)	(36.6)	(-)	(-)	(-)	(-)
Other	1.0	0.0	0.0	1.8	0.0	0.0	0.0	4.5
Facilities: Tap water	98.0	100.0	95.0	98.2	100.0	46.9	75.0	72.7
	(79.5)	(75.0)	(83.3)	(78.5)	(-)	(8.2)	(11.4)	(-)
Electricity	100.0	100.0	100.0	100.0	100.0	97.9	100.0	100.0
	(99.1)	(94.5)	(92.1)	(94.6)	(-)	(55.7)	(63.8)	(-)
Public grid	55.1	31.3	32.5	21.1	15.4	86.5	64.6	54.5
Public grid & 3 phase	39.8	45.3	52.5	56.1	66.7	11.5	8.3	13.6
Telephone	77.6	96.9	90.0	94.7	100.0	19.8	81.3	81.8
	(9.8)	(23.9)	(34.2)	(67.7)	(-)	(0.0)	(6.0)	(-)
Fax	1.0	23.4	2.5	7.0	46.2	1.0	0.0	4.5
Mobile phone	3.1	31.3	17.5	15.8	50.0	1.0	2.1	18.2
Equipment: Hand tools	11.2	6.3	2.5	5.3	0.0	26.0	8.3	9.1
	(17.1)	(7.9)	(2.7)	(8.8)	(-)	(55.3)	(36.3)	(-)
Manual machinery	6.1	4.7	5.0	3.5	6.4	9.4	2.1	4.5
Power-driven	18.4	7.8	15.0	14.0	23.1	13.5	33.3	22.7
Manual & power	64.3	81.3	77.5	77.2	70.5	51.0	56.3	63.6
Access to motorable road:	61.2	37.5	85.0	82.5	89.7	38.5	64.6	95.5

Note: Figures in parentheses refer to the 1991 survey. Figures on premises were not specified for rural areas in the 1991 survey. *Shareholding and LLC.

tools, just as in the earlier survey, but the use of strictly power-driven machinery is actually more common in Hanoi and, surprisingly, also in Ha Tay. It turns out, when classified into ownership groups, that even though hand tools are more common among household firms than among other enterprises in urban areas, this is also where the highest share of power machinery users is found (except for limited liability companies) (Table 2.9). Further, a greater number of rural household and private firms exclusively use power-driven equipment than do their urban counterparts.

Among Long An enterprises, the share having access to a telephone (55 per cent) is even higher than that having access to tap water (Table 2.8), but this is the only surveyed area where this is the case. Ho Chi Minh City offers telephone facilities to almost all businesses, while the coverage is about 80 per cent in Haiphong. And even though it is the household sector that is lagging somewhat compared to other urban forms of ownership in the 1997 survey, one can hardly say that they have been discriminated against, since not even 10 per cent had access to a telephone six years earlier. Rural household industries have, unfortunately, not witnessed the same progress in terms of this facility; around 80 per cent remain without telephones.

The growing access to telephones might well be needed in Long An, since the share of firms having access to roads suitable for motor vehicles has decreased. The change might not be as worrying when looked at in terms of location, as the decrease is very small and concentrated in one area. But when classified by ownership forms, it is found that household industries in the countryside are clearly falling behind. While more than half of these enterprises had access to roads passable for motor vehicles six years ago, the share in the 1997 survey is down to less than 40 per cent. Even though the enterprises included in the two surveys are not the same, and hence a strict comparison cannot be made between the two surveys, this is still not an encouraging sign.

Almost all small enterprises in the survey fully own the machinery used in the business. In Hanoi, Long An and Ha Tay, the equipment has mostly been bought new, while in Ho Chi Minh City and Haiphong some 45 per cent of the firms have bought used machinery (Table 2.10). In terms of ownership form, there is a marginal decrease in the percentage of rural private enterprises buying new machinery, in the 1997

Table 2.10: Details on machinery and equipment by location. Percentages.

	Urban			Rural	
	Hanoi	**Haiphong**	**HCM City**	**Ha Tay**	**Long An**
Possible production increase, with existing machinery:					
Not at all	6.3	8.5	18.0	4.6	12.9
No more than 10%	6.3	4.3	27.9	10.8	7.1
10–25%	29.5	12.8	23.4	20.0	14.3
26–50%	44.6	28.7	18.9	38.5	32.9
51–100%	9.8	29.8	9.9	24.6	28.6
More than 100%	3.6	16.0	1.8	1.5	4.3
Machinery ownership:					
Fully owned	99.1	98.9	99.1	98.5	97.1
Fully hired	0.9	1.1	0.9	1.5	2.9
Machinery acquisition:					
Purchased new	67.6	44.1	38.7	84.6	68.6
	(31.6)	(56.8)	(24.1)	(66.7)	(73.9)
Purchased second-hand	20.7	47.3	43.2	13.8	30.0
Self-constructed	11.7	8.6	18.0	1.5	1.4
	(29.1)	(6.8)	(12.3)	(13.3)	(2.2)
Machinery supply, source:					
Private enterprise	59.5	69.6	72.0	59.4	90.0
State enterprise	25.2	19.6	6.5	39.1	8.6
	(31.8)	(33.8)	(8.9)	(6.5)	(20.8)
Co-operatives	0.9	3.3	0.0	0.0	0.0
Import	9.9	3.3	17.8	1.6	1.4
Other	4.5	4.3	3.7	0.0	0.0
Owned assets:*	547,526	215,387	1,046,828	277,047	84,766

Key: * Value of machinery in use per enterprise, thousand dong, 1997 survey.
Note: Figures in parentheses refer to the corresponding 1991 survey data.

survey (Table 2.11). Other privately owned firms are the main source of supply, as in the 1991 survey, but the share coming from state enterprises has actually increased among rural as well as urban household enterprises, and also among rural private firms. This must be due to the development in Ha Tay, where close to 40 per cent, compared to less than 10 per cent in the earlier survey, got their machinery from state enter-

Table 2.11: Details on machinery and equipment by ownership form. Percentages.

	Urban					Rural		
	Household	Private	Partnership	Co-operatives	Shareholding*	Household	Private	Other form
Possible production increase, with existing machinery:								
Not at all	8.0	10.0	15.8	11.1	12.8	5.6	18.2	0.0
No more than 10%	17.2	16.7	5.3	7.4	14.1	9.9	9.1	5.0
10–25%	21.8	15.0	34.2	16.7	26.9	16.9	15.9	20.0
26–50%	26.4	31.7	31.6	42.6	26.9	38.0	27.3	45.0
51–100%	14.9	20.0	10.5	13.0	17.9	26.8	27.3	25.0
More than 100%	11.5	6.7	2.6	9.3	1.3	2.8	2.3	5.0
Machinery ownership:								
Fully owned	100.0	100.0	97.4	100.0	97.4	97.2	97.7	100.0
Fully hired	0.0	0.0	2.6	0.0	2.6	2.8	2.3	0.0
Machinery acquisition:								
Purchased new	40.2 (29.5)	48.3 (28.3)	36.8 (27.9)	50.0 (45.8)	71.1 (-)	81.7 (64.4)	68.2 (69.6)	75.0 (-)
Purchased second-hand	47.1	33.3	42.1	40.7	21.1	16.9	29.5	25.0
Self-constructed	12.6 (16.8)	18.3 (16.7)	21.1 (16.2)	9.3 (13.3)	7.9 (-)	1.4 (6.7)	2.3 (3.3)	0.0 (-)
Machinery supply, source:								
Private enterprise	79.3	64.3	63.2	58.5	61.8	82.9	72.7	55.0
State enterprise	11.5 (7.6)	16.1 (20.4)	26.3 (17.4)	28.3 (35.9)	11.8 (-)	17.1 (14.2)	27.3 (18.7)	35.0 (-)
Co-operatives	0.0	1.8	2.6	0.0	2.6	0.0	0.0	0.0
Import	2.3	14.3	5.3	9.4	21.1	0.0	0.0	10.0
Other	6.9	3.6	2.6	3.8	2.6	0.0	0.0	0.0
Owned assets:*	31,908	511,702	121,352	321,327	1,927,473	13,586	182,010	908,623

Key: *Value of machinery in use per enterprise, thousand dong, 1997 survey. **Note:** Figures in parenthesis refer to the 1991 survey. *Shareholding and LLC.

prises. The proportion of imported machinery has grown to about 10 per cent in Hanoi and 18 per cent in Ho Chi Minh City (Table 2.10); private enterprises and shareholding and limited liability companies mainly accounted for this development, while imported equipment is still very uncommon in rural areas. The share of self-constructed equipment is rather modest everywhere, but higher in the cities (for instance 18 per cent in Ho Chi Minh City) than in the rural areas; and in terms of forms of urban establishments, it is more common in urban private and partnership enterprises. Among these ownership forms, the shares of self-constructed equipment are actually higher today than in the 1991 survey, which is also the case in Ho Chi Minh City and Haiphong.

Some 18 per cent of the surveyed small-scale industries in Ho Chi Minh City cannot increase production at all, with the equipment to which they currently have access (Table 2.10). By contrast, less than 5 per cent of the surveyed enterprises in Ha Tay are in the same situation. About half of the surveyed firms in Ho Chi Minh City operate on at least 90 per cent capacity utilisation. The corresponding share in the other cities is 13 per cent, while in the rural areas it is marginally higher: 15 per cent in Ha Tay and 20 per cent in Long An. In Haiphong, the existence of unused equipment is of such a magnitude that 16 per cent of the enterprises could double their production, and another 30 per cent could increase production by 50 to 100 per cent without having to undertake further investments. Most firms, regardless of ownership form, are obviously fluctuating somewhere close to 50 per cent of their maximum levels (Table 2.11). The possible increase is somewhat less for urban households, partnerships and shareholding and limited liability companies, and somewhat more among urban private enterprises and in rural areas in general.

Far from all of the small businesses included in the 1997 survey were able to operate continuously throughout the year. In Ho Chi Minh City this share was 87 per cent, while in Long An only 55 per cent were able to avoid breaks in production (Table 2.12). The share of firms with less than continuous operations is higher in rural areas, and more common among household enterprises, irrespective of rural or urban location (Tables 2.12 and 2.13). The differences are large between for instance shareholding and limited liability companies, (where about 10 per cent experienced difficulties) and rural household enterprises (where the

Table 2.12: Continuity of operations by location. Percentages.

	Urban			Rural	
	Hanoi	Haiphong	HCM City	Ha Tay	Long An
Operated all of 1996:	79.5	74.3	87.0	68.7	54.9
Period of closure:					
1 month	0.0	2.0	4.3	0.0	1.2
2 months	6.0	12.9	5.2	6.0	15.9
3–4 months	8.7	9.9	1.7	12.0	18.3
5–6 months	5.1	1.0	0.9	13.2	9.7
over 6 months	0.9	0.0	0.9	0.0	0.0
Reasons for closure:					
Lack of raw material	0.8	0.0	1.7	1.2	10.8
Lack of demand	13.4	20.8	10.3	22.9	16.9
Shortage of labour	0.0	0.0	0.0	1.2	2.4
Other reasons	6.7	5.9	3.4	9.6	26.5
Days worked/week:					
under 5	3.3	5.9	7.7	3.6	3.6
5	12.6	6.9	7.7	3.6	14.5
6	61.3	42.6	73.5	20.5	26.5
7	22.7	44.6	11.1	72.3	55.4
Hours worked/day:					
under 8	12.6	21.8	6.9	26.4	39.7
8–12	74.8	76.3	77.0	65.0	49.3
over 12	12.5	2.0	16.4	8.4	10.8
No. of shifts/day:					
1	85.7	89.0	80.2	84.1	87.8
2	12.6	9.0	15.5	12.2	7.3
3	1.7	2.0	4.3	3.7	4.9

share is more than 40 per cent). Furthermore there are great variations in the period of closure. In Ho Chi Minh City, the closing periods were on average shorter, in most cases limited to two months or less (Table 2.12). In Hanoi and Haiphong, the period was slightly longer, in Hanoi actually five to six months in some cases. In rural areas, firms in Long An suffered interruptions in their production most frequently, but interruptions among firms in Ha Tay tended to last longer, some for five to six months (Table 2.12). Across ownership forms, it is mostly

Table 2.13: Continuity of operations by ownership form. Percentages.

	Urban					Rural		
	Household	Private	Partnership	Co-operatives	Shareholding*	Household	Private	Other form
Operated all of 1996:	72.4	87.3	71.8	80.4	89.6	58.6	79.2	59.1
Period of closure:								
1 month	3.1	3.2	2.6	0.0	1.3	1.0	0.0	0.0
2 months	6.1	4.8	15.4	10.7	6.5	14.6	2.1	13.6
3–4 months	13.2	4.8	5.1	7.2	0.0	19.8	10.4	4.5
5–6 months	4.1	0.0	5.2	0.0	2.6	10.4	8.3	22.7
over 6 months	1.0	0.0	0.0	1.8	0.0	0.0	0.0	0.0
Reasons for closure:								
Lack of raw material	1.0	1.6	0.0	1.8	0.0	0.0	14.6	13.6
Lack of demand	21.4	7.8	25.0	14.0	6.4	27.1	2.1	27.3
Shortage of labour	0.0	0.0	0.0	0.0	0.0	1.0	0.0	9.1
Other reasons	6.1	4.7	5.0	7.0	3.8	20.8	14.6	13.6
Days worked/week								
less than 5	6.1	7.9	5.0	7.0	2.6	5.1	0.0	4.5
5	11.2	9.4	17.5	7.0	3.8	11.5	6.3	4.5
6	40.8	57.8	57.5	70.2	79.5	19.8	27.1	31.8
7	41.8	25.0	20.0	15.8	14.1	63.5	66.7	59.1
Hours worked/day								
less than 8 hours	28.5	6.2	12.5	12.4	1.3	49.0	14.6	4.5
8–12	66.4	82.8	72.5	77.2	83.3	50.0	62.6	77.2
over 12	5.1	11.0	15.0	10.6	15.4	1.0	23.1	18.2
No. of shifts/day								
1	93.9	84.4	87.2	80.4	75.6	97.9	74.5	59.1
2	6.1	9.4	10.3	19.6	19.2	1.0	19.1	27.3
3	0.0	6.3	2.6	0.0	5.1	1.0	6.4	13.6

Note: *Shareholding and LLC.

among household industries that the longer interruptions occur, while partnership enterprises and co-operatives register mainly two-month closures (Table 2.13). It is among the 'other' group that these longer periods of closure appear, while among those private and household enterprises which have been forced to halt production, interruptions lasting three to four months have been more common (Table 2.13).

By far the most common reason for a halt in production is a lack of demand. Only among enterprises in Long An are 'other reasons', not related to raw material or labour, more frequently mentioned (Table 2.12). As will become evident later, this could be an indication of capital shortage prevailing in this area. Moreover rural private enterprises are the only enterprises that regard a lack of raw materials as far more troublesome than a lack of demand (Table 2.13). Nowhere is labour a major bottleneck.

In Hanoi and Ho Chi Minh City most of the enterprises operated six days per week, while operation every day of the week is the most frequent way of running a business in rural areas and in Haiphong (Table 2.12). In the urban areas, it is only among household enterprises that seven days of operations are more common (Table 2.14). Everywhere, eight to twelve hours is the most common length of a workday, though 40 per cent of the industries included in the survey in Long An, 26 per cent of those in Ha Tay and 22 per cent of those in Haiphong do have less than eight-hour workdays. These somewhat shorter days are accounted for by household enterprises, in urban as well as rural areas, although the share is slightly less than 30 per cent among urban household enterprises, but closer to 50 per cent among the rural ones. On the other hand, close to one-quarter of private enterprises in rural areas operate more than 12 hours per day, the highest share among all ownership forms in all areas. Shift work is not very common. In shareholding, limited liability companies and co-operatives, and in rural private enterprises, the share of enterprises with two shifts approaches 20 per cent. In the rural 'other' category, 40 per cent of the firms operated more than one shift per day.

Growth Prospects and Constraints

In terms of how the entrepreneurs view the main constraint to the growth of their enterprises, some very interesting developments have taken place since the 1991 survey was done. At that point in time,

Table 2.14: Main constraint to growth of enterprises by location. Percentages.

	Urban			Rural	
	Hanoi	**Haiphong**	**HCM City**	**Ha Tay**	**Long An**
Shortage of capital	23.5 (43.5)	49.5 (67.5)	17.1 (32.6)	31.3 (27.7)	50.6 (24.6)
Lack of skilled labour	0.0 (0.8)	0.0 (0.0)	0.9 (0.5)	0.0 (0.0)	0.0 (0.9)
Lack of technical know-how	3.4 (2.4)	0.0 (2.2)	0.9 (0.5)	1.2 (0.0)	0.0 (4.8)
Limited demand current output	29.4 (21.8)	25.7 (5.6)	6.8 (15.1)	41.0 (20.5)	4.8 (19.3)
Too much competition	21.8 (12.9)	9.9 (4.5)	51.3 (17.0)	16.9 (2.4)	20.5 (13.2)
Lack of marketing/ transport	0.0 (5.6)	1.0 (4.5)	4.3 (6.4)	1.2 (10.8)	0.0 (0.0)
Lack of modern machinery	0.8 (1.6)	1.0 (6.7)	2.6 (5.0)	1.2 (1.2)	6.0 (1.8)
Lack of raw material	0.0 (3.2)	1.0 (1.0)	1.7 (3.7)	0.0 (0.0)	3.6 (3.5)
Lack of energy (power, fuel)	0.0 (0.0)	0.0 (0.0)	0.9 (7.8)	0.0 (0.0)	0.0 (0.9)
Interference by local officials	0.0 (0.0)	1.0 (0.0)	0.0 (0.0)	0.0 (0.0)	0.0 (2.6)
Uncertain government policies	5.9 (1.6)	3.0 (0.0)	0.0 (1.8)	3.6 (0.0)	0.0 (6.1)
Inadequate premises/ space	3.4 (-)	2.0 (-)	6.8 (-)	1.2 (-)	3.6 (-)
Difficult to get licences, etc.	0.8 (-)	0.0 (-)	0.0 (-)	0.0 (-)	0.0 (-)
Other factors	1.7 (3.2)	2.0 (6.7)	3.4 (8.7)	0.0 (21.7)	6.0 (6.1)
None	9.2 (-)	4.0 (-)	3.4 (-)	2.4 (-)	4.8 (-)

Note: The entrepreneurs were to rank three options at the most. Figures in parentheses refer to the corresponding 1991 survey data. Where marked with a (-), this was not mentioned as an alternative in the 1991 survey. An option at that time was 'cannot afford to hire wage workers', stated by very few then and not mentioned by anyone in the 1997 survey, hence excluded.

capital was the single worst bottleneck in all areas, urban as well as rural, and among all forms of ownership. This is, however, no longer the case. Only in Haiphong, among the cities, is capital still the most frequently mentioned constraint. While almost two-thirds mentioned it in the 1991 survey, only about half do so today (Table 2.14). Meanwhile, a quarter of the small businesses there seem to experience a limited demand for their current output, compared to less than 6 per cent in the 1991 survey. In Ho Chi Minh City more than half of the firms now point to keen competition as the main problem, compared to only 17 per cent in the earlier survey. The share with capital shortages today is only about half what it was in the 1991 survey. Capital is still the main constraint to 24 per cent of the establishments in Hanoi, but limited demand is the single most common answer, cited by approximately 30 per cent of respondents. Heavy competition is the next most common answer, cited by more than 20 per cent.

Even though capital was the single most frequent constraint in rural areas in the 1991 survey, the share mentioning it, approximately one-quarter, was not as high as in the cities (Table 2.14). Today, on the other hand, capital is more of an obstacle to establishments in the countryside, and while the increase is relatively marginal in Ha Tay, more than half of those in Long An mention shortage of capital as the single most important barrier to growth. Enterprises in Long An are far less concerned about limited demand today than six years ago, but opine that the competition they are facing is far heavier today. The entrepreneurs in Ha Tay are not as lucky. If the share facing limited demand was 20 per cent in the 1991 survey, it doubled by the 1997 survey. Difficult competition is mentioned by 17 per cent in the 1997 survey, compared to less than 3 per cent in the 1991 survey. The areas that seem to have improved are market channels and transport facilities.

In terms of ownership forms in the cities, it is among the co-operatives and shareholding and limited liability enterprises that lack of capital is still perceived as the thorniest issue (Table 2.15). Urban household undertakings are more concerned with limited demand for their current products (Table 2.16), while private and partnership enterprises are more worried about the tough competition. In particular, the change in terms of how this is perceived among private enterprises should be noted, since not even 10 per cent mentioned it in

Table 2.15: Main constraints to growth by ownership form in the 1997 survey. Percentages.

	Urban					Rural		
	Household	Private	Partnership	Co-operatives	Shareholding*	Household	Private	Other form
Shortage of capital	25..5	31.8	22.5	32.1	32.5	35.4	41.7	63.6
Lack of skilled labour	0.0	1.5	0.0	0.0	0.0	0.0	0.0	0.0
Lack of technical know-how	1.0	0.0	7.5	1.8	0.0	0.0	0.0	4.5
Limited demand current output	30.6	13.6	22.5	19.6	13.0	28.1	14.6	18.2
Too much competition	24.5	34.8	25.0	26.8	31.2	20.8	18.8	9.1
Lack of marketing/transport	0.0	3.0	0.0	5.4	1.3	1.0	0.0	0.0
Lack of modern machinery	0.0	0.0	0.0	3.6	3.9	4.2	4.2	0.0
Lack of raw material	1.0	0.0	0.0	0.0	2.6	0.0	6.3	0.0
Lack of energy (power, fuel)	0.0	1.5	0.0	0.0	0.0	0.0	0.0	0.0
Interference by local officials	0.0	0.0	0.0	0.0	1.3	0.0	0.0	0.0
Uncertain government policies	1.0	1.5	7.5	1.8	5.2	1.0	2.1	4.5
Inadequate premises/space	5.1	6.1	7.5	1.8	1.3	3.1	2.1	0.0
Difficult get licences, etc.	0.0	0.0	0.0	0.0	1.3	0.0	0.0	0.0
Other factors	2.0	3.0	5.0	1.8	1.3	3.1	4.2	0.0
None	9.2	3.0	2.5	5.4	5.2	3.1	6.3	0.0

Note: The entrepreneurs were to rank up to a maximum of three constraints. *Shareholding and LLC.

Table 2.16: Assistance desired from authorities by urban enterprises by location. Percentages.

	Urban			Rural	
	Hanoi	Haiphong	HCM City	Ha Tay	Long An
Removal of bureaucratic obstacles	6.7 (8.8)	0.0 (6.0)	8.5 (5.2)	9.6 (1.2)	0.0 (12.1)
Provision of premises, power and other infrastructure	1.7 (32.5)	4.0 (19.0)	6.0 (50.5)	8.4 (1.2)	1.2 (4.8)
Provision of easy credit	5.9 (19.3)	22.8 (57.1)	3.4 (7.1)	14.5 (3.6)	13.4 (4.8)
Restriction of imports	5.9 (10.5)	1.0 (2.4)	1.7 (11.3)	0.0 (0.0)	1.2 (2.4)
A more liberal import policy	1.7 (1.8)	0.0 (0.0)	0.0 (3.8)	0.0 (0.0)	0.0 (3.2)
Distribution of raw material	0.0 (1.8)	0.0 (0.0)	0.0 (1.9)	1.2 (0.0)	0.0 (10.5)
Assistance with technical know-how	0.0 (4.4)	0.0 (2.4)	0.9 (0.9)	0.0 (0.0)	0.0 (0.0)
Training facilities for workers	0.0 (0.0)	0.0 (0.0)	0.0 (0.0)	0.0 (0.0)	0.0 (10.5)
Assistance with marketing	1.7 (0.0)	2.0 (0.0)	0.9 (0.0)	15.7 (0.0)	6.1 (0.0)
Clarification of long-term policies	4.2 (11.4)	0.0 (2.4)	1.7 (11.3)	0.0 (43.4)	2.4 (4.0)
Improved macro economic policies	1.7 (0.0)	0.0 (0.5)	0.9 (0.5)	0.0 (1.2)	0.0 (0.8)
Other	0.8 (2.6)	2.0 (3.6)	0.0 (4.7)	7.2 (4.8)	0.0 (8.9)
None	69.7 (-)	68.3 (-)	76.1 (-)	43.4 (-)	75.6 (-)

Note: The entrepreneurs were to rank up to a maximum of three options.
Figures in parentheses refer to the corresponding 1991 survey data. Where marked with a (-), this was not mentioned as an alternative in the 1991 survey.

the 1991 survey, while in the 1997 survey it is the main obstacle for more than one-third of the enterprises in this category. Shortage of capital continues to be the most common hindrance to growth among all rural forms of establishments, and the situation has become worse for household enterprises. The share pointing to capital shortages as the main problem has grown from 25 to 35 per cent since the earlier survey, while remaining at about the same level as in the 1991 survey, for private enterprises. The percentage fighting difficult competition is about twice as high among rural private enterprises today compared to six years ago, and also among rural household firms this share has grown, approximately by 9 percentage points. In sum, competition has increased among all forms of establishments, in the cities as well as on the countryside, while capital has become less of a bottleneck for urban businesses, but more so for rural undertakings.

However, while facing these difficulties, the small businesses included in the survey are still very ambivalent about government assistance. In Ho Chi Minh City, for instance, as many as 76 per cent of the enterprises claim that they want no assistance whatsoever and the shares are almost as high in the other areas (Table 2.16). The most frequently mentioned mode of assistance desired in the cities in the 1991 survey was provision of premises and infrastructure, but since close to every enterprise in these areas now has access to such facilities (Tables 2.8 and 2.9), the demand for these is very small today. Access to credit in urban areas was another troublesome issue in the 1991 survey, especially in the northern areas, but as has become evident earlier in this survey, this is less of a problem today (Table 2.14), and hence the share wanting such assistance has shrunk as well. Although more than one-fifth of the establishments in Haiphong are still interested in receiving credit support from the government, their proportion was close to 60 per cent in the 1991 survey. In addition, what deserves to be pointed out is the lack of interest in undertaking projects with the government as a partner. Even though capital is a constraint, very few want the government to step in as rescuer, but would probably be interested in dealing with a private loan facilitator. Regarding the uncertainty about government long-term policies, which obviously was not too worrying even six years ago as only 10 per cent mentioned it and this in the midst of deregulation, the mist seems to have cleared even more today.

A higher share of the entrepreneurs in rural than in urban areas appreciated credit assistance from the authorities. However, even in the countryside this constraint to growth is not voiced as frequently as the shortage of capital. The latter is in fact, the only thing around which a tangible share, 13 per cent, coalesce in Long An (Table 2.16).

Table 2.17: Assistance desired from authorities by ownership form in the 1997 survey. Percentages.

	Urban					Rural		
	Household	Private	Partnership	Co-operatives	Shareholding*	Household	Private	Other form
Removal of bureaucratic obstacles	1.0	9.1	2.5	8.9	6.5	5.2	0.0	13.6
Provision of premises, power and other infrastructure	0.0	4.5	5.0	10.7	2.6	1.0	12.8	4.5
Provision of easy credit	10.2	15.2	7.5	8.9	7.8	8.3	12.8	40.9
Restriction of imports	3.1	1.5	2.5	5.4	2.6	1.0	0.0	0.0
A more liberal import policy	0.0	1.5	0.0	0.0	1.3	0.0	0.0	0.0
Distribution of raw material	0.0	0.0	0.0	0.0	0.0	0.0	0.0	4.5
Assistance with technical know-how	1.0	0.0	0.0	0.0	0.0	0.0	0.0	0.0
Training facilities for workers	0.0	0.0	0.0	0.0	0.0	0.0	0.0	0.0
Assistance with marketing	2.0	1.5	0.0	0.0	2.6	12.5	12.8	0.0
Clarification of long-term policies	0.0	0.0	2.5	1.8	6.5	1.0	0.0	4.5
Improved macro economic policies	0.0	1.5	2.5	1.8	0.0	0.0	0.0	0.0
Other	1.0	0.0	2.5	0.0	1.3	2.1	4.3	9.1
None	81.6	65.2	75.0	62.5	68.8	68.8	57.4	22.7

Note: The entrepreneurs were to rank up to a maximum of three options. *Shareholding and LLC.

The 10 and 12 per cent, who in the 1991 survey wished for removal of bureaucracy and help with raw material distribution respectively, were not mentioned in the 1997 survey. The need for long-term policy clarification, mentioned by so many in Ha Tay in the earlier survey, is completely gone. Only to a minor extent has this been replaced by calls for credit or assistance with marketing – the latter an issue hardly mentioned six years ago, even in the cities.

In terms of ownership forms, not even 20 per cent of the urban household firms want assistance from the authorities, and like 69 per cent of their counterparts in the countryside, household entrepreneurs prove to be the most sceptical (Table 2.17). It is interesting to note that none of those in this category situated in the cities mentioned premises or infrastructure in the 1997 survey, compared to almost 40 per cent in the earlier survey. Meanwhile, some 13 per cent of the rural respondents would like some help with marketing, an item not mentioned at all in the countryside six years ago. Rural enterprises under 'other' ownership forms are the most inclined to welcome assistance from the authorities, but limit their wishes to capital or removal of bureaucracy.

Notes

1. Chapters 2 to 6 refer to the survey of 'new' enterprises, not surveyed in 1991. For details on the structure of the sample, see Table 1.9. Except where otherwise stated, all monetary figures refer to Vietnamese dong at end-1996 prices. At the time of the 1997 survey, one USD was approximately 11,600 dong. Unless stated otherwise, all data refer to the 1997 survey, as well.

2. There were no shareholding and limited liability enterprises in the 1991 survey, hence data are missing for them for comparisons on ownership basis between 1991 and the 1997 surveys. The group 'other' in rural areas contains partnership enterprises, co-operatives, etc., which are too few to constitute own groups, but which still contribute to a more comprehensive picture of the rural enterprise structure. There were no such groups in the 1991 survey, hence making comparisons impossible.

3. This is due to the large number of repair shops and other small service undertakings located in Long An at that time, undertakings which accordingly had very little equipment, and for which levels of value added, etc. do not really say anything in relation to the 1997 survey data.

3

Origin and Development History

Bhargavi Ramamurthy

In the discussion on the origin and development history of 'new' (i.e., not previously surveyed) enterprises, we consider a number of determinants: the age of enterprises; the profile of the entrepreneurs behind these units; the motivating factors for private entrepreneurship; the major constraints at establishment; the size of initial investments and their sources; any assistance from external agencies at the time of establishment; and whether these enterprises have improved the household incomes of the entrepreneur. All these factors are of vital importance in understanding the proliferation of private sector industries as well as their sustainability over a longer period of time.

Urban Enterprises

The dates of establishment of our sample urban enterprises reflect the natural tendency of private entrepreneurship growth under socialist and more liberal (*doi moi*) conditions very well. Overall, the percentage of enterprises established after reunification in 1976 declined until the period 1986–90, where we notice a sudden spurt of 21 per cent (Table 3.1). This period coincides with the introduction of *doi moi* and the greater participation allowed for the private sector in general. Except for a small 5 per cent established in 1991, the period since 1992 has seen a fairly steady enterprise establishment rate, reflecting the

Table 3.1: Year of establishment of urban enterprises by location. Percentages.

	Hanoi	Haiphong	HCM City	All urban
Before 1976	16.0	10.9	0.9	9.2
1976–80	10.1	5.0	9.4	8.3
1981–85	9.2	5.9	6.8	7.4
1986–90	22.7	22.8	18.8	21.4
1991	2.5	9.9	4.3	5.3
1992	5.9	8.9	17.9	11.0
1993	16.0	14.9	12.0	14.2
1994	6.7	10.9	13.7	10.4
1995	10.9	10.9	16.2	12.8

strong performance of the Vietnamese economy as well as private sector growth in this period.[1]

This broad trend is seen in all three sample cities – Hanoi, Haiphong and Ho Chi Minh City – though we find distinct differences in the individual numbers. Hanoi has the highest share of old enterprises (16 per cent set up before 1976), with an establishment spurt of almost 23 per cent occurring between 1986–90, followed by ups and downs in the period 1991–95 and about 11 per cent of the enterprises in operation for at least one full fiscal year when the 1997 survey was conducted.[2] Haiphong follows the same pattern, and is distinctive with an even representation of the oldest and newest enterprises. About 11 per cent of the enterprises here were set up before 1976 and an equal percentage in 1995. Ho Chi Minh City has very few old enterprises (only 1 per cent of the sample established before 1976) but the highest percentage of its enterprises were set up in the late 1980s. The effects of *doi moi*, showing up in the spurt of almost 19 per cent in the 1986–90 period has continued since, except for a decline in 1991.

Overall, we find only a small percentage (about 9 per cent) of pre-unification enterprises and a majority of the sample enterprises have been in operation only since the *doi moi* era. A quarter of the enterprises were set up before 1986, another quarter between 1986 and 1991 and almost half the sample enterprises were four years old or less at the time of the survey. Next, the presumed effects of *doi moi* are more distinct in Ho Chi Minh City and Haiphong, where a huge 83 and 78

Table 3.2: Year of establishment of urban enterprises by ownership form. Percentages.

	Household	Private	Partnership	Co-operative	Shareholding*
Before 1976	1.0	4.7	5.0	43.9	0.0
1976–80	10.2	1.6	17.5	17.5	0.0
1981–85	10.2	1.6	20.0	8.8	1.3
1986–90	33.7	20.3	37.5	14.0	3.8
1991	5.1	7.8	7.5	1.8	5.1
1992	7.1	23.4	0.0	1.8	17.9
1993	12.2	10.9	5.0	7.0	29.5
1994	9.2	14.1	5.0	0.0	19.2
1995	11.2	15.6	2.5	5.3	23.1

Note: *Shareholding and LLC.

per cent of the enterprises, respectively, were established in the period after 1986, in contrast to a relatively lower 65 per cent in Hanoi.

The above-mentioned trend in establishment history becomes more significant when we look at the ownership forms of the established enterprises. As one might expect, most of the co-operatives (about 70 per cent) and only 1 per cent of the shareholding and limited liability companies were established before 1986 (Table 3.2). Partnerships seem to be the most common ownership form after co-operatives in the pre-1986 period, with more than 40 per cent of these enterprises established then. About 8 per cent of the private enterprises and 21 per cent of the household enterprises pre-date 1986. The first major spurt for all ownership categories is seen in the period 1986–90, except for the shareholding and limited liability companies for which it occurred in 1992. This trend, again, is in conformity with the period of greater admissibility of the private sector. The non-state sector after reunification was largely dominated by co-operatives; private sector growth began with a proliferation of partnership and household enterprises, and only after *doi moi* did the other private entrepreneurial forms grow explicitly. While private, household and partnership enterprises did exist before the *doi moi* era, a drastic increase in the forms and numbers of non-state enterprises has occurred only since the late 1980s .

The pace of establishment of household enterprises has been slow since 1990 (about 45 per cent of the sampled household units have been set up since 1990), relative to the private enterprises, of which almost 72 per cent were set up after 1990. This growth in the number of private enterprises also resulted from a change of ownership forms, mainly from household and co-operative enterprises. In our sample, about 33 per cent of the enterprises previously existed under different forms. About 20 per cent of the private enterprises, 15 per cent of the partnerships and 7 per cent of the co-operatives were previously household enterprises. Almost a third of the shareholding and limited liability companies were originally private enterprises and one of the shareholding companies is a privatised state enterprise. The number of enterprises which have thus changed to more complex ownership forms exceeds the number of enterprises that have moved in the other direction. Only one household enterprise was a private enterprise before, and five household enterprises were previously partnerships.

Table 3.3 presents the profile of the owner-managers of urban household and private enterprises. The overall picture that emerges is that of a middle-aged male with ten or more years of education and previous employment in a position of responsibility, most probably in the state sector. One-fifth of the entrepreneurs are women and there are very few entrepreneurs less than 29 years of age. In fact the age distribution of the owner-managers shows that about 24 per cent are older than 50. The level of education is quite high (almost 37 per cent have more than ten years of education) and this correlates well with their previous experience in a position of responsibility. None of the respondents has been in local or high official cadres. When we combine the advanced age, education and experience, it definitely predicts a positive impact on private entrepreneurship.

However, we find that almost half the owner-managers in the age group 40–49 years and 42 per cent in the over-50 age group are running household enterprises. The implications of this finding are twofold: First, middle-aged, previously employed individuals are voluntarily starting their entrepreneurial careers with household enterprises. This constitutes a 'pull' factor into private sector entrepreneurship. The second interpretation, however, is not so positive. These middle-aged new entrepreneurs might have been forced to stand on their own feet after being dismissed from positions of high responsibility, probably within the state sector. They may well have turned to household enterprises as

Table 3.3: Characteristics of owner-managers of urban household and private enterprises. Percentages.

	Hanoi	Haiphong	HCM City	All urban
Sex:				
Male	83.3	79.5	70.0	80.0
Female	16.7	20.5	30.0	20.0
Age:				
Mean	45.0	45.4	38.2	44.4
Up to 29 years	2.8	0.0	10.0	2.4
30–39 years	33.3	20.5	40.0	28.2
40–49 years	33.3	56.4	50.0	45.9
50 years and over	30.6	23.1	0.0	23.5
Education:				
Up to 4 years	2.8	5.3	0.0	3.6
5–7 years	27.8	39.5	20.0	32.1
8–10 years	25.0	31.6	20.0	27.4
More than 10 years	44.4	23.7	60.0	36.9
Experience:				
Local cadre	0.0	0.0	0.0	0.0
High cadre	0.0	0.0	0.0	0.0
War veteran	2.8	9.4	0.0	5.3
Other position of responsibility	97.2	90.6	100.0	94.7

Note: This table includes responses of owner-cum-managers of household and private enterprises only.

an immediate, alternative income source. We know (as shown in Table 3.4) that nearly 35 per cent of the urban managers have experience in other informal business, and 63 per cent of them list previous experience as the motivating factor for starting their business (Table 3.5). In all, only about 9 per cent of the entrepreneurs said that the main reason for establishing their business was seeing others make a profit. Looking at household enterprises in particular, about 60 per cent of the entrepreneurs have cited previous experience (Table 3.5) as a motivational factor in the establishment of their own business, and nearly 36 per cent of them have worked as employees in other enterprises (Table 3.4). It is, therefore, difficult to discern from this information which of

Table 3.4: Prior experience of managers of urban household and private enterprises in production of similar products/services before establishment of enterprises. Percentages.

	Hanoi	Haiphong	HCM City	Tota l	Household	Private	Partnership	Co-operative	Shareholding
Mainly for own consumption	0.8	4.0	1.7	**2.1**	4.1	0.0	2.5	1.8	1.3
Mainly for sale or exchange †	34.5	29.7	39.3	**34.7**	28.6	40.6	42.5	36.8	32.1
As employee in other enterprise	36.1	40.6	21.4	**32.3**	35.7	28.1	22.5	29.8	38.5
As collective farm member	0.8	1.0	0.9	**0.9**	0.0	0.0	0.0	3.5	1.3
Other form of experience	3.4	0.0	8.5	**4.2**	2.0	4.7	10.0	3.5	3.8
Total	75.6	75.3	71.8	**74.2**	70.4	73.4	77.5	75.4	77.0

Note: *Shareholding and LLC. †Informal

Table 3.5: Main reason for establishing present line of business among urban enterprises. Percentages.

	Hanoi	Haiphong	HCM City	Tota l	Household	Private	Partnership	Co-operative	Shareholding
Previous experience	61.3	62.0	65.0	**62.8**	59.2	63.5	67.5	57.9	67.9
Local tradition	10.1	4.0	4.3	**6.3**	6.1	1.6	5.0	15.8	3.8
Seen others make profit	10.1	11.0	6.0	**8.9**	13.3	9.5	0.0	8.8	7.7
Secure supply/market channels	6.7	3.0	9.4	**6.5**	4.1	4.8	10.0	3.5	11.5
Advised by friends	1.7	7.0	7.7	**5.4**	7.1	9.5	0.0	1.8	5.1
Advised by authorities	0.8	7.0	0.9	**2.7**	0.0	1.6	5.0	10.5	0.0
Financial assistance for this business line	0.0	3.0	3.4	**2.1**	1.0	6.3	0.0	0.0	2.6
Other	9.2	3.0	3.4	**5.4**	9.2	3.2	12.5	1.8	1.3

Note: *Shareholding and LLC

the two possible interpretations is more reasonable. One thing we can be certain of: the ease of establishing household enterprises. It also appears from the data (especially in Table 3.5) that local traditions do not play a major role in initiating private entrepreneurship. Experience gained in previous employment, seeing others making a profit and security of supply or market are the three major 'push factors'. This high percentage of entrepreneurs with previous experience coincides well with their higher average age. The percentage of entrepreneurs who started enterprises at the onset of their career is still small (see Table 3.3).

Nearly 75 per cent of the entrepreneurs have prior experience in production of similar products or services (Table 3.4). About 35 per cent of them have experience in other informal business activities and an almost equal number have previously worked as an employee in another enterprise. Less than 1 per cent have worked in a collective farm and a little more than 2 per cent have engaged in subsistence activities prior to establishing their enterprises. This trend is true of all three cities, with minor variations. Haiphong has more than 40 per cent previously employed in another enterprise and Ho Chi Minh City has the highest percentage (about 28 per cent) without previous experience and this corresponds to the lower average age of its entrepreneur (see Table 3.3).

Managers of household enterprises have previously been employees of other enterprises (36 per cent) or engaged in other informal business activity (29 per cent) (Table 3.4). A majority of private entrepreneurs, however, have prior experience in similar informal business activity (41 per cent) and fewer have moved from being employees of other enterprises (28 per cent). This trend is also true of partnerships and co-operatives. Close to 40 per cent of the managers of the shareholding and limited liability companies, however, had previously been employed in other enterprises. It is interesting to note that collective farm members have moved on to shareholding and limited liability companies, but none of the respondents from household, private and partnership enterprises have previously worked in a collective farm.

As noted earlier, the main reason for establishing their present line of business seems to be some amount of previous experience in the field. This is more so in Ho Chi Minh City, where 65 per cent cited this reason, the comparable figures being 61 per cent in Hanoi and 62 in

Haiphong (Table 3.5). The next factor was the success of other entrepreneurs; 11 per cent of Haiphong entrepreneurs, 10 per cent in Hanoi and a lower 6 per cent in Ho Chi Minh City went into business because they had seen others make a profit. It is interesting that the south, which is recorded as economically more successful in Vietnam, lags behind on this count. On the other hand, the importance of a secure market environment is more clearly borne out in Ho Chi Minh City, where over 9 per cent of the entrepreneurs cited secure supply or market as their main reason. One possible explanation could be that secure environment is more directly visible in the south, whereas in the north this is inferred by seeing others' success stories. In any case, it definitely points to a more comfortable economic environment for private entrepreneurs. Local tradition seems to be responsible for the next highest percentage of entrepreneurs setting up their businesses in Hanoi.

This trend is also found when we examine the motivating factors across the ownership form of the enterprises. Although previous experience is the prime mover across all ownership forms, households and private enterprises have a larger percentage emulating other successful entrepreneurs (13 and 10 per cent), while shareholding and limited liability companies rely more on the observation of more secure supply or market channels (Table 3.5). That these forms of ownership (shareholding and limited liability) are of a fairly recent origin in Vietnam would naturally exclude emulation of other successes as the main reason. The co-operatives (which are of course a longer-established ownership form) cite local tradition (16 per cent) and assistance from authorities (11 per cent) too, highlighting their historical importance to the local economy and stronger ties with the government. Entrepreneurs also seem to rely on their informal ties, with 7 per cent of household enterprises and 10 per cent of private enterprises going into business on the advice of friends. Important to note is the fact that finance for private entrepreneurs is not as readily available, since it is the motivating factor for the smallest percentage of enterprises (2 per cent overall). Availability of financial assistance is not a motivating factor for partnerships and co-operatives, which is a matter of concern since we assume thatcapital availability is a major issue when establishing more complex forms of industrial organisation.

The point on financial assistance mentioned above comes into the discussion once again while discussing the origin of our sample enterprises. It corroborates the finding in Table 3.6 where the highest number of urban enterprises (47 per cent) list lack of capital as a severe difficulty at the time of establishment. Marketing has been difficult for about 18 per cent, in addition to a lack of suitable machinery and premises (14 per cent). Raw materials do not seem to have been as severe a problem for most of the enterprises, since less than 10 per cent cited this as the most difficult area. The same applies to availability of skilled labour, with only 3 per cent experiencing any severe difficulty in this field. Backward linkages seem to be strong, but forward linkages have posed severe difficulties for urban entrepreneurs. Finding a marketing outlet, as noted above, was the most difficult thing for almost a fifth of the enterprises. Cumbersome government regulations, licensing procedures and unfavourable attitudes of officials do not seem to have been a severe problem for most of the enterprises. The high percentage of experienced entrepreneurs and high level of education have probably relegated technical know-how to a lesser problem, since only 6 per cent have mentioned it.

The lack of capital was felt more by Haiphong entrepreneurs (62 per cent), while in Ho Chi Minh City and Hanoi only one half and a third of respondents respectively cited this difficulty. In addition to a shortage of capital, problems with marketing outlets, the supply of raw materials, the availability of premises, and access to machinery constitute the current hierarchy of difficulties for Hanoi's new entrepreneurs. In Haiphong, the order is different: lack of suitable machinery, markets and then technical know-how. For the southern entrepreneurs, finding premises, markets and machinery follow lack of capital as severe difficulties at the time of establishment. The lack of capital is less acute for enterprises on either ends of the spectrum of ownership forms. Less than 20 per cent of the household and shareholding and limited liability companies experienced severe difficulty in this regard, though this has shown itself to be the most severe difficulty among all ownership forms. Lower capital needs of household enterprises and the relative non-dominance of the owner's own capital among shareholding and limited liabilities might explain why this has not been a major problem. Another possibility is that entrepreneurs with a

Table 3.6 Severe difficulties experienced by urban enterprises at the time of establishment. Percentages.

	Hanoi	**Haiphong**	**HCM City**	**Total**	**Household**	**Private**	**Partnership**	**Co-operative**	**Shareholding***
Lack of:									
Capital	31.8	61.8	50.0	**46.5**	17.3	23.4	20.0	31.6	19.2
Raw material	15.2	5.5	5.6	**9.6**	3.1	1.6	15.0	7.0	1.3
Market outlet	24.2	10.9	16.7	**17.8**	10.2	4.7	7.5	10.5	7.7
Technical know-how	3.0	9.1	5.6	**5.7**	3.1	4.7	2.5	3.5	0.0
Suitable machinery	10.6	16.4	16.7	**14.0**	8.2	4.7	15.0	8.8	0.0
Suitable premises	15.2	7.3	22.2	**14.0**	9.2	6.3	5.0	3.5	6.4
Skilled labour	3.0	0.0	5.6	**2.5**	0.0	1.6	2.5	3.5	0.0
Government regulations	10.6	1.8	11.1	**7.6**	0.0	0.0	5.0	5.3	8.9
Attitudes of officials	1.5	0.0	2.8	**1.3**	1.0	0.0	0.0	0.0	1.3
Others	0.0	0.0	2.8	**0.6**	0.0	0.0	0.0	0.0	1.3

Note: The percentages in each column do not add up to 100 since the respondents were asked to list all difficulties that applied to them.
*Shareholding and LLC

significant amount of capital venture into establishing shareholding and limited liability companies, making capital a less serious problem for these ownership forms. Apart from this observation, no trend is visible to explain the nature of severe difficulties across ownership forms.

With regard to other severe difficulties across the various ownership forms the following findings emerged: about 10 per cent of household enterprises experienced difficulties with marketing, since their scale of operations is small; private enterprises had difficulty in finding suitable premises; partnerships listed a lack of raw materials and suitable machinery as severe; and co-operatives also mentioned marketing. Insofar as marketing success depends on the individual entrepreneur's skills, households and co-operatives encounter more problems since household enterprises are dominated by single owners and co-operatives, historically, have little experience in having to look for markets. On the other hand, private enterprises are a scale higher than household enterprises; their investments, and therefore the risk, are higher and so is their requirement of greater entrepreneurial skills.

On the matter of scale, the average start-up investment of Ho Chi Minh City enterprises is higher than the other two cities (Table 3.7), which explains why half the enterprises there experienced difficulty in obtaining capital. The average Ho Chi Minh City enterprise (set up after 1990) is more than two and three times the size of its counterpart in Hanoi and Haiphong respectively. There is clearly a big-scale difference across regions and ownership forms. Even though diverse ownership forms, and therefore capital needs, account for the variations, there are wide variations in the scale of operations of individual units in each ownership category. For instance, less than 50 per cent of the household units have invested 16 million dong, while the average household enterprise has invested over 41 million dong. This individual variation is true of all regions, ownership forms and nature of enterprises. The capital needs of more complex ownership forms increase, with the exception of the average investment of a private enterprise being larger than partnership enterprises. Further, average investments at establishment in agro-processing enterprises are only slightly lower than among manufacturing enterprises, which is a noteworthy finding, implying that the degree of mechanisation has been similar.

Table 3.7: Total investments at the time of establishment of urban enterprises. Thousand dong in 1996 prices.

	Mean	Median	25%	75%	90%
All urban	*654,122*	*207,000*	*29,025*	*528,835*	*1,357,650*
Hanoi	484,407	241,500	25,133	558,650	1,284,780
Haiphong	369,549	64,950	9,576	284,832	812,735
HCM City	1,002,980	333,750	80,850	610,225	2,035,500
Household	41,099	16,170	2,580	43,163	98,420
Private	362,127	186,500	59,100	379,000	1,057,800
Partnership	84,867	41,715	13,670	56,450	489,140
Co-operative	531,040	277,500	117,300	408,600	2,535,036
Shareholding & LLC	1,437,671	555,000	371,700	1,105,290	3,527,700
Agro-processing	538,196	208,950	1,713	643,585	2,131,110
Manufacturing	666,197	207,000	35,200	527,400	1,357,650

Note: The above table excludes units set up before 1990; price inflators were used for those set up in 1990 or later only.

An encouraging finding from Table 3.6 was that most enterprises did not consider cumbersome governmental regulations and official attitudes to be a severe constraint at the time of establishment. On the contrary, about 61 per cent of the urban enterprises received some form of assistance from the government (Table 3.8). Entrepreneurs also obtained more than one form of assistance; 34 per cent received assistance with application and registration formalities and a similar number received some form of temporary tax exemption or reduction. This was more pronounced among enterprises established after 1993, which indicates a more cordial relationship between the government and entrepreneurs. Close to 67 per cent of these enterprises received some assistance at the time of establishment compared to 59 per cent of those established before 1993. Across the cities, an almost equal percentage of enterprises obtained official assistance in Hanoi and Ho Chi Minh City (66 per cent) though this was lower (52 per cent) in Haiphong. The most common form of assistance was with official procedures for applications, registration, etc., followed by temporary tax exemptions and/or reductions. As many as 55 per cent of Ho Chi

Minh City enterprises have been helped with registration procedures. This is similar to the situation in Hanoi, where the most common assistance was in filing applications, etc. (32 per cent), followed closely by temporary tax exemptions or reductions (31 per cent). Haiphong enterprises have more frequently availed themselves of tax concessions (35 per cent) than with procedural assistance (12 per cent).

From the point of view of the government, granting tax concessions reflects greater flexibility with their budgets than in the case of assisting with procedural matters. While the latter plays a major role in reducing enterprise transaction costs, the former kind is more helpful in reducing enterprise production costs. It is clear from Table 3.8 that enterprises in Ho Chi Minh City have obtained greater official assistance in multiple areas, when compared to their counterparts in Haiphong. Except for tax concessions, Ho Chi Minh City has the greatest number of enterprises that have availed themselves of every kind of assistance. It can therefore be inferred that the relations between enterprises and officials are better developed in the south, both in terms of the variety of assistance as well as accessibility to a greater number of enterprises.

Observing the pattern across ownership forms, we find that household enterprises have the lowest percentage with assistance (57 per cent) and co-operatives – again, for historical reasons – the highest (91 per cent) (Table 3.8). Interesting to note is that 47 per cent of the shareholding and limited liability enterprises have obtained official assistance with the procurement of machinery. Almost 60 per cent of the shareholding and limited liability companies are newly established and 22 per cent have previously existed as private enterprises. Combined with the fact that this category also has the largest number of enterprises that have obtained assistance in multiple areas, this is a very encouraging development for the future of private sector entrepreneurship. Table 3.8 also reveals that the most common type of assistance obtained by private enterprises has been official recommendations on what line of business to pursue (33 per cent). Household enterprises, on the other hand, have mainly sought assistance in the form of tax concessions (25 per cent). Shareholding companies, followed by co-operatives, represent the highest percentage of enterprises being assisted in more than one area. The most common types of assistance,

Table 3.8: Official assistance at the time of establishment of urban enterprises. Percentages.

	A	B	C	D	E	F	G	H	No assistance
All urban	*13.4*	*33.8*	*9.2*	*11.6*	*32.0*	*5.0*	*8.9*	*4.7*	*38.3*
Hanoi	8.4	31.9	3.4	5.9	31.1	4.2	8.4	0.8	34.5
Haiphong	11.9	11.9	8.9	12.9	34.7	5.0	6.9	3.0	47.5
HCM City	19.7	54.7	15.4	16.2	30.8	6.0	11.1	10.3	34.2
Household	13.3	14.9	6.5	7.7	25.0	0.0	6.7	0.0	42.6
Private	33.3	21.9	12.9	15.4	18.5	17.6	20.0	31.3	20.2
Partnership	2.2	12.3	9.7	12.8	15.7	0.0	13.3	25.0	12.4
Co-operative	22.2	19.3	38.7	35.9	17.6	35.3	30.0	25.0	8.5
Shareholding & LLC	28.9	31.6	32.3	28.2	23.1	47.1	30.0	18.8	16.3
Enterprises established									
1993–95	18.3	40.5	8.7	10.3	34.1	7.1	7.9	2.4	33.3
Before 1993	10.5	30.0	9.5	12.4	31.0	3.8	9.5	6.2	41.0

Key: A: Recommendation on line of business
B: Assistance with application, registration etc.
C: Assistance with the organisation of the enterprise
D: Assistance with obtaining credits
E: Temporary tax exemption/reduction
F: Assistance with procurement of machinery etc.
G: Assistance in establishing contact with state enterprises.
H: Other assistance.

Note: Respondents were requested to list all areas of assistance obtained. Hence all row percentages exceeding a total of 100 imply assistance in multiple areas.

as seen in Table 3.8, are in organisation of the administrative structure of the enterprise (39 per cent), obtaining credit (36 per cent), machinery procurement (35 per cent), and in establishing contacts with state enterprises (30 per cent). Overall, the typical urban enterprise has received most help from officials in matters of procedural formalities, temporary tax concessions and recommendation on line of business – in that order. Assistance in procuring machinery and other capital equipment is an area where the least number of smaller enterprises have received any official assistance.

An important component of an enterprise's establishment is its financial capital resources. Table 3.9 shows the predominance of owner funds as the capital base of the enterprises. It is clear that most entrepreneurs have invested their own savings in establishing the enterprise and this is the most important source of enterprise capital. External capital is conspicuous by its absence; less than 7 per cent of all urban enterprises have obtained interest-free loans and a little over 2 per cent have taken out bank loans at start-up (column A). For all urban enterprises, about 91 per cent of the enterprise capital comes from own resources, followed by interest-free loans (3 per cent) from friends and relatives, and less than 1 per cent from bank funds (column B). Workers' contributions are features mainly of co-operatives. The figures are not significantly different across the nation.

Lack of reliance on external capital limits the scale of operations of enterprises to the savings of entrepreneurs, and capital becomes a major constraint (a result confirmed by Table 3.6 where almost 47 per cent of the enterprises mentioned lack of capital as the most severe constraint). That this number is not larger might be explained by the fact that the capital needs of household and private enterprises have

Table 3.9: Sources of capital at the time of establishment of urban enterprises by location.

	Hanoi		Haiphong		HCM City		All urban	
	A	B	A	B	A	B	A	B
Own capital	100.0	95.4	96.8	86.6	96.6	90.9	97.8	91.2
Interest-free loan	7.4	3.7	9.7	4.0	4.3	1.7	6.9	3.1
Bank loan	0.9	0.3	3.2	1.2	2.6	0.9	2.2	0.8
Credit co-operative	0.0	0.0	0.0	0.0	0.0	0.0	0.0	0.0
Local authority	0.0	0.0	0.0	0.0	0.0	0.0	0.0	0.0
Workers' contributions	0.9	0.6	8.6	3.0	3.4	3.0	4.1	2.2
Loan from private person	0.0	0.0	6.5	2.9	1.7	1.2	2.5	1.3
Advance against sales	0.0	0.0	0.0	0.0	0.0	0.0	0.0	0.0
Other sources	0.0	0.0	2.2	2.2	3.4	2.4	1.9	1.5

Key: A: Percentage of enterprises that utilised this source of capital.
B: Average contribution to total capital formation for all enterprises

been modest. With a fairly new environment for private enterprises, the tendency toward low-risk, own-capital entrepreneurship is bound to be high. There is a need to develop formal lending sources for private entrepreneurs to counter this restrictive reliance on own funds, as well as to foster an atmosphere for higher-risk investments to grow, thereby increasing employment and productivity in the long run.

While external capital remains the Achilles heel of the Vietnamese private sector, an encouraging feature is the pattern of changes in household income for owner-managers of household and private enterprises. In their own estimation, almost 58 per cent of the owner-managers note that their household incomes have increased since 1990, against 14 per cent of those who report a decline (Table 3.10). The remaining 28 per cent report unchanged earnings which, at least, is more desirable than a decline. It is important to note that all the decline has occurred in household enterprises. Private enterprises have, on the other hand, fared better, with almost 93 per cent registering an increased income since 1990. That 57 per cent of these private enterprises have been in existence since 1990 (see Table 3.1) or earlier points to favourable developments in terms of sustainability as well as growth in private sector entrepreneurship. Hanoi accounts for the largest number of households with reduced incomes (28 per cent); Ho Chi Minh City has fared a little better at 10 per cent and Haiphong has the most impressive growth trend among the cities with less than 3 per cent estimating reductions in income since 1990. Again, while 43

Table 3.10: Estimated change in real income for owner-managers of urban household and private enterprises. Percentages.

	Declined income	Unchanged income	Increased income			
			≤25%	26–50%	51–100%	>100%
All urban	*14.1*	*28.2*	*20.0*	*12.9*	*14.1*	*10.6*
Household	19.4	35.5	17.7	9.7	11.3	6.5
Private	0.0	8.7	26.1	21.7	21.7	21.7
Hanoi	27.8	38.9	8.3	11.1	5.6	8.3
Haiphong	2.6	17.9	30.8	10.3	23.1	15.4
HCM City	10.0	30.0	20.0	30.0	10.0	0.0

per cent of these enterprises were established after 1990, the fact that incomes have grown is a positive sign for private sector entrepreneurship, since they probably do not, in this instance, constitute 'distress industries'.

Rural Enterprises

Similar to their urban counterparts, rural enterprises in our sample display a distinct pattern in establishment rates, namely a sudden spurt of 23 per cent in the period 1986–90, a decline in 1991 and a steady increase since 1992 (Table 3.11). In addition to *doi moi,* rural Vietnam witnessed widespread land reforms in 1987 and it is possible that some of the effects of this reform have translated into an increase in the number of enterprises. A substantial 82 per cent of the enterprises have been set up since 1986 and less than 1 per cent of them were set up in 1986 itself. This points to the strong correlation between the reforms and small enterprise growth. This trend is common to Ha Tay (in the north) as well as Long An (in the south). However, Long An has a slightly larger percentage of old enterprises; the oldest enterprise in our rural sample, one set up in 1937, is from Long An. Ha Tay saw a second spurt of establishment in 1992 with the establishment of 17 per cent of its enterprises, then two successive years of decline in establishment rates, and a recovery in 1995. In fact, Ha Tay has the largest number of new enterprises (16 per cent of its total). Overall, we find a small percentage of pre-unification enterprises, minor ups and downs until a big spurt in the period 1986–90, and a gradual increase since 1992. The reforms and a strengthening economy have resulted in the proliferation of rural enterprises.

Intuitive expectations are confirmed, in our sample, with regard to a lack of diversity among forms of rural enterprises. Household and private enterprises seem to be the most dominant forms of rural enterprises throughout the period from reunification (Table 3.12). Partnerships, co-operatives and limited liability companies constitute the category 'other' but a majority of these are partnerships. There are only five co-operatives in our sample, making up 3 per cent, and two of them were established in the period 1976–80 and three in 1994. The number of limited liability companies is three (or 2 per cent of the total sample), of which one was established in 1994 and the other two in

Table 3.11: Year of establishment of rural enterprises by location. Percentages.

	Ha Tay	Long An	All rural
Before 1976	3.7	6.1	4.9
1976–80	6.1	9.8	7.9
1981–85	1.2	8.5	4.9
1986–90	28.0	18.3	23.2
1991	4.9	8.5	6.7
1992	17.1	6.1	11.6
1993	12.2	13.4	12.8
1994	11.0	15.9	13.4
1995	15.9	13.4	14.6

1995. Surprisingly enough, there are no co-operatives older than from 1976. Further, more than 22 per cent of the household enterprises have been operating for more than 13 years, and 7 per cent have been in existence from pre-unification times. Their numbers have been steadily increasing since *doi moi,* though the rate declined slightly between 1992 and 1994. While there is an indication that some of these household enterprises transform into larger and higher forms of ownership (almost 65 per cent of our private enterprises started out as household enterprises), a large majority seem to retain their initial forms. This contrasts with the urban scenario where a third of the enterprises had changed forms since 1990. Among the private enterprises, two have been privatised from earlier state ownership and two have changed from partnerships. The fairly low degree of penetration of other ownership forms demonstrates the persistent small-scale nature of rural industry. That a majority of the private enterprises started out as household enterprises not only indicates the importance and dominance of household industry as the starting point for rural entrepreneurs, but also shows that conditions have been favourable for growth since 1986, when most of the private enterprises were established.

The profile of a rural entrepreneur is slightly different from the urban entrepreneur. Though on average, the rural manager is also male, and has previous experience in a position of responsibility, he has fewer years of formal education (about seven) and is younger (42 years old

Table 3.12: Year of establishment of rural enterprises by ownership form. Percentages.

	Household	Private	Other
Before 1976	7.4	2.1	0.0
1976–80	10.6	2.1	9.1
1981–85	4.3	8.3	0.0
1986–90	25.5	22.9	13.6
1991	6.4	10.4	0.0
1992	13.8	10.4	4.5
1993	10.6	20.8	4.5
1994	7.4	18.8	27.3
1995	13.8	4.2	40.9

on average) than his urban counterpart (Table 3.13). The gender distribution is not different, with only one-fifth of the entrepreneurs being women (more of them in Long An than in Ha Tay). However, it is encouraging to note that more than 85 per cent of these women entrepreneurs are managing fairly new enterprises – established since 1986. Overall, a third of the entrepreneurs are between 30 and 39 years of age, and there are about a quarter who are older than 50. This is more so in the north than in the south. Almost 87 per cent in the age group 29 years or less manage enterprises that have been established since 1986; the rest manage units established before 1976. It is quite possible that the latter group has taken over traditional family or household enterprises. More than 62 per cent of the entrepreneurs aged 40 and above both own and manage household enterprises.

Like the urban scenario, we cannot conclude positively that this rural picture is a healthy development. It could mean that these individuals have voluntarily been released from the state sector and, given the small capital needs of household industry, this has proved to be the most attractive entrepreneurial option. Another interpretation is that they have been laid off from positions of responsibility and have taken to household enterprises as a ready alternative. In any case, this probable combination of push and pull factors is diversifying the base of the private sector. It remains to be seen if these household enterprises will eventually grow into larger and higher forms of industrial organ-

Table 3.13: Characteristics of owner-managers of rural household and private enterprises. Percentages.

	Ha Tay	Long An	All rural
Sex:			
Male	90.0	69.0	80.4
Female	10.0	31.0	19.6
Age:			
Mean	*42.64*	*41.88*	*42.29*
up to 29 years	12.0	11.9	12.0
30–39 years	34.0	33.3	33.7
40–49 years	22.0	35.7	28.3
50 years and over	32.0	19.0	26.1
Education			
up to 4 years	8.0	14.6	11.0
5–7 years	32.0	36.6	34.1
8–10 years	36.0	24.4	30.8
over 10 years	24.0	24.4	24.2
Experience:			
Local cadre	10.6	0.0	9.8
High cadre	0.0	25.0	2.0
War veteran	21.3	25.0	21.6
Other position of responsibility	68.1	50.0	66.7

isation. If there is greater stability in the economic environment, this may eventually lead to an *evolutionary growth* of private sector firms. Most of the respondents have previous experience in a position of responsibility (almost 67 per cent), probably in the state sector. A minority (2 per cent) has worked in high-level cadres, less than 10 per cent have worked in local cadres and 22 per cent are war veterans. The overall trend is similar in both Ha Tay and Long An, with minor variations. While Ha Tay has more entrepreneurs with up to ten years of education, a majority of Long An entrepreneurs have only seven years of education or less. This might explain why the average age of the entrepreneur in Long An is lower than in Ha Tay.

In addition to a high degree of prior experience in a position of responsibility, 78 per cent of the respondents have experience in pro-

Table 3.14: Prior experience of managers of rural household and private enterprises in production of similar products/services before establishment of enterprises.

	Ha Tay	Long An	All rural	Household	Private	Other
Mainly for own consumption	1.2	6.0	3.6	4.2	2.1	4.5
Mainly for sale or exchange (informal)	48.8	37.3	43.0	42.1	58.3	13.6
As employee in other enterprise	19.5	24.1	21.8	23.2	14.6	31.8
As collective farm member	4.9	0.0	2.4	3.2	0.0	4.5
Other form of experience	11.0	3.6	7.3	6.3	4.2	18.2
Total	*85.4*	*71.0*	*78.1*	*79.0*	*79.2*	*72.6*

duction of similar products (Table 3.14). Among these, 43 per cent have dealt with business work routines and have experience in sales and marketing. This indicates that individuals who were used to business dealings in their earlier employment might have a greater propensity to self-employment in related areas. What is interesting is that about 26 per cent of these experienced entrepreneurs have this exposure at their own or collective farms and a majority of them are running household enterprises. Close to 45 per cent of those who gained this sales experience as employees of state enterprises have gone on to establish private enterprises instead. This trend explains the experiences of 42 per cent of household enterprises and 58 per cent of private enterprises in informal sale and exchange, as set out in Table 3.14.

This trend is more prevalent in Ha Tay, with 49 per cent of managers having indulged in businesses prior to their self-employment. The next overall common feature is the experience gained as employees of other enterprises in related areas. As many as 22 per cent have this experience, with the proportion being greater in Long An than in Ha Tay. Across forms of ownership, both household and private enterprises have a majority with experience in informal sales, more so among the latter. Among other forms of ownership, experience as employees of other enterprises is more prevalent (32 per cent) than other forms of experience.

The motivation behind the start-up of entrepreneurial activities goes a long way towards explaining the economic environment for firms, entrepreneur perceptions, and the sustainability of firms in the long run. Among rural enterprises, previous experience has been the main reason cited for the establishment of firms (about 42 per cent), followed by local tradition (34 per cent) (Table 3.15). It is interesting to note that 69 per cent of those units which mention local tradition as the main reason have been in existence only since 1986. In conformity with expectations, as Table 3.15 shows, over 44 per cent of household enterprises cite local tradition as the motivating factor behind expectations. There is, thus, reason to state that *doi moi* has contributed to a revival of local traditional household industry.

On further examination, it is found that local tradition and previous experience are the only factors motivating entrepreneurs younger than 29 years. Even though these are the main factors for all household entrepreneurs, 10 per cent of those aged between 30 and 49 have also mentioned successful experiences of others and secure supply and marketing channels; for those above 50 years, the prime factor is local tradition. Combining the picture that we get from Table 3.13 and its interpretations (noted earlier), it is likely that most of the entrepreneurs in the age group 40 years and above, who have mainly started household enterprises, are motivated primarily by *pull* rather than *push* factors. With so much previous experience, it is likely that this group would have sought to establish other non-traditional industry, if the scenario were that of distress industries.

Further, across regions, while previous experience is the common motivating factor, local tradition is more a feature in Ha Tay than Long An (Table 3.15). Emulating other successful business ventures, on the other hand, is a more common motivational factor in Long An, in addition to perceptions of secure environment and following advice given by friends. The scenario in Long An is that of a more developed system, with less reliance on tradition and more on other 'push' factors, including linkages with authorities, which is absent in Ha Tay. A significant point is that none of the entrepreneurs has gone into business for reasons of financial availability. This finding lends support to the point discussed earlier, that external credit is one of the weakest institutions in the overall economic environment of start-up

Table 3.15: Main reason for establishing present line of business among rural enterprises. Percentages.

	Ha Tay	Long An	All rural	Household	Private	Other
Previous experience	45.1	39.0	42.1	33.7	61.7	36.4
Local tradition	39.0	28.0	33.5	44.2	14.9	27.3
Seen others make profit	7.3	11.0	9.1	6.3	8.5	22.7
Secure supply/ market channels	4.9	8.5	6.7	7.4	6.4	4.5
Advised by friends	1.2	11.0	6.1	5.3	8.5	4.5
Advised by authorities	0.0	1.2	0.6	0.0	0.0	4.5
Financial assistance for this business line	0.0	0.0	0.0	0.0	0.0	0.0
Other	2.4	1.2	1.8	3.2	0.0	0.0

enterprises. There is a lot of scope for improvement on this count. Across forms of ownership, as one might guess, local tradition is not the main motivating factor among non-household enterprises. An encouraging finding is that apart from previous experience, the example of other successful entrepreneurs has often proved to be a motivating factor, reflecting favourable entrepreneurial conditions. The information in Table 3.15 also indicates that financial non-availability is a feature common to all Vietnamese enterprises, irrespective of their size.

In the development history of enterprises, constraints during establishment determine such important matters as investment scale, legality and their future success and growth potential. Among rural enterprises, not surprisingly, lack of capital was the most severe difficulty experienced at the time of establishment (29 per cent; see Table 3.16), although this is a far lower rate than for their urban counterparts. That the percentage is not higher might be due to the fact that the capital needs of these enterprises, dominated by household forms, have been modest, largely limited to whatever resources the entrepreneur had at the time of establishment. On the other hand, 19 per cent of these

Table 3.16: Severe difficulties experienced by rural enterprises at the time of establishment. Percentages.

	Ha Tay	Long An	All rural	Household	Private	Other
Lack of:						
Capital	27.7	30.1	28.9	28.1	27.1	36.4
Raw material	4.8	3.6	4.2	5.2	4.2	9.1
Market outlet	26.5	12.0	19.3	26.0	10.4	0.0
Technical know-how	1.2	3.6	2.4	2.1	4.2	4.5
Suitable machinery	1.2	7.2	4.2	2.1	8.3	9.1
Suitable premises	1.2	6.0	3.6	1.0	4.2	9.1
Skilled labour	2.4	1.2	1.8	0.0	0.0	4.5
Government regulations	0.0	3.6	1.8	0.0	4.2	0.0
Others	1.2	0.0	0.6	0.0	2.1	0.0

Note: The percentages in each column do not add up to 100 since the respondents were asked to list all difficulties that applied to them.

enterprises experienced a lack of marketing outlets as a severe difficulty. This was in fact the second most common constraint. Since local tradition has been a major factor in establishing rural enterprises, technical know-how does not appear to have been a serious constraint. This might also explain why raw materials have also not figured as severe constraints, since local traditions and practices evolve in response to the relative abundance of one or more local resources. The degree of mechanisation among household enterprises is also usually limited, with the result that suitable machinery has not been a major constraint.

However, with quite a few enterprises involved, finding marketing outlets has naturally been a major concern. Marketing constraints are also due to the disadvantages of being very small scale. This situation is more common in Ha Tay, with nearly 27 per cent of enterprises experiencing marketing difficulties against 12 per cent in Long An. That local traditional activities were found to be more common in Ha Tay may be reiterated here. Long An has a larger number of enterprises experiencing difficulties in finding suitable machinery (7 per cent) and premises (6 per cent).

For all ownership forms, a lack of capital and a lack of marketing outlets – in that order – are the two most common perceived difficulties. Relatively fewer private and other enterprises experienced marketing difficulties, compared to household enterprises. Finding suitable premises and labour has been a constraint for larger-scale enterprises, mainly partnerships and limited liability firms. It is also clear from Table 3.16 that government regulations have not presented severe difficulties for most enterprises, only for private enterprises. Among all the external constraints, capital and marketing deserve closer attention by policy-makers if they wish to remove the hurdles encountered by any new private sector start-up company.

The nature and intensity of establishment constraints, as mentioned above, vary with the size of the firms. Table 3.17 presents the investment profile of private sector enterprises. There is a very distinct scale difference across regions in this regard. The average enterprise at start-up in Ha Tay is almost three times the size of its counterpart in Long An. This may be because 96 per cent of the enterprises are involved in industrial manufacturing in Ha Tay whereas the agro-processing sector is larger, and hence the corresponding percentage is only 66, in Long An. This is a surprising result, since our earlier finding was that local tradition was a greater force in Ha Tay and so one would expect the nature of activity to be smaller-scale, non-industrial manufacturing.

Table 3.17: Total investments at the time of establishment of rural enterprises. Thousand dong in 1996 prices.

	Mean	Median	25%	75%	90%
All rural	*161,880*	*8,000*	*2,000*	*50,000*	*376,800*
Ha Tay	242,434	5,000	1,000	51,750	698,100
Long An	80,319	10,000	3,000	50,000	192,000
Household	6,775	3,000	1,000	9,500	19,400
Private	125,336	50,000	10,000	100,000	434,000
Other	888,573	265,000	36,250	762,500	4,660,000
Agro-processing	89,261	30,000	10,000	100,000	400,800
Manufacturing	179,197	5,000	1,425	31,000	379,000

The investment range is much more homogeneous in Long An, as Table 3.18 shows. The median investment value in Long An is 10 million dong whereas it is 5 million dong in Ha Tay, even though the average Ha Tay enterprise is much larger than its Long An counterpart.

The result across ownership forms is hardly surprising, with average investments increasing substantially with more complex forms of ownership. The scale difference across agro-processing and manufacturing is also distinct – the average manufacturing firms are more than twice the size of the agro-processing firms. However, the investment differences between individual units are high, with less than 50 per cent of the enterprises investing 8 million dong, and the average investment amounting to 16 million dong. This variation is smaller for household enterprises than for other types of business.

Table 3.18 illustrates the sources of capital for rural enterprises at the time of establishment. The data strengthen the arguments made above that external credit has been conspicuous by its absence and that the scale of investments has been limited to the entrepreneur's savings. Own capital formed part of the capital base for all enterprises (shown in column A) and that it has been the most dominant part is shown in

Table 3.18: Sources of capital at the time of establishment of rural enterprises by province.

	Ha Tay		Long An		All rural	
	A	B	A	B	A	B
Own capital	100.0	89.7	100.0	90.8	100.0	90.3
Interest-free loan	8.6	2.3	10.0	5.4	9.3	3.8
Bank loan	9.9	2.9	2.5	0.9	6.2	1.9
Credit co-operative	4.9	1.9	0.0	0.0	2.5	1.0
Local authority	0.0	0.0	1.3	0.6	0.6	0.3
Workers' contribution	2.5	0.2	0.0	0.0	1.2	0.1
Loan from private persons	6.2	2.9	3.8	1.8	4.9	2.3
Advance against sales	0.0	0.0	0.0	0.0	0.0	0.0
Other sources	0.0	0.0	1.3	0.6	0.6	0.3

Key: A: Percentage of enterprises that utilised this source of capital
B: Average contribution to total capital formation for all enterprises

column B. All rural enterprises utilised the entrepreneur's own capital; this constituted a startling 90 per cent of the total capital base for the average enterprise. Interest-free loans from friends and relatives (9 per cent) and bank loans (6 per cent) were the other capital sources at establishment. The reliance on own capital is slightly less, though not significantly so, in Ha Tay than in Long An. In order to reap the potential benefits of private sector entrepreneurship, there is an urgent need to diversify the capital base of enterprises and not limit the scale of operations to the owner's private savings. The number of household enterprises is large in the sample, and this is representative of rural Vietnam. With a bulk of the population living in rural areas, there is a need to diversify the economic base in the region and develop a healthy non-farm sector, by developing the currently weak institutions.

Table 3.19: Official assistance at the time of establishment of rural enterprises. Percentages.

	A	B	C	D	E	F	G	H	No assistance
All rural	*4.2*	*17.6*	*1.2*	*13.3*	*26.7*	*0.0*	*2.4*	*2.4*	*58.2*
Ha Tay	6.0	13.3	1.2	18.1	32.5	0.0	2.4	3.6	57.8
Long An	2.4	22.0	1.2	8.5	20.7	0.0	2.4	1.2	58.5
Household	4.2	9.4	0.0	7.3	20.8	0.0	1.0	0.0	67.7
Private	0.0	29.2	0.0	10.4	22.9	0.0	2.1	6.3	54.2
Other	13.6	27.3	9.1	45.5	59.1	0.0	9.1	4.5	22.7
Enterprises established									
1993–95	4.5	23.9	0.0	19.4	38.9	0.0	2.9	1.5	49.3
Before 1993	4.1	16.3	2.0	9.2	18.4	0.0	2.0	3.1	64.3

Key: A: Recommendation on line of business
B: Assistance with application, registration etc.
C: Assistance with the organisation of the enterprise
D: Assistance with obtaining credits
E: Temporary tax exemption/reduction
F: Assistance with procurement of machinery etc.
G: Assistance in establishing contact with state enterprises.
H: Other assistance.

Note: Respondents were requested to list all areas of assistance obtained. Hence all row percentages exceeding a total of 100 imply assistance in multiple areas.

Linkages with the government at start-up have been less prevalent among rural than urban enterprises. Table 3.19 shows that 58 per cent of the rural enterprises did not avail themselves of any official assistance at this time. The major form of assistance among rural enterprises was with temporary tax exemption or reduction. More than a quarter of the enterprises have taken advantage of this benefit. The next most common form of support was assistance with bureaucratic formalities (18 per cent) and assistance in obtaining credits (13 per cent).

In Long An, more enterprises have sought official assistance with application and registration formalities (22 per cent), followed by tax exemptions (21 per cent); while in Ha Tay the order is assistance with tax concessions (33 per cent), credit (18 per cent) and official formalities (13 per cent). The number of enterprises utilising other forms of assistance has been significantly low. The differing linkages of enterprises with government across ownership forms are also clear from Table 3.19. Private enterprises have shown a greater propensity towards benefiting from official assistance compared to household enterprises, where 68 per cent of enterprises have not sought any assistance. Also enterprises established since 1993 have received more assistance than those established prior to 1993. On the whole, the most common form of official assistance has been tax credits, followed by procedural assistance across regions, ownership forms and dates of establishment, with a few exceptions. Linkages with officials are not as strong in rural areas as in urban ones.

Table 3.20: Estimated change in real income for owner-managers of rural household and private enterprises. Percentages.

	Declined income	Unchanged income	Increased income ≤25%	26–50%	51–100%	>100%
Total	*19.6*	*14.1*	*30.4*	*14.1*	*8.7*	*13.0*
Household	23.9	14.9	32.8	11.9	9.0	7.5
Private	8.0	12.0	24.0	20.0	8.0	28.0
Ha Tay	14.0	4.0	34.0	16.0	12.0	20.0
Long An	26.2	26.2	26.2	11.9	4.8	4.8

Notes

1. 'The overall growth rate has accelerated markedly since the early 1990s, to reach over 9 per cent in 1995 and 1996. As a result, average GDP per capita has grown from about US$140 to US$300 over the same period.' Ari Kokko (1997), *Vietnam 1997. Managing the Transition to Free Trade: Vietnamese Trade Policy for the 21st Century*. Stockholm: Sida, p. 2

2. We may recall from Chapter 1 that one of the sample criteria was to interview units that were established before 31 December 1995 and were in operation for at least one full fiscal year at the time of the survey in 1997.

4

Linkages with the Rest of the Economy

Maud Hemlin

Forward Linkages among Urban Enterprises

The enterprises in Hanoi and Ho Chi Minh City have rather similar sales patterns in the 1997 survey, unlike in the 1991 survey (Table 4.1). In the 1997 survey, non-state enterprises constitute 35 to 40 per cent and individual buyers account for some 32 per cent of sales, on average, in both cities. But while the share sold to state enterprises is slightly higher in Hanoi, 25 as compared to 17 per cent Ho Chi Minh City, the latter has a higher share of exports, about 10 per cent compared to 3 in Hanoi. In Haiphong not even 1 per cent of current sales is exported; instead sales are mainly to individuals. Here, on average, 46 per cent goes to individual buyers and about one-third rely completely on this category of buyers. Approximately one-fifth on average is destined for state enterprises, but very few in Haiphong rely completely on them. Carpentry products, furniture and light engineering goods are among the main products exported, but feature prominently also in sales to individuals, non-state and state enterprises. The latter also buy agricultural processed goods.

This implies that non-state enterprises have become much more important as customers, especially in Hanoi (Table 4.1). Their share of sales is about twice as large today as it was in the 1991 survey. State-owned firms have diminished somewhat in importance but the most remarkable change is that state trading companies have almost disap-

Table 4.1: Type of customers of urban enterprises by location. Percentage share of total sales of main products.

	0	1–24	24–49	50–74	75–99	100	Mean	
Hanoi:							**1997**	**1991**
Individuals	54.6	4.2	7.6	12.6	0.0	21.0	31.3	*34.3*
Non-state enterprises	38.7	7.6	10.9	18.5	2.5	21.8	39.3	*18.1*
State enterprises	63.0	5.9	4.2	8.4	4.2	14.3	24.7	*29.1*
Other state agency	100.0	0.0	0.0	0.0	0.0	0.0	0.0	*9.2*
Local authorities	99.2	0.0	0.0	0.8	0.0	0.0	0.6	*0.7*
Tourists	100.0	0.0	0.0	0.0	0.0	0.0	0.0	-
Export	95.0	0.0	1.7	1.7	1.7	0.0	3.3	*2.6*
Other	99.2	0.0	0.0	0.0	0.0	0.8	0.8	-
Haiphong:								
Individuals	38.6	5.0	6.9	11.9	4.0	33.7	46.2	*38.4*
Non-state enterprises	43.6	12.9	10.9	14.9	4.0	13.9	31.5	*29.0*
State enterprises	63.4	6.9	5.9	11.9	5.0	6.9	21.5	*16.6*
Other state agency	99.0	1.0	0.0	0.0	0.0	0.0	0.2	*8.3*
Local authorities	99.0	1.0	0.0	0.0	0.0	0.0	0.1	*0.0*
Tourists	100.0	0.0	0.0	0.0	0.0	0.0	0.0	-
Export	98.0	1.0	1.0	0.0	0.0	0.0	0.5	*0.0*
Other	100.0	0.0	0.0	0.0	0.0	0.0	0.0	-
HCM City:								
Individuals	41.0	20.5	6.8	5.1	6.8	19.7	32.9	*38.4*
Non-state enterprises	35.0	15.4	10.3	17.1	10.3	12.0	36.6	*29.0*
State enterprises	59.0	17.9	7.7	6.8	4.3	4.3	16.9	*16.6*
Other state agency	97.4	0.0	0.0	0.9	1.7	0.0	2.1	*16.6*
Local authorities	98.3	1.7	0.0	0.0	0.0	0.0	0.1	*0.8*
Tourists	99.1	0.9	0.0	0.0	0.0	0.0	0.1	-
Export	85.5	1.7	0.9	3.4	3.4	5.1	10.8	*5.2*
Other	98.3	0.9	0.9	0.0	0.0	0.0	0.5	-

Note: Figures in italics refer to the corresponding 1991 survey data. 'Tourists' and 'other' categories were not specified in the 1991 survey.

peared from the arena, not just in Hanoi but in all cities. In the earlier survey, these accounted for 16 per cent of sales in Ho Chi Minh City and Haiphong, and slightly less than 10 per cent in Hanoi. Sales to foreign countries are growing, albeit from very low levels. The share of export in average sales, 11 per cent, in Ho Chi Minh City is a 100 per cent increase over the previous level.

Not surprisingly, household enterprises have the highest percentage of individual buyers (Table 4.2). Shareholding companies constitute the category selling least (20 per cent) to individuals, while the corresponding shares from co-operatives, private and partnership enterprises are in the range 25–35 per cent. Non-state enterprises account for some 35–40 per cent of sales for all types of establishments, except for partnership enterprises. Partnerships are instead more tied up with state enterprises, and as much as 43 per cent of the sales of the average partnership enterprise goes to state companies, the highest share among all ownership forms. State enterprises hardly figure in the world of household enterprises, but on the other hand buy about 20–30 per cent of private shareholding enterprises and co-operatives sales. Co-operatives and shareholding and limited liability companies show some similar features in their sales patterns, with non-state enterprises constituting the main buyers, about 37 per cent, followed by state enterprises and individual persons, in that order.

Forward linkages among co-operatives look rather different today compared to the 1991 survey. At that time, state enterprises and trading companies accounted for more than half of the average sales, and more than 40 per cent of the enterprises relied fully on such customers (Table 4.2). Among other ownership forms, such a noticeable change is seen only among private enterprises, where the share of non-state enterprise sales has almost doubled, while that to individual buyers has dropped about 7 percentage points.

On the geographical distribution of sales (see Table 4.3), Haiphong has become the most inward-looking city; on average 83 per cent of its sales were to firms or persons in the same city, in the 1997 survey. Close to 75 per cent of the enterprises here sell only within the city, and both these figures have increased since the 1991 survey. They were selling more locally and more to rural areas than six years earlier. Ho Chi Minh City enterprises, on the other hand, emerged as the most

Table 4.2: Type of customers of urban enterprises by ownership form. Percentage share of total sales of main products.

	0	1–24	24–49	50–74	75–99	100	Mean	
All urban:							**1997**	**1991**
Individuals	45.1	10.1	7.1	9.8	3.6	24.3	36.4	*34.3*
Non-state enterprises	38.9	11.9	10.7	16.9	5.6	16.0	35.8	*23.8*
State enterprises	61.7	10.4	5.9	8.9	4.5	8.6	21.1	*23.8*
Other state agency	98.8	0.3	0.0	0.3	0.6	0.0	0.8	*11.4*
Local authorities	98.8	0.9	0.0	0.3	0.0	0.0	0.3	*0.6*
Tourists	99.7	0.3	0.0	0.0	0.0	0.0	0.0	-
Export	92.6	0.9	1.2	1.8	1.8	1.8	5.1	*3.5*
Other	99.1	0.3	0.3	0.0	0.0	0.3	0.5	-
Household enterprises:								
Individuals	27.6	5.1	7.2	9.1	5.1	45.9	58.8	*55.7*
Non-state enterprises	49.0	8.1	5.1	11.3	5.1	21.4	35.5	*32.2*
State enterprises	91.8	5.1	1.0	0.0	1.0	1.0	2.8	*4.1*
Other state agency	98.0	1.0	0.0	1.0	0.0	0.0	1.0	*4.7*
Local authorities	99.0	1.0	0.0	0.0	0.0	0.0	0.1	*0.0*
Tourists	99.0	1.0	0.0	0.0	0.0	0.0	0.1	-
Export	98.0	0.0	0.0	0.0	2.0	0.0	1.8	*0.0*
Other	100.0	0.0	0.0	0.0	0.0	0.0	0.0	-
Private enterprises:								
Individuals	45.3	15.8	3.2	15.7	6.3	14.1	31.3	*38.2*
Non-state enterprises	26.6	18.8	12.6	17.3	7.9	17.2	40.8	*23.1*
State enterprises	53.1	17.4	9.4	11.1	6.4	3.1	20.7	*18.8*
Other state agency	100.0	0.0	0.0	0.0	0.0	0.0	0.0	*12.1*
Local authorities	100.0	0.0	0.0	0.0	0.0	0.0	0.0	*0.7*
Tourists	100.0	0.0	0.0	0.0	0.0	0.0	0.0	-
Export	90.6	1.6	1.6	0.0	1.6	4.7	7.2	*4.9*
Other	100.0	0.0	0.0	0.0	0.0	0.0	0.0	-

Note: Figures in italics refer to the corresponding 1991 survey data. 'Tourists' and 'other' categories were not specified in the 1991 survey.

Table 4.2: Type of customers of urban enterprises by ownership form. Percentage share of total sales of main products.

	0	1–24	24–49	50–74	75–99	100	Mean 1997	Mean 1991
Partnership enterprises:								
Individuals	45.0	10.0	5.0	12.5	0.0	27.5	37.1	*27.8*
Non-state enterprises	55.0	7.5	12.5	20.0	2.5	2.5	20.3	*22.4*
State enterprises	42.5	0.0	12.5	12.5	10.0	22.5	42.6	*35.2*
Other state agency	100.0	0.0	0.0	0.0	0.0	0.0	0.0	*9.1*
Local authorities	100.0	0.0	0.0	0.0	0.0	0.0	0.0	*0.5*
Tourists	100.0	0.0	0.0	0.0	0.0	0.0	0.0	-
Export	100.0	0.0	0.0	0.0	0.0	0.0	0.0	*1.4*
Other	100.0	0.0	0.0	0.0	0.0	0.0	0.0	-
Co-operatives:								
Individuals	59.6	5.3	8.8	7.0	1.8	17.5	26.4	*12.9*
Non-state enterprises	41.1	8.9	8.9	21.4	1.8	17.9	36.8	*16.8*
State enterprises	50.9	12.4	3.5	12.4	5.3	15.8	30.8	*35.1*
Other state agency	100.0	0.0	0.0	0.0	0.0	0.0	0.0	*21.0*
Local authorities	98.2	1.8	0.0	0.0	0.0	0.0	0.1	*1.2*
Tourists	100.0	0.0	0.0	0.0	0.0	0.0	0.0	-
Export	92.9	0.0	3.6	1.8	0.0	1.8	4.1	*8.0*
Other	98.2	0.0	0.0	0.0	0.0	1.8	1.8	-
Shareholding and limited liability companies:								
Individuals	56.4	15.4	10.3	6.4	2.6	9.1	19.8	-
Non-state enterprises	25.6	16.8	16.7	19.3	7.7	14.1	39.3	-
State enterprises	48.7	15.4	7.7	14.1	3.9	10.3	26.1	-
Other state agency	97.4	0.0	0.0	0.0	2.6	0.0	2.2	-
Local authorities	97.4	1.3	0.0	1.3	0.0	0.0	1.0	-
Tourists	100.0	0.0	0.0	0.0	0.0	0.0	0.0	-
Export	83.3	2.6	1.3	6.5	3.9	2.6	10.9	-
Other	97.4	1.3	1.3	0.0	0.0	0.0	0.7	-

Note: Figures in italics refer to the corresponding 1991 survey data. 'Tourists' and 'other' categories were not specified in the 1991 survey.

Table 4.3: Destination of sales of urban enterprises by location. Percentage share of total sales of main product.

	0	1–24	25–49	50–74	75–99	100	Mean	
Hanoi:							**1997**	**1991**
Same town	19.3	0.8	6.7	18.5	5.0	49.6	66.6	*73.8*
Rural areas	67.2	1.7	5.0	11.8	2.5	11.8	23.4	*9.3*
Other urban areas	80.7	5.9	6.7	5.0	0.0	1.7	7.5	*8.2*
Elsewhere	92.4	1.7	2.5	2.5	0.8	0.0	3.5	*7.2*
Haiphong:								
Same town	9.9	2.0	2.0	6.9	5.0	74.3	83.2	*77.0*
Rural areas	83.2	5.0	3.0	2.0	5.0	2.0	9.0	*4.0*
Other urban areas	84.2	5.9	2.0	5.0	2.0	1.0	6.7	*13.0*
Elsewhere	95.0	4.0	1.0	0.0	0.0	0.0	1.1	*6.8*
HCM City:								
Same town	18.8	9.4	12.0	17.9	11.1	30.8	56.8	*78.7*
Rural areas	68.4	8.5	6.0	7.7	3.4	6.0	16.7	*8.5*
Other urban areas	65.0	10.3	16.2	6.0	1.7	0.9	12.9	*8.0*
Elsewhere	79.5	2.6	2.6	6.0	4.3	5.1	13.5	*2.6*

Note: Figures in italics refer to the corresponding 1991 survey data.

outward bound. In the 1991 survey, on average, close to 80 per cent of sales were within the city, and two-thirds sold all their output within the town area, whereas by the time of the 1997 survey this had reduced, in favour of other rural and urban areas. The establishments in Hanoi fall somewhere in between; while most sales are within Hanoi itself, this percentage has reduced since 1991 and the share of sales to other rural areas has increased.

Examining the geographical distribution of sales across ownership forms, since most of the household enterprise clients are individuals, a high share (78 per cent on average) of the household businesses included in the survey sell all of their output in the same town (Table 4.4). Such nearby clients represent 85 per cent of average sales, and what little is left for other destinations is mainly accounted for by sales to rural areas – a pattern that has not changed much in the inter-survey period. Shareholding and limited liability companies have a structure

Table 4.4: Destination of sales of urban enterprises by ownership form. Percentage share of total sales of main product.

	0	1–24	25–49	50–74	75–99	100	Mean	
All urban:							1997	1991
Same town	16.3	4.2	7.1	14.8	7.1	50.4	68.2	*76.9*
Rural areas	72.4	5.0	4.7	7.4	3.6	6.8	16.4	*7.9*
Other urban areas	76.3	7.4	8.6	5.3	1.2	1.2	9.2	*8.9*
Elsewhere	88.7	2.7	2.1	3.0	1.8	1.8	6.3	*4.6*
Household enterprises:								
Same town	10.2	1.0	1.0	6.1	4.1	77.6	84.5	*87.7*
Rural areas	82.7	4.1	3.1	4.1	0.0	6.1	10.0	*7.5*
Other urban areas	94.9	0.0	1.0	3.1	0.0	1.0	3.0	*3.5*
Elsewhere	96.9	0.0	0.0	1.0	2.0	0.0	2.4	*2.4*
Private enterprises:								
Same town	18.2	7.6	9.1	22.7	7.6	34.8	58.8	*76.1*
Rural areas	71.2	4.5	6.1	10.6	7.6	0.0	15.3	*7.5*
Other urban areas	57.6	15.2	12.1	9.1	3.0	3.0	17.3	*9.5*
Elsewhere	84.8	4.5	1.5	3.0	1.5	4.5	8.6	*8.6*
Partnership enterprises:								
Same town	12.5	2.5	7.5	10.0	7.5	60.0	74.4	*76.2*
Rural areas	67.5	7.5	0.0	12.5	5.0	7.5	19.6	*7.0*
Other urban areas	85.0	5.0	5.0	5.0	0.0	0.0	5.6	*10.8*
Elsewhere	97.5	2.5	0.0	0.0	0.0	0.0	0.5	*3.7*
Co-operatives:								
Same town	25.0	3.6	5.4	19.6	3.6	42.9	60.2	*66.7*
Rural areas	67.9	1.8	3.6	8.9	7.1	10.7	23.0	*10.5*
Other urban areas	75.0	7.1	10.7	3.6	1.8	1.8	9.8	*12.0*
Elsewhere	85.7	5.4	1.8	3.6	1.8	1.8	7.0	*8.6*
Shareholding & limited liability companies:								
Same town	18.2	6.5	14.3	18.2	13.0	29.9	58.0	-
Rural areas	66.2	7.8	9.1	5.2	1.3	10.4	19.0	-
Other urban areas	64.9	11.7	15.6	6.5	1.3	0.0	11.4	-
Elsewhere	79.2	2.6	6.5	6.5	2.6	2.6	11.6	-

Note: Figures in italics refer to the corresponding 1991 survey data.

of forward linkages much in common with private enterprises in the 1997 survey, and although showing the most outward tendencies, they still sell close to 60 per cent within the city area. Private enterprises sell on average slightly less than limited liability companies to other urban areas, but more of them completely depend on sales to such areas. It appears that while co-operatives and partnership enterprises sell about as much within the closest surroundings today as they did in the earlier survey, private enterprises today are reaching much farther. The share among these relying completely on customers within the city is about half as large today, and the share going to other cities and rural areas has doubled over these six years.

As far as the size of the clientele and mode of selling are concerned, most enterprises seem to sell to more than ten customers and commonly produce on order, either sometimes or always. The percentage selling to more than ten customers is highest in Haiphong, followed by Ho Chi Minh City and Hanoi, in that order (Table 4.5). Compared to the 1991 survey, it is seen that more enterprises are increasing their customer base, especially in Haiphong. On average, 80 per cent of the urban enterprises sell to more than ten customers, an increase from 63 per cent in the earlier survey. A similar trend can be seen across ownership forms as well; more than three-quarters sell to more than ten customers. The average number of customers has risen for all ownership forms in the inter-survey period, except household enterprises which register no change.

Production on advance order is the most common mode of selling, more so in Hanoi and Haiphong. Ho Chi Minh City has the highest proportion (a third) that, in the 1997 survey, never sold on order (Table 4.5). Compared to 1991 survey data, the percentage of enterprises *always* selling on the security of an order has decreased. Among the establishments in Hanoi that always produce on order, agricultural processing and bags and covers industries are most common and the same applies for machinery and parts manufacturers in Ho Chi Minh City. Across ownership forms as well, the tendency toward always producing on advance order is decreasing, especially among household enterprises (Table 4.5).

If production on advance order is on the whole common, participation in subcontracting agreements is not. Only in Haiphong does the share of enterprises engaged in such contracts exceed 10 per cent, and

Table 4.5: Number of customers and mode of selling, urban enterprises. Percentages.

	Hanoi	Haiphong	HCM City	All urban	Household	Private	Partnership	Co-operative	Shareholding*
No. of customers:									
1	1.7	2.0	0.9	1.5	1.0	1.6	2.5	1.8	1.3
2–10	30.3	5.0	19.7	19.0	23.5	9.4	27.5	12.3	21.8
over 10	68.1	93.1	79.5	79.5	75.5	89.1	70.0	86.0	76.9
1991	*55.0*	*64.0*	*68.9*	*62.5*	*75.5*	*64.7*	*59.6*	*46.6*	-
Produce on advance order:									
Never	19.3	16.8	29.1	22.0	40.8	18.8	7.5	12.3	15.4
Sometimes	58.8	65.3	47.9	57.0	50.0	59.4	55.0	66.7	57.7
Almost always	21.8	17.8	23.1	21.1	9.2	21.9	37.5	21.1	26.9
1991	*45.9*	*61.6*	*30.0*	*41.0*	*23.5*	*38.8*	*47.6*	*56.5*	-

Note: Figures in italics refer to the corresponding 1991 survey data. *Shareholding and LLC

only in Hanoi does the number of partners exceed one in a majority of cases (Table 4.6).[1]

The establishments with subcontracting agreements are, in terms of ownership, mostly private enterprises. While the figure is 14 per cent for private enterprises, none of the partnership enterprises, less than 3 per cent of the shareholding companies, 6 per cent of household firms and 9 per cent of co-operatives subcontracted in the 1997 survey (Table 4.6). Only among co-operatives does the majority of those subcontracting have two partners, otherwise the subcontracting partnership with other enterprises is limited to one. Assistance from the subcontracting partner, as seen in Table 4.6, was mainly limited to raw materials and credits. The former is the most frequently mentioned form of support in Hanoi and Haiphong and the latter in Ho Chi Minh City. A minority also gets some help with technology and training of workers, but this has only happened in Haiphong, where support otherwise is more uncommon than in the other two cities. In terms of ownership, receiving assistance was most common among co-operatives.

That linkages of the above kind are not more common is actually rather strange, since the intensity of competition is often perceived as 'severe'. In Ho Chi Minh City as well as in Haiphong, 58 per cent of the enterprises in the survey claim they face severe competition from at least one source (Table 4.7). In each of the cities, non-state enterprises present the worst threat; mentioned by 20 per cent of the firms in Hanoi, 44 per cent in Ho Chi Minh City and actually more than 50 per cent in Haiphong. However, the percentage experiencing a severe threat from non-state enterprises was less in the 1997 survey, compared to the earlier one, except in Haiphong. Severe competition from state enterprises has also increased in Haiphong, unlike the other two cities. The enterprises in Haiphong facing severe competition, irrespective of the source, are mostly involved in the manufacture of light engineering and consumer goods, the same industries as those facing severe competition in Ho Chi Minh City, but in the latter case with the addition of furniture and carpentry. In Hanoi it is mainly within agro-processing and light engineering that competition is severe.

It is among partnership enterprises that the share facing such strong competition is the highest, reaching 60 per cent (Table 4.7). It is almost as bad among shareholding and limited liability companies (55 per

Table 4.6: Subcontracting arrangements among urban enterprises. Percentages.

	Hanoi	Haiphong	HCM City	All urban	Household	Private	Partnership	Co-operative	Shareholding*
Subcontracting:	2.5	12.9	5.1	6.5	6.1	13.6	0.0	8.9	2.6
1991	*21.8*	*10.4*	*28.0*	*22.8*	*16.8*	*15.0*	*26.2*	*36.0*	-
No. of partners:									
1	0.0	69.2	100.0	68.2	100.0	66.7	0.0	40.0	50.0
2	100.0	23.1	0.0	27.3	0.0	22.2	0.0	60.0	50.0
3	0.0	7.7	0.0	4.5	0.0	11.1	0.0	0.0	0.0
Partners:									
Non-state enterprises	100.0	92.3	66.7	86.4	83.3	77.8	37.0	100.0	100.0
1991	*34.5*	*28.6*	*46.7*	*50.0*	*52.9*	*47.1*	*37.0*	*38.2*	-
State enterprises	66.7	23.1	33.3	31.8	0.0	44.4	0.0	40.0	50.0
1991	*55.1*	*71.4*	*45.0*	*50.0*	*29.4*	*47.1*	*59.3*	*52.9*	-
Foreign company	0.0	0.0	0.0	0.0	0.0	0.0	0.0	0.0	0.0
Other enterprise	33.3	15.4	0.0	13.6	16.7	11.1	0.0	20.0	0.0
Assistance received:									
Raw materials	66.7	30.8	0.0	27.3	16.7	22.2	0.0	80.0	0.0
Capital/credits	0.0	23.1	95.0	13.6	0.0	11.1	0.0	20.0	0.0
Lease machinery	0.0	0.0	0.0	0.0	0.0	0.0	0.0	0.0	0.0
Technology	0.0	7.7	0.0	4.5	0.0	0.0	0.0	20.0	0.0
Management	0.0	0.0	0.0	0.0	0.0	0.0	0.0	0.0	0.0
Training workers	0.0	7.7	0.0	4.5	0.0	0.0	0.0	20.0	0.0
Other	0.0	0.0	0.0	0.0	0.0	0.0	0.0	0.0	0.0

Note: Figures in italics refer to the corresponding 1991 survey data. *Shareholding and LLC.

Table 4.7: Percentage of urban enterprises experiencing 'severe' competition.

	Hanoi	Haiphong	HCM City	All urban	Household	Private	Partnership	Co-operative	Shareholding*
All urban:	**33.6**	**58.4**	**58.1**	**49.6**	**37.8**	**53.1**	**60.0**	**50.9**	**55.1**
Source of competition:									
Non-state enterprises	21.8	*52.5*	*44.4*	*38.9*	*33.7*	40.6	52.5	40.4	35.9
1991	*37.9*	*44.4*	*52.2*	*46.5*	*52.3*	*35.9*	*54.4*	*44.1*	-
State enterprises	4.2	*24.0*	*14.5*	*13.6*	*6.1*	10.9	15.0	21.1	19.5
1991	*12.9*	*10.0*	*14.2*	*12.9*	*10.8*	*10.9*	*13.2*	*17.2*	-
Legal imports	5.0	*19.0*	*8.5*	*10.4*	*3.1*	9.4	15.0	15.8	14.3
Illegal imports	4.2	*14.0*	*9.4*	*8.9*	*5.1*	6.3	15.0	14.0	9.1
Others	2.5	*0.0*	*7.7*	*3.6*	*2.0*	4.8	2.5	1.8	6.5

Note: Figures in italics refer to the corresponding 1991 survey data. *Shareholding and LLC

cent), followed by private enterprises (53 per cent) and co-operatives (51 per cent). Fewer household enterprises (40 per cent) face severe competition. Here again, irrespective of ownership form, non-state firms pose the worst threat, but more than 20 per cent of the co-operatives mention state enterprises as extremely tough competitors, as do a large number of shareholding and limited liability companies. Severe competition from state enterprises has reduced for household enterprises, remained constant for private enterprises and increased for partnerships and co-operatives in 1990–96. The threat of competition from legal and illegal imports has not changed much.

It is no surprise, therefore, that the percentage of entrepreneurs who believe that there are too many enterprises in the market has risen since the 1991 survey, in all cities. In Haiphong, as much as 66 per cent claim that too many establishments are producing similar goods; this represents an increase of 20 percentage points since the last survey (Table 4.8). An interesting finding is that in Hanoi, while 44 per cent believe there are too many enterprises, an almost equal number feel there are neither too many nor too few. This latter group might explain the relatively fewer enterprises that had accumulated unsold stocks of goods in the 1997 survey.

Meanwhile, 48 per cent of those in Haiphong had stocks of unsaleable goods (a slightly lower percentage than in the 1991 survey). However, this was a smaller percentage than those considering competition as severe or markets oversupplied. This might indicate that even though the situation is more troublesome for entrepreneurs in Haiphong today, with more firms and more competition, they have learned how to handle it, at least in the area of adjusting their output to demand in order not to end up with shelves of unsold goods. Light consumer goods and agricultural processing are industries in which, irrespective of the city, many of the troubled enterprises are found, while carpentry and furniture seems to be a difficult industry in Ho Chi Minh City in particular. In all three cities, the most common reason mentioned for not being able to sell all of the output is an oversupplied market, just as in the 1991 survey. The second most frequent reason is poor sales channels, ranked second also in the earlier survey, but still mentioned by fewer enterprises today than in the 1991 survey.

Table 4.8: Perception of market situation and accumulation of unsold goods among urban enterprises by location. Percentages.

	Hanoi	Haiphong	HCM City	All urban
Too many enterprises	44.1	66.3	61.5	**56.8**
1991	*48.8*	*45.5*	*55.4*	***51.6***
Neither too many nor too few	40.7	25.7	28.2	**31.8**
Too few	13.6	6.9	9.4	**10.1**
No competitors	1.7	1.0	0.9	**1.2**
Unsaleable goods	21.0	47.5	28.2	**31.5**
1991	*32.3*	*51.9*	*34.6*	***37.3***
Main reason:				
Over-supply	66.7	72.9	54.5	**65.7**
1991	*45.2*	*38.5*	*35.1*	***38.5***
Low quality	8.3	4.2	6.1	**5.7**
Poor sales channels	16.7	16.7	24.2	**19.0**
1991	*21.4*	*17.9*	*27.0*	***23.1***
Transport problems	0.0	2.1	0.0	**1.0**
Price too high	0.0	2.1	3.0	**1.9**
Other reason	8.3	2.1	12.1	**6.7**

Note: Figures in italics refer to the corresponding 1991 survey data.

Even though the proportion of household enterprises experiencing severe competition is only 38 per cent (Table 4.7), almost twice as many (70 per cent) say that the number of similar establishments is too high, the latter representing a 10-percentage-point increase since the last survey (Table 4.9). Among partnership enterprises on the other hand, 60 per cent claim to face severe competition, while 50 per cent (just as many as in the 1991 survey) think that there are too many establishments in the market. Perceptions about the severity of competition do not seem to correlate strongly with the feeling of there being too many enterprises in the market. This indicates that while there may be too many in the field, they may not all be efficient enough to pose a threat to the sample enterprises. Since only about one-fifth of the household and partnership enterprises have accumulated stocks of unsold goods, which represents a figure twice as high in the earlier

Table 4.9: Perception of market situation and accumulation of unsold goods among urban enterprises by ownership form. Percentages.

	Household	Private	Partnership	Co-perative	Shareholding*
Too many enterprises	70.4	51.5	50.0	51.8	51.3
1991	*60.4*	*41.8*	*51.8*	*53.3*	-
Neither too many nor too few	23.5	34.8	40.0	35.7	32.9
Too few	6.1	13.6	7.5	12.5	11.8
No competitors	0.0	0.0	2.5	0.0	3.9
Unsaleable goods	19.4	34.8	17.5	48.2	39.0
1991	*34.7*	*37.5*	*37.9*	*38.2*	-
Main reason:					
Over-supply	84.2	30.9	100.0	61.5	53.3
1991	*42.1*	*45.5*	*27.5*	*40.6*	-
Low quality	5.3	4.3	0.0	3.8	10.0
Poor sales channels	0.0	26.1	0.0	30.8	20.0
1991	*36.8*	*22.7*	*22.5*	*9.4*	-
Transport problems	0.0	0.0	0.0	0.0	3.3
Price too high	0.0	0.0	0.0	0.0	6.7
Other reason	10.5	8.7	0.0	3.8	6.7

Note: Figures in italics refer to the corresponding 1991 survey data. *Shareholding and LLC.

survey, it appears that these firms are doing well in facing the severe competition (Table 4.9). By contrast, half of the co-operatives have unsold goods, which represents a 12 percentage point increase since the 1991 survey. Irrespective of ownership form, half the enterprises that have stocks of unsold goods blame an oversupply in the markets. Some co-operatives and private enterprises also have problems finding sales channels, but by no means as many as those who face over-supplied markets.

Forward Linkages among Rural Enterprises[2]

More than half of the establishments in Long An sell only to individuals (Table 4.10). These account for about two-thirds of the average

Table 4.10: Type of customers of rural enterprises by location. Percentage share of total sales of main product.

	0	1–24	25–49	50–74	75–99	100	Mean	
Ha Tay:							1997	1991
Individuals	34.9	14.5	3.6	4.8	1.2	41.0	47.5	*44.5*
Non-state enterprises	50.6	3.6	3.6	7.2	10.8	24.1	39.2	*34.1*
State enterprises	90.4	1.2	1.2	1.2	6.0	0.0	6.6	*13.5*
Other state agency	95.2	0.0	0.0	1.2	1.2	2.4	4.2	*1.8*
Local authority	100.0	0.0	0.0	0.0	0.0	0.0	0.0	*1.6*
Tourists	100.0	0.0	0.0	0.0	0.0	0.0	0.0	-
Export	98.8	0.0	0.0	0.0	1.2	0.0	1.1	*3.5*
Other	97.6	1.2	0.0	0.0	0.0	1.2	1.4	-
Long An:								
Individuals	22.9	8.4	3.6	6.0	3.6	55.4	64.5	*50.1*
Non-state enterprises	62.7	3.6	6.0	6.0	6.0	15.7	27.4	*54.3*
State enterprises	92.8	2.4	1.2	2.4	0.0	1.2	3.6	*0.5*
Other state agency	95.2	1.2	0.0	1.2	0.0	2.4	3.1	*0.0*
Local authority	96.4	2.4	0.0	0.0	1.2	0.0	1.5	*0.0*
Tourists	100.0	0.0	0.0	0.0	0.0	0.0	0.0	-
Export	100.0	0.0	0.0	0.0	0.0	0.0	0.0	*0.0*
Other	100.0	0.0	0.0	0.0	0.0	0.0	0.0	-

Note: Figures in italics refer to the corresponding 1991 survey data. 'Tourists' and 'other' categories were not specified in the 1991 survey.

Long An sales. Although to a lesser degree, individual buyers are also the main clientele for Ha Tay enterprises, accounting for 39 per cent of the average sales, and are the sole buyers for a similar percentage of enterprises.

The firms in Ha Tay have more links to state enterprises and agencies, but the share is still only minor, as not even 7 per cent of sales goes to these clients. Compared to the 1991 survey, Ha Tay records fewer changes than Long An in the sales distribution (Table 4.10). Noticeable changes in Long An include the replacement of non-state enterprises by individual buyers in the average firm's sales.

Table 4.11: Type of customers of rural enterprises by ownership form. Percentage share of total sales of main product.

	0	1–24	25–49	50–74	75–99	100	Mean	
All rural:							1997	1991
Individuals	28.9	11.4	3.6	5.4	2.4	48.2	56.0	*57.7*
Non-state enterprises	56.6	3.6	4.8	6.6	8.4	19.9	33.3	*33.6*
State enterprises	91.6	1.8	1.2	1.8	3.0	0.6	5.1	*5.8*
Other state agency	95.2	0.6	0.0	1.2	0.6	2.4	3.7	*2.0*
Local authority	98.8	0.6	0.0	0.0	0.6	0.0	0.7	*0.8*
Tourists	100.0	00	0.0	0.0	0.0	0.0	0.0	-
Export	99.4	0.0	0.0	0.0	0.6	0.0	0.5	*0.8*
Other	98.8	0.6	0.0	0.0	0.0	0.6	0.7	*0.7*
Household enterprises:								
Individuals	17.7	10.4	1.0	3.1	1.0	66.7	71.0	*60.8*
Non-state enterprises	69.8	1.0	1.0	3.1	10.4	14.6	25.5	*31.0*
State enterprises	97.9	0.0	1.0	0.0	0.0	1.0	1.4	*4.5*
Other state agency	99.0	0.0	0.0	0.0	0.0	1.0	1.0	*2.2*
Local authority	100.0	0.0	0.0	0.0	0.0	0.0	0.0	*1.0*
Tourists	100.0	0.0	0.0	0.0	0.0	0.0	0.0	-
Export	100.0	0.0	0.0	0.0	0.0	0.0	0.0	*1.0*
Other	99.0	0.0	0.0	0.0	0.0	1.0	1.0	-
Private enterprises:								
Individuals	39.6	14.6	6.3	8.3	6.3	25.0	39.0	*56.4*
Non-state enterprises	41.7	4.2	8.3	10.4	8.3	27.1	44.9	*36.4*
State enterprises	87.5	2.1	2.1	4.2	4.2	0.0	7.3	*5.5*
Other state agency	93.8	0.0	0.0	0.0	2.1	4.2	5.9	*1.1*
Local authority	93.8	4.2	0.0	0.0	2.1	0.0	2.5	*0.5*
Tourists	100.0	0.0	0.0	0.0	0.0	0.0	0.0	-
Export	100.0	0.0	0.0	0.0	0.0	0.0	0.0	*0.0*
Other	97.9	2.1	0.0	0.0	0.0	0.0	0.4	-

Note: Figures in italics refer to the corresponding 1991 survey data. 'Tourists' and 'other' categories were not specified in the 1991 survey.

Examining the sales patterns across ownership forms, the picture is not very different. Individual buyers are the largest buyers, more so for household than private enterprises (Table 4.11). Among the latter, a higher share of the average sales goes to non-state enterprises. Since the 1991 survey, this pattern has not changed much, although the increase in individual customer sales for household enterprises and non-state enterprise sales among private enterprises has risen by 10 per cent. The weak linkages with the state sector continue.

Increased sales to individuals have also narrowed the geographical distribution of the market. Sales in the same commune and nearby towns have increased and the share of sales destined for large cities has declined for both Long An and Ha Tay (Table 4.12). The businesses from Ha Tay are increasingly selling to more distant places. The share going to large cities (on average 41 per cent) has grown marginally since the 1991 survey, while the 18 per cent to nearby towns represents a four-fold increase.

Table 4.12: Destination of sales of rural enterprises by location. Percentage share of total sales of main product.

	0	**1–24**	**25–49**	**50–74**	**75–99**	**100**	**Mean**	
Ha Tay:							1997	1991
Same village	83.1	3.6	3.6	3.6	1.2	4.8	9.43	*11.5*
Same commune	79.5	4.8	2.4	2.4	2.4	8.4	13.3	*15.5*
Nearby town	66.3	10.8	4.8	6.0	2.4	9.6	17.9	*4.5*
Large city	49.4	7.2	1.2	2.4	12.0	27.7	41.0	*38.6*
Elsewhere	74.7	3.6	2.4	3.6	7.2	8.4	18.3	*18.3*
Long An:								
Same village	85.2	2.5	1.2	6.2	1.2	3.7	8.6	*14.1*
Same commune	54.3	8.6	2.5	7.4	2.5	24.7	32.5	*14.8*
Nearby town	59.3	1.2	2.5	22.2	2.5	12.3	27.5	*8.4*
Large city	88.9	0.0	1.2	2.5	1.2	6.2	9.0	*21.1*
Elsewhere	67.9	3.7	1.2	9.9	7.4	9.9	22.4	*17.5*

Note: Figures in italics refer to the corresponding 1991 survey data. 'Sales within the same district' was an additional category in the 1991 survey only, hence the mean values do not add up to 100.

The distribution across ownership forms (Table 4.13) shows that household enterprises sell more within the commune borders than do private enterprises. The latter sell more in large cities, 33 per cent on average. Their average sales to large cities have, in fact, doubled since the 1991 survey, and that to nearby towns increased by more than 100 per cent. Household enterprises show a somewhat more dispersed pattern.earlier. Less is sold within the confines of the province, while more is being sold within the commune, or to towns nearby, the latter

Table 4.13: Destination of sales of rural enterprises by ownership form. Percentage share of total sales of main product.

	0	1–24	25–49	50–74	75–99	100	Mean	
All rural:							1997	1991
Same village	84.1	3.0	2.4	4.9	1.2	4.3	9.0	*12.3*
Same commune	67.1	6.7	2.4	4.9	2.4	16.5	22.8	*21.3*
Nearby town	62.8	6.1	3.7	14.0	2.4	11.0	22.6	*5.8*
Large city	68.9	3.7	1.2	2.4	6.7	17.1	25.2	*18.8*
Elsewhere	71.3	3.7	1.8	6.7	7.3	9.1	20.3	*12.8*
Household enterprises:								
Same village	83.3	2.1	2.1	4.2	1.0	7.3	11.4	*13.4*
Same commune	63.5	4.2	1.0	5.2	4.2	21.9	29.1	*20.9*
Nearby town	63.5	5.2	3.1	13.5	3.1	11.5	23.1	*2.4*
Large city	79.2	4.2	0.0	2.1	4.2	10.4	16.0	*21.2*
Elsewhere	68.8	4.2	3.1	9.4	5.2	9.4	20.4	*8.8*
Private enterprises:								
Same village	83.0	4.3	4.3	6.4	2.1	0.0	6.9	*8.1*
Same commune	72.3	6.4	6.4	6.4	0.0	8.5	14.5	*21.7*
Nearby town	57.4	4.3	6.4	19.1	0.0	12.8	26.4	*10.0*
Large city	59.6	2.1	4.3	4.3	4.3	25.5	32.9	*16.6*
Elsewhere	76.6	2.1	0.0	4.3	8.5	8.5	19.4	*14.9*

Note: Figures in italics refer to the corresponding 1991 survey data. Mean values of the 1991 survey data do not add up to 100, since there was an additional destination 'sales within the same district', in the 1991 survey only, not included in the above table.

share having increased from less than 3 to 23 per cent. At the same time, large cities accounted for more than 20 per cent of average sales in the survey.

As a consequence of having their customers somewhat closer, the establishments in Long An are able to handle a larger number of clients. More than 80 per cent of them had over ten customers, compared to some 40 per cent in Ha Tay (Table 4.14). The average number of customers has increased since the 1991 survey; more enterprises are selling to more than ten, although Ha Tay enterprises most commonly sell to 2–10 customers. When looking at the pattern by forms of ownership, we see that household enterprises today tend to sell more to under ten customers, unlike private enterprises.

Production on order seems to be more common in Ha Tay, relatively speaking, where 75 per cent of the enterprises engage in production on such terms at least occasionally, whereas in Long An about 75 per cent never do (Table 4.14). In Long An, on the other hand, the share of 'never producing on order' has grown by 10 percentage points, while the share doing so occasionally, or always, has decreased. Production on order is more frequent among household enterprises, but can no longer be considered the conventional way of operating. More than half of the household firms take part in such arrangements from time to time, while close to 60 per cent of the

Table 4.14: Number of customers and mode of selling among rural enterprises.

	Ha Tay	Long An	All rural	Household	Private
No. of customers:					
1	4.8	1.2	**3.0**	4.2	0.0
2–10	54.2	13.3	**33.7**	44.8	10.4
Over 10	41.0	85.5	**63.3**	51.0	89.6
1991	*29.9*	*69.7*	***78.4***	*83.9*	*73.8*
Produce on advance order:					
Never	24.1	69.9	**47.0**	47.9	58.3
Sometimes	39.8	22.9	**31.3**	30.2	31.3
Almost always	36.1	7.2	**21.7**	21.9	10.4
1991	*56.0*	*14.3*	***25.1***	*22.2*	*24.0*

Note: Figures in italics refer to the corresponding 1991 survey data.

private enterprises never do, and the share of 'always producing on advance orders' has diminished compared to the earlier survey, while the share 'sometimes doing so' has grown.

Subcontracting was a phenomenon that hardly figured in rural areas in the 1991 survey, but became more common by the 1997 survey. The surveyed enterprises in Ha Tay were more involved in subcontracting than those in Long An (Table 4.15). Classified according to ownership forms, 19 and 13 per cent of household and private enterprises respectively had such arrangements. Irrespective of location or form of ownership, the majority had only one partner enterprise, but the share having as many as three is actually higher in Long An than in Ha Tay; these belonged to the 'other' forms. The partners were, both across locations and ownership forms, non-state enterprises for the most part.

Table 4.15: Subcontracting arrangements among rural enterprises. Percentages.

	Long An	Ha Tay	All Rural	Household	Private
Subcontracting:	7.2	33.7	**20.5**	18.8	12.5
No. of partners:					
Only 1	66.6	78.6	**76.5**	77.7	83.3
2	16.7	17.8	**17.6**	16.7	16.7
3	16.7	3.6	**5.9**	5.6	0.0
Partner:					
Non-state enterprises	66.7	96.4	**91.2**	88.9	100.0
State enterprise	0.0	10.7	**8.8**	0.0	0.0
Foreign company	0.0	0.0	**0.0**	0.0	0.0
Other enterprise	33.3	10.7	**14.7**	22.2	16.7
Assistance received:					
Raw materials	16.7	32.1	**29.4**	33.3	0.0
Capital/credits	0.0	42.9	**35.3**	33.3	33.3
Lease machinery	0.0	0.0	**0.0**	0.0	0.0
Technology	0.0	3.6	**2.9**	0.0	0.0
Management	0.0	0.0	**0.0**	0.0	0.0
Training workers	0.0	0.0	**0.0**	0.0	0.0
Other	0.0	0.0	**0.0**	0.0	0.0

Assistance by the subcontracting partner was more common in Ha Tay than in Long An. The form of assistance generally given in Long An centred on the supply of raw materials. In Ha Tay assistance with credits was actually more common than supplying inputs and yet the share assisted with raw materials in Ha Tay, some 30 per cent, was twice as high as the corresponding share in Long An.

The share of enterprises experiencing 'severe' competition has grown as well. In Ha Tay, 57 per cent of the enterprises in the survey said that they faced severe competition, this percentage dropping to 47 in Long An (Table 4.16). In terms of ownership, private enterprises are somewhat worse off than household firms. Irrespective of location or ownership form, this indicates a tremendous increase in the degree of competition perceived, compared to the earlier survey; non-state enterprises still pose by far the worst threat to all forms of enterprises in both rural areas. Even though the share of entrepreneurs experiencing severe competition from state enterprises is still rather limited (6 or 7 per cent in both areas), the share has grown since the 1991 survey. Household undertakings are about as untouched by this threat in the 1997 as in the 1991 survey, but among private enterprises some 10 per cent experience severe competition from state companies in the 1997 survey. In the 1991 survey, this share was less than 1 per cent.

About 70 per cent in Ha Tay and 60 per cent in Long An regard the number of enterprises competing in the same line of business as too

Table 4.16: Percentage share of rural enterprises experiencing 'severe' competition.

	Ha Tay	Long An	*Total*	Household	Private	Other
Total	**62.7**	**44.6**	**53.6**	**47.9**	**58.3**	**68.2**
Source of competition:						
Non-state enterprises	56.6	44.6	**50.6**	47.9	50.0	63.6
1991	*21.7*	*27.2*	***22.8***	*22.3*	*21.8*	-
State enterprises	6.0	7.2	**6.6**	2.1	10.4	18.2
1991	*1.7*	*0.0*	***1.6***	*2.3*	*0.7*	-
Legal imports	2.4	3.6	**3.0**	1.0	6.3	4.5
Illegal imports	1.2	0.0	**0.6**	0.0	2.1	0.0
Others	0.0	1.2	**0.6**	1.0	0.0	0.0

Note: Figures in italics refer to the corresponding 1991 survey data.

high, and 70 per cent of households and 60 per cent of private enterprises hold the same view (Table 4.17). These figures have increased significantly since 1991. The 1997 survey is even more illustrative: one-third of those in Long An and more than half in Ha Tay claimed they had no competitors whatsoever; households being as fortunate in this respect as private enterprises. The industries experiencing severe competition are wide-ranging, but more common among the carpentry and light engineering goods manufacturers.

As a result, more than one-third of Ha Tay enterprises, and slightly less in Long An, have accumulated goods that are proving difficult to sell; here the share of private enterprises (35 per cent) is somewhat higher than for household enterprises (27 per cent) (Table 4.17). This means that the establishments in Ha Tay were doing much better according to the 1997 survey when compared to the 1991 survey, in

Table 4.17: Perception of market situation and accumulation of unsold goods among rural enterprises.

	Ha Tay	Long An	Total Rural	Household	Private
Too many enterprises	71.1	61.4	66.3	71.9	58.3
1991	*53.7*	*37.9*	*32.2*	*34.3*	*27.9*
Neither too many nor too few	16.9	28.9	22.9	21.9	22.9
Too few	10.8	9.6	10.2	6.3	18.8
No competitors	1.2	0.0	0.6	0.0	0.0
1991	*33.3*	*52.9*	*47.9*	*47.2*	*50.0*
Unsaleable goods	32.5	27.7	30.1	27.1	35.4
1991	*48.3*	*17.4*	*21.8*	*20.9*	*22.4*
Main reason:					
Market oversupplied	50.0	66.7	57.8	60.9	56.3
1991	*22.2*	*31.6*	*25.2*	*20.6*	*31.3*
Low quality	12.5	0.0	6.7	8.7	6.3
Poor sales channels	29.2	9.5	20.0	21.7	6.3
1991	*29.6*	*19.0*	*31.7*	*41.1*	*21.9*
Transport problems	0.0	0.0	0.0	0.0	0.0
Price too high	4.2	0.0	2.2	4.3	0.0
Other reason	4.2	23.8	13.3	4.3	31.3

Note: Figures in italics refer to the corresponding 1991 survey data.

Table 4.18: Type of suppliers to urban enterprises by location. Percentage share of total procurement.

	0	1–24	25–49	50–74	75–99	100	Mean
Hanoi:							
Households	73.1	5.0	1.7	5.0	1.7	13.4	18.9
Non-state enterprises	26.1	4.2	15.1	10.9	10.1	33.6	54.7
State enterprises	59.7	10.1	6.7	13.4	1.7	8.4	22.5
Other state agencies	98.3	0.8	0.8	0.0	0.0	0.0	0.5
Collective farms	99.2	0.0	0.0	0.0	0.0	0.8	0.8
Other	97.5	0.0	0.0	0.0	0.0	2.5	2.5
Haiphong:							
Households	69.3	7.9	4.0	6.9	1.0	10.9	18.1
Non-state enterprises	20.8	6.9	5.9	10.9	5.0	50.5	63.4
State enterprises	71.3	5.0	2.0	8.9	5.9	6.9	18.4
Other state agencies	99.0	1.0	0.0	0.0	0.0	0.0	0.1
Collective farms	99.0	1.0	0.0	0.0	0.0	0.0	0.1
Other	100.0	0.0	0.0	0.0	0.0	0.0	0.0
Ho Chi Minh City:							
Households	78.6	6.8	0.0	6.8	1.7	6.0	12.8
Non-state enterprises	20.5	8.5	11.1	12.8	12.8	34.2	57.7
State enterprises	59.8	10.3	12.0	8.5	5.1	4.3	20.0
Other state agencies	99.1	0.0	0.0	0.9	0.0	0.0	0.6
Collective farms	96.6	2.6	0.0	0.9	0.0	0.0	1.0
Other	88.0	1.7	2.6	0.9	3.4	3.4	7.9

adjusting their output to suit buyers' demands, when close to half of them had stocks of unsold goods. The enterprises in Long An are relatively worse off now, and units with unsaleable goods have suffered a 10-per-cent increase. In both areas and regardless of ownership form, oversupplied markets are stated as the main reason, but the lack of proper sales channels is obviously just as much of an obstacle in Ha Tay in the 1997 as in the 1991 survey, the difference between the two rural areas being even in the later survey. In terms of ownership, sales channels are, just as in the 1991 survey, more of a hindrance to household than to private enterprises. The difference is that in the 1991 survey the problem of sales channels was even more of an issue to household entrepreneurs than market oversupply, and the gap in importance between these two obstacles according to private enterprises has widened in the intervening six years.

Backward Linkages among Urban Enterprises

Non-state enterprises stand out as the single most important suppliers of raw materials and other inputs for the enterprises in all the three cities. Their dominance is seen both in the share of non-state enterprises in the purchases of the average urban enterprise (about 50 per cent) as well as in the percentage of enterprises depending solely on them for inputs. On average, a Hanoi firm buys 55 per cent of its main input from non-state enterprises, the corresponding figures being 58 and 64 in Ho Chi Minh City and Haiphong respectively (Table 4.18). Second in importance are state enterprises, which supply, on average, one-fifth of raw materials, and which, for instance, provide all raw materials for 8 per cent of the enterprises in Hanoi. Households are the third most important source, not far behind state enterprises. State agencies and collective farms feature only seldom as suppliers, and in each of the cities as much as 96 per cent of the interviewed businesses have no contact with them.

The importance of non-state enterprises as suppliers is seen across ownership forms as well. Household and private firms buy on average two-thirds of their raw materials and inputs from non-state enterprises, while the share among other forms hovers around 50 per cent (Table 4.19). Households account for more than one-fifth of the average input supply, except for private and shareholding and limited liability companies. In general, it appears that the greater the complexity of ownership, the less the reliance on household enterprises as input suppliers. The same trend can be observed across manufacturing and agro-processing enterprises.

Irrespective of the ownership form of supplier, the source and user of the input are mostly situated in the same town. In Haiphong, as high a share as 90 per cent get all of their inputs from suppliers located in the same town, while in Hanoi and Ho Chi Minh City, the share is some 75 per cent (Table 4.20). On average, sources in the same town

Table 4.19: Type of suppliers to urban enterprises by ownership form. Percentage share of total procurement

	0	1–24	25–49	50–74	75–99	100	Mean
All urban from:							
Households	73.9	6.5	1.8	6.2	1.5	10.1	16.5
Non-state enterprises	22.6	6.5	11.0	11.6	9.5	38.9	58.4
State enterprises	63.4	8.6	6.8	10.4	4.2	6.5	20.4
Other state agencies	98.8	0.6	0.3	0.3	0.0	0.0	0.4
Collective farms	98.2	1.2	0.0	0.3	0.0	0.3	0.6
Other	95.0	0.6	0.9	0.3	1.2	2.1	3.7
Household enterprises from:							
Households	65.3	7.1	3.1	5.1	0.0	19.4	24.3
Non-state enterprises	26.5	3.1	4.1	8.2	11.2	46.9	63.4
State enterprises	76.5	6.1	8.2	4.1	0.0	5.1	11.4
Other state agencies	99.0	0.0	1.0	0.0	0.0	0.0	0.4
Collective farms	99.0	0.0	0.0	1.0	0.0	0.0	0.5
Other	100.0	0.0	0.0	0.0	0.0	0.0	0.0
Private enterprises from:							
Households	75.4	10.6	0.0	7.6	1.5	4.6	12.4
Non-state enterprises	13.8	9.0	13.8	13.8	13.8	35.4	61.0
State enterprises	55.4	12.1	9.1	15.2	7.5	1.5	21.8
Other state agencies	100.0	0.0	0.0	0.0	0.0	0.0	0.0
Collective farms	95.4	4.6	0.0	0.0	0.0	0.0	0.9
Other	93.8	0.0	1.5	1.5	3.0	0.0	3.8
Partnership enterprises from:							
Households	62.5	7.5	0.0	10.0	0.0	20.0	27.0
Non-state enterprises	37.5	5.0	12.5	2.5	10.0	32.5	46.9
State enterprises	65.0	10.0	0.0	7.5	2.5	15.0	23.6
Other state agencies	100.0	0.0	0.0	0.0	0.0	0.0	0.0
Collective farms	100.0	0.0	0.0	0.0	0.0	0.0	0.0
Other	97.5	0.0	0.0	0.0	0.0	2.5	2.5

Table 4.19: Type of suppliers to urban enterprises by ownership form. Percentage share of total procurement (continued)

	0	1–24	25–49	50–74	75–99	100	Mean
Co-operatives from:							
Households	71.9	0.0	3.6	8.9	5.3	10.5	21.6
Non-state enterprises	26.3	7.1	14.2	12.3	5.3	35.1	52.8
State enterprises	61.4	8.9	1.8	14.3	5.3	8.8	23.1
Other state agencies	100.0	0.0	0.0	0.0	0.0	0.0	0.0
Collective farms	100.0	0.0	0.0	0.0	0.0	0.0	0.0
Other	94.7	1.8	1.8	0.0	0.0	1.8	2.6
Shareholding and limited liability companies from:							
Households	88.5	7.8	0.0	2.6	1.3	0.0	3.4
Non-state enterprises	16.7	10.3	15.4	16.7	9.0	32.1	56.0
State enterprises	48.7	10.4	11.7	15.4	6.4	7.7	28.6
Other state agencies	96.2	2.6	0.0	1.3	0.0	0.0	1.2
Collective farms	97.4	1.3	0.0	0.0	0.0	1.3	1.4
Other	88.5	1.3	1.3	0.0	2.6	6.4	9.4
Agro-processing enterprises from:							
Households	51.2	7.3	4.9	7.3	0.0	29.3	36.9
Non-state enterprises	31.7	7.3	12.2	9.8	9.8	29.3	48.2
State enterprises	73.2	4.9	12.2	7.3	2.4	0.0	11.9
Other state agencies	97.6	2.4	0.0	0.0	0.0	0.0	0.1
Collective farms	87.8	9.8	0.0	2.4	0.0	0.0	2.9
Other	100.0	0.0	0.0	0.0	0.0	0.0	0.0
Manufacturing enterprises from:							
Households	77.0	6.4	1.4	6.1	1.7	7.4	13.7
Non-state enterprises	21.3	6.4	10.8	11.8	9.5	40.2	59.8
State enterprises	62.0	9.2	6.1	10.8	4.4	7.5	21.6
Other state agencies	99.0	0.3	0.3	0.3	0.0	0.0	0.4
Collective farms	99.7	0.0	0.0	0.0	0.0	0.3	0.3
Other	94.3	0.7	1.0	0.3	1.4	2.4	4.2

Table 4.20: Location of suppliers to urban enterprises by city. Percentage share of total procurement

	0	1–24	25–49	50–74	75–99	100	Mean
Hanoi:							
Same town	7.6	1.6	3.4	8.9	3.4	74.8	84.4
Other rural	84.9	2.4	3.3	5.0	0.8	3.4	8.6
Other urban	90.8	3.3	4.0	0.0	0.0	1.7	3.8
Elsewhere	95.0	0.8	0.8	1.7	0.0	1.7	3.2
Haiphong:							
Same town	3.0	1.0	2.0	2.0	2.0	90.1	93.7
Other rural	95.0	2.0	0.0	2.0	0.0	1.0	2.3
Other urban	94.1	1.0	0.0	3.0	1.0	1.0	3.5
Elsewhere	99.0	0.0	0.0	1.0	0.0	0.0	0.5
HCM City:							
Same town	5.1	6.2	5.3	4.4	3.6	76.1	84.1
Other rural	89.7	0.0	1.8	5.3	2.6	0.9	6.9
Other urban	89.7	3.6	4.3	0.0	0.0	2.6	4.7
Elsewhere	94.9	0.0	0.0	0.9	3.6	0.9	4.2

provide about 85 per cent of the raw materials, while suppliers in rural areas account for about half of what is left. The surveyed enterprises thus have very strong backward linkages with their own cities. Nearby sources supply household and partnership enterprises and co-operatives to more than 90 per cent on average, indicating very strong backward linkages (Table 4.21).

The most important criterion for selecting suppliers appears to be input prices; it is affirmed by two-thirds of all urban enterprises and is the main criterion both across locations and ownership forms (Table 4.22). This pattern has not changed much in the inter-survey period. However, while more than 80 per cent of the undertakings in Hanoi mention a competitive price as being most important, the proportion is lower at 58 per cent in Ho Chi Minh City and 61 per cent in Haiphong. Quality aspects are completely overshadowed by price as the main criterion among those selecting suppliers in Hanoi, while 28 per cent

Table 4.21: Location of suppliers to urban enterprises by ownership form. Percentage share of total procurement.

	0	1–24	25–49	50–74	75–99	100	Mean
Household enterprises:							
Same town	3.1	0.0	0.0	6.0	0.0	90.8	94.2
Other rural	93.9	0.0	2.0	2.0	0.0	2.0	3.9
Other urban	96.9	0.0	2.0	0.0	0.0	1.0	1.8
Elsewhere	100.0	0.0	0.0	0.0	0.0	0.0	0.0
Private enterprises:							
Same town	6.3	6.3	4.7	4.8	3.2	75.0	83.2
Other rural	87.5	1.6	1.6	7.8	1.6	0.0	6.7
Other urban	87.5	3.2	3.2	1.6	1.6	3.1	7.0
Elsewhere	95.3	0.0	0.0	3.2	1.6	0.0	3.1
Partnership enterprises:							
Same town	2.5	0.0	2.5	2.5	2.5	90.0	94.3
Other rural	92.5	2.5	0.0	2.5	0.0	2.5	4.9
Other urban	97.5	0.0	2.5	0.0	0.0	0.0	0.9
Elsewhere	100.0	0.0	0.0	0.0	0.0	0.0	0.0
Co-operatives:							
Same town	0.0	1.8	5.2	3.5	7.1	82.5	92.3
Other rural	91.2	0.0	1.8	5.3	1.8	0.0	4.8
Other urban	89.5	8.9	1.8	0.0	0.0	0.0	2.0
Elsewhere	98.2	0.0	0.0	1.8	0.0	0.0	0.9
Shareholding & limited liability companies:							
Same town	12.8	6.5	6.5	7.8	3.9	62.8	73.9
Other rural	83.3	3.9	2.6	3.9	2.6	3.8	10.0
Other urban	85.9	2.6	5.2	2.6	0.0	3.8	7.5
Elsewhere	88.5	1.3	1.3	1.3	3.9	3.8	8.7

of the firms in Ho Chi Minh City and 23 per cent of those in Haiphong actually put quality before prices. Next in importance is the secure supply of inputs. There are also variations in the criteria for selecting suppliers, across ownership forms. Price is more an issue among 80 per cent of partnerships and co-operatives, while quality is paramount for one-third of the private and shareholding companies and one-fifth of the household enterprises.

In the search for suppliers, informal methods like personal contacts and own search processes dominate. Personal contacts are more prevalent in Hanoi while it is own search processes in Haiphong; an almost equal number of entrepreneurs use these two methods in Ho Chi Minh City (Table 4.22). The picture is similar across ownership forms; as much as 60 per cent of the partnership enterprises use mainly personal contacts in identifying suppliers. It appears that personal knowledge of the supplier offers some kind of a guarantee as far as quality of the input is concerned. Personal contacts may also prove useful in negotiating prices.

Although personal knowledge of suppliers offers better quality guarantees, entrepreneurs are dissatisfied, to differing degrees, with the current raw materials situation. Very few establishments in Hanoi claim to have any difficulties at all in securing adequate quantities of raw materials; reliance on imports is the most common among those that actually do experience quantity problems. The inputs in short supply cover several categories without any clear pattern. The numbers are slightly higher in Ho Chi Minh City and Haiphong (about 15 per cent), and it is the erratic nature of supply that is the biggest problem. In both these cities it is mostly wood products, cane, bamboo and timber that are difficult to procure. It appears to be private and share-holding enterprises that suffer most from shortages, since they account for 31 and 36 per cent of those suffering from insufficient quantities of inputs. Household, private and partnership enterprises seem to manage better with their supplies, and although they constitute 30 and 12 per cent of the survey sample, respectively, their share among the enterprises encountering difficulties is 18 and 3 per cent. Comparing the 1997 with the 1991 survey, one must say that the developments are very encouraging. Hanoi, the city with previously the greatest raw material shortages reported by its enterprises, hardly shows any such cases today. In terms of ownership, it is household and partnership enterprises that have experienced the greatest relief. An examination of the enterprises with difficulties in securing inputs shows that about two-thirds get all of their inputs from within the same town, and more than 80 per cent get no inputs whatsoever from other areas, rural or urban.

Table 4.22: Main criteria and method of selecting suppliers among urban enterprises.

	Hanoi	Hai-phong	HCM City	House-hold	Private	Partner-ship	Co-operative	Share-holding*	Total	
Main criteria:									1997	1991
Competitive prices	82.4	61.0	57.8	67.3	61.9	79.5	77.2	59.0	67.1	*73.7*
Terms of credit	0.8	3.0	1.7	2.0	3.2	0.0	0.0	2.6	1.8	*0.0*
Quality standards	7.6	23.0	28.4	18.4	27.0	7.7	10.5	26.9	19.3	*15.4*
Secure supply	5.0	6.7	7.8	8.2	6.3	10.3	8.8	5.1	7.4	*4.5*
Know supplier personally	0.8	6.7	3.4	4.1	0.0	0.0	3.5	1.3	2.1	*1.4*
Located nearby	0.0	1.0	0.0	0.0	1.6	0.0	0.0	0.0	0.3	*0.3*
Government agent	0.8	0.0	0.0	0.0	0.0	0.0	0.0	1.3	0.3	*0.3*
No choice	2.5	0.0	0.9	0.0	0.0	2.6	0.0	3.8	1.2	*4.2*
Method:										
Personal contacts	59.7	21.8	43.1	45.9	33.3	60.0	31.6	4.9	42.4	-
Marketing by supplier	2.5	15.8	6.9	7.1	11.1	2.5	10.5	7.7	8.0	-
Government agencies	7.6	5.9	0.0	2.0	1.6	2.5	10.5	6.4	4.5	-
Own search process	30.3	55.4	45.7	43.9	50.8	32.5	47.4	38.5	43.0	-
Other	0.0	1.0	4.3	1.0	3.2	2.5	0.0	2.9	1.8	-

Note: Figures in italics refer to the corresponding 1991 survey data. 'Co-operatives' is based on less than 20 observations as for mode of identification. Regarding method, there was no similar variable calculated on a total basis in the 1991 survey. *Shareholding and LLC.

Table 4.23: Percentage of urban enterprises experiencing difficulties with supply of inputs..

	Hanoi	Haiphong	HCM City	Household	Private	Partnership	Co-operative	Shareholding*
Quantity problems*	5.1	14.9	15.5	7.1	19.0	2.5	8.8	18.2
1991	*37.8*	*30.7*	*25.0*	*22.0*	*36.5*	*33.3*	*35.2*	-
Import dependency	66.7	20.0	38.9	14.3	58.3	100.0	20.0	42.9
Inadequate or erratic supply	16.7	53.3	55.6	85.7	50.0	100.0	40.0	28.6
No local suppliers	0.0	20.0	27.8	14.3	33.3	0.0	40.0	7.1
Seasonal supply	16.7	26.7	27.8	0.0	25.0	0.0	20.0	42.9
Poor transportation	16.7	0.0	0.0	0.0	0.0	0.0	0.0	7.1
Bureaucratic difficulties	50.0	6.7	33.3	28.6	25.0	0.0	40.0	21.4
Quality problems	9.2	14.9	23.9	9.2	18.8	7.5	15.8	26.9
1991	*27.8*	*31.2*	*42.2*	*25.3*	*36.5*	*29.3*	*38.0*	-
Insufficient power	5.9	5.0	37.1	21.6	23.8	2.5	7.0	17.9
1991	*17.7*	*14.2*	*42.2*	-	-	-	-	-

Note Figures in italics refer to the corresponding 1991 survey data. *Shareholding and LLC.

Key: * The number of observations for tabulating quantity problems, in the 1997 survey, upon which the above table is based were: 6 for Hanoi, 18 for Ho Chi Minh City, 15 for Haiphong; 7 household enterprises, 12 private enterprises, 1 partnership enterprise, 5 co-operatives and 14 shareholding and limited liability companies. Hence the percentages should be interpreted with some caution. Where marked with a (-), this was not specified in the 1991 survey.

As far as quality problems are concerned, the situation has improved since the 1991 survey (Table 4.23). Even then, Ho Chi Minh City entrepreneurs were plagued to a greater extent by this problem than were entrepreneurs in the other cities. In terms of ownership form, quality problems were more common among shareholding and limited liability companies; they account for close to 40 per cent of those experiencing problems with the quality of their inputs. The purchasing pattern among the enterprises with quality problems is not very different from the whole group of enterprises. Non-state enterprises account for the bulk of supplies while households and state enterprises account for some 20 per cent each. However, while the average share of sources within the city is 87 per cent for the entire urban sample, it is 75 per cent among those having quality problems.

Among the cities covered, Ho Chi Minh City reveals the greatest difficulties with energy supply (Table 4.23). Here, as many as 37 per cent report an inadequate supply of energy, compared to less than 6 per cent in the other cities. There is no observable correlation between those using power-driven machinery and those experiencing an inadequate energy supply. Although this is a problem, two-thirds say the effect is negligible, and less than 3 per cent rate it as very serious.

Backward Linkages among Rural Enterprises

In very general terms, the nature of backward linkages does not differ much between the two rural areas. Non-state enterprises are the most important source of the main inputs in Ha Tay as well as in Long An, and households have a stronger position in rural than in urban areas accounting for, on average, 37 and 34 per cent in Long An and Ha Tay respectively (Table 4.24). However, state enterprises play a somewhat more important part in the supply to Ha Tay. While about 13 per cent of the establishments buy from state suppliers, none in Long An does. On the other hand, collective farms do not feature at all as suppliers in Ha Tay, while in Long An, those that purchase from collective farms procure 75–99 per cent of their raw materials from them. Although non-state enterprises dominate as suppliers, the share of households has increased since 1990. They have doubled their share in the average Ha Tay enterprise's purchases in 1996. State enterprises

Table 4.24: Type of suppliers to rural enterprises by location. Percentage share of total procurement.

	0	1–24	25–49	50–74	75–99	100	Mean	
Ha Tay:							1997	1991
Households	59.0	3.6	2.4	3.6	3.6	27.7	34.4	*17.8*
Non-state enterprises	30.1	8.4	3.6	4.8	3.6	49.4	57.6	*72.9*
State enterprises	86.7	2.4	1.2	4.8	4.8	0.0	7.5	*6.8*
Other state agencies	96.4	2.4	1.2	0.0	0.0	0.0	0.6	*1.0*
Collective farms	100.0	0.0	0.0	0.0	0.0	0.0	0.0	*0.4*
Other	97.6	2.4	0.0	0.0	0.0	0.0	0.0	*2.5*
Long An:								
Households	55.4	3.6	3.6	3.6	0.0	33.7	37.2	*29.8*
Non-state enterprises	37.3	0.0	0.0	8.4	2.4	51.8	58.6	*64.2*
State enterprises	100.0	0.0	0.0	0.0	0.0	0.0	0.0	*6.7*
Other state agencies	97.6	1.2	0.0	0.0	0.0	1.2	1.3	*0.0*
Collective farms	98.8	0.0	0.0	0.0	1.2	0.0	1.1	*0.1*
Other	97.6	0.0	0.0	1.2	0.0	1.2	1.8	*0.0*

Note: Figures in italics refer to the corresponding 1991 survey data. The share from 'households' in the 1997 survey is comapred to 'individuals' in the 1991 survey, while 'other state agencies' above are compared with the 'state trading companies' share respectively.

have completely disappeared from the Long An arena, but kept about the same position in Ha Tay as they held in the 1991 survey.

Across ownership forms, a similar pattern emerges. Non-state enterprises constitute 58 per cent of the rural firm's average purchases of inputs, while households provide about 30 per cent (Table 4.25). It appears that households took over some share of state enterprises, while non-state establishments have held their position since the earlier survey. The linkages with state that did exist were mainly found among private enterprises. Next, the share relying completely on one particular source of raw material is higher among household firms, where 37 per cent purchase all of their inputs from other households, and 54 per cent rely completely on non-state undertakings. For the representative agro-processing enterprise, household suppliers are

Table 4.25: Type of suppliers to rural enterprises by ownership form. Percentage share of total procurement

	0	1–24	25–49	50–74	75–99	100	Mean	
All rural from:							1997	1991
Households	57.2	3.6	3.0	3.6	1.8	30.7	35.8	*30.5*
Non-state enterprises	33.7	4.2	1.8	6.6	3.0	50.6	58.1	*58.5*
State enterprises	93.4	1.2	0.6	2.4	2.4	0.0	3.7	*8.0*
Other state agencies	97.0	1.8	0.6	0.0	0.0	0.6	0.9	*1.1*
Collective farms	99.4	0.0	0.0	0.0	0.6	0.0	0.5	*0.5*
Other	97.6	1.2	0.0	0.6	0.0	0.6	0.9	*2.0*
Household enterprises from:								
Households	57.3	3.1	0.0	2.1	1.0	36.5	38.9	*28.5*
Non-state enterprises	37.5	2.1	0.0	3.1	3.1	54.2	58.6	*59.6*
State enterprises	99.0	0.0	0.0	0.0	1.0	0.0	0.9	*9.0*
Other state agencies	99.0	0.0	0.0	0.0	0.0	1.0	1.0	*2.0*
Collective farms	100.0	0.0	0.0	0.0	0.0	0.0	0.0	*0.9*
Other	97.9	1.0	0.0	1.0	0.0	0.0	0.5	*1.7*
Private enterprises from:								
Households	47.9	6.3	10.4	8.3	0.0	27.1	36.1	*31.5*
Non-state enterprises	33.3	4.2	4.2	14.6	4.2	39.6	53.8	*54.6*
State enterprises	87.5	2.1	0.0	6.3	4.2	0.0	7.4	*9.8*
Other state agencies	95.8	2.1	2.1	0.0	0.0	0.0	0.8	*0.0*
Collective farms	97.9	0.0	0.0	0.0	2.1	0.0	1.9	*0.4*
Other	100.0	0.0	0.0	0.0	0.0	0.0	0.0	*3.2*
Agro-processing enterprises from:								
Households	25.8	6.5	3.2	3.2	0.0	61.3	64.8	*28.6*
Non-state enterprises	61.3	0.0	0.0	6.5	6.5	25.8	35.3	*61.3*
State enterprises	100.0	0.0	0.0	0.0	0.0	0.0	0.0	*6.8*
Other state agencies	100.0	0.0	0.0	0.0	0.0	0.0	0.0	*0.0*
Collective farms	100.0	0.0	0.0	0.0	0.0	0.0	0.0	*2.3*
Other	100.0	0.0	0.0	0.0	0.0	0.0	0.0	*0.0*

Table 4.25: Type of suppliers to rural enterprises by ownership form. Percentage share of total procurement (continued)

	0	1–24	25–49	50–74	75–99	100	Mean	
Manufacturing enterprises from:								
Households	64.4	3.0	3.0	3.7	2.2	23.7	29.1	*32.1*
Non-state enterprises	27.4	5.2	2.2	6.7	2.2	56.3	63.4	*56.6*
State enterprises	91.9	1.5	0.7	3.0	3.0	0.0	4.6	*7.3*
Other state agencies	96.3	2.2	0.7	0.0	0.0	0.7	1.2	*0.6*
Collective farms	99.3	0.0	0.0	0.0	0.7	0.0	0.7	*0.4*
Other	97.0	1.5	0.0	0.7	0.0	0.7	1.1	*4.1*

Note: Figures in italics refer to the corresponding 1991 survey data. The share procured from 'households' in the 1997 survey is compared to 'individual persons' in the 1991 survey, while 'other state agencies' above are compared with the 'state trading companies' respectively.

dominant, supplying two-thirds of its inputs, while non-state enterprises are in the same position when it comes to selling to manufacturing establishments. There is thus evidence of an increased importance of households as suppliers to agro-processing units.

Geographically, on average, 36 per cent of the inputs to enterprises in Long An come from large cities, compared to one-fifth in the 1991 survey; this indicates extended backward linkages (Table 4.26). In Ha Tay, this share, which was about one-third in 1991, is today slightly higher than 20 per cent; it is instead the nearby towns that supply about 30 per cent, which denotes closer availability of inputs. In both rural areas, a very small percentage – less than one-tenth – of raw materials are procured from sources within the same village, but still more than in the earlier survey. It would thus appear as if the enterprises in Ha Tay are concentrating on closer surroundings today compared to the 1991 survey, for their raw material and input needs. The establishments in Long An, on the other hand, are turning to large cities rather than nearby towns. However, it must be remembered that the sets of enterprises interviewed in 1991 and 1997 and used in this chapter are not the same; hence the pattern[3] of changes might not be very helpful in determining the flexibility of firms.

Table 4.26: Location of suppliers to rural enterprises by area. Percentage share of total procurement.

	0	1–24	25–49	50–74	75–99	100	Mean	
Ha Tay:							1997	1991
Same village	84.3	4.8	1.2	2.4	1.2	6.0	9.1	*2.7*
Same commune	68.7	8.4	3.6	2.4	4.8	12.0	20.0	*18.2*
Nearby town	55.4	7.2	7.2	3.6	7.2	19.3	31.0	*29.6*
Large city	65.1	9.6	2.4	7.2	4.8	10.8	21.7	*34.1*
Other	69.5	8.4	3.6	6.0	7.2	4.9	17.3	*17.3*
Long An:								
Same village	90.4	0.0	0.0	2.4	0.0	7.2	8.5	*0.5*
Same commune	69.9	4.8	0.0	6.0	1.2	18.1	22.6	*11.3*
Nearby town	75.9	4.8	1.2	2.4	0.0	15.7	18.3	*62.0*
Large city	61.4	0.0	0.0	3.6	4.8	30.1	36.2	*20.0*
Other	80.7	0.0	3.6	4.8	2.4	8.4	14.4	*4.1*

Note: Figures in italics refer to the corresponding 1991 survey data.

Looking across ownership forms, the average private enterprise is getting the same percentage of its inputs from within the commune (20 per cent) but other sources (imports etc.) have reduced the share nearby towns had, in the earlier survey (Table 4.27). Household firms are instead moving in exactly the opposite direction from private enterprises, and have increased their local raw material supply, especially from sources within the village, over the past six years. Large cities, however, continue to account for 30 per cent of the purchases by the average household enterprise.

The criteria for identifying potential suppliers do, however, differ very much between Long An and Ha Tay. Enterprises in Long An pay more attention to the price – 72 per cent mentioning this as the main criterion – compared to 49 per cent in Ha Tay, and also whether the supplier might be able to give credit (Table 4.28). One-third of the enterprises in Ha Tay state quality aspects as the main criterion for selecting suppliers, as against only 5 per cent in Long An. That raw materials can be supplied in adequate quantities continuously also

Table 4.27: Location of suppliers to rural enterprises by ownership form. Percentage share of total procurement.

	0	1–24	25–49	50–74	75–99	100	Mean	
Household enterprises:							1997	1991
Same village	83.3	3.1	0.0	3.1	1.0	9.4	12.1	*4.3*
Same commune	67.7	6.0	3.1	3.0	2.0	17.7	23.0	*17.8*
Nearby town	61.5	7.1	3.0	3.1	5.1	19.8	28.0	*31.2*
Large city	67.7	2.0	0.0	3.1	3.0	23.9	28.7	*31.2*
Other	88.4	1.1	2.2	4.2	2.2	2.1	7.3	*16.2*
Private enterprises:								
Same village	97.9	0.0	0.0	2.1	0.0	0.0	1.1	*1.4*
Same commune	70.8	6.3	0.0	8.4	2.1	12.5	19.1	*19.5*
Nearby town	62.5	6.3	6.3	4.2	2.1	18.8	26.5	*48.0*
Large city	68.8	6.3	0.0	6.3	2.1	16.7	23.3	*26.1*
Other	58.3	2.1	8.4	8.4	8.4	14.6	30.0	*3.7*
Other enterprise forms:								
Same village	81.8	4.5	4.5	0.0	0.0	9.1	10.9	-
Same commune	72.7	9.0	0.0	0.0	9.1	9.1	18.8	-
Nearby town	90.9	0.0	4.5	0.0	0.0	4.5	5.9	-
Large city	31.8	13.6	9.0	13.6	18.1	13.6	42.5	
Other	54.5	22.6	0.0	4.5	9.0	9.1	21.9	-

Note: Figures in italics refer to the corresponding 1991 survey data.

receives more weight in Ha Tay. The methods used to identify suppliers continue to be informal. Relatively, more Long An enterprises (53 per cent) have used their own search processes in order to identify suppliers. While the same percentage used personal contacts, marketing efforts of suppliers were more visible in Ha Tay.

Input price is the main criterion for identifying suppliers, even across ownership forms, although a few variations exist. About 60 per cent rate this as most important followed by the quality of inputs (4.28). A secure supply is more an issue among household enterprises, than the others. The methods used to identify suppliers show that

Table 4.28: Main criteria and methods of selecting suppliers among rural enterprises.

	Ha Tay	Long An	Household	Private	Other
Main criteria:					
Competitive prices	48.2	72.3	59.4	60.4	63.6
Terms of credit	0.0	7.2	4.2	2.1	4.5
Quality standards	33.7	4.8	15.6	25.0	22.7
Secure supply	13.3	4.8	12.5	4.2	4.5
Know supplier personally	2.4	4.8	3.1	4.2	4.5
Located nearby	1.2	3.6	4.2	0.0	0.0
Government agent	0.0	0.0	0.0	0.0	0.0
No choice	1.2	2.4	1.0	4.2	0.0
Method:					
Personal contacts	44.6	44.6	37.5	57.4	40.0
Marketing by supplier	12.0	1.2	5.2	4.3	20.0
Government agencies	0.0	0.0	0.0	0.0	0.0
Own search process	39.8	53.0	57.3	29.8	40.0
Other	3.6	1.2	0.0	8.5	0.0

Note: The number of 'other' observations is 8, constituting 13 per cent of the rural enterprises sample.

household enterprises rely more on their own search processes while private enterprises are more reliant on personal contacts.

Households seem to be suppliers when price is what matters most, and their share is almost halved when quality issues are considered to be more important. Non-state enterprises do take a step forward in the latter case as well, but the biggest change is that involving state enterprises. These supply close to nothing to those caring mainly for price, but grow to a 12 per cent share when focusing on quality. It might be in order to look at the kind of raw materials that make price and quality respectively. Wood is represented in both categories, but while such inputs represent 47 per cent in the quality group, the share is 19 per cent where price matters more. In the latter group, steel, iron, rice and maize figure as well.

A higher share of enterprises in Ha Tay than in Long An experienced problems in the supply of raw materials in the 1997 survey (Table 4.29). In the former province 24 per cent of the enterprises experienced problems with the quality of inputs and 20 per cent with the quantity of the inputs, compared to 10 per cent in Long An being discontent with the quantity, and 17 per cent with the quality. There are some difficulties in interpreting this question and determining an appropriate response, since if quality is important, and there are difficulties securing raw materials that meet with the requirements, then insufficiencies in quantity are bound to surface as well. While problems with supply in Long An are invariably linked to seasonal fluctuations, erratic supply is a worse problem in Ha Tay. The input affected most gravely in short supply is timber, and, in the case of insufficient quantities, also beverages. But these answers reveal something rather interesting. In terms of quantity, the situation has improved in both rural areas and for all ownership forms since the 1991 survey, but the problems are still worse in Ha Tay than in Long An. The quality of the inputs has instead become more of a problem than it was earlier, irrespective of location or form of ownership, and also in this aspect, the establishments in Ha Tay are more discontent than those in Long An.

The enterprises which are unable to secure enough quantities of inputs have a purchasing pattern that, geographically, differs somewhat from the average one. As mentioned before, while the entrepreneurs in Long An acquire inputs from larger cities, those in Ha Tay purchase from nearby towns. The establishments experiencing shortfalls in quantity do, however, rely mostly on sources within the commune. The rural enterprises that have difficulty in finding sufficient raw material rely on sources within the same village or commune for, on average, 40 per cent of raw materials, and one-fifth of them get all of their supplies from within the commune. It should, however, be noted that their share bought from 'other' areas, mainly imports, is higher than for rural enterprises in general, which explains the problem.

Ha Tay has a slightly greater incidence of enterprises with quality problems, 24 as against 17 per cent in Ha Tay (Table 4.29). Also, a higher percentage of private enterprises mentioned this problem compared to household enterprises. The group with such problems appears to be reaching farther in their search for inputs that meet their requirements.

Table 4.29: Percentage of rural enterprises experiencing difficulties with supply of inputs.

	Ha Tay	Long An	Household	Private	Other
Quantity problems	20.5	10.0	14.6	15.2	19.0
1991	*44.6*	*26.6*	*40.7*	*35.0*	-
Import dependency	0.0	37.5	7.1	14.3	25.0
Inadequate or erratic supply	64.7	37.5	57.1	42.9	75.0
No local suppliers	17.6	37.5	14.3	28.6	50.0
Seasonal supply	23.5	100.0	35.7	100.0	0.0
Poor transportation	5.9	12.5	0.0	14.3	25.0
Bureaucratic difficulties	29.4	12.5	28.6	0.0	50.0
Quality problems	24.1	16.9	17.7	25.0	22.7
1991	*14.5*	*7.3*	*9.5*	*9.0*	-
Insufficient power	3.9	26.8	15.6	15.2	18.2
1991	*22.9*	*29.0*	*20.1*	*35.0*	-

Note: Figures in italics refer to the corresponding 1991 survey data. The number of observations (firms with difficulties) regarding quantity upon which the above table is based is: 17 for Ha Tay, 8 for Long An, 14 household enterprises, 7 private enterprises and 4 'other' enterprises; hence the percentages should be interpreted with some caution.

On average, one-fifth of the inputs are bought within the village or commune, 28 per cent from nearby towns and 30 per cent from large cities, which is a pattern quite distinct from both Ha Tay and Long An in general. This group is also quite different from the rest with regard to the kind of establishment from which they get their inputs. As much as 75 per cent is bought from non-state enterprises, to be compared with a share less than 60 per cent for the rural areas in general. The ones with quality problems buy about half as much from households (19 per cent) as the average for the rural survey, but their criteria and methods when selecting suppliers do not differ much from the average. A somewhat lower share (50 per cent compared to 60 per cent for the whole rural survey) mention competitive prices as the main criteria, and 17 per cent, compared to 9 per cent in general, think that a secure supply is the most important when choosing supplier.

Almost all enterprises in Long An and Ha Tay have access to electricity. In Long An, some 71 per cent are connected to the public grid, while the share is 81 per cent in Ha Tay. However, more establishments in Long An (27 per cent) than in Ha Tay (4 per cent) have problems securing adequate supplies of power (Table 4.29). This difference in supply of electricity might partly be explained by the fact that Long An enterprises use power-driven machinery to a greater degree than in Ha Tay. However, the problem does not seem to be too serious as at least half of those with insufficient electricity rate the problem as negligible.

Notes

1. The comparison is not exact, as subcontracting was somewhat more loosely defined in the 1991 survey.

2. The comparison made on ownership basis should be interpreted with some caution. The 1991 survey included more areas than just Ha Tay and Long An, areas from which observations are included in the earlier survey among the respective forms of ownership. These observations are also included in all the general 'rural' tables and where 'all rural' values are calculated for the 1991 survey data.

3. The generalisations about improvements and deterioration, as mentioned earlier, should be treated with caution since we are not dealing with the same set of enterprises in the 1991 and 1997 surveys.

5

Payment of Taxes and Fees

Carmina Cortés

Data comparisons between the enterprises surveyed in 1991 and the 'new' enterprises surveyed in 1997 reveal that tax collection among non-state enterprises is rather small regardless of location, form of ownership or period of time. The average tax payment in the 1997 survey, as a percentage of income, was 3.9 per cent (Table 5.1). There has been no significant change in this figure since the 1991 survey when the mean for tax payment was 4.2 per cent of income; however, the number of enterprises completely exempted from tax payment decreased slightly by the 1997 survey. Earlier, 9.8 per cent of the enterprises did not pay any taxes and 34.2 per cent of them paid less than 2 per cent of their income. In the 1997 survey, only 7 per cent were exempted and the percentage paying less than 2 per cent of their income had increased to 37.2 per cent.[1]

Tax payment varied according to different regions and types of enterprises. Variations could be noticed particularly in three respects:

- tax collection was higher in the urban areas than in the rural;
- taxation seems to favour small enterprises, particularly household enterprises, regardless of location;
- in the south, tax collection policies were more strictly enforced than in the north, where more relaxed practices could be observed.

Table 5.1: Taxes paid as percentage of total income in the 1997 survey.

	Mean	Median	% of enterprises paying:	
			no tax	less than 2%
All enterprises	**3.9**	**3.3**	**7.0**	**30.1**
Urban areas:	**4.6**	**4.7**	**2.8**	**23.9**
Hanoi	3.6	3.3	3.4	32.8
Haiphong	4.1	2.8	5.0	35.6
HCM City	6.3	5.5	0.0	3.4
Rural areas:	**2.4**	**1.5**	**15.3**	**46.7**
Ha Tay	1.1	0.3	30.5	54.9
Long An	3.4	2.7	0.1	38.6
Type of enterprise:				
Household	2.8	1.7	13.5	40.4
Private	4.9	3.9	1.8	27.7
Partnership	3.8	3.5	7.4	24.1
Co-operative	4.2	3.9	1.6	29.0
Shareholding & LLC	4.9	4.8	2.5	13.1

Note: Data for 'All enterprises' and for the different ownership forms are the combined aggregates of both urban and rural enterprises.

While there were significant differences between the north and south in both surveys, in the 1997 survey there seemed to be greater contrasts between urban and rural enterprises than in the past. Changes in tax collection practices had favoured rural enterprises greatly by the second survey, resulting in lower taxes and a higher share of enterprises paying no taxes at all or only very little. In the 1997 survey, the urban areas had a mean tax collection of 4.6 per cent of income while the rural areas averaged only 2.4 per cent. Enterprises in Long An appear to have benefited during this period, in which the average tax payment dropped to 3.4 per cent of income, from over 6 per cent in the 1991 survey. In Ha Tay this indicator was very low and it remained at low levels with almost all enterprises being exempted from payment in the 1997 survey. By contrast, enterprises in Ho Chi Minh City paid an average of 4.1 per cent in the earlier and 6.3 per cent in the later survey (Table 5.1). Such contrasts arose mainly because of the different forms of ownership that exist in the rural and urban locations. In the rural areas the majority of the enterprises are household or small private enterprises with very low levels of income, while in the cities the array of enterprises is more varied and includes larger companies. The location of the enterprise also plays a part in taxation because enterprises located in more remote and inaccessible areas have a more favourable taxation.[2] The results of the 1997 survey suggest an attempt by fiscal authorities to give rural enterprises a more competitive position and the opportunity to develop at levels similar to their urban counterparts. However, there remain many inconsistencies.

Tax collection favours small enterprises and particularly household enterprises regardless of location or period of time. This can be observed in Table 5.1, which shows how household enterprises had the lightest tax burden among all forms of ownership. The average payment for this type of enterprise in the 1991 survey was 3.3 per cent of the income and only 2.8 per cent in the 1997 survey. By the latter survey, over 13 per cent of these enterprises were completely exempt from tax payment and more than half of them paid amounts below 2 per cent of their total income. Private enterprises are the second smallest form of ownership; however this group does not enjoy the same benefits as households. The mean tax payment in this group was 4.9 per cent of income and only 1.7 per cent of these enterprises were completely exempt. Household enterprises would appear to receive preferential treatment in the tax system. The other forms of ownership are considered more capitalistic; therefore controls and taxation are stricter for these enterprises, resulting in higher rates of payment, regardless of income or value added taxes.

Differences between the north and south were significant in both surveys, with a more uniform and comprehensive tax collection in the south than in the north. However, the contrast was more widespread in the 1997 survey. The average tax payments in the 1991 survey were 4 per cent and 4.4 per cent of the income, in the north and south respectively (Table 5.2). In the 1997 survey, Ho Chi Minh City had the heaviest tax burden. All the enterprises surveyed in this location paid some tax, over 96 per cent paid taxes above 2 per cent of their total income and the mean was 6.3 per cent. In the northern cities average tax payments were much lower, 4 per cent in Haiphong and 3.6 per cent in Hanoi; the percentage of enterprises paying more than 2 per cent of income were 67.2 per cent for the latter and 64.4 per cent in the former.

Table 5.2: Taxes as percentage of total income in 1991 and 1997 surveys.

	1991 survey	1997 survey
All enterprises:	***3.9***	***4.1***
Urban	4.7	4.2
Rural	2.4	4.0
North:	***4.0***	***2.9***
Urban	4.4	3.8
Rural	3.7	1.1
South:	***4.4***	***4.9***
Urban	4.1	6.3
Rural	4.5	3.4

In the rural areas the differences were also striking in this respect, and although the gap between north and south decreased considerably in the inter-survey period, it was still quite notable. At the time of the 1997 survey, in the province of Long An a great majority of the enterprises paid some tax and over 60 per cent of all enterprises paid taxes above 2 per cent of their income. The average payment was 3.4 per cent, which was similar to that of the northern cities. Ha Tay seemed to be the most favoured region in this respect because 30.5 per cent of the enterprises in this area were exempt from tax payment and almost 55 per cent paid less than 2 per cent with a mean of only 1.3 per cent and median of 0.3 per cent of income. It is worth noticing that while Ho Chi Minh City had a heavier tax burden in the 1997 survey, rising from 4.1 per cent to 6.3 per cent, Long An reduced the rate of tax payment by almost 50 per cent in the same period. These changes gave enterprises in Long An a more competitive edge by the time of the second survey, when the tax burden was excessive in comparison with their counterparts in the north; instead, enterprises in Ho Chi Minh City were placed at a disadvantage.

From the results of the 1997 survey, it can be concluded that tax collection is more uniform and better structured in the south than in the north regardless of the type of enterprise or its urban or rural location.

Classification of Taxes

In the 1997 survey, over 60 per cent of all taxes collected were sales taxes, with only a few variations across the different forms of ownership and location. Profit taxes amounted to 20 per cent of all taxes, licence fees were almost 10 per cent and property taxes accounted for 6.5 per cent. The rest fell in the category of other taxes since registration fees were almost non-existent.

Variations across ownership form were relatively small. The pattern described above was true for all except in the case of household enterprises, where licence fees and property constituted a greater percentage of total taxes than profit tax (Table 5.3). This variation is another consequence of the special regulations that apply in the case of household enterprises.

The same basic pattern was valid regardless of city or province. However, variations were more pronounced when looking at particular locations. In Long An sales tax amounted to 74 per cent of all taxes while in Ha Tay, the same tax accounted for only 46 per cent and property tax for 23.5 per cent. Ho Chi Minh City also showed significant

Table 5.3: Type of tax as percentage of total taxes in the 1997 survey, by form of ownership.

Ownership form	Sales tax	Profit tax	Licence fees	Registration fees	Property tax	Other taxes
Household						
Mean	56.7	8.6	16.0	0.6	13.2	4.6
Median	70.5	0.0	11.9	0.0	0.0	0.0
Private						
Mean	68.8	20.3	6.5	0.1	2.2	2.1
Median	73.6	16.0	3.7	0.0	0.0	0.0
Partnership						
Mean	57.6	27.7	7.6	0.0	2.6	2.5
Median	57.6	33.0	4.7	0.0	0.0	0.0
Co-operatives						
Mean	65.7	20.9	6.8	0.2	5.9	0.4
Median	57.5	32.1	1.4	0.0	0.0	0.0
Shareholding and LLC						
Mean	54.4	31.7	5.7	0.0	1.8	6.4
Median	57.5	32.1	1.4	0.0	0.0	0.0
All enterprises						
Mean	60.6	19.1	9.8	0.2	6.5	3.5
Median	64.9	12.2	4.3	0.0	0.0	0.0

Table 5.4: Type of tax as percentage of total taxes in the 1997 survey, by location.

Location	Sales tax	Profit tax	Licence fees	Registration fees	Property tax	Other taxes
Hanoi						
Mean	62.9	21.3	10.0	0.1	2.8	2.9
Median	59.6	21.4	5.1	0.0	0.0	0.0
Haiphong						
Mean	58.4	11.0	12.0	0.9	12.2	5.5
Median	66.7	1.0	6.4	0.0	2.6	0.0
HCM City						
Mean	57.2	35.5	2.3	0.1	0.4	4.6
Median	57.7	35.2	1.2	0.0	0.0	0.0
Ha Tay						
Mean	46.3	12.8	12.7	0.0	23.5	2.9
Median	56.3	0.0	5.2	0.0	0.4	0.0
Long An						
Mean	74.2	6.7	15.8	0.0	0.0	0.0
Median	74.2	0.0	15.3	0.0	0.0	0.0
All enterprises						
Mean	60.6	19.1	9.8	0.2	6.5	3.5
Median	64.9	12.2	4.3	0.0	0.0	0.0

variations because profit tax accounted for over 35 per cent of the taxes there, while in the rest of the locations it averaged only 13 per cent of total taxes (Table 5.4).

In the 1991 survey the same pattern was observed, but the sales tax was even more important than in the 1997 survey constituting on average almost 68 per cent of total taxes paid.[3] Profit taxes accounted for 15 per cent, licence fees for 11 per cent and other taxes and registration fees for 6 per cent.[4] Property tax was not considered in the 1991 survey.

Tax Collection Authorities

Taxes are primarily collected by district authorities, who ,according to the 1997 survey data, collected an average of 75 per cent of all taxes. Town authorities, in the same survey, accounted for approximately 15 per cent of the total, particularly from payments of household enterprises, while the rest was collected by national or other authorities.

The district authorities collected over 90 per cent of total taxes from all forms of ownership, except in the case of household enterprises where the figure dropped to 51 per cent in the 1997 survey (Table 5.5). This is again due to the particular characteristics of households and the regulations that apply to this form of ownership, which remits a greater percentage of payment to town authorities, mainly as licence fees.

The percentages of tax collection by the different kinds of authorities varied widely between north and south. In Ho Chi Minh City and Long An, district authorities collected over 90 per cent of all taxes while in the cities of the north they collected only 70 per cent and in Ha Tay this rate was as low as 46 per cent in the 1997 survey. In the north the rest of the taxes were collected mainly by town authorities, with an average collection of 22 per cent of all taxes. National authorities had a very small percentage of collection in both areas (Table 5.6).

Table 5.5: Tax authorities collecting payment by form of ownership. Percent of total taxes paid.

Ownership form	Town authority	District authority	National authority	Other authority
Household				
Mean	31.3	51.1	0.8	0.3
Median	0.0	72.0	0.0	0.0
Private				
Mean	4.1	93.1	1.0	0.0
Median	0.0	100.0	0.0	0.0
Partnership				
Mean	18.6	76.0	1.9	1.7
Median	0.0	100.0	0.0	0.0
Co-operative				
Mean	1.9	96.3	0.0	0.1
Median	0.0	100.0	0.0	0.0
Shareholding &LLC				
Mean	.08	92.9	7.0	0.0
Median	0.0	100.0	0.0	0.0
All enterprises				
Mean	15.2	75.5	1.8	0.3
Median	0.00	100.0	0.00	0.0

There are two main reasons for the high proportion of taxes collected by district authorities. First, district authorities collect sales tax which, as mentioned earlier, is the main tax paid in Vietnam; second, all forms of ownership, except household enterprises, must submit tax payments, licence and registration fees to district authorities.

While the district authorities had the greatest share of tax collection, even in the earlier survey, the national authority had a more significant participation in the past, accounting for an average of almost 25 per cent of all taxes; by contrast, town authorities did not participate very actively and averaged less than 2 per cent.

The former pattern was the general rule for all locations in the 1991 survey except in the case of Long An, where almost 80 per cent of taxes were paid to the national authority and only 20 per cent to the district authority. This general tendency persisted for all forms of

Table 5.6: Tax authorities collecting payment by location. Percentage of total taxes paid in the 1997 survey.

Location	Town authority	District authority	National authority	Other authority
Hanoi				
Mean	26.9	67.4	2.4	0.0
Median	0.0	100.0	0.0	0.0
Haiphong				
Mean	22.4	72.7	2.0	0.0
Median	0.0	100.0	0.0	0.0
HCM City				
Mean	1.5	94.3	2.4	0.1
Median	0.0	100.0	0.0	0.0
Ha Tay				
Mean	18.1	46.4	0.8	1.9
Median	0.0	30.5	0.0	0.0
Long An				
Mean	6.0	92.8	1.2	0.0
Median	0.0	100.0	0.0	0.0
All enterprises				
Mean	15.2	75.5	1.8	0.3
Median	0.0	100.0	0.0	0.0

ownership, but it is interesting to note that national authorities collected almost 40 per cent of all taxes paid by household and private enterprises while the other forms of ownership paid over 90 per cent to district authorities.

It can be inferred from these figures that the increasing participation of town authorities in total collection during the 1997 survey was due to a delegation of these functions by national authorities, particularly in the case of household enterprises whose payments are made directly to the commune.

Taxes and Informal Costs of Operation

Informal costs of operation are payments made to government officials, which according to owners and managers are necessary in order to operate the company. These payments cannot be counted as formal taxes and there is no official record. Therefore, the information given by enterprises may not be entirely accurate. In the 1997 survey, the average informal payments amounted to 2.4 per cent of income, which is quite high when compared to tax payments, which averaged 3.9 per cent. However, the median was only 0.2 per cent which means that general payments were much lower. Over 30 per cent of all enterprises did not pay informal fees and of those who did, the great majority declared payments below 3.9 per cent of their total income. Only a few cases, 12.2 per cent of all the enterprises in the survey, paid higher informal fees than taxes.

One might expect informal fees to serve as a substitute for tax payments in some instances. However, there is no negative correlation between these two expenditures and there is no consistent pattern of payments with regard to location or form of ownership. For instance, partnership enterprises had relatively low rates of tax payment as a percentage of total income or value added. By contrast, this form of ownership had the highest rates of informal costs of operation. But in the case of private enterprises, rates of tax payment as well as informal fees were high, reaching 3.1 and 4.9 per cent respectively (Table 5.7).

The same picture can be drawn when looking at locations. Ha Tay had the lowest rates for tax payment and very high informal fees, 50 per cent above tax payment levels. By contrast, Ho Chi Minh City had the heaviest tax burden but also the highest informal costs of operation

Table 5.7: Taxes and informal cost of operation by form of ownership in the 1997 survey.

Ownership form	Taxes as % of income	Taxes as % of value added	Informal costs as % of income	Informal costs as % of value added
Household				
Mean	2.8	7.3	0.6	1.3
Median	1.7	4.2	0.1	0.2
Private				
Mean	4.9	13.7	3.2	7.5
Median	3.9	11.0	0.3	0.3
Partnership				
Mean	3.8	11.1	4.7	8.9
Median	3.5	8.8	0.1	0.4
Co-operative				
Mean	4.2	12.8	3.1	8.5
Median	3.9	11.5	0.2	0.7
Shareholding &LLC				
Mean	4.9	13.8	3.7	15.6
Median	4.8	12.9	0.8	2.3
All enterprises				
Mean	3.9	10.9	2.4	6.7
Median	3.2	8.8	0.2	0.5

(Table 5.8). The lack of patterns and correlation between tax payment and informal fees indicates that these practices are completely arbitrary and do not generally serve as a substitute for tax payment.

The majority of the enterprises that paid higher informal fees than taxes were located in urban areas, particularly in Ho Chi Minh City. Haiphong accounted for 20 per cent and Hanoi for 16 per cent of these enterprises and the rural locations for only 6 per cent each. According to form of ownership, private and limited companies had the highest percentages of approximately 31 per cent each (Figure 5.1 and 5.2). It should be noticed that the sample of enterprises considered in this analysis was rather limited, the results may not be representative.In the 1991 survey, informal fees appear to have been less frequent and smaller. Only 20 per cent of the enterprises paid informal fees, 4 per cent paid higher informal fees than taxes and almost 80 per cent of all

Figure 5.1: Enterprises paying informal fees (by location), 1996.

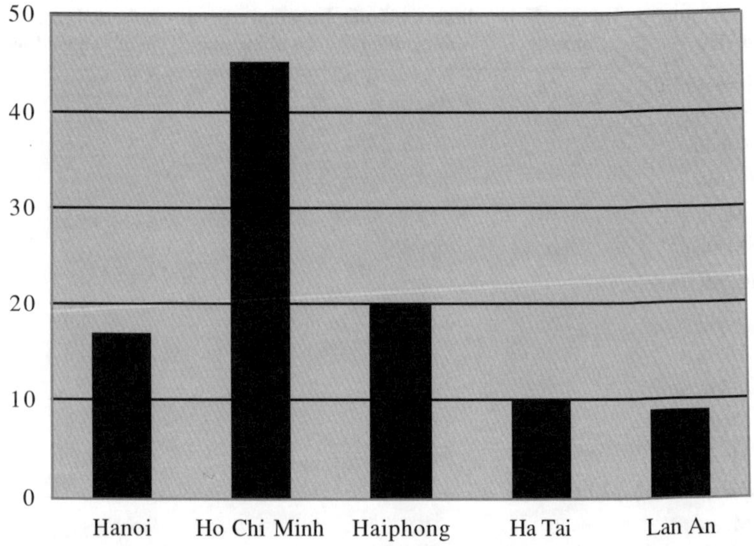

Figure 5.2: Enterprises paying informal fees (by form of ownership), 1996.

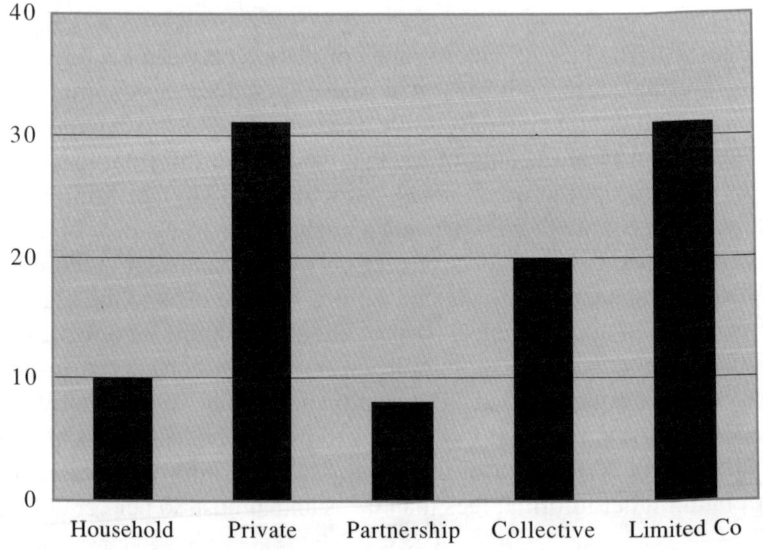

Table 5.8: Taxes and informal costs of operation in the 1997 survey, by location.

Location	Taxes as % of income	Taxes as % of value added	Informal costs as % of income	Informal costs as % of value added
Hanoi				
Mean	3.6	10.6	1.3	4.0
Median	3.3	9.8	0.2	0.6
Haiphong				
Mean	4.0	10.5	2.5	5.9
Median	2.8	8.1	0.1	0.5
HCM City				
Mean	6.3	18.2	4.1	13.9
Median	5.5	16.1	0.8	2.0
Ha Tay				
Mean	1.3	3.0	3.0	6.6
Median	0.3	0.5	0.0	0.0
Long An				
Mean	3.4	9.1	1.1	2.4
Median	2.7	8.8	0.2	0.5
All enterprises				
Mean	3.9	10.9	2.4	6.7
Median	3.2	8.8	0.2	0.5

payments were made in the urban areas. Although the figures shown in the analysis for the 1997 survey are still rather low, special attention should be paid in this respect, because these practices have become a lot more common as the economy has grown and eventually informal fees could be a major constraint to development.

Notes

1. The comparison of tax payments between the 1991 and 1997 surveys was based on the published results of the 1991 survey in Per Ronnås (1992), *Employment Generation through Private Entrepreneurship in Vietnam* (New Delhi: ILO-ARTEP/SIDA, p. 111, Table 4.30).

2. National Assembly of the Socialist Republic of Vietnam (1997), *Luat Thue Gia Tri Tang – Luat Thue Thu Nhap Doanh Nghiep* [Law on Value Added Tax – Law on Business Income Tax] (Hanoi: The National Political Publishing House).

3. The results of the 1991 survey used in the comparison of classification of taxes between the 1991 and 1997 surveys, as well as for the rest of the analysis, were based on the data collected from the enterprises surveyed in 1991 that operated in the locations of the 1997 survey.

4. Property tax was not considered in the 1991 survey.

6

Employment, Labour and Wages

Per Ronnås

The average labour force in the urban enterprises during the month prior to the 1997 survey ranged from 14.2 persons in Haiphong to 27.0 in Ho Chi Minh City, with Hanoi in an intermediate position with 20.0 workers[1] on average (Table 6.1). In Hanoi and Haiphong half of the enterprises had ten workers or more, but there were relatively fewer enterprises with a large labour force in Haiphong than in Hanoi. In Hanoi a quarter of the enterprises had at least 25 workers and 10 per cent had more than 50 workers. In Haiphong there were only a few enterprises with more than 50 workers in the sample. The enterprises in Ho Chi Minh City were on the whole larger than in the two northern cities; half of them had at least 16 workers and 25 per cent had 33 workers or more.

As might be expected, there were large differences in the size of the labour force between the ownership forms. The urban household enterprises had an average labour force of 5.8 persons, as against 24.9 in the private enterprises, 28.4 in the co-operative enterprises and 34.8 in the shareholding and limited liability companies, but only 12.8 in the partnership enterprises (Table 6.2). However, except for the household enterprises (which by definition are small), there were also large differences in the labour force within the individual ownership forms. Thus, among the private enterprises 25 per cent had less than ten workers, while at the upper end 25 per cent had a workforce of 32 or

Table 6.1: Size and structure of labour force by location of enterprise. Average number of workers.

	Hanoi	Haiphong	HCM City	Ha Tay	Long An
Total labour force	20.3	14.2	27.0	16.0	8.0
female	6.8	4.9	11.7	8.6	1.4
Unpaid	1.6	1.4	1.2	2.8	2.0
female	0.6	0.5	0.5	1.1	0.6
Regular	18.1	13.2	24.0	14.1	7.4
female	5.9	4.8	9.6	6.3	1.3
Casual	1.9	0.7	3.1	1.9	1.1
female	0.8	0.1	2.0	0.6	0.4
Skilled	16.8	10.8	18.3	13.7	5.2
female	5.3	3.8	7.2	5.9	0.7

more and 10 per cent had more than 67 workers. Co-operatives and shareholding and limited liability companies also displayed a wide spread in the size of the labour force. However, there were few large partnership enterprises; less than 10 per cent of the enterprises in this category had 25 workers or more.

By and large, the enterprises in the two rural areas covered by the survey had a smaller labour force than those in the urban areas. The average size of the labour force in enterprises in Ha Tay was 16 and in Long An only 8. This large discrepancy in the average labour force between the two provinces was entirely accounted for by the incidence of a small number of quite large enterprises in Ha Tay. In both provinces half of the enterprises had no more than five workers. However, in contrast to the situation in Long An, a considerable number of quite large enterprises were included in the sample in Ha Tay. In this province, 10 per cent of the enterprises had more than 55 workers and 25 per cent had more than 17 workers. Just as in the urban areas, there was a large difference in the average size of the labour force in the household enterprises on the one hand (3.8 persons) and in the private enterprises (19.2 persons) and other forms of enterprises (32.4 persons) on the other (Table 6.3).

Except for the household enterprises, which by virtue of their small size depend largely on the labour of unpaid household members, wage

Table 6.2: Size and structure of labour force in urban enterprises by ownership form. Average number of workers.

	Household	Private	Partnership	Co-operatives	Shareholding*
Total labour force	5.8	24.9	12.8	28.4	34.8
female	1.9	9.4	4.1	11.6	13.5
Unpaid	2.0	1.7	0.9	0.8	1.1
female	0.8	0.6	0.4	0.2	0.3
Regular	5.5	23.6	11.9	25.1	29.9
female	1.9	9.0	3.9	10.5	10.3
Casual	0.2	1.2	1.1	2.4	5.1
female	0.0	0.4	0.3	0.8	3.2
Skilled	4.7	17.6	10.1	22.8	23.8
female	1.4	6.2	3.1	9.6	8.3

Note: *Shareholding and LLC.

workers who are engaged in the enterprise on a regular and usually full-time basis make up the core of the workforce in both urban and rural areas. Casual workers – defined as those hired on a daily or short-term basis – play a totally insignificant role, except in some urban co-operatives and shareholding and limited liability companies and in the co-operatives in the rural areas (Tables 6.2 and 6.3).

The main distinction between household enterprises on the one hand and private and other forms of non-state enterprises on the other is ostensibly that while the former rely primarily on the labour of the owner household, the latter are based on wage labour. By and large, the survey bears out this distinction. Virtually all private enterprises and all partnership, co-operative and shareholding and limited liability enterprises have at least some wage labour. However, the distinction is not absolute. Almost 80 per cent of the household enterprises in the urban areas and nearly half of those in the rural areas supplemented the labour of household members with wage workers. Still, the number of wage workers was quite small. It averaged 3.7 in the urban enterprises and only 1.1 in the rural enterprises. Thus, unpaid household members on average made up one-third of the labour force of the household enterprises in the urban areas and over 60 per cent in the rural enterprises.

Table 6.3: Size and structure of labour force in rural enterprises by ownership form. Average number of workers.

	Household	Private	Other forms
Total labour force	3.8	19.2	32.4
female	1.0	7.5	10.9
Unpaid	2.3	2.7	2.0
female	0.9	1.1	0.6
Regular	3.5	18.1	26.4
female	0.9	6.9	9.5
Casual	0.7	1.1	6.0
female	0.3	0.6	1.2
Skilled	3.3	13.8	27.0
female	0.8	5.4	9.0

On the other hand, most private enterprises also had one or two, but seldom more than three, unpaid household members in their workforce. Thus, this category of labour was quite important in the many small private enterprises, but their importance declined rapidly with the size of the enterprise. In the co-operative, partnership and shareholding and limited liability enterprises they played an altogether insignificant role.

The share of females in the labour force in the urban enterprises varied, on average, between one-third in Hanoi and Haiphong and 43 per cent in Ho Chi Minh City. They accounted for a slightly larger share of the labour force in the co-operative, limited liability and private enterprises than in the household and partnership enterprises (Table 6.2). Among rural enterprises, there was a marked difference between those in Ha Tay, where more than half the labour force was female, and those in Long An, where women made up a mere 17.5 per cent of the labour force on average. This difference may largely be explained by differences in the branch structure of the enterprises. In Long An, agro-processing and light engineering predominate, while in Ha Tay more than three-quarters of the enterprises were engaged in carpentry and furniture making, arts and handicraft or textile manufacturing. In particular the latter branches have traditionally belonged to the realm of female labour.

Apart from hiring wage workers to work in the enterprise itself, many enterprises also resort to hiring out work to persons working outside the enterprise, typically in their own home. This practice was most common in Ha Tay, where one-quarter of enterprises hired out work in the 1997 survey. In about two-thirds of the cases, work was farmed out on a casual basis, suggesting that it was used as a means of meeting occasional production peaks. Yet 12 per cent of the enterprises in this province farmed out work on a regular basis, suggesting that it was used as a regular mode of production. Elsewhere this practice was much less prevalent, although in Ho Chi Minh City and Haiphong 12 per cent and in Long An 13.5 per cent of the enterprises had farmed out work in the 1997 survey. As in Ha Tay, it was done primarily, but not exclusively, on a casual basis. In Hanoi only 6 per cent of the enterprises had farmed out work in the same survey, in all but one case on a regular basis.

Tables 6.4–6.6 show the size and mobility of the wage labour force in the 1997 survey by location and ownership form of the enterprises. As may be seen from these tables, the vast majority of enterprises in Ho Chi Minh City had more than five, but not more than 50 wage workers, while in Hanoi there was a large share of enterprises with no more than five wage workers. The large difference in the size structure of the labour force in enterprises in Ha Tay and Long An, commented upon above, is shown very clearly in Table 6.4. In Long An, more than half of the enterprises had between one and five wage workers. Only a quarter of them had no wage workers at all, while few had more than ten. In Ha Tay, on the other hand, almost half of the enterprises did not have any wage workers at all, but there was also a high proportion of enterprises with more than ten wage workers.

Table 6.5 underscores the fact that the non-state manufacturing sector is not primarily a source of self-employment, but of wage employment. Most urban private enterprises have between five and 50 wage workers. Somewhat surprisingly, the size of most urban co-operatives and shareholding and limited liability enterprises is not much larger than that of the private firms. Half of the partnership enterprises have between six and ten workers, while almost none has more than 25. The private enterprises in the rural areas are generally

Table 6.4: Number and mobility of wage workforce in urban enterprises by location of enterprise. Percentages and mean.

	Hanoi	Haiphong	HCM City	Ha Tay	Long An
No. of wage workers:					
0	6.7	12.9	0.0	46.3	25.3
1–5	31.1	25.7	10.3	14.6	54.2
6–10	15.1	22.8	22.2	8.5	10.8
11–25	22.7	23.8	38.5	14.6	8.4
26–50	15.1	10.9	14.5	9.8	1.2
51–75	6.7	1.0	9.4	2.4	0.0
Over 75	2.5	3.0	5.1	3.7	0.0
Mean	17.9	13.6	25.9	11.6	4.4
Net change in past year:					
Decrease in wage workers	4.2	8.9	17.9	9.8	2.4
Unchanged no. of wage workers	89.1	81.2	60.7	73.2	97.6
Increase in wage workers	6.7	9.9	21.4	17.1	0.0
Mean change	0.34	-0.08	1.32	0.43	-0.13
Gross change in past year:					
Workers who left	10.1	22.8	47.0	29.3	4.8
Workers fired	0.8	5.0	2.6	4.9	1.2
Workers left at end of contract	2.5	8.9	7.7	6.1	0.0
Workers resigned	7.6	13.9	41.9	28.0	4.8
Hired workers	11.8	22.8	46.2	31.7	2.5

smaller than those in the urban areas. The vast majority have less than 25 wage workers and about 15 per cent employ no wage workers at all.

By and large the turnover rate of the labour force appears to be quite low, suggesting a considerable stability. However, there is a marked difference between the two northern cities of Hanoi and Haiphong on the one hand and Ho Chi Minh City in the south on the other. In Hanoi a little more than 10 per cent of the enterprises lost any wage workers in the 1997 survey, for whatever reason, and almost as few recruited any new workers in the period, while in Ho Chi Minh City almost half of the enterprises lost workers and an equal proportion

Table 6.5: Number and mobility of wage workforce in urban enterprises by ownership form. Percentages and mean.

	House-hold	Private	Partner-ship	Co-operatives	Share-holding*
No. of wage workers:					
0	21.4	0.0	0.0	0.0	0.0
1–5	53.1	15.6	15.0	7.0	3.8
6–10	18.4	15.6	50.0	14.0	14.1
11–25	7.1	40.6	32.5	42.1	33.3
26–50	0.0	17.2	0.0	21.1	29.5
51–75	0.0	7.8	0.0	12.3	10.3
Over 75	0.0	3.1	2.5	3.5	9.0
Mean	3.8	23.0	11.7	27.4	34.2
Net change in past year:					
Decrease in wage workers	4.1	15.6	2.5	14.0	20.4
Unchanged no. of wage workers	90.8	57.8	95.0	71.9	69.2
Increase in wage workers	4.1	21.9	2.5	14.0	16.7
Mean change	-0.07	1.86	0.65	-0.39	0.91
Gross change in past year:					
Workers who left	8.2	48.4	17.5	22.8	39.7
Workers fired	0.0	6.3	0.0	1.8	5.1
Workers left at end of contract	0.0	9.4	0.0	12.3	11.5
Workers resigned	8.2	39.1	17.5	25.8	29.5
Hired workers	7.1	50.0	17.5	24.6	39.8

Note: *Shareholding and LLC

hired new workers. It is unclear if the reason behind the much higher labour mobility in Ho Chi Minh City is due to a more developed and flexible labour market or to other factors. In the rural areas the picture was the reverse. Enterprises in Ha Tay in the north had a much higher turnover rate of the wage labour force than those in Long An. Among the different ownership forms in the urban areas, the private enterprises registered by far the highest labour mobility, followed by the shareholding and limited liability companies and the co-operatives.

Table 6.6: Number and mobility of wage workforce in rural enterprises by ownership form. Percentages.

	Household	Private	Other
No. of wage workers:			
0	53.7	14.6	4.5
1–5	41.1	31.3	13.6
6–10	5.3	18.8	9.1
11–25	0.0	20.8	40.9
26–50	0.0	10.4	18.2
51–75	0.0	2.1	4.5
Over 75	0.0	2.1	9.1
Mean	1.4	13.2	25.0
Net change in past year:			
Decrease in wage workers	1.1	6.3	27.3
Unchanged no. of wage workers	95.8	77.1	59.1
Increase in wage workers	3.1	16.5	13.6
Mean change	0.06	0.50	-0.27
Gross change in past year:			
Workers who left	3.2	25.0	59.1
Workers fired	0.0	2.1	18.2
Workers left at end of contract	1.1	6.3	4.5
Workers resigned	3.2	25.0	54.5
Hired workers	4.2	29.2	45.5

The mobility of the wage labour force in the household enterprises was very low, both in the urban and in the rural areas. In the rural areas there was a pronounced contrast between the very high degree of stability of the wage labour force in the household enterprises and the high proportion of co-operatives and partnership enterprises (lumped together under the category 'other' in Table 6.6) which lost and/or hired new wage workers in the 1997 survey.

Job security would also seem to be quite good. Very few of the enterprises in the 1997 survey fired any workers. The main exceptions were the rural co-operatives and partnership enterprises in Ha Tay, where approximately one out of five enterprises fired workers. Among the private and shareholding and limited liability enterprises there were also a few instances of workers being fired. However, these appear to have been exceptions to the rule. There were also few cases of workers being forced to leave because their contracts had expired. Instead, in the vast majority of cases the initiative to leave the firm seem to have come from the worker and not from the enterprise.

The average urban private enterprise expanded its workforce by 1.9 persons or 8 per cent in 1996. Slightly more than one-fifth of the private enterprises increased their workforces in the 1997 survey, while 15 per cent registered a decrease. Among the shareholding and limited liability companies one-fifth of the enterprises decreased their workforce, but only 17 per cent increased it. Yet, on the whole this category of enterprises registered a net increase in their labour force. The overwhelming majority of household and partnership enterprises did not register any net change at all in their labour force, although a few partnership enterprises substantially increased their labour force. The urban co-operative enterprises on balance saw a small decline in the workforce, but in more than 70 per cent of the enterprises the workforce remained constant.

The pattern in the rural areas was similar to that of the urban areas. The overwhelming majority of household enterprises (95.8 per cent) neither increased nor decreased their labour force. The only expansion took place among the private enterprises, where the number of enterprises increasing their workforce outweighed those which decreased the workforce and as a result, the average workforce increased by 0.5 persons or 4 per cent. Among the 'other' rural enterprises, that is primarily co-operatives and partnerships, rather more enterprises decreased their workforce (27.3 per cent) than increased it (13.6 per cent).

From the viewpoint of location, it may be seen that the enterprises in Ho Chi Minh City and in Ha Tay were the most dynamic in the 1997 survey. In Ho Chi Minh City more than one-fifth of the enterprises expanded their workforce, while 18 per cent decreased it. The average increase in the labour force in this city was 5 per cent. In Ha Tay no less than 17 per cent of the enterprises increased their wage labour force in the 1997 survey, which is a remarkably high figure in view of

Table 6.7: Predominant way of recruiting workers by location of enterprise. Percentages.

	Hanoi	Haiphong	HCM City	Ha Tay	Long An
Advertisement	0.0	1.2	0.9	0.0	0.0
Labour exchanges	7.2	0.0	1.7	0.0	1.5
Recommendations by friends/relatives	30.6	31.8	72.6	68.1	22.1
Recommendations by local authorities	8.1	1.2	4.3	0.0	1.5
Personal contacts	53.2	60.0	19.7	25.5	72.1
Other means	0.9	5.9	0.9	6.4	2.9

Table 6.8: Predominant way of recruiting workers for urban enterprises by ownership form. Percentages.

	Household	Private	Partnership	Co-operatives	Shareholding*
Advertisement	0.0	0.0	0.0	0.0	2.6
Labour exchanges	0.0	3.1	0.0	9.3	3.8
Recommendations by friends/ relatives	39.0	62.5	42.5	24.1	59.0
Recommendations by local authorities	0.0	3.1	0.0	14.8	6.4
Personal contacts	61.0	29.7	52.5	44.4	28.2
Other ways	0.0	1.6	5.0	7.4	0.0

Note: *Shareholding and LLC.

Table 6.9: Predominant way of recruiting workers for rural enterprises by ownership form. Percentages.

	Household	Private	Other forms
Advertisements	0.0	2.2	0.0
Labour exchanges	0.0	0.0	0.0
Recommendations by friends/relatives	33.3	33.3	72.7
Recommendations by local authorities	0.0	0.0	4.5
Personal contacts	64.6	57.8	18.2
Other ways	2.1	6.7	4.5

the predominance of household enterprises. In Long An, by contrast, there were virtually no changes in the labour force.

Recommendations by friends, relatives and other workers, and personal contacts remain by far the most important ways of recruiting new labour (Tables 6.7–6.9). Recruitment through labour exchanges and placement offices occurs almost only in Hanoi and primarily among co-operatives. By and large, local authorities play a minor role as intermediaries on the labour market. Only in Hanoi and, to a much lesser extent in Ho Chi Minh City, do they show up in the data, and again, primarily for the co-operatives. It is noteworthy that local authorities appear to play virtually no role at all in the recruitment of labour in the rural areas.

Despite the lack of more formal and impersonal mechanisms of labour mediation, few enterprises state that they have difficulties in finding and recruiting labour with the requisite skills. In Hanoi and Ho Chi Minh City less than 5 per cent and in Haiphong less than 10 per cent of the enterprises professed to have such difficulties. The only exception to this rule was Ha Tay, where the larger co-operative and partnership enterprises reported difficulties in recruiting labour with appropriate skills. However, the small share of enterprises expressing such a problem may be somewhat deceptive as most enterprises had not recruited any labour in the past year. Indeed, among the urban and rural private enterprises, which are the most dynamic in terms of hiring new labour, 10 per cent stated that they found it difficult to find and hire labour with the necessary skills.

Most of the skills listed as being in short supply were technical or vocational in nature rather than professional. A wide variety of skills were listed, such as carpentry, smithy, embroidery and printing, but in only three cases did an enterprise list a professional skill (viz. chemical technician). Some 59 per cent of the enterprises complaining about a skills shortage stated that the problem was severe, 9 per cent that it was very severe and 32 per cent did not consider the problem to be very acute. In most cases (64 per cent) the shortage was perceived to be due to an absolute shortage of the desired skills rather than to problems of affordability. It seems likely that the very small number of firms complaining about shortages of managerial, technical or other professional skills reflects a perceived lack of need for such skills in the enterprises rather than any abundant supply.

The practice of requiring the worker to make a contribution in cash or kind to the enterprise at the time of recruitment is not very common, except in the co-operatives and, to a lesser degree, in the partnership enterprises. In the urban areas half of the co-operatives stated that they required such contributions from the workers always (22.6 per cent) or sometimes (27.4 per cent). For the urban partnership enterprises the percentages were 5.6 (always required a contribution) and 14.8 (sometimes required it). These contributions are almost always redeemable upon termination of the employment and they usually also entitle the worker to a share in the profit of the enterprise. They can therefore be seen as an investment, albeit not always voluntary, by the worker in the enterprise rather than as an entrance fee for a job.

It would appear that the practice of requesting a contribution from workers upon recruitment has become less common in the 1990s. Among the urban partnership and co-operative enterprises covered by the 1991 survey, about 58 per cent always or sometimes requested such contributions. By the 1997 survey, this percentage had fallen to 20 for the urban partnership enterprises and 50 for the urban co-operatives. In the rural areas it is uncommon for enterprises to request contributions from their workers. None of the household or private enterprises covered by the survey and a mere 18 per cent of the other (i.e. mainly partnership and co-operative enterprises) sometimes or always requested contributions from their workers.

Labour Force Characteristics

A survey of the workers in the enterprises covered confirms the importance of this sector as a source of employment creation. A vast majority of the workers had been recruited outside the owner household, as wage workers and on a regular and full-time basis. By and large, this is true for all areas and ownership forms. In Hanoi and Ho Chi Minh City well over 90 per cent of the workers had been recruited outside the owner household. In Haiphong this percentage was only slightly lower, while in the two rural areas – Ha Tay and Long An – it exceeded 70 per cent (Table 6.10).[2] The proportion of workers recruited outside the household is obviously related to the

Table 6.10: Main employment characteristics by location of enterprise. Percentages and mean/median.

	Hanoi	Haiphong	HCM City	Ha Tay	Long An
Work status:					
Head of household	0.8	0.0	0.3	0.1	0.3
Other household member	7.4	14.1	5.2	29.8	25.8
Worker recruited elsewhere	91.9	85.9	94.5	70.1	73.8
Engagement in enterprise:					
Full-time	92.6	83.3	93.1	80.4	72.7
Part-time	6.4	13.5	6.0	12.8	14.7
Seasonal	0.4	0.6	0.9	1.3	10.6
Casual	0.6	2.5	0.1	5.5	2.0
Payment status:					
Cash only	91.1	89.0	92.2	62.4	60.3
Cash and kind	1.0	1.8	4.2	10.0	13.7
Unpaid	7.9	9.2	3.7	27.6	26.0
Wage basis:					
Time rate	36.8	39.2	59.7	27.2	28.7
Piece rate	61.7	48.4	28.6	61.4	57.3
Combined	1.5	11.8	11.0	11.4	13.3
Other	0.0	0.6	0.7	0.0	0.6
Days worked last month:					
Mean	24.7	24.3	24.5	24.4	23.5
Median	25	26	26	25	25

Note: Based on the total labour force, excluding owner/manager, engaged in the enterprise at the time of the survey. In cases where the total workforce exceeded ten, a random sample of ten was made.

size of the enterprise. The larger the size of the labour force, the higher the proportion of workers recruited from outside. However, even among the urban household enterprises, three out of four workers are recruited outside the owner household (Table 6.11).

In the rural areas the reliance on household labour is typically higher than in the urban areas. Still, less than half of the labour force in

Table 6.11: Main employment characteristics in urban enterprises by ownership form. Percentages and mean/median.

	Household	Private	Partnership	Co-operative	Shareholding*
Work status:					
Head of household	0.0	0.0	2.7	0.2	0.1
Other household member	24.7	8.3	4.5	3.3	1.5
Worker recruited elsewhere	75.3	91.7	92.8	96.5	98.3
Engagement in enterprise:					
Full-time	85.4	89.9	91.0	81.3	94.5
Part-time	12.4	9.2	8.7	15.7	3.9
Seasonal	0.9	0.5	0.0	0.7	1.5
Casual	1.3	0.4	0.3	2.2	0.1
Payment status:					
Cash only	76.2	93.3	94.3	97.2	95.3
Cash and kind	2.0	3.2	0.0	0.4	4.4
Unpaid	21.9	3.4	5.7	2.4	0.3
Wage basis:					
Time rate	64.4	45.0	47.0	46.7	49.2
Piece rate	31.1	39.4	46.4	51.2	47.8
Combined	4.5	13.6	5.3	1.9	3.0
Other	0.0	2.0	1.3	0.2	0.0
Days worked last month:					
Mean	25.0	24.4	23.4	23.8	24.9
Median	26	26	24	25	26

Note: Based on the total labour force, excluding owner/manager, engaged in the enterprise at the time of the survey. In cases where the total workforce exceeded ten, a random sample of ten was made. *Shareholding and LLC.

the rural household enterprises consists of household members and in the rural private enterprises the share of this category falls to less than one in five (Table 6.12). As a rule, workers recruited from outside the household work for wages, while household members do not. However, there are instances where household members, too, receive wages for their work.

Table 6.12: Main employment characteristics in rural enterprises by ownership form. Percentages and mean/median.

	Household	Private	Other forms
Work status:			
Head of household	0.0	0.0	0.5
Other household member	47.5	18.9	8.7
Worker recruited elsewhere	52.5	81.1	90.8
Engagement in enterprise:			
Full-time	72.8	81.1	86.4
Part-time	21.1	9.6	1.9
Seasonal	1.9	9.1	6.8
Casual	4.2	0.3	4.9
Payment status:			
Cash only	44.4	71.5	69.4
Cash and kind	7.3	13.1	22.8
Unpaid	48.3	15.5	7.8
Wage basis:			
Time rate	25.7	21.8	47.9
Piece rate	44.1	70.5	40.6
Combined	30.2	7.7	11.6
Other	0.0	0.0	0.0
Days worked last month:			
Mean	22.5	25.1	25.7
Median	24	26	26

Note: Based on the total labour force, excluding owner/manager, engaged in the enterprise at the time of the survey. In cases where the total workforce exceeded ten, a random sample of ten was made.

Similarly, full-time work is the rule in all types of enterprises and in all locations. In Hanoi and Ho Chi Minh City over 90 per cent of the workers are employed full-time. In Haiphong this share is slightly lower at 83 per cent, dropping further in Ha Tay (80 per cent) and Long An (73 per cent). In the urban areas the proportion of full-time workers is universally very high in all types of enterprises. Only in the co-operative enterprises does it fall to 81 per cent. In the rural areas, too, full-time work is the rule, but there are also some part-time workers, particularly in the household enterprises (21 per cent), but also in the private enterprises (10 per cent). Seasonal employment is insignificant everywhere except in Long An where it accounts for 11 per cent of the total employment. Casual labour is very rare. Only in Ha Tay does it account for slightly more than 5 per cent of the workforce.

Compared to the situation in the 1991 survey, it would appear that full-time, remunerated and non-household labour has become more important in all types of enterprises, both urban and rural. Part-time employment has declined sharply, from 17.5 to 6.4 per cent in Hanoi, from 19.3 to 6.0 per cent in Ho Chi Minh City and from 24.1 to 12.8 per cent in Ha Tay. However, in Haiphong part-time employment appears to have increased slightly from 9.1 to 13.5 per cent.[3] In the urban areas, the decline in part-time work took place in all ownership forms.

Similarly, the recruitment of labour from outside the owner/manager household increased significantly between 1991 and 1997. The share of 'other household members' in the workforce of the urban enterprises fell sharply in Hanoi and Ho Chi Minh City from 17.1 to 7.4 per cent and from 18.7 to 5.2 per cent respectively. The decline was most striking in the urban household enterprises, where it fell from 64.0 to 24.7 per cent. However, it fell in the private and partnership enterprises, too. Comparisons for the rural enterprises are more difficult to make because of methodological differences in the samples, but it would appear that the same tendency to rely increasingly on workers from outside the household is true of rural areas also. Thus, in Ha Tay the share of 'other household members' in the enterprise workforce fell from 49.7 to 29.8 per cent.

This development may be interpreted as a welcome sign that the private manufacturing sector is maturing and becoming increasingly important not only as a source of self-employment, but also of wage employment. However, it should also be noted that with the increasing reliance on workers recruited from outside the household and on wage labour, the cost structure of the enterprises may change and this may increase the financial vulnerability of the enterprise.When faced with economic difficulties, unpaid household members working in the enterprise will typically put in longer hours to ensure that the enter-

Table 6.13: Social characteristics of labour force by location of enterprise. Percentages and mean.

	Hanoi	Haiphong	HCM City	Ha Tay	Long An
Sex:					
Male	64.9	64.6	68.8	55.7	83.0
Female	35.1	35.4	31.2	44.3	18.0
Age (years):					
19 and under	3.9	4.3	4.8	16.5	8.3
20–29	49.0	53.0	37.1	41.7	43.5
30–39	28.3	30.6	29.6	21.6	31.8
40–49	12.9	9.5	17.8	13.2	12.6
50 and over	5.9	2.7	10.6	7.0	3.8
Mean age	31.0	29.9	34.0	29.7	30.2
Education (years):					
6 or less	6.3	21.9	9.6	15.7	38.6
7–9	31.7	34.8	35.7	59.9	39.4
10 or over	62.0	43.2	54.7	24.4	22.0
Mean	9.7	9.1	9.5	8.3	7.5
Prior work experience:					
Production worker	65.6	52.7	32.8	48.9	24.5
Other non-farm	11.8	22.4	10.5	5.2	7.0
Agriculture	4.1	6.4	0.6	20.9	28.3

Note: Based on the total labour force, excluding owner/manager, engaged in the enterprise at the time of the survey. In cases where the total workforce exceeded ten, a random sample of ten was made.

prise stays afloat. As the proportion of household members in the workforce goes down, much of the traditional resilience and flexibility of the small enterprises may be lost.

The average worker is male, around 30 years old and has nine years of education. In the urban areas there is little difference in the social characteristics between the three cities and in the different ownership types. Women account for slightly more than a third of the labour force in the urban enterprises (Table 6.14). The share of females in the

Table 6.14: Social characteristics of the labour force in urban enterprises by ownership form. Percentages and mean.

	Household	Private	Partnership	Co-operative	Shareholding*
Sex:					
Male	64.9	68.1	68.9	61.7	67.2
Female	35.1	31.9	31.1	38.3	32.8
Age (years):					
19 and under	11.0	2.2	4.8	1.3	2.5
20–29	52.3	53.6	46.4	27.7	52.7
30–39	22.7	28.3	29.0	35.5	30.2
40–49	9.7	12.3	12.6	23.1	9.9
50 and over	4.1	3.6	7.2	12.3	4.7
Mean age	28.9	30.5	31.6	36.5	30.6
Education (years):					
6 or less	18.8	16.4	14.1	10.2	8.0
7–9	40.0	36.3	30.5	34.8	26.6
10 or over	41.3	47.3	55.4	55.1	65.4
Mean	8.7	9.4	9.2	9.3	10.4
Prior work experience:					
Production worker	37.3	48.4	50.0	55.5	55.6
Other non-farm	10.1	17.1	14.7	14.6	22.5
Agriculture	6.0	6.7	3.0	1.1	5.2

Note: Based on the total labour force, excluding owner/manager, engaged in the enterprise at the time of the survey. In cases where the total workforce exceeded ten, a random sample of ten was made. *Shareholding and LLC.

labour force is somewhat higher in the co-operative and household enterprises than in the private and partnership enterprises. The higher share of females in household enterprises may also partly explain the fact that a rather higher percentage of the female than of the male labour work as unpaid household members: 17.5 as against 10.1 per cent. In the rural areas there is a distinct difference in the gender structure of the labour force between Ha Tay, where 44 per cent of the labour force is female, and Long An, where only 18 per cent is female

(Table 6.13). This difference appears to be largely due to variation in the branch structure. In Ha Tay there is much handicraft and garment manufacturing, which are traditional domains for women, while in Long An male preserves such as agro-processing and light engineering predominate.

Generally speaking, females are under-represented in the labour force of the surveyed enterprises, when compared to the industrial labour force as a whole. According to the 1996 official labour force survey, women made up about 44 per cent of the industrial labour force in Hanoi, Ho Chi Minh City and Haiphong.[4] Only in Ha Tay did the proportion of females in the sample exceed the official labour force survey estimate. Compared to the 1991 survey, it would appear that the gender structure of the labour force has changed little, if at all.

The vast majority of the workers are in the age bracket 20–39 years. Compared to the 1991 survey, the workforce has become younger in Hanoi and Haiphong, but not in Ho Chi Minh City. However, the difference is too small to be statistically significant. A close comparison reveals an increase of the labour force aged 20–39 and a decrease of those below the age of 20 and above the age 40 in Hanoi and Haiphong. However, in Ho Chi Minh City no such trend is discernible. The decline in the proportion of workers under the age of 20 may be related to the general relative decline in the proportion of household members in the workforce, as it appears to be rather uncommon to hire wage workers under the age of 20. Among the different ownership forms in the rural areas, the household enterprises tend to have the youngest workforce. In this category, 63 per cent of the workforce is below the age of 30, of which 11 per cent is below 20. However, the private and limited liability firms, too, have an overwhelmingly young labour force. In these firms more than half of the workers are in their twenties. By contrast, a vast majority of the workers in the co-operatives are in their thirties or forties. The rather younger labour force in the private enterprises is probably linked to the fact that these enterprises tend to be more dynamic and expansive and, as a consequence, a larger share of the workforce is recently hired.

In the rural areas, too, the labour force is predominantly young. In Ha Tay some 16.5 per cent of the workers are still in their teens and an additional 41.7 per cent are in their twenties. In Long An the workers

Table 6.15: Social characteristics of the labour force in rural enterprises by ownership form. Percentages and mean.

	Household	Private	Other forms
Sex:			
Male	70.9	67.7	68.9
Female	29.1	32.3	31.1
Age (years):			
19 and under	15.3	11.7	6.3
20–29	41.8	44.8	43.7
30–39	25.7	25.6	27.7
40–49	9.6	13.9	16.5
50 and over	7.6	4.0	5.8
Mean age	29.9	29.5	31.6
Education (years):			
6 or less	33.7	32.3	11.7
7–9	52.5	45.1	43.2
10 or over	13.8	22.7	45.1
Mean	7.2	7.8	9.2
Prior work experience:			
Production worker	28.4	41.3	38.3
Other non-farm	2.7	6.4	12.6
Agriculture	31.0	25.9	27.7

Notes: Based on the total labour force, excluding owner/manager, engaged in the enterprise at the time of the survey. In cases where the total workforce exceeded ten, a random sample of ten was made.

tend to be somewhat older, yet in both provinces less than 20 per cent of the workers are over 40.

The educational level of the labour force is quite high. In the urban areas it ranges from nine to ten years of formal education on average. In Hanoi and Ho Chi Minh City well over half of the workforce has at least ten years of formal education and less than 10 per cent have not completed six years of primary education. In Haiphong the educational level is considerably lower, which seems to be linked to the higher proportion of older workers in this city. The workforce in the smaller household enterprises tends to have a somewhat lower level of education than in the larger shareholding and limited liability firms (Table 6.15). In the latter, almost two-thirds of the workforce have ten years of education or more and a mere 8 per cent have no more than six years of school. From the point of view of formal education, the urban household enterprises obviously have a disadvantage *vis-à-vis* the other ownership forms.

The educational level of the workforce is markedly lower in the rural areas than in the urban. In particular, workers with higher education (viz. ten years or more) make up a much smaller share of the workforce in the rural than in the urban firms. In Ha Tay the bulk of the labour force has seven to nine years of formal education, while in Long An almost 40 per cent have not even completed seven years of school. In the rural areas there is a marked difference between the relatively lower educational level in the household and private enterprises and the much higher level of education in the other firms, that is, in co-operatives and partnerships.

Compared to the situation in the 1991 survey, it may be seen that the educational level has increased in general, no doubt reflecting an improvement in the educational level in society as a whole. In other words, younger and better-educated workers have replaced older workers with less education. It is interesting to note that differences in educational level of the labour force in the northern and southern parts of the country (due to historical differences in the respective educational systems), which were quite pronounced in the 1991 survey, appear to have more or less disappeared in the urban areas in the 1997 survey. In Ho Chi Minh City the average level of education increased from 8.5 years in the 1991 survey to 9.5 years in the 1997 survey and the share of the workforce with less than seven years of education fell in this city from 29.3 to 9.6 per cent. This is a remarkable change, which, among other things, implies that enterprises in the north have lost their educational edge over those in the south. In the rural areas the difference in education between the south and the north is still in evidence. Indeed, while the mean educational level of the workforce in Ha Tay increased from 7.5 to 8.3 years between the 1991 and the 1997 surveys, it actually declined in Long An from 8.8 to 7.5 years.[5]

From the point of view of employment creation, it is important to note that the private manufacturing sector offers job openings not only for those with secondary education, but also for those who have finished primary school but have no secondary education. As educational requirements for state employment tend to be quite high, the latter is a group which has traditionally had poor access to wage employment; hence, the employment opportunities offered by the private sector are particularly welcome. Seen from an international perspective, the educational level of the workforce, not least in the rural areas, is remarkably high. This should give rural industries in Vietnam a potential long-term advantage over similar enterprises in other developing Asian countries.

A high proportion of the workers, particularly in the north, have prior experience as production workers or of other forms of non-farm work. In the two northern cities three out of five workers and in Ha Tay one out of two workers have such prior experience, while in Ho Chi Minh City and in the southern province of Long An less than half of the workers have prior work experience outside agriculture. The very high figures in the north are somewhat surprising, considering the relatively young age of most workers and the low rate of labour turnover in the surveyed enterprises. The most likely explanation would seem to be that many workers have previously been employed in state enterprises. If this indeed is the case, then it would have important implications for employment policies, not least in a situation where state enterprises are forced to shed labour as a consequence of structural reform and hardening budget constraints. As will be discussed later, many, if not most, enterprise managers and owners are recruited from the ranks of former state employees. As might be expected, the highest shares of workers with prior experience of non-farm work are found in the larger firms. However, even among the urban household enterprises the share is remarkably high.

Even in the rural enterprises, prior experience as a production worker tends to be more common than a background exclusively in agriculture. In Ha Tay only one-fifth of the workers have an employment history in agriculture, while in Long An this figure is somewhat higher. Rural household enterprises have a higher share of workers with an agricultural background than other types of rural enterprises, but even within this category less than one-third of the workers are recruited from agriculture.

Several conclusions may be drawn from this finding. On the positive side, it suggests that rural non-farm enterprises do not serve as a safety-valve for an over-populated agriculture. In other words, labour is not pushed into non-farm activity by an inability to make ends meet in agriculture. The high proportion of workers with experience as production workers also implies that rural firms are not very disadvantaged *vis-à-vis* urban firms with regard to worker skills. On the negative side it should be noted that the evidently poor employment linkages between agriculture and rural industries imply a lack of dynamism and occupational flexibility in the rural labour market, which would be an important complement to a dynamic agricultural development.

Employment Practices and Wages

An examination of the wage structure by location and ownership form of the enterprise and gender and education of the worker yields more or less an expected pattern. Wages tend to be higher in the south than in the north and higher in urban than in rural areas. Moreover private enterprises and shareholding and limited liability firms usually pay better wages than household enterprises and co-operatives. Similarly, men receive higher wages than women and those with higher education earn more than those with less education. The average wage per working day in Hanoi was 20,300 dong, 5,900 dong less than in Ho Chi Minh City, but 3,100 dong more than in Haiphong (Table 6.16). Assuming 25 working days per month, this would amount to 507,500 dong or US$ 44 per month in Hanoi, US$ 56 in Ho Chi Minh City and US$ 37 in Haiphong.[6]

Among the urban enterprises the average wage ranged from 445,000 to 474,000 dong (US$ 38–41) per month in Haiphong and Hanoi to 640,000 dong (US$55) per month in Ho Chi Minh City. Both the wage floor and the wage ceiling are higher in Ho Chi Minh City than in the two northern cities. In Ho Chi Minh City 90 per cent of the workers earn more than 15,400 dong per day as against 75 per cent in Hanoi and no more than 50 per cent in Haiphong. Similarly, only slightly more than 10 per cent of the workers in Haiphong and about

Table 6.16: Wage structure in urban enterprises, 1,000 dong/day. Percentiles and mean.

	Percentiles					Mean
	10	25	50	75	90	
Location:						
Hanoi	12.1	15.4	19.2	23.1	30.0	*20.3*
Haiphong	9.6	11.5	15.0	20.0	26.9	*17.2*
Ho Chi Minh City	15.4	18.7	25.0	31.8	39.3	*26.2*
Ownership form:						
Household	11.5	15.0	18.8	25.0	32.4	*20.3*
Private	12.2	16.7	22.2	30.8	38.3	*24.1*
Partnership	11.5	15.4	20.0	26.4	30.4	*21.0*
Co-operative	9.6	12.5	16.7	23.3	30.7	*18.9*
Shareholding & LLC	12.9	16.0	20.8	28.1	39.3	*23.8*
Sex:						
Male	11.5	15.4	20.8	27.3	37.0	*22.8*
Female	11.5	13.8	18.5	24.9	32.0	*20.3*
Education:						
up to 6 years	10.0	13.8	20.0	26.4	31.7	*20.7*
10 years or more	12.5	15.4	20.0	26.9	37.0	*22.9*

20 per cent of those in Hanoi earn more than 25,000 dong per day, as against half of the workers in Ho Chi Minh City.

By comparison, the wage differences between the various ownership forms of the urban enterprises are rather small (Table 6.16). In the private and shareholding and limited liability companies the average wage is around 24,000 dong per day and the median wage 20,000–21,000 dong. This can be compared with an average wage of 18,900 and a median wage of 16,700 dong in the co-operatives. Wages in household and partnership enterprises are only slightly below those of the private firms. Except for the co-operatives, the wage floor, if defined as the level above which 90 per cent of the workers are found, is about US$1 per day, or 11,600 dong.

Wages in the urban areas are on average 12 per cent higher for men than for women. This wage difference is approximately the same for all percentiles, except the lowest 10 per cent. Thus, the starting wage for the 25 per cent best paid is about 15 per cent higher for men than for women, while the gap for the 25 per cent with the lowest wage is 11 per cent. Haiphong displays the largest gender difference in wages. In this city the average male wage is 20 per cent higher than the average female wage, while this discrepancy is only 15 per cent in Hanoi and 12 per cent in Ho Chi Minh City. In the urban private enterprises and co-operatives the wage difference between men and women appears to be negligible, a mere 5 and 3 per cent respectively. In the urban household and partnership enterprises it is in the range of 14–16 per cent, while in the shareholding and limited liability companies it is as much as 20 per cent.

The impact of education on the wage level in the urban areas is similarly small. Those with ten years of education earn on average only 2,700 dong (11 per cent) more than those with no more than six years of formal education. It is only among the top earners that education seems to pay off in terms of higher remunerations. However, in reality the educational impact on wages is likely to be larger than the figures in Table 6.16 indicate, as the educational level in the south, where wages are generally higher, is lower than in the north.

The wage patterns in the rural areas resemble those in the urban areas. Wages in Ha Tay are notably lower than in Long An: 15,400 versus 22,400 dong per day (Table 6.17). However, the wage differences between the different ownership forms in the rural areas are quite negligible. Household enterprises appear to pay approximately the same wages as the private enterprises, while both of these ownership forms pay better wages than those in the 'other' category, that is, primarily partnerships and co-operatives. Gender difference in wages tend to be larger in the rural than in the urban areas. Thus, in Ha Tay the average male wage is 38 per cent higher than the average female wage.[7] The largest wage difference is found in the private enterprises, 44 per cent, while in the rural partnerships and co-operatives it is 28 per cent.[8]

Lastly, it should be noted that there are no significant differences in wage levels between the enterprises established since 1991 and those

Table 6.17: Wage structure in rural enterprises, 1,000 dong/day. Percentiles and mean.

	Percentiles					Mean
	10	25	50	75	90	
Location:						
Hanoi	9.0	10.0	13.5	19.2	25.0	*15.4*
Haiphong	14.9	17.9	20.0	25.0	30.0	*22.4*
Ho Chi Minh City						
Ownership form:	10.0	14.0	18.2	21.7	26.8	*18.2*
Household	10.0	13.5	19.2	23.0	27.6	*19.7*
Private	10.0	11.7	16.4	20.6	29.1	*17.9*
Partnership						
Co-operative	11.5	15.0	20.0	23.3	27.7	*20.1*
Shareholding & LLC	8.0	10.0	13.0	17.9	24.0	*14.9*
Sex:						
Male	9.5	12.9	19.2	20.4	26.7	*17.8*
Female	11.4	14.6	19.2	2.3	34.5	*20.6*

established earlier, either for the 1997 survey sample as a whole or in the individual locations. Thus, to the extent that the more recently established firms are larger and more modern, this is not reflected in higher wages. The only exception to this rule is Haiphong, where the newer enterprises pay somewhat higher wages than the older ones.

While the wage pattern described above is very much in line with already known wage differentials and reveal no surprises, the same cannot be said about the changes which seem to have occurred between the 1991 and 1997 surveys. A comparison between the wage data from the 1991 and 1997 surveys results in two main and important conclusions.

First, there has been a substantial increase in real wages, by and large. This is encouraging as it shows that a general increase in economic development and in the well-being of the private manufacturing sector has been translated into improved incomes for the workers in these enterprises. It also refutes any notion of an unlimited supply of labour, which would make the supply price of labour very inelastic and ensure a steady supply of labour even at very low wage levels.

Second, there appears to have been a remarkable equalisation of wages between the two surveys. This is perhaps the most important finding of all. In the 1991 survey there were extremely large wage differences between the north and the south, between rural and urban areas as well as between men and women. By the 1997 survey these differences had diminished greatly, with the notable exception of the rural–urban differences (Tables 6.18 and 6.19).

While in the 1991 survey average wages in the two northern cities were about half of those in Ho Chi Minh City, by the 1997 survey the wage gap had been reduced to 30–50 per cent. Similarly, while the average wage in Long An was almost three times as high as in Ha Tay in the earlier survey,[9] this gap had been reduced to 50 per cent in the 1997 survey. Wage differences across ownership forms were also considerably lower in the 1997 survey than in the 1991 survey. By the second survey, wages in urban household enterprises had more or less caught up with those paid in other types of urban enterprises. However, the most significant relative change in wages took place in the co-operatives. While real wages in household, private and partnership enterprises increased by about 30 per cent between the 1991 and 1997 surveys, they remained constant in the co-operatives. As a consequence, co-operatives lost their position as a wage leader and actually ended up at the bottom of the scale (Table 6.18).

In rural areas too, there was a pronounced equalisation of wages between household and private enterprises, as real wages in rural household enterprises increased by more than twice as much as in the private enterprises (see Table 6.19). The vast gap in wages between men and women in the 1991 survey was also dramatically reduced, as female wages in rural areas almost doubled in real terms over the period while male wages increased by a mere 10 per cent.

However, the rural–urban wage gap seems to have persisted over the period. In the 1991 survey, wages in Hanoi were on average 30 per cent higher than in the neighbouring rural province of Ha Son Binh. By the 1997 survey, the gap had actually widened somewhat, to 32 per cent. However, this marginal relative change should be seen against the backdrop of very sharp increases in real wages in both areas. In Long

Table 6.18: Wage structures in urban enterprises in 1991 and 1997 surveys. Thousand dong at 1997 prices.

	1991 survey		1997 survey		% change 1991–97
	Mean	V	Mean	V	
Location:					
Hanoi	10.8	58.5	20.3	40.8	*88.0*
Haiphong	13.0	85.3	17.2	37.6	*10.6*
Ho Chi Minh City	23.6	161.5	26.2	54.3	*32.2*
Ownership form:					
Household	15.6	42.2	20.3	40.6	*30.1*
Private	18.2	71.9	24.1	41.5	*32.6*
Partnership	16.3	64.3	21.0	34.7	*28.7*
Co-operative	19.0	246.9	18.9	48.4	*-0.8*
Sex:					
Male	13.8	81.0	20.3	44.3	*46.7*
Female	19.6	70.6	22.8	45.1	*16.3*
Education:					
up to 6 years	20.5	114.1	20.7	43.8	*0.7*
over 10 years	16.5	53.2	22.9	45.4	*38.8*

Key: V: Coefficient of variation. **Note:** Figures from the 1991 survey were inflated by a factor of 2.108 to bring them up to 1997 prices.

An the average wage was actually somewhat higher than in Ho Chi Minh City, while by the 1997 survey it had decreased in real terms and was some 15 per cent lower than in Ho Chi Minh City.

Wage differences have decreased not only across locations, ownership forms and gender, but also within each sub-category. As shown in Tables 6.18 and 6.19, the coefficient of variation decreased, often dramatically, between the two surveys for all sub-categories of enterprises and labour. Thus, there is persuasive evidence of a general equalisation of wages within the non-state manufacturing sector. The survey data do not permit any detailed analysis of the causes behind this remarkable development. However, it may tentatively be concluded that the main factors are likely to be a generally more dynamic eco-

Table 6.19: Wage structures in rural enterprises in 1991 and 1997 surveys. Thousand dong at 1997 prices.

	1991 survey		1997 survey		% change 1991-97
	Mean	V	Mean	V	
Location:					
Ha Tay	8.3	56.6	15.4	43.0	*85.5*
Long An	23.5	126.5	22.4	65.5	*-4.7*
Ownership form:					
Household	16.3	48.6	18.2	34.9	*11.7*
Private	18.6	46.3	19.7	76.9	*5.9*
Sex:					
Male	18.2	37.3	20.1	61.7	*10.4*
Female	7.6	60.0	14.9	58.1	*96.1*
Education:					
up to 6 years	11.6	60.2	17.8	37.8	*80.5*
10 years or more	17.5	70.8	20.6	70.8	*17.7*

Key: V:Coefficient of variation. **Note:** Figures from the 1991 survey were inflated by 2.108 to bring them up to 1997 prices. The 1991 survey figures on incomes by sex and education refer to the provinces of Ha Son Binh and Long An only.

nomic development in the north (particularly in and around Hanoi) than in the south and a much better functioning of the labour market. At the same time, it also seems reasonable to conclude that a rather unimpressive development of real incomes in agriculture is a main reason why the rural–urban wage gap remains unchanged.

In absolute terms there were also some remarkable developments in wages. The most important of these was probably the very large increase in real wages (86–88 per cent) in Hanoi and in neighbouring Ha Tay. This increase stands in sharp contrast to a mere 10.6 per cent increase in Ho Chi Minh City, a slight decrease in Long An and a 32-per-cent increase in Haiphong. The other extraordinary increase is that of female wages, which in real terms increased by 47 per cent in the urban areas and by a staggering 96 per cent in the rural areas.[10]

The most common basis for establishing wages, according to the enterprise managers/owners themselves, is the paying capacity of the

Table 6.20: Main basis for determining wage rates by location of enterprise. Percentages.

	Hanoi	Haiphong	HCM City	Ha Tay	Long An
Wage rates in other firms	21.6	18.4	35.0	23.4	23.5
Wage rates in local state enterprises	3.6	1.1	7.7	4.3	2.9
Wages set by authorities	0.0	1.1	0.9	0.0	0.0
Earnings in agriculture	0.0	0.0	0.0	0.0	1.5
Wage rates in agriculture	0.0	0.0	0.0	0.0	7.4
Individual negotiations	31.5	27.6	24.8	14.9	54.4
Paying capacity of enterprise	42.3	51.7	29.9	55.3	10.3
Other basis	0.9	0.0	1.7	2.1	0.0

enterprise. Some 42 per cent of the enterprises in Hanoi, 30 per cent of those in Ho Chi Minh City and well over half of those in Haiphong and Ha Tay state that this is the most important basis for setting the wages (Table 6.20). Only in Long An does this factor seem to carry rather little weight. There do not seem to be any large differences across ownership forms in this regard (Tables 6.21 and 6.22).

This statement is borne out by a simple correlation between wage rates on the one hand and other enterprise characteristics on the other. Thus, there is a significant positive correlation between the value added per worker and the wage rate at the enterprise level.[11] There is also a somewhat weaker, but still significant correlation between profits and wage rates.[12] When broken down by locations, these correlations become somewhat stronger, particularly in the rural areas. Thus, the correlation between labour productivity, measured as value added per worker, and the wage rate is 0.82 in Ha Tay and 0.4 in Long An, while it is only 0.30 in Hanoi.[13] In Ho Chi Minh City and Haiphong there does not seem to be any significant correlation at all between labour productivity and wage rates.

Compared to the situation in the 1991 survey, the link at the enterprise level between labour productivity and remuneration appears to have weakened considerably in the urban areas, but not in the rural areas. A possible explanation behind the weakening of this link in the

Table 6.21: Main basis for determining wage rates in urban enterprises by ownership form. Percentages.

	House-hold	Private	Partner-ship	Co-operative	Share-holding*
Wage rates in other firms	14.3	34.4	15.0	28.1	33.8
Wage rates in local state enterprises	3.9	4.7	0.0	8.8	3.9
Wages set by authorities	0.0	0.0	2.5	0.0	1.3
Earnings in agriculture	0.0	0.0	0.0	0.0	0.0
Wage rates in agriculture	0.0	0.0	0.0	0.0	0.0
Individual negotiations	40.3	18.8	45.0	15.8	23.4
Paying capacity of enterprise	41.6	42.2	37.5	45.6	35.1
Other basis	0.0	0.0	0.0	1.8	2.6

Note: *Shareholding and LLC.

urban areas is the establishment of a more efficient labour market in the main cities. As a consequence, the individual enterprises have become wage-takers, instead of being wage-setters. In other words, they can no longer set the wage rates themselves, but have to accept the going market rate. This could also be a factor behind the pronounced equalisation of wages between enterprises, discussed above.

As can be seen from Table 6.23, the linkage between labour productivity and wage rates appears to have been strengthened in the rural areas, in sharp contrast to the situation in the urban areas. There is an obvious reason behind this development in the rural areas, but the figures should be interpreted with some caution as there was little wage employment in the rural enterprises in the 1991 survey.

The increasing dependence of the individual urban enterprises on the going wage is also confirmed by the statements of the enterprise managers/owners themselves. Thus, in Ho Chi Minh City, which arguably has the most developed labour market, more than a third of the enterprise managers/owners state that wage rates in other firms provide the main basis for setting the wage rates. In Hanoi and Haiphong the proportion of enterprises stating this as the main basis for wage determination is lower, but far from insignificant. It deserves to

Table 6.22: Main basis for determining wage rates in rural enterprises by ownership form. Percentages.

	Household	Private	Other forms
Wage rates in other firms	22.9	17.8	36.4
Wage rates in local state firms	0.0	4.4	9.1
Earnings in agriculture	2.1	0.0	0.0
Agricultural wages	2.1	6.7	4.5
Individual negotiations	43.8	35.6	31.8
Paying capacity of enterprise	29.2	33.3	18.2
Other basis	0.0	2.2	0.0

be noted that it is the wage level in other *non-state* enterprises rather than in state enterprises which sets the benchmark.

The figures in Tables 6.22 are as interesting for what they do not show as for what they do. First, it should be noted that authorities no longer play any role in determining wage rates. Indeed, this was generally also the case in the 1991 survey. Second, it is remarkable that even in the rural areas, incomes in agriculture do not seem to have any major influence on the wage rates in the enterprises. This tendency was noted already in the 1991 survey, but became more pronounced by the 1997 survey. This confirms the conclusion drawn above that the labour flows between agriculture and rural small-scale manufacturing are quite small and that there is a division between the agricultural and the non-agricultural labour markets in the rural areas. Only in Long An does a minority of the enterprises (9 per cent) state that earnings or wage rates in agriculture provide the main basis for determining the wages in the rural enterprises.

In contrast to the state sector, where social benefits such as paid sick leave, maternity leave and annual leave are taken more or less for granted, the provision of such benefits is largely optional for the non-state enterprises. Still many enterprises provide basic social benefits to their workers. However, there are large differences both across locations and ownership types in the benefits offered. Thus, four out of five firms in Ho Chi Minh City, but only between one in ten and one in five enterprises elsewhere, grant their workers paid sick leave (Table

Table 6.23: Correlation between labour productivity and average wage at the enterprise level in 1991 and 1997 surveys.

	Hanoi	Haiphong	HCM City	Ha Tay	Long An
1991 survey	0.710*	0.734*	0.812*	(-)	(-)
1997 survey	0.299*	(-)	(-)	0.818*	0.434*

Key: * Significant at the 1 per cent level. **(-)** No significant correlation even at the 5 per cent level.

6.24). Similarly, almost half of the firms in Ho Chi Minh City offer their employees paid annual leave, in contrast to the situation in the other locations, where few workers enjoy this benefit. Paid maternity leave is also more common in Ho Chi Minh City than elsewhere. Unpaid maternity leave is the rule in Hanoi, while female workers in most enterprises in Haiphong, Ha Tay and Long An have to make do without any leave at all.

As might be expected, social benefits are more commonly given by larger private, co-operative and shareholding and limited liability firms than by the smaller household enterprises. Compared to the situation in the 1991 survey, the share of urban household and private enterprises offering their workers social benefits has increased substantially, while social benefits in the co-operative sector have deteriorated (Table 6.25). There is a large discrepancy between urban and rural areas in terms of social benefits. Generally speaking, social benefits are the exception rather than the rule in the rural enterprises (Table 6.26). Only a small proportion of the household and private firms grant their workers paid sick leave, while maternity leave and paid annual leave is unheard of in the rural household enterprises and very rare in the rural private firms. However, among the rural co-operative and partnership enterprises, there is a minority of firms granting these benefits.

Except for Ha Tay, it is rather uncommon for enterprises to resort to wage reductions or wage postponements. Less than 5 per cent of the enterprises with wage labour in Hanoi, Ho Chi Minh City and in Long An resorted to such drastic measures in the 1997 survey. In Haiphong some 5.7 per cent of the enterprises postponed payment of wages and an additional 4.5 per cent both reduced wages and postponed their

Table 6.24: Enterprises granting social benefits by location. Percentages.

	Hanoi	Haiphong	HCM City	Ha Tay	Long An
Paid sick leave	11.6	11.4	80.3	21.3	17.4
Paid maternity leave	8.9	6.8	24.8	6.4	0.0
Unpaid maternity leave	63.4	9.1	6.0	8.5	4.3
Paid annual leave	14.3	6.8	48.7	4.3	5.8

Table 6.25: Urban enterprises granting social benefits by ownership form. Percentages.

	Household	Private	Partnership	Co-operative	Shareholding*
Paid sick leave	16.7	45.3	25.0	35.1	57.7
Paid maternity leave	2.6	10.9	2.5	22.8	28.2
Unpaid maternity leave	12.8	14.1	30.0	38.6	42.3
Paid annual leave	2.6	26.6	10.0	36.8	44.9

Note: *Shareholding and LLC.

Table 6.26: Rural enterprises granting social benefits by ownership form. Percentages.

	Household	Private	Other forms
Paid sick leave	12.5	19.6	31.8
Paid maternity leave	0.0	0.0	13.6
Unpaid maternity leave	0.0	8.7	13.6
Paid annual leave	0.0	4.3	18.2

payment. In Ha Tay, no less than 38.3 per cent of the enterprises postponed wage payments in the 1997 survey, but only 2.1 per cent resorted to wage reductions (Table 6.27).

Generally speaking, these measures are most common among the co-operatives in the urban areas, and among the co-operatives and partnerships in the rural areas (Tables 6.28 and 6.29). More than 10 per cent of the urban co-operatives and 41 per cent of the enterprises in the category 'other' in the rural areas postponed wage payments in the

Table 6.27: Enterprises resorting to wage postponement/reduction in the 1997 survey by location. Percentages.

	Hanoi	Haiphong	HCM City	Ha Tay	Long An
Wage postponement	3.6	5.7	1.7	38.3	1.4
Wage reduction	0.0	0.0	0.9	2.1	0.0
Both postponement and reduction	0.0	4.5	0.0	0.0	0.0

Table 6.28: Urban enterprises resorting to wage postponement/reduction in the 1997 survey by ownership forms. Percentages.

	Household	Private	Partnership	Co-operatives	Shareholding*
Wage postponement	2.6	4.7	2.5	7.0	1.3
Wage reduction	0.0	0.0	0.0	1.8	0.0
Both postponement and reduction	3.8	0.0	0.0	1.8	0.0

Note: *Shareholding and LLC.

Table 6.29: Rural enterprises resorting to wage postponement/reduction in 1996 by ownership forms. Percentages.

	Household	Private	Other forms
Wage postponement	8.3	13.0	40.9
Wage reductions	2.1	0.0	0.0
Both postponement and reduction	0.0	0.0	0.0

1997 survey. Some 10 per cent of the rural and 6.4 per cent of the urban household enterprises also resorted to wage postponement or reduction or both in the 1997 survey. Among the other types of enterprises such measures were much more infrequent.

In fact this problem would seem to be less acute than the figures in Tables 6.27 to 6.29 suggest, as in a third of the cases the stated reason was 'delayed payment as per contract', suggesting that the postponed payment was not an extraordinary measure. Apart from these cases, the most common reason for postponing or reducing wages was liquidity problems due to the failure of the enterprise to collect payments owed by customers on time. Other, less frequently stated reasons were lack of demand and poor profitability. There were also a few cases in which the first month's wage of a worker was withheld as a matter of course. Hence, it may be concluded that it is mainly in times of unforeseen liquidity crisis that enterprises resort to postponing the payment of wages.

Notes

1. The terms 'labour force' and 'workers' are used synonymously and refer to the entire workforce, both paid and unpaid, while the term 'wage workers' is used to denote paid workers.

2. Excluding the managers/owners themselves.

3. For Long An it is difficult to make comparisons because of the large share of non-manufacturing enterprises in the sample in this province in the 1991 survey.

4. *Thuc trang Lao Dong – Viec Lam o Viet Nam 1996* [Status of Labour – Employment in Vietnam 1996]. (Hanoi: Statistical Publishing House, 1997), pp. 123–134.

5. However, comparisons for Long An should be made with caution as a very high proportion of the firms surveyed in 1991 were involved in services and not in manufacturing.

6. At an exchange rate of 11,600 dong per US$.

7. The small number of female wage workers in the sample in Long An makes it difficult to draw any conclusions for this province.

8. The small number of female wage workers in the rural household enterprises in the sample makes it difficult to draw any conclusions for this ownership form.

9. Then Ha Son Binh.

10. However, it should be noted that the figures for the rural areas are based on a rather limited sample.

11. The correlation coefficient is 0.21 and significant at the 1 per cent level.

12. The correlation coefficient is 0.12 and significant at the 3-per-cent level.

13. All three correlations are significant at the 1-per-cent level.

7

The Transformation of the Non-state Manufacturing Sector in the 1990s

Per Ronnås

The comprehensive surveys of the non-state manufacturing sector in Vietnam conducted in 1991 and 1997, as described in Chapter 1, provide unique data sets for analysing the changes that have taken place in the non-state manufacturing sector in Vietnam in the 1990s. As a quick recapitulation, the surveys consisted of

(i) a survey of 923 enterprises in Hanoi, Haiphong, Ho Chi Minh City and in the provinces of Ha Son Binh, Vinh Phu, Quang Ninh, Long An and Cuu Long in 1991,

(ii) a repeat survey in 1997 of some 371 of the enterprises surveyed in 1991 in Hanoi, Ho Chi Minh City, Haiphong, Long An and Ha Tay (previously Ha Son Binh), and

(iii) a survey in 1997 of some 500 enterprises in Hanoi, Ho Chi Minh City, Haiphong, Long An and Ha Tay that had not been previously surveyed.

As the sampling and stratification procedures as well as the questionnaires were virtually identical in the surveys, the data obtained (i) and (iii) make it possible to analyse developments in the sector as a whole between 1991 and 1997, while data from surveys (i) and (ii) can be used to examine the development and changes of a randomly selected cohort of enterprises over a period of six years.[1]

A comparison of the general characteristics and behaviour of the two different sets of enterprises from surveys (i) and (iii), was made at various levels in Chapters 2, 4 and 5. The results describe a dynamic private manufacturing sector, with a new profile (in the 1997 survey) of the enterprises, registering remarkable growth in size, capital intensity and labour productivity in the 1990s, with moderate increases in the workforce.Thus, the average value added increased almost three-fold among the enterprises in Hanoi and by almost as much in Ho Chi Minh City (Tables 2.1, 2.2). In Ha Tay, the only province for which comparable data are available, the value added per enterprise increased more than four-fold. The increase in production was accompanied by an equally impressive growth of the capital stock. The average asset base increased by more than three times among the enterprises in Hanoi and by an almost incredible 13 times in Ha Tay. Among the enterprises in Ho Chi Minh City, the increase in assets was more modest, while among the enterprises in Haiphong the asset base declined somewhat.[2]

By way of summing up the sectoral comparisons made in Chapters 2, 4 and 5, it may be emphasised that the non-state manufacturing sector has registered a considerable consolidation in terms of size, capital base, capital intensity and labour productivity in the 1990s and that this process has been accompanied by a sharp reduction in the regional differences in these regards. The enterprises in the 1997 survey were not only larger than in the 1991 survey, they also displayed different characteristics. The capital/labour ratio, measured as assets per worker, among Hanoi enterprises had nearly doubled; in Ha Tay it was a staggering 7.7 times higher, which suggests that a fundamental restructuring had indeed taken place between the two surveys. Labour productivity was also higher as a result of this increased capital intensity, and in turn translated into higher wages.

As both surveys (in 1991 and 1997) were stratified similarly by ownership forms, the large differences in size and operational characteristics cannot be explained by changes in the ownership structure of enterprises. The comparisons made earlier show that the average value added, asset base and labour force of rural and urban enterprises have increased significantly for both household and private enterprises (see Tables 2.1, 2.3). The increase in assets was made possible partly through increased indebtedness[3] but mainly through own capital.

The increases in size, capital intensity and labour productivity of the enterprises were most pronounced in the areas where enterprises were previously weakest, notably Hanoi and Ha Tay. The traditional large differences in the level of development between the north and south and between rural and urban areas had narrowed significantly by the 1997 survey, as reflected in improved industrial infrastructure (Tables 2.8, 2.9), extended forward linkages (Chapter 4) and equalisation of wages (Tables 6.18, 6.19), among other things.

This transformation can basically have taken place through two non-exclusive processes. First, through the appearance of new enterprises that are fundamentally different from existing enterprises with regard to size, capital intensity and labour productivity, and, second, through growth and transformation of existing enterprises. In the case of Vietnam, both of these processes have clearly been at work. The rest of the present chapter is devoted to detailed, individual analysis of each of these processes on the basis of the data from the 1991 and 1997 surveys.

Old versus New Enterprises

In order to determine to what extent the much larger size of the enterprises in the 1997 survey than in the 1991 survey was due to the establishment of increasingly larger enterprises, the enterprises surveyed in 1997 were divided into two groups; those established prior to 1991 and those established in or after 1991. Table 7.1 reveals a striking difference between the two categories of enterprises. Generally speaking, the newer enterprises were found to be much larger than the older ones. In Hanoi the more recently established enterprises had, in the 1997 survey, on average about three times larger production and more assets than the older enterprises and 64 per cent more labour.[4] Labour productivity was also almost 50 per cent higher in the newer enterprises in Hanoi than in the older ones. In Haiphong and Ho Chi Minh City, too, the newer enterprises were considerably larger than the older ones. However, the differences in labour productivity between the two categories of enterprises were less pronounced in these two cities.[5]

The large differences in average size between the newer and the older enterprises were also found in the rural areas covered by the sur-

Table 7.1: Main characteristics of enterprises in the 1997 survey by period of establishment and location.

	Income	Value added	Assets	Debts	Labour force	VA /worker	Assets / worker
Hanoi:							
Before 1991 (A)	470,941	140,069	457,132	15,861	13.8	9,741	33,216
1991 and after (B)	1,559,153	413,849	1,304,538	173,261	22.7	14,454	56,133
B as % of A	331	295	285	1,092	164	148	169
Haiphong:							
Before 1991 (A)	234,153	85,322	332,327	7,588	10.2	7,936	30,783
1991 and after (B)	415,729	134,229	545,394	39,636	14.1	8,590	33,810
B as % of A	178	157	164	522	138	108	110
Ho Chi Minh City:							
Before 1991 (A)	1,503,955	449,792	639,323	35,782	20.7	22,120	32,019
1991 and after (B)	2,161,715	619,633	1,343,784	97,694	25.4	24,266	59,312
B as % of A	144	138	210	273	122	110	185
Ha Tay:							
Before 1991 (A)	256,630	77,744	282,085	7,580	9.7	7,945	17,945
1991 and after (B)	394,866	159,100	393,755	50,889	15.8	7,840	18,283
B as % of A	154	205	140	671	163	99	102
Long An:							
Before 1991 (A)	153,888	61,584	144,246	1,515	5.6	10,491	23,609
1991 and after (B)	453,209	115,484	224,802	1,442	8.2	13,758	24,098
B as % of A	294	188	156	95	146	131	102

Note: All figures refer to 5 per cent trimmed means. Output, assets, debts and value added are expressed in thousand dong. The percentage of enterprises with debts was 15.9 and 34.0 respectively for the old and the new enterprises, in Hanoi, 29.5 and 41.1 in Haiphong, 26.2 and 22.7 in Ho Chi Minh City, 19.4 and 38.0 in Ha Tay and 25.7 and 17.0 in Long An. **Key**: VA: Value added.

Table 7.2: Enterprises by period of establishment and location. Percentages.

	Hanoi	Haiphong	HCM City	Ha Tay	Long An
Before 1991	58.0	44.0	35.9	38.3	42.7
1991 and after	42.0	56.0	64.1	61.7	57.3

vey. In both Ha Tay and Long An the more recently established enterprises produced almost twice as much value added on average as the older enterprises in the 1997 survey. They were also about 50 per cent larger in terms of both size of capital and labour. However, in contrast to the situation in the urban areas, the newer enterprises in the two rural areas were on the whole no more capital-intensive than the older ones. There was virtually no difference in labour productivity between the two categories of enterprises in Ha Tay, while in Long An labour productivity in the newer enterprises was about 30 per cent higher than in the older enterprises.

This picture clearly shows that the establishment of increasingly large enterprises has been a main factor behind the general increase in the size of enterprises between the 1991 and 1997 surveys. The increasing size of newly established enterprises is also reflected in the age structure of the various ownership types of the enterprises. Generally speaking, the private and limited liability enterprises covered by the survey tend to be more recently established than, in particular, the partnerships and co-operatives. In the urban areas almost three out of four private enterprises were established after 1990, as against less than one out of every five partnership and co-operative enterprises (Table 7.3). Among the urban household enterprises, slightly more than half had been established after 1990. In the rural areas the proportion of newer enterprises was slightly lower than in the urban areas (Table 7.3). Approximately two-thirds of private enterprises and half of the household enterprises had been established since 1991. Somewhat surprisingly, among the other types of enterprises in the rural areas (primarily partnerships and co-operatives) the vast majority were new.

In terms of location, Ho Chi Minh City had the highest proportion of new enterprises, followed by Ha Tay, Long An and Haiphong, while in Hanoi the majority of the enterprises had been established before 1991 (Table 7.2).

Table 7.3: Enterprises by period of establishment and ownership form. Percentages.

	Urban					Rural		
	House-hold	Private	Partner-ship	Co-operative	Share-holding*	House-hold	Private	Others
Before 1991	55.1	27.0	60.0	84.2	5.1	47.3	35.4	22.7
1991 and after	44.9	73.0	20.0	15.8	94.9	52.7	64.6	77.3

Note: *Shareholding and LLC.

However, the increasing share of private and shareholding and limited liability firms among newly established enterprises does not entirely explain the larger size of new enterprises. An examination of the average size of enterprises by age group and ownership form in the urban areas reveals that among both the household and the private enterprises the newer enterprises tend to be larger than the older ones (Table 7.4). Thus, the more recently established household enterprises produced on average 33 per cent higher value added than the older household enterprises in the 1997 survey. Among the private enterprises the difference was even larger at 62 per cent. It is interesting to note that among private enterprises the average labour force was much larger in the newer enterprises than in the older ones, while there was hardly any difference between the two groups with regard to assets. This suggests that the newer private enterprises are rather more labour-intensive than the older ones. Yet labour productivity was on average 13 per cent higher in the newer enterprises, indicating that they are more efficient. Among the urban household enterprises the picture is somewhat different: both the capital stock and the labour force is on average larger in the newer than in the older enterprises, as is labour productivity and capital intensity. Thus, not only do these two types of enterprises appear to be rapidly increasing in number, but the size of the newly established enterprises has also increased over time.

Among partnerships as well as co-operatives in the urban areas the picture is exactly the reverse.[6] The older partnerships and co-operatives tend to be much larger than the more recently established ones.

Table 7.4: Main characteristics of urban enterprises by period of establishment and ownership form.

	Income	Value added	Assets	Debts	Labour force	VA/ worker	Assets / worker
Household enterprises:							
Before 1991 (A)	171,181	60,676	134,243	979	5.2	10,522	25,475
1991 and after (B)	260,316	80,897	182,880	967	6.3	11,589	33,649
B as % of A	152	133	136	99	121	110	132
Private enterprises:							
Before 1991 (A)	723,517	300,839	1,016,777	43,304	15.8	16,155	71,250
1991 and after (B)	1,549,046	486,906	1,011,248	86,120	25.6	18,332	40,850
B as % of A	212	162	99	192	161	113	57
Partnerships:							
Before 1991 (A)	398,718	143,820	371,585	1,250	11.7	11,951	31,553
1991 and after (B)	133,503	67,032	165,081	0	7.9	8,670	22,267
B as % of A	33	47	44	0	68	73	71
Co-operatives:							
Before 1991 (A)	1,255,710	356,238	786,728	73,483	27.0	14,468	30,191
1991 and after (B)	337,308	153,314	558,572	94,444	22.5	8,041	32,349
B as % of A	27	43	71	129	83	56	107
Shareholding & LLC:							
Before 1991 (A)	–	–	–	–	–	–	–
1991 and after (B)	2,457,213	682,351	2,063,660	240,044	31.0	21,234	72,700
B as % of A	–	–	–	–	–	–	–

Note: All figures refer to 5 per cent trimmed means. Output, assets, debts and value added are expressed in thousand dong. The percentage of enterprises with debts was 14.8 and 15.1 respectively for the older and the newer firms, among household enterprises, 23.5 and 41.3 among private enterprises, 12.5 and 0.0 among partnerships, 37.5 and 55.6 among co-operatives and 35.1 among the limited liability firms. As there were only four limited liability firms established before 1991 in the sample, figures for this category were not included. **Key:** VA: Value Added.

The magnitude of the difference is more than one to two with regard to value added and even more with regard to total income. The older enterprises also tend to have a larger labour force than the newer ones, although the difference is not as pronounced as in assets. It is interesting to note that labour productivity, measured as value added per worker, is also considerably lower in the more recently established partnership and co-operative enterprises than in the older ones. Indeed, it is much lower than the labour productivity both in the private enterprises, and in the household enterprises. While this might be interpreted as an indication that partnership and co-operative enterprises grow rapidly after they have been established, a more likely interpretation is that the very nature of these enterprise forms has changed in the 1990s and that the size at the time of establishment has become much smaller than it used to be. The relative importance of these types of enterprises has declined considerably in the past decade and the number of new establishments has been quite small.

The rural enterprises present quite a different picture from those in the urban areas (Table 7.5). Among both household and private enterprises in rural areas, the capital base is on average larger in the older than in the newer enterprises. The more recently established rural private enterprises produced somewhat more value added on average than the older enterprises did in the 1997 survey, while among the rural household enterprises the picture was the reverse. Furthermore, there was hardly any difference in labour productivity between the more recent and the older household and private enterprises in the rural areas. Among the other forms of enterprises in the rural areas, it may be seen that the newer enterprises were much larger in terms of production and assets, but not of labour force, than the older enterprises. However, it is difficult to draw any firm conclusions from this as the enterprises found in this category are quite diverse.

It deserves to be noted that among urban enterprises in general, the size of debts is much larger among the more recently established enterprises (Table 7.6). This suggests two things. First, that bank loans have increasingly become available to non-state manufacturing enterprises and, second, that loans are predominantly taken at the time of establishment.

It should be noted that within each ownership form the debts of the newer enterprises on the whole are no larger than those of the older

Table 7.5: Main characteristics of rural enterprises by period of establishment and ownership form.

	Output	Value added	Assets	Debts	Labour force	VA/ worker	Assets / worker
Household enterprises:							
Before 1991 (A)	62,055	30,127	53,755	580	3.9	7,559	13,428
1991 and after (B)	63,748	26,669	40,470	335	3.3	7,906	12,034
B as % of A	103	89	75	58	120	105	90
Private enterprises:							
Before 1991 (A)	821,713	193,895	530,216	42,353	13.8	13,680	40,233
1991 and after (B)	909,684	233,856	420,726	30,287	19.1	13,700	23,714
B as % of A	111	121	79	72	138	100	59
Other forms:							
Before 1991 (A)	653,221	223,969	1,125,669	8,333	28.7	10,743	46,856
1991 and after (B)	2,002,717	512,035	1,630,565	192,549	30.6	16,466	52,339
B as % of A	307	229	149	2,311	107	153	112

Note: All figures refer to 5 per cent trimmed means. Output, assets, debts and value added are expressed in thousand dong. The percentage of enterprises with debts was 18.2 and 14.3 respectively for the older and the newer firms among the household enterprises, 35.3 and 32.0 among the private enterprises, and 80.0 and 58.8 among the other types of enterprises. **Key:** VA:Value Added.

Table 7.6: Indebtedness by period of establishment and location.

	Hanoi		HCM City		Haiphong		Long An		Ha Tay	
	1990	**1991**	**1990**	**1991**	**1990**	**1991**	**1990**	**1991**	**1990**	**1991**
Av. debt	15,862	173,261	35,782	97,694	7,588	39,636	1,516	1,442	7,581	50,889
Share with no debt	84.1	66.0	73.8	77.3	70.5	58.9	74.3	83.0	80.6	62.0

Note: Average debt in thousand dong. Averages refer to 5 per cent trimmed mean for all enterprises.

enterprises, but that the difference in indebtedness is explained by a higher proportion of firms with debts among the more recently established enterprises and, in particular, a rather large number of limited liability companies with large debts among the newer enterprises. It is noteworthy that the difference in the incidence of debts between newer and older enterprises is largest among the private enterprises, which in the past had very little access to formal credit. Among the household enterprises the level of indebtedness is generally very low.

Although there are some differences in the branch structure of the enterprises established before and after 1991, the picture differs from city to city and the only general pattern that appears to have emerged is an increasing diversification in the branch structure (Table 7.7). Thus, in Hanoi there was a relative decrease in the establishment of enterprises producing light engineering, general consumer goods, cloth and garments, while the proportion of new firms in almost all other branches increased slightly. In Ho Chi Minh City there was a relative decline in the number of new establishments in the fields of agro-processing, arts and handicrafts, and paper and stationery production. In Haiphong, the relative number of establishments in agro-processing and in carpentry and furniture production declined sharply.

In the rural areas, the two provinces covered by the survey display quite opposite pictures (Table 7.8). In Long An, in the south, more than half of the firms established since 1991 are engaged in agro-processing, as against less than 29 per cent of the firms established prior to 1991. In Ha Tay, by contrast, only 8 per cent of the firms established since 1991 are in the field of agro-processing. Here, arts and handicrafts, and cloth and garment production account for more than half of the firms estab-

Table 7.7: Branch structure of urban enterprises in 1991 and 1997 surveys, by period of establishment. Percentages.

	Hanoi		Haiphong		HCM City	
	–1990	1991–	–1990	1991–	–1990	1991–
Agricultural processing	11.6	14.0	27.3	13.3	19.0	13.3
Chemicals	0.0	0.0	0.0	6.7	2.4	6.7
Machinery & parts	5.8	8.0	6.8	6.7	7.1	6.7
Ceramics	0.0	2.0	0.0	0.0	0.0	0.0
Bags & covers	2.9	6.0	0.0	16.0	7.1	16.0
Carpentry & furniture	11.6	14.0	25.0	9.3	7.1	9.3
Light engineering and consumer goods	36.2	20.2	25.0	25.3	23.8	25.3
Medicine and medical equipment	2.9	4.0	0.0	4.0	2.4	4.0
Bricks & tiles	0.0	6.0	0.0	0.0	0.0	0.0
Paper & other stationery	4.3	8.0	0.0	2.7	7.1	2.7
Arts & handicrafts	4.3	6.0	9.1	5.3	16.7	5.3
Cloth, garment & accessories	14.5	4.0	6.8	5.3	4.8	5.3
Heavy engineering	0.0	2.0	0.0	1.3	0.0	1.3
Services	2.9	2.0	0.0	4.0	2.4	4.0
Construction and building materials	2.9	4.0	0.0	0.0	0.0	0.0

lished since 1991, while the share of new establishments in traditional local industries such as carpentry and furniture has declined sharply.

There has been quite a pronounced shift in the type of people who set up enterprises since the beginning of the 1990s. In the past, most managers were recruited from the ranks of blue-collar workers, particularly in the north. Thus among the enterprises established prior to 1991 in the north, more than half of the managers had an employment history as manual non-farm workers (Table 7.9). Only in Ho Chi Minh City did this category not predominate among the managers of the older enterprises. In Hanoi the employment history of the managers was centred in the professional, technical, administrative or

Table 7.8: Branch structure of rural enterprises, by period of establishment. Percentages.

	Ha Tay		Long An	
	–1990	**1991–**	**–1990**	**1991–**
Agricultural processing	12.9	8.0	28.6	55.3
Chemicals	3.2	2.0	0.0	0.0
Machinery & parts	3.2	0.0	11.4	2.1
Ceramics	0.0	2.0	2.9	0.0
Bags & covers	0.0	0.0	0.0	2.1
Carpentry & furniture	41.9	24.0	14.3	14.9
Light engineering and consumer goods	12.9	8.0	28.6	17.0
Medicine & medical equipment	0.0	0.0	0.0	2.1
Bricks & tiles	0.0	0.0	0.0	2.1
Paper & other stationery	0.0	0.0	2.9	0.0
Arts & handicrafts	16.1	34.0	2.9	2.1
Cloth, garment and accessories	9.7	22.0	5.7	0.0
Heavy engineering	0.0	0.0	0.0	0.0
Services	0.0	0.0	0.0	0.0
Construction and building materials	0.0	0.0	2,9	2.1

managerial fields in less than 20 per cent of the older enterprises. In the other locations, managers with such a background were more common, but they did not make up a majority anywhere. Among the more recently established enterprises, the picture is dramatically different. There has been a pronounced trend everywhere towards a higher proportion of managers with a professional, technical, administrative or managerial background. The change has been most dramatic in Hanoi, where almost two-thirds of the managers in the enterprises established since 1991 have come from the ranks of white-collar workers, as against only 21 per cent prior to 1991.[7] By contrast, only 18 per cent of the managers in the newly established enterprises have a background as manual workers. The only location showing a slightly divergent trend is Ha Tay, where the main shift has been from managers with a background as non-farm manual workers to managers

Table 7.9: Previous occupation of manager by period of establishment of enterprise and location.

	Hanoi		Haiphong		HCM City		Ha Tay		Long An	
	-1990	1991-	-1990	1991-	-1990	1991-	-1990	1991-	-1990	1991-
A	10.7	35.3	25.0	28.1	30.0	30.8	10.0	15.2	18.2	25.0
B	7.1	11.8	4.2	9.4	10.0	19.2	10.0	6.1	3.0	13.6
C	3.6	17.7	4.2	9.4	25.0	28.8	3.3	6.1	3.0	15.9
D	7.1	5.9	0.0	0.0	0.0	0.0	10.0	21.2	30.3	15.9
E	57.1	17.6	54.2	40.6	20.0	11.5	60.0	42.4	42.4	20.5
F	14.3	11.8	12.5	12.5	15.0	7.7	6.7	9.1	3.0	9.1
G	0.0	0.0	0.0	0.0	0.0	1.9	0.0	0.0	0.0	0.0

Key: **A** Professional, technical and related
B Administrative and managerial
C Clerical, sales, services
D Agriculture, animal husbandry, forestry, fisherman, hunter
E Manual worker (manufacturing, construction, transport etc.)
F Other
G Did not work

Note: Figures refer to household, private and shareholding and limited liability companies only.

with a background in agriculture. By contrast, Long An displays the same trend as the three urban locations, with an increasing share of managers with white-collar background.

The trend towards managers with experience in managerial, professional or administrative positions is the same in both household and private enterprises, although the proportion of managers with such a background remains smaller in the household enterprises (Table 7.10). Hence, this development seems to be unrelated to any changes in the ownership structure of newly established firms. The trend seems to be equally pronounced in the rural areas and in the urban areas, although the somewhat divergent picture in the two rural areas covered by the survey suggests that conclusions regarding the rural areas must be read with care.

The tendency towards a higher proportion of enterprises whose managers hold a professional, managerial or administrative background, underscores that the transformation of the non-state manufacturing

Table 7.10: Previous occupation of manager by period of establishment of enterprise and enterprise form. Percentages.

	Urban areas				Rural areas			
	Household		Private		Household		Private	
	–1990	1991–	–1990	1991–	–1990	1991–	–1990	1991–
A	16.7	25.6	35.3	32.6	6.8	12.2	29.4	35.7
B	3.7	4.7	11.8	18.6	4.5	6.1	11.8	17.9
C	9.3	25.6	11.8	16.3	2.3	6.1	0.0	21.1
D	3.7	2.3	0.0	0.0	27.3	26.5	5.9	3.6
E	50.0	30.2	35.3	20.9	54.5	40.8	41.2	10.7
F	16.7	11.6	5.9	9.3	4.5	8.2	5.9	10.7
G	0.0	0.0	0.0	2.3	0.0	0.0	0.0	0.0

Key: **A** Professional, technical and related
B Administrative and managerial
C Clerical, sales, services
D Agriculture, animal husbandry, forestry, fisherman, hunter
E Manual worker (manufacturing, construction, transport etc.)
F Other
G Did not work

sector in the 1990s has been towards larger enterprises with a higher capital intensity and labour productivity, but it has also entailed a qualitative change requiring managerial skills beyond those obtained on the shop-floor. Seen from a different angle, this development also indicates that changes in the overall economic environment are making it increasingly difficult for blue-collar workers to set up and run their own enterprises.

Patterns of Growth of Enterprises

Overall Development

An examination of the entire cohort of enterprises surveyed in both 1991 and 1997, including those no longer in operation by the latter date, yields, at first sight, a somewhat disheartening picture.[8] By the latter date only 66.9 per cent of the enterprises were still in existence, while the rest had closed down for one reason or another.[9] Although the total combined value added produced by these enterprises had in-

Table 7.11: Aggregate change of key variables of the cohort of enterprises between the 1991 and 1997 surveys by location. Percentages.

	Hanoi	Haiphong	HCM City	Ha Tay	Long An	All areas
Value added	67.3	112.5	-19.8	-40.5	-32.2	12.1
Income	85.2	100.5	-55.9	-23.6	-14.6	-7.6
Assets	188.9	64.5	-52.2	16.1	246.1	74.8
Employment	7.0	-48.8	3.4	-56.9	-31.7	-28.3
Wage labour	15.7	-49.7	18.8	-53.3	-11.7	-16.6
No. of enterprises	-30.4	-43.2	-20.5	-33.3	-40.0	-34.1

Note: The figures refer to the entire cohort of enterprises, including those no longer in existence in the 1997 survey. The figures exclude state enterprises. Value added, income and assets are expressed in real terms.

creased by 12 per cent in real terms over the period, total employment had fallen by no less than 28 per cent and wage employment by 17 per cent. The value of the combined assets of the enterprises had, by contrast, increased by no less than 75 per cent in real terms (Table 7.12). The decline in employment was primarily due to the loss of employment following the closure of a large number of the enterprises.

Generally speaking, the enterprises in Hanoi fared best. Although some 30 per cent of the surveyed enterprises in this city closed down during the period, the strong growth of a large number of the remaining enterprises ensured an overall increase in value added for the cohort as a whole of 67 per cent and a net increase in total and wage employment of 7 and 16 per cent respectively. Thus, it may be concluded that the enterprises in this city went through a considerable consolidation over the period. The asset base, in aggregate terms as well as by enterprise and by worker, increased considerably, as did labour productivity measured as value added produced per worker.

The enterprises in Haiphong, too, went through a process of consolidation, albeit of a more drastic nature. Although a record 43 per cent of the enterprises in this city closed down during the period, aggregate value added for the whole cohort more than doubled in real terms. This is all the more remarkable as employment fell by almost 50 per cent. This apparently contradictory development would seem to be due to the closure of a number of primarily co-operative enterprises with large labour force, but very low productivity.[10]

Table 7.12: Aggregate change of key variables in the cohort of urban enterprises surveyed between the 1991 and 1997 surveys by ownership form. Percentages.

	Household	Private	Partnership	Co-operative	All urban
Value added	17.0	48.1	-7.8	-31.1	22.8
Income	12.7	-19.1	-19.3	-21.5	-5.9
Assets	122.1	88.3	101.0	-41.3	73.3
Employment	-9.8	29.0	8.5	-49.3	-20.5
Wage labour	183.6	38.9	-1.0	-49.3	-9.6
No. of enterprises	-35.7	-23.3	-29.7	-39.2	-31.7

Note: The figures refer to the entire cohort of enterprises, including those no longer in existence in the 1997 survey. The figures exclude state enterprises. Value added, income and assets are expressed in real terms. The categorisation by ownership form refers to the situation in the 1991 survey.

Enterprises in Ho Chi Minh City had the lowest mortality rate of the five locations, but also a rather poor performance of the surviving enterprises. Although 'only' one-fifth of the enterprises in this city disappeared, aggregate value added fell by almost as much. The sharp fall in aggregate assets and incomes among the enterprises in this city was exclusively due to very large assets among some of the enterprises that closed down.[11] Generally speaking, the private enterprises performed better than the other types of enterprises in the urban areas. Relatively fewer enterprises of this category were closed down and this group of enterprises as a whole increased its production by nearly 50 per cent as well as its total and wage employment by 29 and 40 per cent, respectively.

Generally speaking, the private enterprises performed better than the other types of enterprises in the urban areas. Relatively fewer enterprises of this category were closed down and this group of enterprises as a whole increased its production by nearly 50 per cent as well as its total and wage employment by 29 and 40 per cent, respectively.

The urban household enterprises, too, performed rather well. Even though some 36 per cent of these enterprises were closed down, value added increased by some 17 per cent and assets by an impressive 184 per cent, while total employment fell by 10 per cent. Although the mortality rate among these enterprises has been high, those that have survived have apparently, by and large, been able to consolidate themselves. Their asset base has been considerably strengthened and they have also increased production. The urban private enterprises also display the same indications of having gone through a process of weeding, which has left the survivors fitter and stronger, although this process would seem to have been much more pronounced for the urban household than for the urban private enterprises.

By contrast, the development of the urban co-operative enterprises shows few such redeeming features. Not only were 39 per cent of these enterprises closed down, but also value added produced, assets and, not least, employment fell by just as much or more for the group as a whole. The main reason for this dismal overall performance was the large size of many of the closed down units.

By and large, the rural enterprises fared much worse than the urban during the period. A somewhat lower proportion of the rural than of the urban enterprises were still in operation by the 1997 survey (63 versus 68 per cent), but more importantly, growth of the surviving enterprises did not make up for the loss of production and employment of those that closed down. The loss of employment was to a large extent due to the closure of a few rather large co-operative and partnership enterprises at the same time as the remaining enterprises generated little if any new employment. The rather dismal development of the rural enterprises was not altogether unexpected (Table 7.13). The rural enterprises covered by the survey in 1990, apart from a number of seemingly moribund co-operatives and a large number of rather primitive household enterprises which were poorly endowed, suffered from low productivity. They were scarcely capable of producing anything more than a subsistence income for the household members employed in them. With the opening up of the rural markets and increased competition, it was to be expected that many of them had little chance of developing and prospering. On the positive side it should be noted that the asset base has been considerably strengthened among those enterprises that have survived. It appears that the rural enterprises have gone through a period of rather forceful restructuring, driven by increasingly fierce competition, where the fittest have adapted and become stronger, but which has also resulted in many casualties. This would seem to have been the case both in Ha Tay and

Table 7.13: Aggregate change of key variables in the cohort of rural enterprises between the 1991 and 1997 surveys by ownership form. Percentages.

	Household	Private	All rural
Value added	-2.1	-40.1	-36.0
Income	-22.5	-6.0	-18.0
Assets	62.4	215.3	94.4
Employment	-13.4	-40.8	-50.6
Wage labour	129.9	-41.5	-47.7
No. enterprises	-36.8	-29.3	-36.6

Note: The figures refer to the entire cohort of enterprises, including those no longer in existence in 1997. Apart from household and private enterprises, the rural total also includes a few partnership and co-operative enterprises. Value added, income and assets are expressed in real terms. The categorisation by ownership form refers to the situation in the 1991 survey.

in Long An. The effects have generally been more drastic in Ha Tay, although the share of discontinued enterprises has been higher in Long An, mainly because closures in the former province affected a number of large co-operative and partnership enterprises while in the latter mainly household enterprises were closed down.

That enterprises in Ha Tay generally fared worse than those in Long An is hardly surprising, considering that the enterprises in Ha Tay were generally much weaker and poorer than those in Long An in the 1991 survey. Although the mortality rate has been higher among the household than private enterprises in the rural areas, it is the latter group that has registered the most severe overall decline in production and employment. In a way this is not surprising, as the scope for decline of either income or employment in most household enterprises must have been very small, considering the very low levels of production at the starting point.

Survival and Development Patterns

By the time of the 1997 survey 65.5 per cent of the enterprises surveyed in 1991 were still in operation.[12] This proportion varied between location and ownership forms. The highest proportion of surviving enterprises was found in Ho Chi Minh City (78 per cent), followed by Hanoi (68 per cent), and Ha Tay (63 per cent); however, in Long An and Haiphong only 58 and 52 per cent, respectively, of the enterprises were still in existence. Generally speaking, the rate of survival was somewhat higher in the urban than in the rural areas (Table 7.14).

Both in urban and in rural areas the private enterprises registered the lowest number of closures.[13] In urban areas more than three-quarters and in rural areas more than two-thirds of the private enterprises surveyed in 1991 were still in operation in 1997. Among the household enterprises the survival rate was somewhat lower: 64 per cent in the urban and 62 per cent in the rural areas. Among the partnership enterprises, 68 per cent of the urban, but only one in six rural, still existed in 1997. The lowest rate of survival was found among the co-operative enterprises, where 61 per cent of the urban, but none of the rural units, were operating in 1997.[14] In the rural areas relatively more manufacturing than agro-processing enterprises were still in operation in 1997: 66 as against 54 per cent.

However, the survival ratio provides only a part of the picture of the development of the enterprises. When the rate of survival is combined with the growth performance in terms of value added created of the enterprises still in operation in 1997 (Tables 7.14 to 7.16), an intriguing picture emerges. It would appear that the vast majority of enterprises fall into two distinct categories: those that have grown at a very rapid pace (by more than 10 per cent per year in real terms) and those that have closed down or suffered pronounced decline.[15]

The proportion of less successful enterprises, which either closed down or declined in terms of value added by more than 2.5 per cent per year, ranged from 44 per cent in Hanoi to no less than two-thirds in Haiphong and Long An. In Ho Chi Minh City and in the province of Ha Tay a clear majority of the enterprises (58 and 56 per cent), also fell into this category. It is interesting to note that when lumped together in this manner, the differences across locations becomes much smaller than when the categories 'closed down' and 'declining' are examined individually. It would appear that in Ho Chi Minh City a considerably smaller share of the less successful enterprises closed down than in the other locations. Thus, while this city had the lowest proportion of discontinued enterprises, it had the highest share of (still surviving) enterprises registering sharp decline.

An examination by ownership forms reveals the same pattern. Thus, in the urban areas, the household and co-operative enterprises had

Table 7.14: Development of enterprises between the 1991 and 1997 surveys by location. Average annual percentage change of value added.

	Hanoi	Haiphong	HCM City	Ha Tay	Long An
Closed down	31.6	47.5	22.4	36.6	41.7
Decline over 2.5%	12.3	18.8	35.5	19.7	23.6
-2.5 to 2.5%	8.8	3.8	5.3	9.9	8.3
2.6% to 10.0%	10.5	6.3	10.5	7.0	6.9
Growth over 10.0%	36.8	23.8	26.3	26.8	19.4

Table 7.15: Development of urban enterprises between the 1991 and 1997 surveys by ownership form. Average annual percentage change of value added.

	Household	Private	Partnership	Co-operative	State
Closed down	35.7	24.6	31.6	39.2	(100.0)
Decline over 2.5%	19.6	31.1	34.2	11.8	(0.0)
-2.5% to 2.5%	3.6	8.2	2.6	7.8	(0.0)
2.5% to 10.0%	8.9	8.2	5.3	13.7	(0.0)
Growth over 10.0%	32.1	27.9	26.3	27.5	(0.0)

Note: There were only six state enterprises in the sample. All closed down during the period.

Table 7.16: Development of rural enterprises between the 1991 and 1997 surveys by ownership form. Average annual percentage change of value added.

	Household	Private	Partnership	Co-operative
Closed down	38.4	32.8	(83.3)	(100.0)
Decline over 2.5 %	17.8	29.5	(0.0)	(0.0)
-2.5% to 2.5%	11.0	8.2	(0.0)	(0.0)
2.6% to 10.0 %	4.1	9.8	(16.7)	(0.0)

Note: There were only six partnership and two co-operative enterprises in the sample.

the highest share of closed-down enterprises, but the lowest share of declining enterprises among those still in operation. On the whole, it would appear that among the urban enterprises, partnership enterprises had the poorest performance, with two-thirds of the enterprises either discontinuing their operation or registering a sharp decline. The pattern across ownership forms in rural areas is broadly similar. Although the incidence of closure was higher among household than private enterprises, the former had a much smaller share of surviving, albeit declining enterprises.

At the other end of the scale is a rather high proportion of enterprises registering very rapid growth indeed. Some 37 per cent of the enterprises in Hanoi, about a quarter of the enterprises in Ho Chi Minh City, Haiphong and Ha Tay and a fifth of the enterprises in Long An, increased their value added by more than 10 per cent per year in real terms between the two surveys.

This reinforces the impression that the 1990s was a decade of dramatic structural change amidst growth. This environment offered great possibilities of growth for those astute and adaptable enough to exploit these opportunities, at the same time as it was merciless on those enterprises that failed to adapt and change with the times. Table 7.14 reinforces the impression gleaned from Table 7.11 that these changes were generally more dramatic in the north than in the south. Thus, Hanoi had a much higher proportion of rapidly growing enterprises (37 per cent) than the other cities, as well as a rather high mortality rate. Haiphong would seem to differ from Hanoi in that it offered a harsher economic environment and/or that its enterprises were less viable. Thus, the mortality rate among the repeat enterprises was higher, while the share of fast growing enterprises (those growing more than 10 per cent per year) was lower than in either Hanoi or Ho Chi Minh City.[16]

Similarly, despite the much weaker economic base of enterprises in Ha Tay than in Long An, the former generally fared better. Thus, the enterprises in Ha Tay not only registered a lower mortality rate than those in Long An, but a higher proportion of them were fast-growing enterprises. Moreover Ha Tay benefited from a smaller number of declining enterprises.

An examination of growth by ownership forms of enterprises shatters several common prejudices. First, it may be noted that the highest proportion of fast-growing enterprises is found among household enterprises, both in the urban and in the rural areas. While it may be argued that the modest starting-point makes even modest absolute growth look impressive in relative terms, small household enterprises often face organisational, managerial and operational barriers to growth. Not least, the inevitable increase in wage labour as the enterprise expands dramatically changes the cost structure of production and greatly increases the need for managerial and organisation skills. Seen in this light, the fact that 32 per cent of the urban and 29 per cent of the rural household enterprises grew by more than 10 per cent per year is both impressive and encouraging (Tables 7.15 and 7.16). That this growth was associated with an increased use of wage labour is clearly demonstrated by the fact that the net wage employment in the urban household enterprises which were still in operation by the time of the 1997 survey was 142 persons, or 3.7 persons on average per enterprise. This should be seen against the fact the most of the enterprises did not employ any wage labour in 1991.[17] The fast-growing enterprises accounted for most of this increase.

From a policy perspective, the finding that quite a large proportion of the household enterprises grow rapidly and hire wage labour is important. As the overwhelming majority of non-state enterprises in Vietnam are household enterprises, it must be concluded that the dynamic household enterprises do indeed constitute a major source of industrial growth and employment generation. One relatively easy way of promoting this dynamism would be to facilitate the change of an enterprise from one ownership form to another; for example, from household to private. In the present sample only four out of 36 urban, but nine out of 45 rural household enterprises graduated to a 'higher' form of enterprise, although many more obviously had the characteristics of a private rather than a household enterprise by 1997.

Another popular conception, which the data belie, is that the co-operatives in the 1990s were moribund. While this may largely have proved to be true in the rural areas where the co-operative, as well as partnership enterprises in the survey all fared badly, the urban co-operatives had a much more mixed performance. Although close to 40 per cent of them closed down during the period, more than a quarter increased production by more than 10 per cent per year. Thus, the negative overall performance notwithstanding (Table 7.15), a fair share of the co-operatives have apparently managed to adapt to the more market-oriented environment and have prospered. Some of these success stories were transformed into other ownership forms, mainly to limited liability companies, but the majority remained co-operatives.[18]

A more detailed analysis of the growth pattern in terms of value added of the repeat enterprises still operating in 1997 reinforces the picture depicted above. The average rate of growth was almost three times higher in Hanoi and Haiphong than in Ho Chi Minh City (Table 7.17). In Hanoi only a quarter of the repeat enterprises registered a decline in value added produced between the 1991 and 1997 surveys, as against half of the enterprises in Ho Chi Minh City. In Hanoi half of the enterprises grew by more than 11 per cent per year and almost a quarter of them grew by more than 20 per cent per year. The performance was similarly impressive in Haiphong. In Ho Chi Minh City, too, almost a quarter of the enterprises grew by more than 20 per cent per year, but the performance of the remaining 75 per cent was much more dismal than in Hanoi or Haiphong.

The enterprises in rural areas, on average, grew at a slower rate than in the urban areas. To be more precise, while the average growth rate of the enterprises in the southern province of Long An was about the same as that of Ho Chi Minh City, the enterprises in the northern province of Ha Tay on average grew more slowly than those in the neighbouring cities of Hanoi and Haiphong. The development of the enterprises in Ha Tay presents a very polarised picture. At the bottom end, it can be seen that a quarter of the enterprises decreased by 10 per cent or more per year, while at the top end a quarter of the enterprises grew at a staggering rate of 25 per cent or more per year. By comparison, the picture in Long An was much less dramatic.

Among the various ownership forms, the surviving household enterprises would seem by and large to have enjoyed the most impressive development, both in the urban and in the rural areas (Tables 7.18 and 7.19). Their average rate of annual growth was 13 per cent in the urban and 8 per cent in the rural areas. In the urban areas, two-thirds of them registered positive growth rates. Almost half of them grew by 10 per cent per year or more, thus clearly qualifying as fast-growing enterprises, and a quarter of them grew by a staggering 30 per cent or more per year.

In the rural areas the growth of household enterprises was somewhat less impressive than in the urban areas. The proportion of enterprises with positive growth was smaller at 59 per cent. Yet half of the enterprises grew by more than 7 per cent per year and a quarter grew

Table 7.17: Average annual rate of growth of value added of enterprises between 1991 and 1997 surveys by location.

	Hanoi	Haiphong	HCM City	Ha Tay	Long An
Mean	*12.5*	*13.2*	*4.6*	*5.3*	*4.6*
Percentiles:					
10	-12.6	-22.1	-21.9	-26.1	-19.1
25	-1.2	-4.6	-14.6	-9.8	7.8
50	11.1	7.6	-0.4	4.4	0.7
75	19.7	23.3	18.6	24.8	15.0
90	39.4	61.4	34.5	30.1	31.3

Table 7.18: Average annual rate of growth of value added of urban enterprises between 1991 and 1997 surveys by ownership form.

	Household	Private	Partnership	Co-operatives
Mean	*13.2*	*6.7*	*2.9*	*13.5*
Percentiles:				
10	-16.5	-20.7	-33.2	-13.2
25	4.0	-10.4	-13.9	-1.2
50	9.8	1.4	-2.0	9.1
75	29.9	13.6	16.2	19.7
90	42.0	43.2	28.3	54.6

Table 7.19: Average annual rate of growth of value added of rural enterprises between the 1991 and 1997 surveys by ownership form and area of activity.

	Household	Private	Agro-processing	Manufacturing
Mean	*7.8*	*1.9*	*10.9*	*3.9*
Percentiles:				
10	-19.1	-28.6	-24.9	-24.8
25	-6.2	-15.7	-10.2	-9.5
50	7.2	-1.0	3.3	0.7
75	20.5	23.6	29.6	21.9
90	29.1	33.1	64.6	29.7

by more than 20 per cent per year. Those in Ha Tay seem to have performed slightly better than those in Long An, but this difference is hardly significant.

The urban co-operatives performed quite well, too. Almost three-quarters of the surviving enterprises registered positive growth, half of them grew by more than 9 per cent per year and a quarter of them by 20 per cent per year or more.[19] The high average rate of growth of the urban co-operatives (13.5 per cent per year) was influenced by a small number of very rapidly growing enterprises.

The development of the urban co-operatives contrasts with the much poorer performance of partnership enterprises. More than half of the urban partnerships actually declined, many of them significantly, and the performance of the most successful partnership was much less impressive than that of its counterpart among other forms. In the rural areas, development of the few partnership enterprises found in the sample was, as noted above, dismal.

The performance of the private enterprises, both in urban and in rural areas, was mixed. Although the performance in urban areas was somewhat better than in rural areas, it should be noted that in both areas about half of the enterprises either declined or did not grow at all. Although a small minority of private enterprises in the urban areas performed extremely well, rapid growth was much less broad-based and involved relatively fewer enterprises than among the household and co-operative enterprises. In the rural areas, however, the private enterprises equalled the household enterprises with regard to the proportion of fast-growing enterprises.

An examination of the enterprise performance by branches does not yield a very conclusive picture. Most branches had both declining and rapidly growing enterprises, suggesting that line of activity was not a major determinant of growth. Still, enterprises in some branches would seem to have fared better than others. In the urban areas, the sectors 'construction and building materials', 'machine building' and 'services' performed better, while 'carpentry and furniture making' and, in particular, 'cloth and garment production' performed worse than average.

In the rural areas a somewhat more clear-cut, but also different, picture emerges. Hence, enterprises involved in 'construction and building materials' and 'arts and handicraft' performed much above average. 'Carpentry and furniture' had a number of very successful as well as a number of declining enterprises, while the performance of the enterprises engaged in 'services' and in 'light engineering', in particular, but also in 'food production' was clearly below average. With regard to the latter it should also be noted that agro-processing firms registered a very high rate of closures at 46 per cent.

On Accumulation, Growth and Employment

More than any other factors, the ability to accumulate capital at a rapid pace has determined the survival and growth of the small-scale manufacturing enterprises in the 1990s. The correlation between accumulation of capital and growth in terms of value added produced is remarkably high.[20] While this link may seem trivial at first, the nature of the link and its implications show that it is not.

First, the enterprise data clearly show that what might be considered as a modest, but respectable rate of capital accumulation of, say, 10 per cent, does not suffice. The threshold in terms of capital accumulation needed in order for an enterprise to achieve a take-off and grow was very high indeed. In the urban areas, even enterprises growing by a modest rate of 2.5 to 10 per cent per year had an average annual rate of capital accumulation of 23 per cent, while the fast-growing enterprises with growth rates in excess of 10 per cent per year had an average rate of capital generation of 38.2 per cent per year (Table 7.20). Among the latter, only a quarter had a rate of capital accu-mulation of less than 15 per cent per year.

In the rural areas, the rate of capital accumulation needed for growth was even higher. Even among the enterprises with a modest growth rate of 2.5 to 10 per cent per year it averaged 43 per cent and among the faster-growing enterprises it was an extraordinary 56 per cent per year (Table 7.20).

The finding that growth requires very high levels of capital accumulation is supported by the fact that the declining enterprises, too, generally registered net increases in capital, although at much lower rates (Table 7.20).

Second, as discussed above, the enterprises display a pronounced dualistic pattern in terms of performance. At the lower end, 50–60 per

Table 7.20: Average annual rate of growth of assets, employment and labour productivity by growth categories of enterprises.

	I	II	III	IV	All enterprises
Urban:					
Assets	3.0	11.3	22.6	38.2	21.5
Employment	-5.3	-3.4	1.6	8.6	1.9
Productivity	-8.6	4.1	5.6	21.4	7.4
Rural:					
Assets	10.7	37.5	43.2	56.2	35.1
Employment	-5.8	3.5	3.1	6.6	1.2
Productivity	-9.7	-3.1	2.9	20.6	4.2

Key: I: Enterprises with an average annual decline of value added of more than 2.5 per cent.
II: Enterprises with an average annual change of value added between -2.5 and +2.5 per cent.
III: Enterprises with an average annual increase of value added between 2.5 and 10.0 per cent.
IV: Enterprises with an average annual increase of value added of more than 10 per cent.
Note: All figures refer to percentage average annual change. Labour productivity calculated as value added per worker.

cent of the enterprises either closed down or declined significantly during the six-year period between the two surveys (Tables 7.14 to 7.16). It can reasonably be assumed that in the long run the majority of the declining enterprises, too, will close down. At the upper end, 25–35 per cent of the enterprises grew at more than 10 per cent per year. Remarkably few enterprises registered zero or only modest growth. Hence, the ability to achieve very high rates of capital accumulation would, by and large, seem to be a prerequisite not only for growth, but also for the long-term viability of the enterprise.

Third, in the virtual absence of access to credits, accumulation of capital has to be self-generated and hence is tantamount to very high profit margins. In other words, just making ends meet or achieving modest profits is not enough for long-term viability of the enterprise.

This does not imply that credits have not played any role at all as a means of capital accumulation. By the 1997 survey some 26 per cent of the urban and 21 per cent of the rural enterprises had some debt, more often than not in the form of bank loans. However, even among those with debts, the level of indebtedness was quite modest. Both

Table 7.21: Average annual rate of growth of assets, employment and labour productivity by growth categories and location of enterprises.

	Hanoi	Haiphong	HCM City	Ha Tay	Long An
All enterprises:					
Assets	24.6	27.8	14.8	38.1	31.7
Employment	2.2	2.6	1.1	0.7	1.6
Productivity	10.7	10.0	3.4	5.3	2.9
Declining enterprises:					
Assets	5.4	5.0	1.3	3.1	17.4
Employment	-5.5	-8.5	-3.5	-8.0	-3.9
Productivity	-4.5	-5.1	-11.4	-11.1	-8.5
Growing enterprises:					
Assets	33.2	42.8	27.7	61.1	43.4
Employment	6.5	9.7	5.0	5.0	6.7
Productivity	14.8	19.5	18.8	18.2	14.4
Fast-growing enterprises:					
Assets	37.7	52.3	23.8	65.6	44.0
Employment	7.4	12.5	6.2	6.7	6.5
Productivity	17.7	22.7	24.2	20.9	20.2

Note: *Declining enterprises* are defined as enterprises with an average annual decline of value added in excess of 2.5 per cent. *Growing enterprises* are defined as all enterprises with an average annual increase of value added in excess of 2.5 per cent. *Fast-growing enterprises* are defined as enterprises with an average annual increase in value added in excess of 10 per cent. *Productivity* is defined as value added produced per worker. *Employment* refers to total employment.

among the urban and the rural enterprises with debts, the share of debts in total capital was only 20 per cent. The enterprises growing by at least 2.5 per cent per year had a higher incidence of debts than average, suggesting both that credit was generally given on a commercial basis to sound enterprises rather than to support declining ones, and that the importance of credits to growth was larger than the above figures might suggest. Thus, some 36 per cent of the growing urban enterprises had debts, as against only 12.5 per cent of the declining ones. For the rural enterprises the corresponding figures were 31 and 12.5 per cent, respectively. As might be expected, credit was primarily extended to the larger enterprises. Both in the urban and the rural areas between 27 and

32 per cent of the private, partnership and co-operative enterprises had debts, as against only 11–13 per cent of the household enterprises.

The need for consolidation and continuous strengthening of the asset base may be expected to be greatest for the small enterprises and in the areas where technological change is fastest. Indeed, the average rate of capital accumulation among the enterprises in Ho Chi Minh City has been significantly lower than in the other locations (Table 7.21). Thus, this rate was only 24 per cent per year among the fast-growing enterprises in Ho Chi Minh City, as against 38 per cent in Hanoi, 52 per cent in Haiphong and a staggering 66 per cent in Ha Tay. An additional factor behind this discrepancy may well be a strong pressure, as markets become more integrated, to reduce the technological gap between the comparatively stronger and more advanced enterprises in Ho Chi Minh City and those in the north. Other findings, such as the decreasing wage gap between the north and the south, may be interpreted to support this view.

Similarly, the generally much smaller household enterprises not only need to achieve higher rates of capital accumulation than other types of enterprises in order to survive and grow, but also, it would seem, find it easier to do so. Thus, in the urban areas household enterprises growing by more than 2.5 per cent per year had an average rate of capital accumulation of 49 per cent, compared to 20 per cent for the private, 36 per cent for the partnership and 32 per cent for the co-operative enterprises (Table 7.22). However, even for the comparatively large co-operative enterprises, a very high rate of capital accumulation was a precondition for growth.

In the rural areas, the rate of capital accumulation was generally higher than in the urban areas, and the threshold to achieve growth was generally much higher. Among the rural enterprises growing by more than 2.5 per cent per year (i.e. about a third of the enterprises), the average annual rate of capital accumulation was 58 per cent for the household enterprises and 48 per cent for the private enterprises (Table 7.23).

A comparison of the enterprise environment in the rural areas at the time of the survey in 1991 and in 1997 reveals that fundamental changes have taken place both with regard to the nature of the enterprises and the economic environment in which they operate.

Table 7.22: Average annual rate of growth of assets, employment and labour productivity by growth categories and ownership form of urban enterprises. Percentages.

	Household	Private	Partnership	Co-operative	All urban
All enterprises:					
Assets	36.6	10.3	18.8	22.9	21.5
Employment	4.8	2.2	-0.9	0.1	1.8
Productivity	7.4	4.9	3.9	14.0	7.4
Declining enterprises:					
Assets	14.1	-0.6	-0.1	-0.1	3.0
Employment	-3.8	-5.1	-8.7	-1.3	-5.3
Productivity	-7.6	-8.6	-8.2	-10.7	-8.6
Growing enterprises:					
Assets	49.0	19.9	36.0	32.3	34.3
Employment	9.4	9.5	6.6	1.6	6.9
Productivity	15.3	16.2	16.5	22.5	17.6
Fast-growing enterprises:					
Assets	56.0	24.1	39.4	31.0	38.2
Employment	12.2	11.0	7.2	2.1	8.6
Productivity	17.1	19.8	19.0	30.8	21.4

Note: *Declining enterprises* are defined as enterprises with an average annual decline of value added in excess of 2.5 per cent. *Growing enterprises* are defined as all enterprises with an average annual increase of value added in excess of 2.5 per cent. *Fast-growing enterprises* are those enterprises with an average annual increase in value added in excess of 10 per cent. *Categorisation by ownership form* refers to the situation in the 1991 survey. *Productivity* defined as value added produced per worker. *Employment* refers to total employment.

In the 1991 survey most firms in Ha Tay operated with exceedingly little capital and with very poor technology. The majority (52 per cent) did not even have electricity. As a consequence, labour productivity was also low and many enterprises barely managed to provide sufficient income to meet the basic needs of the owner family.[21] The produce was mainly sold locally. Poorly developed markets and rather weak competition made the existence of these enterprises possible. By the time of the 1997 survey the picture had changed dramatically. By then, virtually all enterprises had electricity, and they were substantially stronger in terms of capital and technology.[22] The average asset

Table 7.23: Average annual rate of growth of assets, employment and labour productivity by growth categories and ownership form of rural enterprises. Percentages.

	Household	Private	All rural
All enterprises:			
Assets	39.4	29.4	35.0
Employment	3.2	-1.3	1.1
Productivity	5.4	3.0	4.2
Declining enterprises:			
Assets	8.4	12.4	10.7
Employment	-1.8	-9.0	-5.8
Productivity	-10.1	-9.3	-9.7
Growing enterprises:			
Assets	58.1	47.5	53.1
Employment	6.2	5.7	5.8
Productivity	16.8	16.5	16.5
Fast-growing enterprises:			
Assets	61.0	48.2	56.2
Employment	7.1	5.7	6.6
Productivity	18.0	25.2	20.6

Note: For definition of terms used, see Table 7.22.

base of the private and household enterprises surveyed in 1997 in Ha Tay was 331 thousand dong, compared to only 77 thousand dong in the 1991 survey.[23] Labour productivity, too, had increased substantially, as had competition. This development was intrinsically linked to the development and integration of markets. By the 1997 survey the enterprises in Ha Tay were much more exposed to competition from urban enterprises and to imports than in the 1991 survey, but they also sold their produce further afield. Much of this development took place through the replacement of weak and inefficient enterprises by enterprises that tended to be technically and economically stronger. Some 62 per cent of the enterprises covered by the survey in Ha Tay in 1997 had been established after 1990.

This very dynamic external development no doubt goes a very long way to explain the extraordinarily high rates of capital accumulation of the growing enterprises in Ha Tay. In order not only to grow, but to survive, enterprises have had to keep pace with the rapid changes in the environment in which they operate. Anything less would inevitably result in decline and, sooner or later, closure.

The same link between rapid changes in the overall economic environment and pressure on existing enterprises to develop or succumb to market forces obviously also existed elsewhere. As markets have become more integrated, this pressure will have been strongest in the least developed areas. This is borne out by the survey results and helps to explain the higher mortality rates as well as the higher rates of capital accumulation in the north than in the south and in the rural areas than in the urban areas.

The pivotal role of high rates of capital accumulation as a prerequisite for growth is also reflected in the nature of growth. Increases in labour productivity have generally accounted for a higher share of the increase in value added than have increases in employment. Among the fast-growing enterprises, labour productivity increased by more than 20 per cent on average in both rural and urban areas, while employment increased at a much slower rate.

.In view of the very high rates of capital accumulation among the growing enterprises, it comes as no surprise that growth has been capital-intensive rather than labour-intensive. The asset base per worker more than doubled from an average 23.025 million dong per worker in the 1991 survey to 55.801 million dong in the 1997 survey among the urban enterprises growing by more than 2.5 per cent per year (Table 7.24).[24] The increase was fastest in the two northern cities of Hanoi and Haiphong, which in this regard not only caught up with Ho Chi Minh City, but substantially surpassed it. The most remarkable development was registered in Hanoi, where the average capital base per worker increased from 20.0 to 65.5 million dong. In the 1991 survey the capital/labour ratio varied widely between the various ownership forms. Broadly speaking, it was more than twice as high in the private enterprises as in any of the other ownership forms.

The low capital/labour ratio in the household enterprises could readily be explained by the small size of these firms and the fact that they relied primarily on both own capital and own labour. The similarly low ratio in the co-operative enterprises was no doubt due to the fact that

Table 7.24: Changes in absolute and relative capital intensity of growing urban enterprises between 1991 and 1997 surveys.

	Assets/worker (1,000 dong)		Index: 1990=100	Index: All urban enterprises = 100	
	1991 survey	1997 survey		1991 survey	1997 survey
Hanoi	20,048	65,508	*327*	87	117
Haiphong	20,570	57,058	*277*	123	81
HCM City	28,001	45,365	*162*	89	102
Household	17,167	56,223	*327*	75	101
Private	38,032	55,004	*145*	165	99
Partnership	18,748	63,639	*339*	81	114
Co-operative	15,450	51,734	*335*	67	93
All enterprises	23,025	55,801	*242*	100	100

Note: All absolute figures in 1996 prices. *Growing enterprises* are defined as those with an average annual increase in value added produced of more than 2.5 per cent.

these enterprises had inherited from their past as 'socialist' enterprises a weak economic base as well as an unjustifiably large labour force. By the 1997 survey, these differences had by and large disappeared, through remarkable increases in the capital/labour ratio in the household, partnership and co-operative enterprises (Table 7.24). The outstanding increase in the capital/labour base of the household enterprises is particularly noteworthy, not least in view of the fact that 40 per cent of the household enterprises covered by the survey in 1991 belong to the category of growing enterprises to which the figures refer.

The increase in the capital intensity of rural enterprises was even more rapid than that of the urban enterprises and, as a result, the wide gap in capital intensity between the rural and the urban enterprises registered in the 1991 survey narrowed considerably (Table 7.25). Similarly, and as in the case of the urban enterprises, the gap between the north and the south of the country decreased substantially. In Ha Tay the capital per worker in the growing enterprises (which amounted to a third of the enterprises in this province) increased almost tenfold from 1.6 million to 14.7 million dong between the two surveys. The fact that the asset base in these enterprises was very weak indeed in the

Table 7.25: Changes in absolute and relative capital intensity of growing rural enterprises between the 1991 and 1997 surveys.

	Assets/worker (1,000 dong)		Index: 1990=100	Index: All rural enterprises = 100	
	1991 survey	1997 survey		1991 survey	1997 survey
Ha Tay	1,569	14,691	*937*	30	49
Long An	9,889	49,340	*499*	189	164
Household	4,580	26,301	*574*	87	88
Private	6,374	36,137	*567*	122	120
All enterprises	5,244	30,000	*572*	100	100

Note: All absolute figures in 1996 prices. *Growing enterprises* here refer to those with an average annual increase in value added produced of more than 2.5 per cent and include fast-growing enterprises.

1991 survey does not make this achievement any less impressive. While the prospects for the generally very weak and impoverished enterprises in this province seemed very bleak in the 1991 survey, we find that six years later at least a third of them had performed very well indeed, to the extent that they have more or less been able to cast their legacy of indigence aside. In the southern province of Long An the increase in the capital/labour ratio has been less remarkable than in Ha Tay, although it has by no means been unimpressive. The less dramatic development in Long An than in Ha Tay should be seen in the light of the fact that the capital base in the former province was much stronger than in the latter in the 1991 survey.

In light of the above, it comes as no surprise that growth has been achieved through increased labour productivity rather than through increased employment. In the urban areas, labour productivity increased by an average annual rate of 18 per cent among the growing enterprises and 21 per cent among the fast-growing enterprises (Table 7.22).[25] Among the rural enterprises the corresponding rates of growth were 17 and 21 per cent (Table 7.23). At the same time, employment increased by 6–7 per cent among the growing and 7–9 per cent among the fast-growing enterprises. However, there were considerable differences between the different types of enterprises. In the urban areas, the rate of employment growth among the growing enterprises was by far

Table 7.26: Employment elasticity of growth by location of enterprise.

	Hanoi	Haiphong	HCM City	Ha Tay	Long An
Growth over 2.5% per year:					
Total employment	0.25	0.13	0.13	0.19	0.26
Wage employment	0.33	0.14	0.22	0.61	0.91
***Incremental capital/ labour ratio** (1,000 dong)*	88,709	94,236	75,179	38,233	121,204
Decline over 2.5% per year:					
Total employment	-0.25	0.59	0.01	0.72	0.42
Wage employment	-0.01	0.79	0.22	0.86	0.35

Note: Calculated as percentage increase of each indicator divided by percentage increase in value added between 1991 and 1997 surveys for each subset of enterprises.

Table 7.27: Employment elasticity of growth in urban enterprises by ownership form.

	Household	Private	Partnership	Co-operative	All urban
Growth over 2.5% per year:					
Total employment	0.31	0.18	0.38	0.08	0.17
Wage employment	2.56	0.22	0.41	0.10	0.21
***Incremental capital/ labour ratio** (1,000 dong)*	88,303	73,451	59,136	216,086	89,797
Decline over 2.5% per year:					
Total employment	-0.21	4.00	0.30	0.48	0.11
Wage employment	1.79	5.30	0.75	-0.55	0.26

Table 7.28: Employment elasticity of growth in rural enterprises by ownership form.

	Household	Private	All rural
Growth over 2.5% per year:			
Total employment	0.35	0.20	0.24
Wage employment	3.33	0.48	0.78
***Incremental capital/labour ratio** (1,000 dong)*	39,042	88,389	64,290
Decline over 2.5% per year:			
Total employment	0.40	0.73	0.65
Wage employment	0.28	0.86	0.79

highest in the household and private enterprises sector, where it generally exceeded 10 per cent per year (Table 7.23). By contrast, even among the fast growing co-operatives, employment only increased by a mere 2 per cent per year on average. In the rural areas, the rate of employment growth among the expansive household and private enterprises was considerably lower than among their urban counterparts and averaged only 6 per cent (Table 7.2).

The capital-intensive rather than labour-intensive nature of the growth is also reflected in rather low employment elasticities of growth (Tables 7.26–7.28). Among the growing urban enterprises, the overall employment elasticity was only 0.17. The wage employment elasticity was slightly higher (0.21), reflecting the fact that most incremental employment takes the form of wage employment rather than additional unpaid household labour. The highest employment elasticities were found in the household and partnership enterprises, followed by private enterprises.[26] For the co-operative enterprises it was virtually zero, because of a relative abundance of labour to start with.

In the rural areas the employment elasticity was slightly higher than in the urban areas; 0.35 for household and 0.20 for private enterprises. The higher overall employment elasticity among the rural than among the urban enterprises was primarily due to the absence of growing co-operatives in the rural areas.

Among the declining enterprises, the employment elasticities – that is the decline in employment relative to the decline in production – present a rather more complex pattern. Generally speaking, they were as high as or higher than the employment elasticity for the growing enterprises, suggesting that enterprises that decline generally also shed labour. The elasticity was particularly high in the rural areas and among private enterprises.[27] Only among the co-operative enterprises has decline not generally been associated with a reduction in employment.

Nine out of ten enterprises in both the urban and rural areas either increased or decreased their labour force between the 1991 and 1997 surveys, while only about 10 per cent of the enterprises did not register any change in the size of their labour force (Tables 7.29–7.31).[29] The proportion of enterprises decreasing and increasing their labour force was almost equal at 44 and 47 per cent respectively. Although growing enterprises had a higher propensity to increase their labour force than

Table 7.29: Net change in labour force and wage labour force between the 1991 and 1997 surveys by location. Percentages.

	Hanoi	Haiphong	HCM City	Ha Tay	Long An
All enterprises					
Labour force:					
Decrease	46.2	42.9	42.4	50.0	35.7
Unchanged	5.1	9.5	11.9	10.9	9.5
Increase	48.7	47.6	45.7	39.1	54.8
Wage labour:					
Decrease	43.6	35.7	32.2	21.7	28.6
Unchanged	7.7	16.7	16.8	37.0	23.8
Increase	48.7	47.6	51.0	41.3	47.6
Growing enterprises					
Labour force:					
Decrease	33.3	25.0	21.4	41.7	10.5
Unchanged	3.7	8.3	10.7	8.3	10.5
Increase	63.0	66.7	67.9	50.0	79.0
Declining enterprises					
Labour force:					
Decrease	71.4	78.6	69.3	66.7	64.7
Unchanged	0.0	7.1	11.5	20.0	5.9
Increase	28.6	14.3	19.2	13.3	29.4

Note: *Growing enterprises* defined as those with a more than 2.5 per cent annual increase in value added. *Declining enterprises* refers to those with a more than 2.5-per-cent annual decline of value added.

had the declining enterprises, while the latter were more inclined to decrease their labour force than the former, this link was far from clear cut. Thus, some 28 per cent of the growing urban enterprises actually decreased their labour force, while 63 per cent increased it. Among the declining urban enterprises two-thirds reduced their labour force, while 22 per cent actually increased it (Table 7.30). The picture in the rural areas was in this regard rather similar to that in the urban areas (Table 7.31).

The pattern varied substantially between the various ownership forms of enterprises and, to a much lesser extent, between localities. A more detailed examination reveals that between 30 and 42 per cent of

Table 7.30: Net change in labour force and wage labour force in urban enterprises between the 1991 and 1997 surveys by ownership form. Percentages.

	Household	Private	Partnership	Co-operative	All urban
All enterprises:					
Labour force					
Decreased	22.0	46.8	65.4	45.2	43.6
Unchanged	19.4	8.5	3.8	3.2	9.3
Increased	58.6	44.7	30.8	51.6	47.1
Wage labour:					
Decreased	8.3	40.4	53.8	48.4	36.4
Unchanged	19.4	8.5	7.7	3.2	10.0
Increased	72.2	51.1	38.5	48.4	53.6
Growing enterprises					
Labour force:					
Decreased	4.3	30.4	41.7	38.1	26.6
Unchanged	13.0	8.7	0.0	4.8	7.6
Increased	82.6	60.9	58.3	57.1	65.8
Declining enterprises					
Labour force:					
Decreased	63.6	66.7	100.0	50.0	72.3
Unchanged	18.2	11.1	0.0	0.0	8.5
Increased	18.2	22.2	0.0	50.0	19.2

Note: *Growing enterprises* defined as those with more than 2.5-per-cent annual increase in value added. *Declining enterprises* refers to those with a more than 2.5-per-cent annual decline of value added.

the growing private, partnership and co-operative enterprises in the urban areas actually reduced their labour force, while only 57–61 per cent increased it. The combination of growth and decrease of the labour force suggests a quite dramatic restructuring of the enterprises in question in the context of increasing wages and a highly competitive environment. This conclusion is supported by the fact that the proportion of growing enterprises shedding labour was lowest in Ho Chi Minh City, where wage increases between the 1991 and 1997 surveys were much lower than in the two cities in the north. The growing household enterprises in the urban areas differed markedly from the rest in as much as very few (a mere 4 per cent) of them decreased their labour force, while no less than 83 per cent increased it. The fact that

Table 7.31: Net change in labour force and wage labour force in rural enterprises between the 1991 and 1997 surveys by ownership form. Percentages.

	Household	Private	All rural
All enterprises			
Labour force:			
Decreased	40.0	46.3	43.2
Unchanged	17.8	2.4	10.2
Increased	42.2	51.3	46.6
Wage labour:			
Decreased	8.9	41.5	25.0
Unchanged	51.1	7.3	30.7
Increased	40.0	51.2	44.3
Growing enterprises			
Labour force:			
Decreased	37.5	11.1	27.9
Unchanged	12.5	5.6	9.3
Increased	50.0	83.3	62.8
Declining enterprises			
Labour force:			
Decreased	42.9	83.3	65.6
Unchanged	28.6	0.0	12.5
Increased	28.6	16.7	21.9

Note: *Growing enterprises* defined as those with more than 2.5-per-cent annual increase in value added. *Declining enterprises* refers to those with a more than 2.5-per-cent annual decline of value added.

most of these enterprises hired little or no wage labour in the 1991 survey no doubt explains why so few shed labour.

In the rural areas it can be seen that the vast majority of the private enterprises (83 per cent) increased their labour force, while only 11 per cent reduced it (Table 7.31). Among the household enterprises, however, no less than 37.5 per cent reduced their labour force, while only half of them increased it. However, a closer look at those that reduced their labour force reveals that in the majority of cases this entailed using fewer unpaid household members in the enterprise and in only two instances did it involve a reduction of wage labour. Seen in this light, the figures are not as surprising, as it can be assumed that a large number of household members working in the enterprise at the beginning of the period may reflect a lack of alternative employment opportunities as much as a need for labour in the enterprise.

The overwhelming majority of the declining enterprises also reduced their labour force. In the urban areas, decline in production also resulted in a decrease of the labour force in 72 per cent of the cases, while in the rural areas 65 per cent of the declining enterprises also reduced their labour force. By contrast, less than 20 per cent of the declining enterprises in the urban areas and 22 per cent of those in the rural areas increased their labour force. The only exceptions to this rule were the co-operatives, where an equal number of the declining enterprises increased and decreased the labour force.

Notes

1. Generalisations of the survey results should obviously be done with some caution, as the surveys did not cover the entire country. However, the inclusion of the three main cities suggests that at least as far as the urban subset is concerned, the surveys are likely to have covered main trends in development.

2. Haiphong stands as the ‘odd man out’. As discussed in Chapter 2, it appears that restructuring in this city has largely taken the form of replacement of large, inefficient firms by smaller, but more efficient and productive enterprises.

3. By the 1997 survey, the average level of indebtedness, measured as debts per unit of asset, had increased from 3.2 to 5.4 per cent among private enterprises and from 0.2 to 0.7 per cent for household enterprises. In 1990, few enterprises had any debts.

4. Hence, the capital/labour ratio was much higher in the more recently established enterprises, particularly in Hanoi and in Ho Chi Minh City.

5. For the urban survey as a whole, the differences in size between the two age groups of enterprises were statistically significant. A t-test shows that the differences with regard to income, assets, labour force, debts and value added were significantly different between the two groups at the 1 per cent level, while the difference in value added per worker was significant at the 7 per cent level.

6. The comparisons for the partnership and co-operative enterprises should be interpreted with some caution as there were only eight partnership and nine co-operative enterprises established since 1991 in the sample.

7. White-collar workers are defined as categories A, B and C in Table 7.9.

8. Excluding state enterprises.

9. The reasons behind their closure are analysed in greater detail in Chapter

10. Three of the discontinued enterprises in Haiphong had over 100 employees in 1991.

11. One of the enterprises which had closed down in Ho Chi Minh City ostensibly had a total turnover of 25.7 billion dong (at 1990 prices) in 1990, while another enterprise had 1 billion dong in both assets and turnover in the 1991 survey.

12. The repeat survey of the enterprises surveyed in 1991 was confined to non-state manufacturing enterprises in Hanoi, Ho Chi Minh City, Haiphong and the provinces of Long and Ha Tay (previously Ha Son Binh). For details, see Chapter 1.

13. Ownership form throughout this section refers to that stated at the time of the survey in 1991.

14. There were only two co-operative enterprises in the rural sample of repeat enterprises.

15. Value added was chosen as the key indicator of growth as it was perceived to be more relevant than alternative indicators, such as total income, assets or employment. As shown below, value added generally also has the highest positive correlation with other relevant indicators.

Correlation of average annual rate of change between the 1991 and 1997 surveys, of key economic indicators.

	Value Added	Assets	Labour	Wage Labour
Urban areas				
Income	0.85*	0.49*	0.55*	0.42*
Value Added		0.57*	0.64*	0.48*
Assets			0.49*	0.40*
Labour				0.79*
Rural areas				
Income	0.85*	0.55*	0.52*	0.54*
Value Added		0.51*	0.48*	0.41‡
Assets			0.51*	0.33
Labour				0.44*

Key: * Significant at the 0.1 per cent level.
‡ Significant at the 1 per cent level.

16. The large increase in aggregate value added in this city was largely due to the very impressive performance of a few enterprises.

17. In the 1991 survey these enterprises had a combined total wage labour force of 31, i.e. less than one per enterprise.

18. Ten out of 14 fast growing co-operatives did not change ownership form.

19. It should be remembered that the co-operatives had the highest mortality rate among all the ownership forms.

20. The correlation coefficient was 0.85 for both urban and rural enterprises, at 0.1 per cent significance level.

21. For details, see Per Ronnås (1992), *Employment Generation through Private Entrepreneurship in Vietnam* (New Delhi: ILO-ARTEP / Sida), chapters 2 and 5. Also Chapter 2 in the present volume.

22. The comparison is between the sample of enterprises surveyed in 1991 and the new representative sample of enterprises surveyed in 1997. Thus, the comparison refers to changes in the population of enterprises as a whole and not to changes over time in individual enterprises. See Chapter 2 of the present volume for details.

23. Both figures refer to 1997 prices.

24. All figures are in 1997 prices.

25. *Growing enterprises* defined as all those growing by more than 2.5 per cent per year and *fast-growing enterprises* defined as those growing by more than 10 per cent per year.

26. The figure for the partnership enterprises should be interpreted with some caution, as the absolute number of enterprises involved was quite small.

27. The very high figures for the urban private enterprises are strongly influenced by a very sharp decline of employment in a few enterprises.

28. The fact that the size of the labour force remained the same in these enterprises clearly does not imply that the same workers remained in the enterprise over the period.

29. The fact that the size of the labour force remained the same in these enterprises clearly does not imply that the same workers remained in the enterprise over the period.

8

The Non-state Manufacturing Sector in Vietnam 1991–97: An Analysis of the Winners

Bhargavi Ramamurthy

Vietnam has witnessed a dynamic restructuring of its non-state enterprises in the 1990s, observable at both micro and macro levels. The 1991 survey of 923 of these enterprises and the repeat survey of 371 units in 1997 are an attempt to capture some of the micro-level dynamism. As seen in Table 8.1, a vast majority of resurveyed enterprises fall into two distinct categories: those that have grown at a very rapid pace (by more than 10 per cent per year in real terms) and those that have closed down or suffered a pronounced decline. In this chapter we shall focus on the former category, termed the 'winners' or 'fast-growing enterprises', which have recorded more than 10 per cent annual average rate of growth of value added in the inter-survey period. The analysis attempts to answer two kinds of questions. First, how have they behaved in terms of various internal and external determinants of firm survival and growth, in the 1991 and 1997 surveys, particularly in light of the changes that have occurred in the intervening period? Second, by looking at how they have behaved and changed, can we determine why some enterprises succeeded?

In achieving this goal, we also record the performance of all 'surviving enterprises' (i.e., those that had not closed down, including the fast-growing category) in the 1991 and 1997 surveys in an attempt to give the reader a perspective of the position of fast-growing units

Table 8.1: Distribution of resurveyed units by location and performance between 1991–97 surveys. Average annual percentage change of value added.

	Total	Urban				Rural		
		Hanoi	Hai-phong	HCM City	Total urban	Ha Tay	Long An	Total rural
Total	356	57	80	76	213	71	72	143
Closures	129	18	38	17	73	26	30	56
Declining	80	7	15	27	49	14	17	31
Stagnant	25	5	3	4	12	7	6	13
Growing	29	6	5	8	19	5	5	10
Fast-growing	93	21	19	20	60	19	14	33

Note: Declining, stagnant, growing and fast-growing enterprises are classified according to the annual average rate of growth of value added, which is -2.6 or more, -2.5 to 2.5%, 2.6 to 10% and more than 10% respectively in the period 1991–97. The number of resurveyed enterprises was 371, but data for computing value added were not available for 14 urban and one rural surviving units; hence the total number of enterprises came down to 356.

vis-à-vis all survivors. The analysis is also done separately for urban and rural firms; the terms 'surviving' and 'fast-growing' enterprises refer, accordingly, to urban and rural firms in their respective sections.

Urban Enterprises

The urban surveys in 1991 and 1997 were held in the three major cities in Vietnam, namely Hanoi and Haiphong in the north and Ho Chi Minh City in the south. The sample is, therefore, reasonably representative of the urban scene in Vietnam. Among the enterprises resurveyed, 34 per cent had closed down by the 1997 survey and 37 per cent had grown in excess of 2.5 per cent a year. The fast-growing enterprises accounted for 26 per cent of the whole sample and 41 per cent of the surviving enterprises (Table 8.1).

Location and Organisational Structure

The number of urban fast-growing units was 60, almost equally distributed among Hanoi, Ho Chi Minh City and Haiphong (Table 8.1). In the 1997 survey, 37 per cent of these units were household enterprises, 25 per cent co-operatives, 17 per cent were private, 13 per cent were shareholding and 8 per cent partnerships and limited liability companies.[1] Compared to the 1991 survey, 70 per cent of the fast-growing enterprises retained their original ownership forms, while 30 per cent changed. As far as transformation is concerned, the private and partnership enterprises have been most dynamic – more than 44 per cent of private and 57 per cent of partnership enterprises changed ownership forms.[2] However, 11 per cent of private and 14 per cent of partnership enterprises moved to lower categories in the hierarchy of organisational forms; they have become household enterprises. In the short run, as their growth record shows, this change does not seem to have been for the worse. However, in the long run, as formality, size and benefits from external sources could go hand in hand, this move might have to be reversed. Household enterprises and co-operatives dominated Hanoi and Haiphong, while in Ho Chi Minh City it was household and private enterprises. Five of the eight limited liability companies were located in Haiphong; eight of the ten private enterprises were located in Ho Chi Minh City. There were no partnership units in Haiphong, but there were four in Hanoi and one in Ho Chi Minh City.

Nature of Activity

In the 1991 survey the distribution of fast-growing enterprises by activity was as follows: for agro-processing there was none; for manufacturing 87 per cent; for trading 14 per cent. This distribution altered to 3, 77 and 20 per cent respectively by the 1997 survey, mainly due to the 19 per cent of enterprises that shifted their main area of activity in the intervening period. As a result, in the 1997 survey, manufacturing activity had reduced by the movement of five units, agro-processing had made its appearance, and trading units had increased by three. Ho Chi Minh City had only manufacturing units; Hanoi had apart from manufacturing also four trading units; and Haiphong was the most diversified city in terms of nature of activity, with both the agro-processing units, eight of the trading units in addition to nine manufacturing units.

Across ownership forms, in the 1991 survey, household enterprises followed by private enterprises dominated manufacturing activity, accounting for 34 and 32 per cent respectively. However, in the 1997 survey, with the movement of eight units out of private ownership forms,[3] the share of private manufacturing units decreased but was compensated by the entry of limited liability units. Thus the order of constitution was household enterprises, co-operatives and private enterprises for manufacturing activity (approximately 35, 24 and 20 per cent respectively).

Enterprise History

The stability of an enterprise and the sector as a whole may be inferred by noting how long the firms stay in operation. Particularly in the case of small entrepreneurs, being in the same or similar lines of activity can help to develop a lot of useful linkages with other firms, the government, etc., not to mention the benefits of a pool of entrepreneurial experience in dealing with production as well as organisational matters in the long run. Table 8.2 presents the age distribution of urban fast-growing enterprises and years of establishment. It is very clear from the table that a majority of enterprises were set up in the *doi moi* era; close to 60 per cent of the enterprises were set up after 1985.

Since the surveys were conducted in 1991 and 1997, the youngest enterprise in the sample was at least seven years old by the later date. As the second half of the table shows, a little more than half of the enterprises fall in the category of five to ten years of age, which means an equal amount were very young at the time of the 1991 survey. However, the proportion of older enterprises is not insignificant, with almost a quarter being in operation (and doing well) for more than 15 years. Most of these older enterprises were located either in Hanoi or Ho Chi Minh City, whereas the youngest enterprises were in Haiphong.

Household enterprises constitute a significant proportion of every age category, except for the oldest units where the co-operatives, for historical reasons, dominate. All the other ownership forms are less than 20 years old, with most units being established in the period 1981–85. Only six enterprises[4] (constituting 10 per cent of the sample) had changed owners since the 1991 survey, all through inheritance.

Further, about 22 per cent of the enterprises had changed the location of their enterprises (within the same city) since the 1991 survey; 46 per cent of them were in Haiphong, 31 per cent in Hanoi and the rest were in Ho Chi Minh City. The reasons given for changing

Table 8.2: Year of establishment and age of urban fast-growing enterprises in the 1997 survey.

Year of establishment	%	Age in the 1997 survey	%
Before 1976	11.7	Less than 5 years	0.0
1976–80	8.3	5–10 years	51.7
1981–85	21.7	11–15 years	25.0
1986	6.7	16–20 years	8.3
1987	6.7	21–25 years	5.0
1988	5.0	Over 25 years	10.0
1989	30.0		
1990	10.0		

locations were the requirement for larger premises (46 per cent), better equipped premises (15 per cent), less expensive premises (8 per cent) and no choice (31 per cent). A majority of the units that changed location of premises were involved in manufacturing (77 per cent) and were limited liability companies (39 per cent). This finding confirms that with graduation into higher ownership forms, the scale and hence the requirement for larger premises also increased.

Entrepreneurial Characteristics

Data regarding owner characteristics of enterprises were collected only from *owners* of household and private enterprises. In the urban sample, male entrepreneurs were more common in both the 1991 and 1997 surveys. The amount of women entrepreneurs increased from 24 to 30 per cent.[5] Table 8.3 presents the entrepreneurial profile in the 1997 survey of fast-growing enterprises as well as the entire cohort of surviving enterprises.

The entrepreneurial profile has changed between the two surveys for the following reasons: the six years between 1991–97 have altered the age distribution, the number of household and private enterprises has changed and finally, in a few cases, the respondents have not all been owners in the 1997 survey, even though the same units have been resurveyed. Despite these differences, most entrepreneurs in the 1997 survey belonged to the category 40–49 years, as before. The percentage in the category 50 years and older changed from 21 to 35 in the

Table 8.3: Characteristics of owner-managers of urban fast-growing enterprises in the 1997 survey.

Characteristics:	% all surviving enterprises	% fast-growing enterprises
Sex:		
Male	71.8	70.0
Female	28.2	30.0
Age:		
Mean	45.59	47.17
29 years and less	4.7	0.0
30–39 years	28.2	20.7
40–49 years	35.3	44.8
50 years and over	31.8	34.5
Education:		
4 years or less	2.4	0.0
5–7 years	18.8	30.0
8–10 years	31.8	20.0
Over 10 years	47.1	50.0
Prior experience:		
Local cadre	2.5	0.0
War veteran	2.5	12.5
State enterprise employee	5.0	0.0
Other position of responsibility	90.0	87.5
Other	0.0	0.0

1997 survey, and these entrepreneurs were mainly managing household enterprises.[6] The average age, as a result of these changes, rose from 43 to 47 years by the 1997 survey.

Half the entrepreneurs had more than ten years of education and almost nine out of ten had prior experience in a position of responsibility, not as a state enterprise employee. Across regions, the number of women entrepreneurs was equally distributed between Hanoi and Ho Chi Minh City (four in each), while only one woman entrepreneur was located in Haiphong. On the whole, it appears that the typical entrepreneur representing the fast-growing urban enterprises was male, between 40–49 years old with more than ten years of education and previous employment in a position of responsibility. The characteristics of owner-managers of fast-growing household and private enterprises are not noticeably different from those of all surviving enterprises. As Table 8.3 shows, the typical entrepreneur of a resurveyed *surviving* enterprise in the 1997 survey had exactly the same profile.

Primary Income Source

Data on income sources of the entrepreneur household were also collected from household and private enterprises only. Most enterprises were reportedly the primary income sources to the entrepreneur household (Table 8.4). Compared to the 1991 survey, we find that the importance of the enterprise to the owner-household has increased drastically; almost 70 per cent of the fast-growing enterprises were the sole income sources in the 1997 survey. These enterprises have thus transformed into more independent, commercial units. The fast-growing enterprises had also a slightly higher incidence of second income in the 1997 survey compared to all survivors, which might have helped in ploughing back enterprise earnings without diversions for household expenditure.

Further, not only have other incomes reduced, but household involvement in the enterprises in the form of unpaid household labour has also noticeably reduced; from 81 per cent in the 1991 survey to 45 per cent in the 1997 survey. Reflecting the growing importance and the performance of the enterprises, we find that 90 per cent of the household and private enterprise owners report that their household incomes have increased since the previous survey.

Scale of Operations

The urban fast-growing enterprises covered a wide range in the scale of operation, measured by initial investments and asset growth rates (Table 8.5). The average fast-growing urban enterprise invested 126 million dong at establishment, and its assets had grown to 310 million dong by the 1991 survey and to 1.6 billion dong by the 1997 survey. For the average surviving, resurveyed enterprise, these values were slightly different – 217 million dong of initial investment, reduced to 153 million dong in assets by the 1991 survey (mainly due to the declining and stagnant categories) and about a three-fold rise in assets by the 1997 survey to 657 million (mainly due to the fast-growing enterprises).

Table 8.4: Sources of household income in the 1991 and 1997 surveys. Urban enterprises.

	% all surviving enterprises		% fast-growing enterprises	
Income source:	**1991**	**1997**	**1991**	**1997**
Enterprise as sole source	52.4	76.2	31.6	70.0
Wage employment	20.7	19.6	44.7	30.0
Farming	0.7	0.0	0.0	0.0
Others	26.2	4.2	23.6	3.3

Note: Where the sum of a column is greater than 100, it implies some enterprises have more than two sources of income; where the sum is less than 100, data are not available for those units; where the sum equals 100, the enterprises have at most one additional source of income.

Whatever the initial investment (calculated in terms of gold ounces invested, at 1996 prices), most units moved to the categories over 150 million dong in assets by the 1991 survey and further to the more than 500 million category by the 1997 survey, reflecting very impressive asset growth rates. The percentage reaching this latter category by the 1997 survey was higher among fast-growing enterprises than other survivors, indicating higher growth rates. This is confirmed by Table 8.6, which clearly shows a higher percentage of fast-growers experiencing growth rates over 20 per cent per year between the two surveys. If we examine the distribution of growth rates from establishment to the 1991 survey, we find there were only a few differences between survivors and fast-growers.

Haiphong had the largest units, assets averaging 2.4 billion dong in the 1997 survey while Hanoi had the smallest units, with 1.7 billion dong (Table 8.7). The performance of enterprises with regard to asset growth rates across location and ownership forms is also given in Table 8.7. While the two sets of asset growth rates are incomparable owing to different bases, one can form an idea of the comparative performmance of each location and ownership form in each set. Ho Chi Minh City enterprises have recorded fairly steady, although lower, growth rates (between 25 and 30 per cent per year) while Haiphong and Hanoi have witnessed greater pressures to grow. This is very clear from Table 8.7, which profiles the size of the representative firm across all regions and ownership categories.

Table 8.5: Initial investment (at establishment) and total assets in 1990 and 1996. Urban enterprises. Thousand dong (all values at 1996 prices).

Investment and assets:	% all surviving enterprises	% fast-growing enterprises
Initial investment at establishment:		
1,000 and less	2.2	1.8
1,001–10,000	31.1	21.8
10,001–50,000	28.1	32.7
50,001–100,000	5.9	12.7
100,001–500,000	25.9	23.6
Over 500,000	6.7	7.3
Total assets in the 1991 survey:		
1,000 and less	0.7	0.0
1,001–25,000	14.9	16.9
25,001–75,000	12.8	10.2
75,001–100,000	4.3	8.5
100,001–150,000	14.2	8.5
150,001–500,000	29.8	32.2
Over 500,000	23.4	23.7
Total assets in the 1997 survey:		
1,000 and less	0.7	0.0
1,001–25,000	3.5	3.4
25,001–75,000	4.9	0.0
75,001–100,000	7.6	6.8
100,001–150,000	7.6	5.1
150,001–500,000	34.7	28.8
Over 500,000	41.0	55.9

Across ownership forms, household enterprises were at the lowest end of the spectrum, although they experienced the highest growth rates between the two surveys. In terms of assets, as Table 8.7 shows, the gap between household and non-household forms widened. From Tables 8.6 and 8.7 it is clear that the best performance in the period between the surveys has been from enterprises that were the weakest

Table 8.6: Distribution of annual average asset growth rates among urban enterprises. Percentages.

Nature of growth rate:	% all surviving enterprises	% fast-growing enterprises
Growth rates from establishment to 1991 survey:		
Zero	34.4	38.5
1–10%	5.2	2.6
11–20%	4.2	7.7
21–50%	19.8	20.5
51–75%	8.3	2.6
76–100%	7.3	0.0
Over 100%	20.8	28.2
Growth rates 199197 surveys:		
Negative	27.7	13.8
Zero	0.0	0.0
1–10%	10.8	3.4
11–20%	10.8	13.8
21–50%	32.3	37.9
51–75%	12.3	20.7
76–100%	4.6	6.9
Over 100%	1.5	3.4

Note: Growth rates from establishment to 1991 were calculated in terms of actual gold ounces invested between establishment and mid 1991. Growth rates 1991–97 surveys were calculated in terms of monetary value of assets (in 1996 prices) at the end of 1990 and 1996.

in the 1991 survey – Haiphong and household enterprises. A great factor in the success of the fast-growing enterprises has therefore been the capacity of enterprises to catch up with the relatively advanced areas. In this endeavour, the north has not only caught up, but has surpassed the south by the 1997 survey.

Related to capital accumulation and investments are the sources of finance for these, both at establishment and for expansion purposes. More than half of the fast-growing enterprises financed their establishment investments exclusively from their own savings/resources (Table 8.8). Clearly, banks and other formal credit institutions have not been

Table 8.7: Size structure and growth rates of the average enterprise by location and ownership form. Urban fast-growing enterprises. Thousand dong.

	Monetary value of assets		Average annual growth rates of asset (%)
	1991*	1997†	1990–96
Hanoi	214.4	1,720.0	37.7
Haiphong	360.2	2,490.0	52.3
HCM City	366.4	613.0	23.8
Household	273.9	428.3	56.0
Private	402.8	783.8	24.1
Partnership	192.6	891.4	39.4
Co-operative	312.7	1,709.7	31.0
Shareholding & LLC	–	6,083.4	59.4

Key: * Calculated in terms of investment of gold ounces in the period establishment to 1991; ownership forms refer to those stated in the 1991 survey.

† Calculated in terms of monetary values of assets at the end of 1990 and 1996; ownership forms refer to those stated in the 1997 survey.

significant sources for establishment investment. Household enterprises, as expected, accounted for most units using 100 per cent own resources (48 per cent) followed by private enterprises (34 per cent). This reliance on own resources was most prevalent in Ho Chi Minh City and was least obvious in Haiphong. This trend of very strong reliance on own resources was also found for financing investments between establishment and the 1991 survey. The second half of Table 8.8 records the distribution of sources for expansionary investment incurred between the 1991 and 1997 surveys. About 66 per cent of the units reported making major investments in machinery and equipment in this period and the sources of finance show a slightly altered pattern as far as formal financing sources are concerned. While a major chunk of the investment came from capital generated from within the firm and the entrepreneur's own resources, the percentage of units securing bank finances rose sharply from those at establishment, from under 4 per cent to 18 per cent.

The improvement is found not only in the number of units using this source, but also in the share of banks providing finance for the total

Table 8.8: Percentage distribution of investment finance by source. Urban fast-growing enterprises.

Sources:	0	1–25	26–50	51–75	76–99	100
Sources for investment at establishment:						
Own resources	15.1	3.8	5.7	9.4	11.3	54.7
Friends and family	81.8	10.9	3.6	0.0	1.8	1.8
Banks	96.4	0.0	1.8	1.8	0.0	0.0
Credit co-operatives	98.2	1.8	0.0	0.0	0.0	0.0
Local authorities	100.0	0.0	0.0	0.0	0.0	0.0
Employees	75.9	3.7	9.3	0.0	0.0	11.1
Private moneylenders	94.5	3.6	1.8	0.0	0.0	0.0
Advance from sales	100.0	0.0	0.0	0.0	0.0	0.0
Others	100.0	0.0	0.0	0.0	0.0	0.0
Sources for investment finance between surveys (1991–97):						
Own resources	2.6	5.2	5.2	7.8	2.6	76.9
Banks and other financial institutions	82.1	2.6	7.8	2.6	5.2	0.0
Loans from other sources	94.9	2.6	0.0	0.0	0.0	2.6
Interest-free loans from friends and family	94.9	2.6	2.6	0.0	0.0	0.0
Other sources	100.0	0.0	0.0	0.0	0.0	0.0

costs of improvement: 5 per cent of the fast-growing enterprises secured between 76 and 99 per cent of their investment from bank resources (Table 8.8). It is well known that banks require a track record to approve financing, and units that have been in operation for a reasonable number of years (like our sample, between 1990 and 1997) stand a better chance of securing funding than new units with no performance record. This throws a whole new light on the relationship of non-state units with the banking system. It is not only a problem of availability of bank funds, but also eligibility and access to funding that determine the extent to which the banking sector is aiding private enterprises. The more the enterprise relies on internally generated capital, the greater the pressure on short-term profits and capital accumulation. In the absence of a generous financial market, as our data show, firms with lower capital accumulation will most likely meet an early demise or stagnation.

Further, the data on expansionary investment sources show that none of the household enterprises and co-operatives benefited from the increased share of banks in the investment funding. An interesting point is that most units that secured bank assistance were located in Haiphong (71 per cent); formal financing, contrary to our expectations, has not been a feature of the more developed southern Vietnam.

Mechanisation

The high volume of investment and assets is reflected well in the degree of mechanisation among fast-growing urban enterprises. Table 8.9 presents the distribution of fast-growing as well as all resurveyed surviving enterprises in 1991 and 1997 surveys, according to the kind of machinery used. Fast-growing enterprises account for a majority of the resurveyed enterprises (43 per cent) using both power-driven and manually-operated machinery.

As Table 8.9 also shows, a clear majority of fast-growing firms (61 per cent) used both power-driven and manually-operated machinery in the manufacture of their product, in both the 1991 and 1997 surveys. The percentage using hand tools only remained at 7 per cent, while those using power-driven machinery climbed by 3.3 per cent, compensating for the corresponding fall among those who relied exclusively on manually-operated machinery. However, these 3.3 per cent enterprises are not the only ones to have changed (for the better), as the numbers show. Far from it: 25 per cent of the enterprises have changed the kind of machinery they used, and those that increased mechanisation owe it to increased investments. However, the reasons for reduced mechanisation are not very clear. The extent of mechanisation was greatest in Haiphong, followed by Ho Chi Minh City and Hanoi, in that order. Following the general trend, units using both power-driven and manually-operated machinery dominated every ownership form; none of the shareholding and limited liability companies relied solely on hand tools or manually-operated machinery.

Employment

In the period between the two surveys, wage employment increased among fast-growing enterprises (both in number as well as in proportion to total employment), particularly in the north, though not in proportion to the increase in value added. The asset base per

Table 8.9: Type of machinery used in 1991 and 1997 surveys. Urban enterprises.

	% all surviving enterprises		% fast-growing enterprises	
Type of Machinery:	**1991**	**1997**	**1991**	**1997**
Only hand tools, no machinery	8.5	4.9	6.8	6.8
Manually-operated machinery only	14.1	12.6	16.9	13.6
Power-driven machinery only	16.9	15.4	15.3	18.6
Both manually-operated and power-driven machinery	60.6	67.1	61.0	61.0

worker doubled, indicating that overall growth among these units has been attained through increased labour productivity, rather than by a major increase in employment (Table 8.10).[7]

As far as individual enterprises are concerned, 23 per cent of the fast-growing units reduced their labour force between the 1991 and 1997 surveys, 12 per cent did not change the number of wage employees, but a majority of 65 per cent of the enterprises increased their total (wage) labour force. The average increase in number of workers among firms that increased their employment since the 1991 survey (excluding two outliers who added 182 and 290 workers in Haiphong and Hanoi respectively) is 21, which is slightly higher than the average reduction (among firms that reduced their labour force) of 12 employees. This has resulted in a net increase in the number of employees to nine for a typical fast-growing enterprise. Including the two outliers, the average number of wage employees increased from 12 to 28 workers in a period of six years (Table 8.10).

In percentage terms, while the value added of the average enterprise grew at 26 per cent, its wage employment grew by 45 per cent (excluding the outliers), which indicates that employment elasticity was very high (2.4) among fast-growing units as a whole in the inter-survey period. However, a major factor responsible for this high employment elasticity is the change in the large number of units (27 per cent) that did not use any wage labour at all in the 1991 survey, thus undermining any conclusion that there has been a marked effect on total employment. It is clear from the table that fast-growing enterprises as a group were not much different from the surviving enterprises in the

Table 8.10: Wage employment in the 1991 and 1997 surveys. Urban enterprises.

	% all surviving enterprises		% fast-growing enterprises	
No. of wage employees:	**1991**	**1997**	**1991**	**1997**
0	22.9	7.1	26.7	6.7
1–10	34.3	54.3	35.1	50.0
11–25	25.0	21.4	16.1	18.3
26–50	16.4	10.0	22.1	13.3
51–70	0.0	0.7	0.0	1.7
Over 70	1.4	6.4	0.0	10.0
Mean	*12.9*	*20.1*	*12.2*	*28.1*

1991 survey; by the 1997 survey, the average fast-growing enterprise had only slightly more employees than its counterpart survivor.

Not surprisingly, household enterprises accounted for 75 per cent of the units without wage labour; the maximum number of wage employees was nine for this category. The co-operatives were the largest employers; their average number comprised 28 workers. Across cities, surprisingly, Ho Chi Minh City had the largest number of enterprises working without wage labour (35 per cent) and also had the greatest number of enterprises in the second category (one to ten wage workers). Haiphong dominated the third category (11–25 workers) and Hanoi had some of the largest employers. In the 1997 survey, shareholding and limited liability companies along with co-operatives were the biggest employers, employing more than 70 workers, while the other ownership forms continued their previous performances.

As a result of the increase in the number of wage employees hired, the percentage of wage workers in proportion to the total labour force rose from 62 per cent in the 1991 survey to 81 per cent in the 1997 survey among fast-growing enterprises. Relative to the numbers employed, Haiphong had, on average, the highest percentage of wage employment in the 1997 survey, followed by Ho Chi Minh City and Hanoi.

Production Flexibility

In this section we shall describe the production flexibility among firms in terms of changes to their product mix in the two years prior to the 1991 survey and thereafter. The data show improvements undertaken as well as the introduction of new products. According to Table 8.11, firms have displayed more flexibility since the 1991 survey. However, it should be remembered that the latter time-frame (1991–97) is longer. In the period 1989–91, roughly half of the fast-growing enterprises introduced some form of change (either new products or improvements to existing products). Of these, 26 per cent introduced new products only, 33 per cent only made improvements to existing products, and the remaining 41 per cent introduced both types of changes.

The introduction of changes was most common in Ho Chi Minh City and among private enterprises. By the 1997 survey, the percentage introducing either of the changes rose to 72, of which 51 per cent implemented both types of changes, 16 per cent introduced new products only, and the remaining 33 per cent only made improvements to existing products.

Hanoi was most flexible, Ho Chi Minh was least flexible and co-operatives and shareholding and limited liability companies (in terms of highest flexibility) replaced the private enterprises. In fact, household enterprises followed only slightly behind in the introduction of new products; they led all the other ownership forms in terms of making improvements to existing products. Another finding is that firms established after 1985 (especially in 1989) have made the maximum changes to the product mix. Their percentage was somewhat lower in the 1991 survey, probably because the enterprises were too young at that time to be changing their products.

As Table 8.11 also shows, the reasons for undertaking changes have altered significantly for all enterprises, including fast-growing enterprises. In the 1991 survey most changes were made in order to overcome a difficulty in selling existing products. However, in the later survey the changes were mostly undertaken in response to purchaser requests. Since many of the units were still young in the 1991 survey, they had not yet achieved a performance record. However, six years later, they had probably established themselves in the market so that their product mix was steady and the only changes that were made were reflections of evolving customer tastes. If this is the case, then it is a very strong indicator of the improvement in the reliability and stability in the output markets for these enterprises. For mature, low-

Table 8.11: Product changes and their impact in the 1991 and 1997 surveys. Urban enterprises.

	% all surviving enterprises		% fast-growing enterprises	
	1991	**1997**	**1991**	**1997**
Introduced new products	34.0	49.0	30.0	50.0
Made improvements to existing products	38.2	52.0	33.3	58.3
Reason for change:				
Difficult to sell current product	37.5	31.1	48.0	34.5
Increasing competition from producers	30.6	18.9	24.0	13.8
Increasing competition from imports	5.6	6.8	4.0	0.0
Requested by purchasers	12.5	36.5	20.0	48.3
Other	6.9	6.8	4.0	3.4
Degree of success:				
Unsuccessful	4.3	1.4	4.3	3.4
Not very successful	8.7	21.6	8.7	6.9
Quite successful	65.2	63.5	60.9	75.9
Very successful	21.7	12.2	26.1	10.3
Too early to tell	0.0	1.4	0.0	3.4

Note: The 1991 survey referred to product changes in the 1989–91 period, while the 1997 survey referred to product changes in the 1991–97 period.

risk enterprises with a well-established market, most changes will not be initiated to change this relationship with a stable market unless the firms plan a drastic change in their mode of operations.

That there was a drastic reduction in the number of firms that felt increasing competition from domestic producers in this period also strengthens our argument that most of these fast-growing enterprises have established themselves in the output markets. The optimism surrounding these changes correlates well with the main reason for change. When the change is a result of customer requests, the degree of success is high, as opposed to changes initiated by the producer (where success is by no means as certain). The optimism of entrepreneurs was slightly tempered by the time of the 1997 survey, though the number that believed the changes were unsuccessful had dropped among fast-growing enterprises. For the surviving enterprises as a whole, the number of pessimists increased by the 1997 survey, owing to the declining and stagnant categories of enterprises.

Continuity of Operations

For sustained long-term profits and reliable employment generation, continuous functioning of an enterprise is of paramount importance. Discontinuous operations imply instability in both internal and external conditions and, in this context, we find that the overall environment has been more stable in the 1997 than in the 1991 survey, as Table 8.12 shows. The percentage of fast-growing enterprises that operated throughout the year increased significantly from 59 to 88 by the 1997 survey.[8]

Though the average period of closure for the remaining enterprises has remained at 2.7 months in both years, we find that the maximum period of closure has come down from six to four months. The lack of demand, however, narrowed down from being the main reason to the only reason in the 1997 survey. Improved continuity in operations is true in the case of all surviving enterprises also (Table 8.12). The difference between fast-growing enterprises and all surviving enterprises, which was significant in the earlier survey, had reduced by the 1997 survey. The number of fast-growing enterprises with discontinuous operations was seven in the 1991 survey; hence no generalisation is attempted.

Capacity Utilisation

Related to the extent of the problem of lack of demand is the extent of production capacity utilisation. As Table 8.13 shows, the percentage of fast-growing units operating at full capacity doubled by the 1997 survey. This is in conformity with the decrease in the number of units that reported a lack of demand in the 1997 survey and consequently shut down operations temporarily. This growing percentage of enterprises operating at or near full capacity reflects better and more stable output market conditions. None of the industries reported input market problems in either survey, indicating that stability in input markets has continued in the period between the two surveys. The increasing capacity utilisation becomes even more significant when we recall that most units (66 per cent) have made major additions to machinery and equipment and the annual average asset growth rate[9]

Table 8.12: Continuity of operations in the 1991 and 1997 surveys. Urban enterprises.

Months operated and reasons for closure:	% all surviving enterprises		% fast-growing enterprises	
	1991	1997	1991	1997
Operated throughout the year*	66.9	86.1	59.2	88.3
Closed for:				
1 month	8.1	1.4	8.2	0.0
2 months	11.3	4.2	10.2	5.0
3 months	6.5	3.5	12.2	5.0
4 months	3.2	2.8	4.1	1.7
5 months	1.6	0.0	4.1	0.0
6 months	0.8	2.1	2.0	0.0
Over 6 months	1.6	0.0	0.0	0.0
Reasons for closure:				
Lack of raw material	7.9	5.3	0.0	0.0
Lack of demand	60.5	89.4	70.0	100.0
Other reasons	31.6	5.3	30.0	0.0

Key: *The 1991 survey refers to the whole year of 1990 and the 1997 survey refers to the whole year of 1996. **Note:** Percentages for reasons for closure are based on the number of units that did not operate throughout the year. Enterprises established in 1990 have been excluded from calculations for the 1991 survey columns only.

has been 38 per cent for a typical urban fast-growing enterprise. Thus, it is clear that these enterprises attained capacity utilisation of machinery and equipment owned in the 1991 survey, as well as the additions since then.

Despite this rising number, almost 36 per cent of the (fast-growing) sample reported they could increase their production by 25 to 50 per cent. Among the units that had full capacity utilisation in the 1991 survey, 60 per cent reported under-utilisation in the 1997 survey, most likely due to the additional capacity they created in the intervening six years. At the other end, most units that expressed a belief in the 1991 survey that their capacity utilisation could be doubled, later went on to improve their performance (22 per cent of them even reported full capacity utilisation) in the 1997 survey. As Table 8.13 shows, the higher capacity utilisation in the second survey is spread among the entire set of surviving enterprises, with minor differences.

Table 8.13: Capacity utilisation in the 1991 and 1997 surveys. Urban enterprises.

	% all surviving enterprises		% fast-growing enterprises	
Extent of utilisation:	**1991**	**1997**	**1991**	**1997**
Operating at full capacity	9.9	13.3	8.9	16.4
If employing all machinery & equipment, can increase production by:				
Up to 10%	10.7	14.1	10.7	14.5
11–25%	23.7	19.3	14.3	18.2
26–50%	26.0	34.1	28.6	36.4
51–100%	16.8	11.9	17.9	12.7
Over 100%	13.0	7.4	19.6	1.8

We find that capacity utilisation is best among those enterprises which had an initial investment of 10 to 50 million dong (in 1996 prices) and among those with annual asset growth rates higher than 20 per cent. Across regions, capacity utilisation was most homogeneous (and efficient) in Hanoi, where 59 per cent of the enterprises reported working at 50 to 75 per cent of their capacity, and all the other units had even better utilisation. Ho Chi Minh City also had most units belonging to this category (35 per cent), and the least percentage (5) operating at full capacity. Haiphong registered a very mixed performance.

Across ownership forms, household enterprises and co-operatives reported the best rates of capacity utilisation and the former group was also the most diverse in terms of the rates. None of the private and partnership enterprises operated at full capacity, and the co-operatives generally performed best on this count. This situation is similar to the 1991 survey except that Ho Chi Minh City enterprises and co-operatives have witnessed the greatest transformations. Haiphong had the greatest number of enterprises operating at full capacity even then, and Hanoi had the most homogeneous enterprises (a quarter of its enterprises reported operating at a minimum of 90 per cent capacity). It is clear that, on the whole, the urban enterprise in the 1997 survey was operating closer to its capacity compared to the 1991 survey.

Forward Linkages

Forward linkages of enterprises are measured here by the destination of main product sales, in terms of category and location of buyers. From the data on category of buyers in Table 8.14, the following observations may be noted. First, there is ample evidence of changes in the main category of 'buyer' between the 1991 and 1997 surveys – private enterprises replaced individuals as the main customers of the average fast-growing urban enterprise in the latter survey. The percentages of sales of the main product (of the average enterprise) to individual buyers and private enterprises were 34 and 25 per cent in the earlier survey, and they changed to 28 and 44 per cent respectively, in the latter.[10] Second, significant changes also occurred in the enterprises' linkages with the state sector – 53 per cent of the enterprises sold a certain percentage of their main product to the state sector (including state enterprises and other state agencies) in the 1991 survey and this reduced significantly to 40 per cent by the 1997 survey. The percentage of enterprises selling exclusively to the state also halved in this period, from 18 to 9 per cent. Third, while sales to tourists had ceased by the 1997 survey (only 2 per cent of the enterprises sold 25–49 per cent in the 1991 survey), the share of exports increased noticeably, from 2.6 per cent to 4.4 per cent of the main product sales, in the average enterprise. However, the 2 per cent of units that exported all of their main products in the earlier survey have since diversified in favour of other domestic categories.

The significance of these linkages is clearer when we consider the nature of the main products. A majority of the enterprises traded in light engineering and consumer goods (including spare parts, aluminium and glass items, detergents, electrical wires, etc.); other products were medical equipment and devices, furniture, handicrafts, garments and construction materials. Since most of these are goods of everyday consumption by the population, we find that most sales are within the same town. However, as the second half of Table 8.14 shows, the linkages with the location of sales have also altered. The average enterprise sold 77 per cent of its main product within the same city in the 1991 survey and this dropped to 58 per cent in the 1997 survey. Also, the number of enterprises selling exclusively within the same town dropped from 58 to 45 per cent in the same period. The share of other rural and urban areas (in the sales distribution of the average enterprise) doubled correspondingly; from about 9 per cent each in the 1991 survey, to 18 per cent each in the 1997 survey. On the whole, it is clear that the urban fast-growing enterprises have displayed

Table 8.14: Forward linkages of main product in 1991 and 1997 surveys. Urban fast-growing enterprises. Percentages.

Destination and location	0	1–24	25–49	50–74	75–99	100	Mean
Destination of main product sales 1991 survey:							
Individual buyers	46.9	12.2	8.2	8.2	4.1	20.4	*33.7*
Private enterprises	57.1	2.0	20.4	4.1	4.1	12.2	*25.3*
State enterprises	59.2	2.0	10.2	4.1	6.1	18.4	*29.3*
Other state agency	87.8	4.1	2.0	2.0	0.0	4.1	*6.3*
Local authority	98.0	0.0	0.0	2.0	0.0	0.0	*1.2*
Tourists	98.0	0.0	2.0	0.0	0.0	0.0	*0.9*
Export	95.9	0.0	2.0	0.0	0.0	2.0	*2.7*
Other	98.0	2.0	0.0	0.0	0.0	0.0	*0.5*
Destination of main product sales 1997 survey:							
Individual buyers	49.1	22.6	3.8	0.0	3.8	20.8	*28.2*
Private enterprises	41.5	5.7	5.7	11.3	15.1	20.8	*43.7*
State enterprises	60.4	15.1	9.4	1.9	3.8	9.4	*19.0*
Other state agency	100.0	0.0	0.0	0.0	0.0	0.0	*0.0*
Local authority	96.2	0.0	1.9	0.0	0.0	1.9	*2.6*
Tourists	100.0	0.0	0.0	0.0	0.0	0.0	*0.0*
Export	92.5	0.0	3.8	1.9	1.9	0.0	*4.4*
Other	98.1	0.0	0.0	0.0	0.0	1.9	*1.9*
Geographical distribution of main product sales 1991 survey:							
Same town	6.3	6.3	8.3	14.6	6.3	58.3	*76.7*
Other rural	75.0	6.3	10.4	4.2	4.2	0.0	*8.9*
Other urban	75.0	8.3	12.5	2.1	0.0	2.1	*9.5*
Elsewhere	93.8	0.0	2.1	0.0	0.0	4.2	*4.9*
Geographical distribution of main product sales 1997 survey:							
Same town	26.4	7.5	1.9	17.0	1.9	45.3	*58.1*
Other rural	67.9	1.9	9.4	13.2	3.8	3.8	*17.8*
Other urban	67.9	5.7	7.5	7.5	3.8	7.5	*17.8*
Elsewhere	84.9	3.8	5.7	3.8	1.9	0.0	*6.3*

a significant amount of adaptability (especially with regard to the state sector) and have diversified their sales not only in terms of selling to more categories of buyers, but also in terms of selling to outside locations as well. Their forward linkages definitely diversified, and to that extent, improved in the period between the two surveys.

On the whole, we notice that household enterprises have displayed the most remarkable diversity in linkages in both years and that their behaviour patterns have not changed much (except for the inclusion of exports in the 1997 survey). They sold to almost every category of buyers and the proportions altered only slightly in the six inter-survey years. The co-operatives have undergone major adaptations, halving the share of exports and increasing sales to the state sector and private enterprises. Regarding the geographical location of sales, percentage sales in the same town of the average household and partnership enterprise declined, while that of the private and co-operative enterprise increased. It is, therefore, clear that the diversity in linkages has not only increased in terms of categories of buyers, but also in terms of increasing the reach of the products in terms of geographical location; and the performance of household and co-operative enterprises stand out, in this respect. This adaptation is seen in all the three cities. Ho Chi Minh City behaved a bit unlike the other two (it increased its sales to individual buyers[11] and reduced the share of private enterprises); all three reduced the share of state sector overall between the two surveys. All exporting units were located in Ho Chi Minh City in the 1991 survey, but were also seen in the other two by the 1997 survey. Linkages with the state were highest in Haiphong in both years, it was least in Hanoi in the 1997 survey and in Ho Chi Minh City in the 1991 survey. The high growth of the urban fast-growing enterprises has been accompanied by extending the reach of both buyers and their location.

Backward Linkages

Backward linkages describe the role of enterprises in creating demand for inputs, which form the output of other supplying agents. The extent of backward linkages, thus, also determines the usefulness of enterprises in creating income and employment among these supplying agents. The greater the linkages to the local economy, the greater is the symbiotic relationship between providers of inputs and output which help in their mutual growth. However, very high backward linkages to the local economy could also mean that (national) markets are segmented, with the result that the industries have no choice but to depend on the local suppliers, even though it means encouraging inefficient production. Typical factors causing segmented markets include poor infrastructure, insufficient information, high transport costs, etc. The nature of inputs also determines the extent of backward linkages with the local economy. In our sample of urban fast-growing enterprises the main raw materials ranged from iron and steel, sand, paper, chemicals, rubber, timber, leather etc. to bread flour. Agro-processing industries were few, and so the share of manufacturing inputs was higher.

Table 8.15 presents the nature of backward linkages of fast-growing enterprises in the 1991 and 1997 surveys in terms of the category of main input suppliers and their location. From this table we find that the linkages have varied only slightly between the surveys except for the drastic reduction in the share of households (from 33 to 5 per cent) and a corresponding increase in the share of private enterprises (20 to 59 per cent) as suppliers to the average enterprise. These changes have not resulted from changes in the kind of inputs purchased; the main inputs listed above were common to both 1991 and 1997 surveys. Rather, it reflects the overall proliferation of private enterprises in the cities (true of all of Vietnam, too) and the possible transformation of many household sales into registered formal enterprise transactions.

Also noticeable in Table 8.15 is the reduced dependence on the state sector for main raw materials – the number of enterprises buying from the state sector reduced from 41 per cent in the 1991 survey to 26 in the 1997 survey, the major change is among units that bought solely from the state before. While there is this noticeable change in the categories of input suppliers, their location has not significantly altered, strengthening the earlier statement that household sales might have transformed into private enterprise transactions. Even though the percentage of enterprises buying solely from the same town reduced from 88 to 81 per cent between the 1991 and 1997 surveys, the overall share of local suppliers in the purchases of the average enterprise dominated other locations in both years, falling by 4 percentage points. An important development is the increase in the share of other rural suppliers, which implies that the success of these urban enterprises trickles down better to the rural areas. On the whole, the enterprises appear to be more reliant on a single source, but less reliant on a single location; they are buying more from fewer categories of input suppliers

Table 8.15: Backward linkages of main raw material in the 1991 and 1997 surveys. Urban fast-growing enterprises. Percentages.

Supplier and location	0	1–24	25–49	50–74	75–99	100	Mean
Main input supplier 1991 survey:							
Individuals	50.0	3.7	1.9	7.4	3.7	33.3	*42.2*
Private enterprises	61.0	7.4	3.7	5.6	1.9	20.4	*27.4*
State enterprises	68.5	1.9	3.7	9.3	3.7	13.0	*22.2*
Other state agency	90.7	1.9	1.9	1.9	1.9	1.9	*5.7*
Collective farms	98.1	1.9	0.0	0.0	0.0	0.0	*0.2*
Other	96.3	1.9	0.0	0.0	0.0	1.9	*2.2*
Main input supplier 1997 survey:							
Individuals	82.8	1.7	1.7	6.9	1.7	5.2	*11.9*
Private enterprises	13.8	5.2	5.2	12.1	5.2	58.6	*72.7*
State enterprises	74.1	5.2	6.9	5.2	0.0	8.6	*14.9*
Other state agency	100	0.0	0.0	0.0	0.0	0.0	*0.0*
Collective farms	96.6	3.4	0.0	0.0	0.0	0.0	*0.4*
Other	100.0	0.0	0.0	0.0	0.0	0.0	*0.0*
Location of main input supplier 1991 survey:							
Same town	4.0	0.0	4.0	2.0	2.0	88.0	*92.2*
Other rural	96.0	2.0	0.0	0.0	0.0	2.0	*2.2*
Other urban	92.0	0.0	0.0	6.0	0.0	2.0	*5.6*
Elsewhere	100.0	0.0	0.0	0.0	0.0	0.0	*0.0*
Location of main input supplier 1997 survey:							
Same town	5.2	0.0	5.2	6.9	1.7	81.0	*88.3*
Other rural	93.1	0.0	0.0	5.2	0.0	1.7	*4.8*
Other urban	87.9	3.4	3.4	3.4	0.0	1.7	*5.2*
Elsewhere	98.3	0.0	0.0	0.0	0.0	1.7	*1.7*

but the locations are more diverse. The reducing importance of households and state has increased the reliance on private enterprises, but the geographical reach has widened significantly.

Across ownership forms, in the 1997 survey, household enterprises (especially in Ho Chi Minh City) had the greatest tendency to buy from other households, while non-household forms relied on private enterprises. Surprisingly, an equal number of private enterprises, shareholding and limited liability companies and co-operatives bought from the state sector. However, relative to the total numbers in each category, shareholding and limited liability companies had the strongest linkages to the state sector, followed by private and lastly the co-operatives. They were mainly located in Hanoi and Haiphong. This scenario has changed slightly since the 1991 survey, when household enterprises in Haiphong bought mainly from households, while non-household firms in Ho Chi Minh City and Haiphong bought primarily from private enterprises. The linkages of co-operatives and private enterprises, particularly in Hanoi, were greatest with the state sector.

Horizontal Linkages

Subcontracting relationships were the only form of horizontal linkages measured in both 1991 and 1997 surveys. Used synonymously here, the data on urban enterprises reveal very poor and reduced horizontal linkages in the inter-survey period. The number of subcontracting units halved from 14 to seven in this period, and only one of the 14 units[12] continued subcontracting until the 1997 survey. However, a major reason for this drop is the narrower definition used for subcontracting in the second survey.[13] As a result of this, a comparison between the two years is not attempted.

The units subcontracting in the 1997 survey were three household enterprises (two in Hanoi and one in Ho Chi Minh City), two co-operatives (in Hanoi and Ho Chi Minh City) and one private enterprise (in Ho Chi Minh City) and a limited liability company (in Haiphong). The main subcontracting partner was a private enterprise in the same town for five units, the remaining two were linked to a state enterprise and a foreign company. All the subcontracting units had at least two partners, while two units had three partners. The duration of the contracts in the survey ranged from one to twelve months. The effects of short-term contracts seem to have been offset by an increase in the number of partners. The major form of assistance was in procuring raw material (as secured by five units); one other unit received managerial assistance. From the above description, it is clear that subcontracting linkages were not significant in the 1997 survey.

Production Relations

Production relations describe the client–producer contracts. Generally, the fewer the number of customers, the greater the incidence of

Table 8.16: Production relations in the 1991 and 1997 surveys. Urban enterprises.

	% all surviving enterprises		% fast-growing enterprises	
Nature of relations:	**1991**	**1997**	**1991**	**1997**
No. of annual customers:				
1	8.1	2.1	7.3	3.3
2–10	30.9	30.1	36.4	21.7
More than 10	61.0	67.8	56.4	75.0
Production on advance order:				
Never	18.8	22.7	20.8	18.6
Sometimes	25.8	47.5	39.6	55.9
Always or almost always	30.5	16.3	23.5	13.6
Subcontracting	25.0	13.5	27.5	11.9

producing on advance order. In our fast-growing sample, Table 8.16 shows that since the 1991 survey, the number of annual customers increased but so has the tendency to produce on advance order. Since the increase in annual customers has been in the more-than-ten category, it is reasonable that the frequency of always producing on advance order has fallen; and the units that occasionally produce on advance order have increased. With an increase in the volume of customers, the impact of a purchaser breaching the contract is smaller on the producer; hence the lesser reliance on advance orders. Another factor in explaining this relationship is the size of the enterprise. If the productive capacity and working capital of the unit are quite high, it is possible to manufacture and create stocks whereby production time is substantially reduced when the customer arrives. This practice also reduces the frequency of producing on advance order. Elsewhere (see Table 8.17), only a third of the units have mentioned problems with shortage of capital in the 1997 survey, which supports our conclusion that the presence of stocks might have caused the lesser reliance on advance orders.

Almost all the fast-growing trading and commercial units sold to more than ten customers,[14] while manufacturing units had the greatest propensity to sell to under ten customers. This trend is similar to the 1991 survey, except for the larger percentage of manufacturing units selling to one customer only. Across cities, sales to one customer only was characteristic of Hanoi in the 1991 survey, but it reduced to one unit each in Hanoi and Haiphong in the 1997 survey. Sales to between two and ten customers were more common in Ho Chi Minh City in the later survey, though almost equally distributed in the former survey. Most units in the 1997 survey sold to more than ten customers, but in the 1991 survey, selling to under ten customers was more common among co-operatives and private enterprises. There are no noticeable differences between the fast-growing enterprises, discussed so far, and the whole set of surviving enterprises.

Constraints

The respondents' perceptions of the main constraints to the growth of the enterprise were collected in both the surveys. The nature of the growth of fast-growing enterprises in the intervening six years had noticeably altered these perceptions by the 1997 survey. Shortage of capital leads the list of main constraints in both years but the number of enterprises citing it fell from 41 to 33 percent by the time of the 1997 survey (Table 8.17). This reduction has probably been the result of the high rate of internally generated capital between the 1991 and 1997 surveys and the greater access and use of external formal financing for investments in the same period (see the section on scale of operations). The next major constraint was too much competition, in line with the 1991 survey. Two new constraints have appeared – lack of raw materials[15] (1.7 per cent) and lack of premises or industrial space (10 per cent, equally distributed in Ho Chi Minh City and Haiphong, indicating growth pains).

As the enterprises have grown at high rates, their output has risen correspondingly and hence the need for growing markets. The shortage of markets becomes more acute when the proliferation of private sector industries continues at the rate found in Vietnam. Hence it is understandable that markets and competition have become more serious constraints for enterprises; that their forward linkages are expanding is proof of their efforts to adapt to the changing situation.

Interestingly, the constraints mentioned by fast-growing enterprises were more homogeneous in the south. No enterprise in Ho Chi Minh City mentioned shortage of capital as a main constraint; competition (55 per cent) and limited demand (25 per cent) were most frequently cited in the 1997 survey. Haiphong continued to lead the

Table 8.17: Main constraint to enterprise growth, in the 1991 and 1997 surveys. Urban enterprises.

	% all surviving enterprises		% fast-growing enterprises	
Nature of the constraint:	**1991**	**1997**	**1991**	**1997**
Shortage of capital	42.1	34.7	41.4	33.3
Cannot afford to hire wage labour	2.9	0.7	1.7	0.0
Lack of technical know-how	2.1	2.8	3.4	1.7
Limited demand for products	15.7	18.1	15.0	18.3
Too much competition	12.9	24.3	15.0	25.0
Lack of marketing and transport facilities	5.0	0.0	3.4	0.0
Lack of modern machinery/equipment	5.7	3.5	10.3	3.3
Lack of raw materials	1.4	0.7	0.0	1.7
Lack of energy	4.3	0.0	3.4	0.0
Uncertain government policies	2.1	2.8	1.7	1.7
Inadequate premises/space	0.0	8.3	0.0	10.0
Other	5.7	2.1	3.4	1.7
No constraint	0.0	2.1	0.0	3.3

cities in terms of the frequency of capital constraints (along with Hanoi). Across ownership forms, shortage of capital was felt by an equal number of household enterprises and shareholding and limited liability companies in the 1997 survey. However, while capital shortage was almost the only constraint mentioned by two-thirds of the latter; competition proved a greater constraint to household enterprises. Overall, we notice that contrary to expectations, the problem of lack of capital has been less common among household enterprises, and its severity has decreased in the last six years. While there is evidence of adaptability among all these urban units, more efforts are needed to break the extreme reliance on local markets and the concomitant growing number of producers within the same markets.

Competition

Confirming the growing importance of competition as a constraint, data show that the number of fast-growing enterprises that feel there are too many enterprises producing similar goods and services was high in both 1991 and 1997 surveys (at 58 and 60 per cent respectively). However, an interesting development is in the perception of the intensity of the competition – the percentage of enterprises that experienced 'severe' competition actually reduced from 70 to 42.[16] About 56 per cent of the enterprises experienced severe competition from private enterprises in the 1991 survey but the number reduced drastically to 15 per cent in the 1997 survey. Across cities, Haiphong registered the least incidence of severe competition; Hanoi and Ho Chi Minh City had an equal number of firms mentioning severe competition. In the 1997 survey, competition from private enterprises was felt most in Hanoi while competition from state enterprises was more common in Ho Chi Minh City. Interestingly, the firms that felt most threatened by state enterprises were (four) co-operatives, followed by (three) private enterprises. Limited liability companies mentioned severe competition the least among ownership categories.

Government Assistance

At the time of establishment, almost 67 per cent of the fast-growing enterprises received government assistance. The most common forms of support, in ranked order, were: completing application procedures (70 per cent); tax exemptions (35 per cent); recommendations on line of business (25 per cent); introductions to state enterprises or organisations for collaboration (18 per cent); assistance in the set-up and organisation of the enterprise (13 per cent); and help in procuring machinery (10 per cent). Most units received assistance in more than one category. While some forms of assistance like tax exemptions and application procedures fall fully within the 'formal' purview of the state, we do not know if informal ties with government officials played a part in securing assistance in other areas.

Further, the number of enterprises reporting government assistance rose dramatically between the 1991 and 1997 surveys, indicating that many enterprises benefited from government assistance in the intervening period. In the 1991 survey, only ten units reported procuring assistance while this number rose to 26 in the 1997 survey. The most common form of assistance reported in the 1991 survey was in solving managerial difficulties, procuring inputs and marketing. In the later survey, however, legal advice topped the list (42 per cent). That most of this legal advice has been received by co-operatives and limited liability companies is, no doubt, related to the issues of transformation of ownership forms; this also highlights the role of the government in assisting private sector units in their transition process.

The data on enterprises receiving assistance indicate that enterprises on either extremes of the scale had the lowest tendency toward obtaining government assistance. This is true of assistance both at start-up and during the lifetime of the enterprise. Further, government assistance at start-up was most common in Hanoi, followed by Ho Chi Minh City and Haiphong. Hanoi continued to lead the other two with regard to assistance at other times, but Ho Chi Minh City entrepreneurs obtained the least assistance. It is apparent that while legal and bureaucratic assistance in forming and establishing the enterprise was received, help in other areas (e.g. marketing, inputs, workers etc.) has not been very significant. Either the enterprises did not seek advice in these matters or the officials had no way of rendering assistance in these areas. Even when they did assist, slightly larger enterprises (but not the largest) seemed to be better placed to take advantage of government support.

Rural Enterprises

The overall growth performance among rural resurveyed units in the inter-survey period was quite polarised. By the 1997 survey, 40 per cent of the enterprises surveyed in 1991 had closed down and 30 per cent of the enterprises had been growing at a rate over 2.5 per cent per year (See Table 8.1). The category of fast-growing rural enterprises (which grew in excess of 10 per cent a year), in fact, comprised 23 per cent of the whole rural sample resurveyed in 1997, and an overwhelming 77 per cent of the enterprises which grew over 2.5 per cent a year between the 1991 and 1997 surveys.

Location and Organisational Structure

As shown in Table 8.1, the number of rural fast-growing enterprises resurveyed was 33, and these were slightly more concentrated in Ha Tay than Long An. There was a clear dominance of household enterprises in the 1997 survey; non-household firms accounted for only a third of the whole sample. Specifically, the share of household enterprises was 67 per cent, followed by private enterprises (27 per cent) and a partnership and a co-operative (accounting for 3 per cent each). This lack of diversity in the 1997 survey shows that the extent of change in the inter-survey period in terms of organisational struc-ture of firms was very small. In the 1991 survey, the situation was even more polarised; there were only household enterprises (78 per cent) and private enterprises (22 per cent). In the intervening period, about seven enterprises changed ownership forms, six for the better.[17] All the new ownership forms were found in Ha Tay, while Long An continued to host only household and private enterprises.[18]

Nature of Activity

Manufacturing industry dominated the activities of rural fast-growing enterprises in both the 1991 and 1997 surveys. In percentage terms, 60, 16 and 24 per cent of the enterprises were involved in manufacturing, agro-processing and services in the 1991 survey and this distribution altered to 67, 18 and 15 per cent respectively by the 1997 survey. Ha Tay had only manufacturing (89 per cent) and agro-processing units (11 per cent) in 1997. Long An recorded greater diversity in the nature of business activity in the 1997 survey. Manufacturing and services (e.g. repair shops, catering, transport etc.) accounted for 36 per cent (each) of the enterprises there; the remaining 28 per cent were in the business of agro-processing.

A total of 11 units changed their lines of activity between the two surveys, ten in Long An and one in Ha Tay. It appears that there were more changes in Ha Tay in ownership forms while Long An witnessed most changes in lines of activity. Changes in both ownership form and lines of activity have been more common among household enterprises (in their 1991 survey form), reflecting their larger numbers in the sample.

Enterprise History

The increasingly liberal environment for the private sector in Vietnam, since the 1980s, is well reflected in the dates of establishment of rural enterprises. A large number of enterprises (34 per cent) were set up in 1990 and so were only one year old at the time of the 1991 survey (Table 8.18). The table also shows that a majority of

Table 8.18: Year of establishment and age of rural enterprises.

Year of establishment	%	Age in 1997 survey	%
Before 1976	12.5	Less than 5 years	0.0
1976–80	0.0	5–10 years	68.8
1981–85	12.5	11–15 years	18.8
1986	6.3	16–20 years	0.0
1987	6.3	21–25 years	3.1
1988	15.6	More than 25 years	9.3
1989	12.5		
1990	34.4		

enterprises were set up during the late 1980s. Correspondingly, the second half of Table 8.18 shows that close to 70 per cent of the enterprises were less than ten years old in the 1997 survey, indicating that they were very young in 1991.[19] The period before 1976 accounts for the establishment of nearly 13 per cent of the enterprises. Household enterprises have historically been the oldest and most dominant form of organisation among fast-growing rural enterprises. Their importance has not diminished even after other ownership forms emerged during the 1980s; a third of them were set up in 1990. It is thus clear that the fastest-growing units were established in the *doi moi* era and were, typically, less than three years old in the 1991 survey and between five and ten years old in the 1997 survey.

Entrepreneurial Characteristics

Data on entrepreneurial characteristics were collected from owners of household and private enterprises only, which covered all but two units among rural fast-growers. The profiles of entrepreneurs from the two surveys (Table 8.19) differ slightly because the number of household and private enterprises reduced from 33 to 31 units by the 1997 survey;[20] moreover the 1991 survey data covered all the units' owners, while in the 1997 survey some of the respondents of household and private enterprises were only managers and hence were excluded from tabulations on entrepreneurial characteristics. The percentage of male entrepreneurs among fast-growing enterprises increased from 76 to 85 in the period 1991–97. However, the average

Table 8.19: Characteristics of rural owner-managers in the 1997 survey.

Characteristics:	% all surviving enterprises	% fast-growing enterprises
Sex:		
Male	78.0	77.4
Female	22.0	22.6
Age:		
Mean (years)	48.23	42.90
29 years or under	13.8	15.4
30–39 years	13.8	19.2
40–49 years	32.2	42.3
50 years or more	40.2	23.1
Education:		
4 years or less	6.9	7.7
5–7 years	25.3	23.1
8–10 years	34.5	23.1
Over 10 years	33.3	46.2
Prior experience:		
Local or other cadre	10.0	10.0
War veteran	24.0	20.0
Other position of responsibility	66.0	70.0

age of these entrepreneurs fell from 49 years to 43 years, indicating that the owners of units that changed ownership forms or who had not been the respondents in the 1997 survey must have been over 50 years old at the time of the 1991 survey. This is confirmed by the data. Also, a significant percentage of owners were over 50 years in both 1991 and 1997 surveys. The youngest entrepreneurs owned only household enterprises in both years (all in Ha Tay), while most private enterprises belonged to owners between 40 and 49 years of age (mostly in Long An). The oldest entrepreneurs, like the youngest, owned only household enterprises in both years (almost all in Ha Tay), except for one household-turned-private enterprise owner in Long An in the 1997 survey.

Regarding their educational background, a majority of entrepreneurs had received more than ten years of formal education. Table 8.19 also shows that most entrepreneurs of fast-growing enterprises had prior experience in a position of responsibility, including the state sector. Compared to the full set of surviving enterprises, managers of more fast-growing entreprises were younger, had more years of education and prior experience in a position of responsibility.

Primary Income Source

Related to entrepreneurial characteristics is the structure of household income among household and private enterprises. Table 8.20 presents the distribution of all surviving and fast-growing rural enterprises by source of primary income. It reveals some dramatic changes in the structure of household income between the 1991 and 1997 surveys, especially among fast-growing enterprises. The role of the enterprise as the sole source of household income rose ten-fold, among fast-growers. However, since the percentages do not include land holdings and income from agriculture among these enterprises, the figures in both 1991 and 1997 surveys might not accurately reflect the entire income structure.

While the importance of the enterprise as the main income source increased, there was a corresponding reduction in the involvement of unpaid household members in the inter-survey period. In the 1991 survey, 85 per cent of the enterprises (fast-growing as well as all surviving) used unpaid household labour (an average 2.5 relatives per unit) but this number had reduced to 74 per cent (an average of 1.6 relatives) by the 1997 survey. The extent of involvement of houschold labour was lower in Long An, where only 1.4 household members were unpaid labourers in the fast-growing enterprises, compared to two in Ha Tay (in the 1997 survey).

Consistent with the reduction in other income sources, almost 23 per cent of the entrepreneurs reported that their household income had declined since 1991. The excellent performance of the enterprise in terms of assets and value added (and therefore, income) apparently compensated for any such reduction among 65 per cent of the units that reported an increased household income since 1991.[21]

Scale of Operations

This section presents the distribution of initial investment and assets (and their growth) in the 1991 and 1997 surveys for fast-growing and other surviving rural units (Tables 8.21 and 8.22). As Table 8.21

Table 8.20: Sources of household income in the 1991 and 1997 surveys. Rural enterprises.

	% all surviving enterprises		% fast-growing enterprises	
Income source:	**1991**	**1997**	**1991**	**1997**
Enterprise as sole source	9.1	36.7	6.1	63.6
Wage employment	5.7	26.4	12.1	6.1
Farming	25.3	14.9	33.3	24.2
Others	14.9	12.6	27.3	15.2

Note: Data on income from family farm have not been included. The income from farming is calculated on the basis of the household members gainfully employed in agriculture.Where the sum of a column is greater than 100, it implies that some enterprises have more than two sources of income; where the sum is less than 100, data are not available for those units; where the sum equals 100, the enterprises have at most one additional source of income.

shows, a majority of fast-growing enterprises (65 per cent) invested between 1 and 10 million dong (in 1996 prices) at the time of starting the enterprise. The average amount invested by a fast-growing enterprise at start-up was 8 million dong. The average value of its assets by the 1991 and 1997 surveys was 21 and 213 million dong respectively. This phenomenal growth in assets between the two surveys is a striking feature among fast-growing enterprises as well as for all surviving enterprises. The average surviving enterprise also invested 8 million dong at establishment. Its assets in the 1991 survey (at 33 million dong) were greater than those of the fast-growing enterprise but by the time of the 1997 survey these assets (at 160 million dong) had failed to keep pace with those of its fast-growing counterpart.

There was a ten-fold increase in asset investments in the inter-survey period. Some 16 per cent of the fast-growing enterprises moved to higher categories of assets (when compared to their initial investments) by the 1991 survey; and 87 per cent had done so by the 1997 survey, indicating that the inter-survey period was a very successful period of growth for the rural fast-growers.

Across regions, the average fast-growing Long An firm (with 11 million dong) was almost twice the size of its Ha Tay counterpart (with 6 million dong) at start-up. Its assets in the 1991 survey were 35 million dong compared to 11 million dong in Ha Tay. This absolute difference in size became more conspicuous by the 1997 survey, when

Table 8.21: Initial investment (at establishment) and total assets in the 1991 and 1997 surveys for rural enterprises. Thousand dong.

	% all surviving enterprises	% fast-growing enterprises
Initial investment at establishment:		
1,000 and less	9.5	9.7
1,001–10,000	67.9	64.5
10,001–50,000	19.0	22.6
50,001–100,000	3.6	3.2
100,001–500,000	0.0	0.0
More than 500,000	0.0	0.0
Total assets in the 1991 survey:		
1,000 and less	4.6	12.1
1,001–25,000	58.6	60.6
25,001–75,000	24.1	18.2
75,001–100,000	4.6	3.0
100,001–150,000	4.6	6.1
150,001–500,000	3.4	0.0
More than 500,000	0.0	0.0
Total assets in the 1997 survey:		
1,000 and less	1.1	3.0
1,001–25,000	23.0	6.1
25,001–75,000	27.6	30.3
75,001–100,000	10.3	12.1
100,001–150,000	10.3	9.1
150,001–500,000	20.7	30.3
More than 500,000	6.9	9.1

Note: All monetary values are in 1996 prices.

the average Long An firm was worth 272 million while the Ha Tay firm had 166 million in assets. Although this difference widened, Ha Tay has grown faster, in percentage terms.[22] The annual average growth of assets of the typical enterprise in Ha Tay between the two surveys was 66 per cent, compared to 44 in Long An. The growth rate between establishment and the 1991 survey was also higher in Ha Tay (19 per cent) than in Long An (1 per cent).

The regional differences in the size of an enterprise at establishment were greater than differences across ownership forms. The aver-

Table 8.22: Distribution of annual average asset growth rates among rural enterprises. Percentages.

Nature of growth rate:	% all surviving enterprises	% fast-growing enterprises
Growth rates from establishment to 1991 survey:		
Zero	51.3	63.0
1–10%	17.9	25.9
11–20%	7.7	0.0
21–50%	9.0	3.7
51–75%	9.0	3.7
76–100%	1.3	0.0
More than 100%	3.8	3.7
Growth rates 1991–97 survey:		
Negative	12.8	0.0
Zero	8.1	3.1
1–10%	16.3	9.4
11–20%	34.9	37.5
21–50%	9.3	9.4
51–75%	14.0	28.1
76–100%	4.7	12.5
More than 100%	0.0	0.0

Note: Data for computing growth rates from establishment up to the 1991 survey and between the 1991 and 1997 surveys are not available for six units and one unit respectively. Growth rates from establishment to the 1991 survey were computed on the basis of gold ounces invested in the period of establishment to mid-1991; those from the 1991 to 1997 survey were based on monetary values of assets at the end of the years 1990 and 1996 respectively.

age private enterprise was only slightly larger (8.3 million dong) than its household counterpart at establishment (7 million dong); its assets in the 1991 survey were 26 million dong (compared to 16 million dong for the household enterprise), but by the 1997 survey, there was a clear difference in the size of firms across owner-ship forms. Assets of the average private enterprise were worth 370 million dong in the 1997 survey compared to 101 million dong for the household enterprise. Even though the number of private enterprises is much less than household enterprises, the rate of growth in assets shows that the former have grown faster. Table 8.22 elaborates on the distribution of growth rates of assets among fast-growing as well as all surviving rural enterprises.

.Although the two growth rates cannot be strictly compared, we find that a majority did not increase their assets between establishment and the 1991 survey, probably because most were very young and none of the fast-growing enterprises experienced negative growth rates between the 1991 and 1997 surveys. The average annual growth rate in the inter-survey period works out to 56 per cent for rural fast-growers, and is more homogeneous in Long An than Ha Tay. There is a very high correlation between growth in value added and growth in assets between 1990–96,[23] leading us to believe that growth in assets was a prerequisite condition for growth in value added, and that overall growth has been capital-intensive.[24]

Closely linked to capital accumulation and capital-intensive growth is the availability of capital. On the one hand, there is evidence of a very high rate of capital accumulation among rural fast-growing enterprises. On the other hand, there is evidence of a major shortage of external sources for investment funding, both for start-ups and for expansion. Table 8.23 presents the distribution of investment sources (at establishment and for the inter-survey years) by the percentage of enterprises procuring them. The importance of own resources – entrepreneurial savings and the firm's internally generated revenue – is clearly shown in the table. An astounding 61 per cent of the units relied solely on entrepreneurial savings for investment needs at start-up. Borrowing from a bank was conspicuous by its near-absence. The average enterprise, as Table 8.23 shows, financed 83 per cent of its initial capital investment from its own resources, 11 per cent from friends and family and a mere 2 per cent from banks.

Further, although 97 per cent of the fast-growing enterprises registered positive growth in the value of assets between the 1991 and 1997 surveys (Table 8.22), only 48 per cent reported an additional purchase of machinery and equipment since the 1991 survey.[25] The sources for this investment are even less varied than at the time of establishment. Almost 81.3 per cent of the enterprises financed 100 per cent of their expansionary investment through their own resources (Table 8.23). The average expanding fast-growing enterprise depended on its internally generated revenue for close to 92 per cent of its investment needs,

Table 8.23: Percentage distribution of investment finance by source. Rural fast-growing enterprises.

Sources:	0	1–24	25–49	50–74	75–99	100	Mean
Sources for investment at establishment:							
Own resources	3.2	0.0	6.4	12.9	16.1	61.4	*83.3*
Friends and family	74.2	9.7	3.2	9.7	0.0	3.2	*11.3*
Banks	96.8	0.0	0.0	3.2	0.0	0.0	*2.0*
Credit co-operatives	100.0	0.0	0.0	0.0	0.0	0.0	*0.0*
Local authorities	100.0	0.0	0.0	0.0	0.0	0.0	*0.0*
Employees	100.0	0.0	0.0	0.0	0.0	0.0	*0.0*
Private moneylenders	93.5	3.2	3.2	0.0	0.0	0.0	*1.8*
Advance from sales	96.8	0.0	0.0	3.2	0.0	0.0	*1.6*
Other	100.0	0.0	0.0	0.0	0.0	0.0	*0.0*
Sources for investment finance 1991–97 surveys:							
Own resources	0.0	0.0	6.2	12.6	0.0	81.3	*91.9*
Banks and other financial institutions	93.8	0.0	0.0	6.2	0.0	0.0	*3.3*
Loans from other sources	87.5	0.0	6.2	6.2	0.0	0.0	*4.8*
Interest-free loans from friends	100.0	0.0	0.0	0.0	0.0	0.0	*0.0*
Other sources	100.0	0.0	0.0	0.0	0.0	0.0	*0.0*

and procured less than 5 per cent from banks and other sources. It is very clear from this data that the high rates of capital accumulation achieved by rural fast-growing firms between the 1991 and 1997 surveys were funded predominantly by own sources. That this kind of a growth occurred is very impressive and also offers clues to the non-viability of several others in the same period.

Mechanisation

Capital accumulation, in terms of addition to existing assets, is reflected in the extent of mechanisation. Table 8.24 presents the extent of mechanisation among fast-growing and all surviving enterprises in the 1991 and 1997 surveys. Considering power-driven machinery as a better mode of production than manually-operated machinery, we find that a majority of fast-growing enterprises used better modes of production, and this 'revolutionary' change occurred in the period 1991–97, coinciding with the high rates of capital accumulation. As Table 8.24 points out, the percentage using power-driven machinery more

Table 8.24: Type of machinery used in the 1991 and 1997 surveys. Rural enterprises.

	% all surviving enterprises		% fast-growing enterprises	
Type of machinery:	**1991**	**1997**	**1991**	**1997**
Only hand tools, no machinery	49.4	23.8	65.5	31.3
Manually-operated machinery only	7.4	7.1	6.9	3.1
Power-driven machinery only	8.6	17.9	3.4	18.8
Both manually-operated and power-driven machinery	34.6	51.2	24.1	46.9

than doubled since the 1991 survey, while the percentage using hand tools only halved (or thereabouts) in that period. However, when compared to all surviving enterprises, we find that the fast-growing enterprises lagged behind in the 1991 survey on all counts.[26]

Two-thirds of the fast-growing enterprises changed the kind of machinery they used, between the 1991 and the 1997 surveys. A majority of them (71 per cent) shifted to higher forms of machinery. Further, most changes are found among the category that used only hand tools in the 1991 survey. However, about 47 per cent of the manufacturing enterprises still used only hand tools in the 1997 survey; on the whole, this percentage remains unchanged since the 1991 survey. Ha Tay witnessed more changes; more than half of the enterprises used only hand tools in the 1991 survey and many of them did not even have electricity. By the 1997 survey, the number using only hand tools halved and the number using power-driven machinery increased significantly. Across ownership forms, this trend was predominant among household enterprises.

Employment

Total employment among rural fast-growing enterprises increased from 176 in the 1991 survey to 287 in the 1997 survey, which represents a 63-per-cent increase. The annual average growth rate of total employment in the period between the surveys is 6.6 per cent, almost equal in Ha Tay and Long An.[27] The average number employed per enterprise correspondingly rose from five to nine, in that period. Most

Table 8.25: Wage employment in the 1991 and 1997 surveys. Rural enterprises.

	% all surviving enterprises		% fast-growing enterprises	
No. of wage employees:	**1991**	**1997**	**1991**	**1997**
None	43.7	32.2	48.5	21.2
1–10	47.1	55.2	48.5	57.6
11–25	4.6	10.3	3.0	18.2
26–50	3.4	2.3	0.0	3.0
51–70	1.1	0.0	0.0	0.0
More than 70	0.0	0.0	0.0	0.0
Mean	4.51	4.72	1.82	6.18

of the fast-growing units employed wage labour, in varying proportions. It is clear from Table 8.25 that the average number of wage employees increased from less than two to over six by the 1997 survey. The number of units employing wage labour rose from 52 to 79 per cent in the intervening six years.

Fast-growing enterprises lagged behind all surviving enterprises in the 1991 survey in respect to wage employees; they employed a maximum of 15 wage employees, compared to 67 among the latter; but they almost doubled it to 29 wage employees in the 1997 survey, compared to 33 among all the survivors.[28] Across regions, in both years, Ha Tay accounted for 66 per cent of units without wage labour, but was more diverse in its representation among employment categories than Long An. However, in both regions and years, a majority of enterprises (with wage labour) belonged to the category of one-to-ten wage employees (Table 8.25). Further, household enterprises accounted for 84 and 100 per cent of the units without wage labour in the 1991 and 1997 surveys respectively.

Growth in employment is also reflected in the percentage of wage employees to total labour force; it rose from 25 to 55 per cent in the inter-survey period. Interestingly, none of the fast growing enterprises used 100 per cent wage labour, implying that they used some amount of unpaid (mainly household) labour full-time, in both years.

Production Flexibility

Production flexibility is measured by the changes introduced to the product mix, whether these comprise new products or improvements

Table 8.26: Product changes and their impact. Rural enterprises.

	% all surviving enterprises		% fast-growing enterprises	
Nature of flexibility:	**1991**	**1997**	**1991**	**1997**
Introduced new products	17.4	27.6	6.3	30.0
Improved existing products	30.2	40.2	25.0	42.4
Reason for change:				
Difficult to sell current product	32.0	4.2	22.2	0.0
Increasing competition from producers	36.0	12.5	44.4	30.0
Increasing competition from imports	0.0	0.0	0.0	0.0
Purchaser requests	24.0	75.0	33.3	60.0
Other	8.3	8.3	0.0	10.0
Degree of success:				
Unsuccessful	7.7	0.0	11.1*	0.0
Not very successful	23.1	8.3	11.1*	0.0
Quite successful	61.5	87.5	11.1*	0.0
Very successful	0.0	4.2	0.0	0.0
Too early to tell	7.7	0.0	0.0	0.0

Key: * Data for the remaining 67 per cent of units not avaiable. **Note:** The 1991 survey referred to changes in the period 1989–91; the 1997 survey referred to changes since the 1991 survey. Data on reason for change and success of change are based only on those enterprises that initiated change.

to existing products. Table 8.26 shows the nature of flexibility among fast-growing and all surviving enterprises in the two surveys. It is seen that the percentage of enterprises introducing new products/ improvements increased significantly in the 1997 survey, especially among fast-growing enterprises and in Ha Tay.[29] In both time periods and categories of enterprises, improvements to existing products were more common than the introduction of new products.

Interesting developments in production flexibility are evidenced in the different reasons given for initiating product mix changes and the perception of their success. Among fast-growing enterprises in the 1991 survey, competition from other producers was the dominant reason cited for initiating change, followed by difficulties in selling existing products. In 1997, customer requests replaced the threat of competition as the dominant reason; and all enterprises regarded the changes as quite successful.

Table 8.27: Continuity of operations in the 1991 and 1997 surveys. Rural enterprises.

Months operated and reasons for closure:	% all surviving enterprises		% fast-growing enterprises	
	1991	1997	1991	1997
Operated throughout the year*	52.9	70.1	33.3	75.8
Closed for:				
1 month	1.1	0.0	0.0	0.0
2 months	5.7	6.9	9.1	9.1
3 months	11.5	9.2	15.2	6.1
4 months	5.7	3.4	6.1	3.0
5 months	2.3	2.3	3.0	0.0
6 months	0.0	8.0	0.0	6.1
Over 6 months	1.1	0.0	0.0	0.0
Reasons for closure:				
Lack of raw material	16.7	30.8	9.1	37.5
Lack of demand	29.2	34.6	45.5	50.0
Other reasons	79.2	46.2	90.0	25.0

Key: *The 1991 survey refers to the whole year of 1990 and the 1997 survey refers to the whole year of 1996. **Note:** Percentages for reasons for closure are based on the number of units that did not operate throughout the year. Enterprises established in 1990 have been excluded from calculations for 1990 only.

Continuity of Operations

The ability of an enterprise to remain in operation throughout the year is an important indicator of its stability. Relevant data are presented in Table 8.27 for rural enterprises, in relation to both fast-growing and all surviving enterprises. The percentage of enterprises operating throughout the year increased for both groups in the inter-survey period. The average period of closure, however, increased from 3.3 months per year to 3.9 for all survivors and from 3.1 to 3.5 for fast-growing enterprises within the same period.

Next, the percentage of units that closed down temporarily owing to a lack of raw materials and product demand increased between the two surveys for both fast-growing and all surviving enterprises. 'Other reasons' (including agricultural peak season and personal reasons) were mostly cited by fast-growing enterprises in the 1991 survey but reduced drastically by the 1997 survey, implying, among other things, a more independent non-farm unit.

Most of the fast-growing units with discontinuous operations were located in Ha Tay in the 1991 survey (73 per cent), and in Long An (75 per cent) in the 1997 survey. Household enterprises were more prone to shut down temporarily; but this was probably due to their larger numbers in the fast-growing sample. It is clear that the impact of agricultural seasonality reduced in the period between the two surveys. When we combine it with our earlier finding regarding the growing importance of the enterprise as main source of income (Table 8.20), it is clear that enterprises no longer compete as strongly for the household resources (money, labour, etc.) as in the 1991 survey.

Capacity Utilisation

The extent of capacity utilisation is based on the respondents' perception of a possible increase in production if all machinery and equipment were to be employed. Lack of data for a large number of units in the 1991 survey reduces the comparability of data in the two years. In the 1997 survey it is clear from Table 8.28 that the fast-growing enterprises were working at least at half their production capacity, since none of them reported the possibility of increasing production by more than 100 per cent. There were no noticeable regional differences across Ha Tay and Long An; none of the private and partnership units reported working at full capacity. Half the units that reported the possibility of increasing production by more than 25 per cent also

Table 8.28: Capacity utilisation in the 1991 and 1997 surveys. Rural enterprises.

	% all surviving enterprises		% fast-growing enterprises	
Extent of utilisation:	**1991***	**1997**	**1991†**	**1997**
Operating at full capacity	12.2	23.8	0.0	22.7
If using all machinery & equipment, can increase production by:				
Up to 10%	17.1	11.1	9.1	13.6
11–25%	22.0	11.1	27.3	4.5
26–50%	24.0	25.4	27.3	27.3
51–100%	14.6	22.2	18.2	31.8
Above 100%	9.8	6.3	18.2	0.0

Key:* Data for 53 per cent of all surviving enterprises not included due to non-availability.† Data for 67 per cent of fast-growing enterprises not included due to non availability.

had asset growth rates in excess of 20 per cent, implying that the additional capacity created had not been fully utilised.

Forward Linkages

Forward linkages of rural fast-growing enterprises are analysed in terms of destination and location of sales of main product. Table 8.29 presents the linkages in both the 1991 and 1997 surveys for fast-growing enterprises. On the whole, forward linkages altered only marginally between the two surveys. A majority of enterprises sold solely to individual buyers in both the 1991 (45 per cent) and 1997 (41 per cent) surveys. Also, the share of individual buyers in the sales of the average fast-growing enterprise continued to be the largest; it dropped only slightly from 50 to 49 per cent in the inter-survey period. Correspondingly, the share of private enterprises in the average firm's sales increased while the percentage of enterprises selling solely to private enterprises dropped by the 1997 survey. Sales to the state sector, already thin in the 1991 survey, reduced even further in the 1997 survey. Not only did the number of enterprises selling to the state sector drop from 7 to 4 per cent, but they sold only 1–24 per cent of their main product to the state by the latter date. Next, the percentage of enterprises selling solely to one category of buyers reduced from 80 to 74 per cent; clearly, greater assets and production capacity made it necessary to diversify sales.

The main product manufactured and sold by the fast-growing enterprises consisted mainly of carpentry and furniture, agricultural processing, arts and handicrafts, light engineering and consumer goods, construction and building materials and garments. The linkages in terms of destination of sales thus appear to be strong with individual buyers and private enterprises.

There were some noticeable changes among fast-growing enterprises regarding geographical distribution of sales since the 1991 survey. As the second half of Table 8.29 shows, the share of large cities in the average firm's sales almost doubled from 25 to 48 per cent between the two surveys. The percentage of enterprises selling solely to large cities also increased, although by a lesser extent, from 25 to 30 per cent. Correspondingly, the share of rural areas (including same village, commune and district) in the average firm's sales dropped from 18 to 11 per cent in the same period. The geographical proximity

Table 8.29: Forward linkages of main product in the 1991 and 1997 surveys. Rural fast-growing enterprises. Percentages.

Destination and location	0	1–24	25–49	50–74	75–99	100	Mean
Destination of sales of main product in 1991 survey:							
Individuals	41.1	3.4	3.4	6.9	0.0	44.8	*50.3*
Private enterprises	51.7	0.0	0.0	10.3	3.4	34.5	*43.5*
State enterprises	96.6	0.0	3.4	0.0	0.0	0.0	*1.4*
Other state agency	96.6	0.0	0.0	3.4	0.0	0.0	*1.7*
Local authority	96.6	0.0	0.0	3.4	0.0	0.0	*1.7*
Tourists	100.0	0.0	0.0	0.0	0.0	0.0	*0.0*
Export	96.6	0.0	3.4	0.0	0.0	0.0	*1.4*
Other	100.0	0.0	0.0	0.0	0.0	0.0	*0.0*
Destination of sales of main product in the 1997 survey:							
Individuals	40.7	11.1	0.0	0.0	7.4	40.7	*48.7*
Private enterprises	48.1	3.7	0.0	3.7	14.8	29.6	*45.0*
State enterprises	96.3	3.7	0.0	0.0	0.0	0.0	*0.7*
Other state agency	100.0	0.0	0.0	0.0	0.0	0.0	*0.0*
Local authority	92.6	3.7	3.7	0.0	0.0	0.0	*1.9*
Tourists	100.0	0.0	0.0	0.0	0.0	0.0	*0.0*
Export	96.3	0.0	0.0	0.0	0.0	3.7	*3.7*
Other	100.0	0.0	0.0	0.0	0.0	0.0	*0.0*
Geographical distribution of main product sales in 1991 survey:							
Same town	78.6	3.6	0.0	7.1	3.6	7.1	*14.3*
Same commune	75.0	0.0	10.7	3.6	0.0	10.7	*16.4*
Same rural district	64.3	3.6	3.6	10.7	3.6	14.3	*24.5*
Nearby town	82.1	7.1	3.6	3.6	0.0	3.6	*8.0*
Large city	75.0	0.0	0.0	0.0	0.0	25.0	*25.0*
Elsewhere	82.1	3.6	0.0	7.1	0.0	7.1	*11.8*
Geographical distribution of main product sales in 1997 survey:							
Same town	88.9	7.4	0.0	3.7	0.0	0.0	*3.3*
Same commune	70.4	7.4	7.4	3.7	0.0	11.1	*16.7*
Same rural district	70.4	7.4	7.4	3.7	3.7	7.4	*15.4*
Nearby town	40.7	3.7	0.0	14.8	11.1	29.6	*47.9*
Large city	70.4	7.4	3.7	11.1	0.0	7.4	*16.7*

to Hanoi and Ho Chi Minh City probably accounted for the high shares of sales to large cities among fast-growing enterprises. Especially in Ha Tay, the average share of large cities increased from 26 to 51 per cent by the 1997 survey. In the 1991 survey, there was a clear dichotomy between firms that sold in the local area and those that sold entirely in cities. This distinction had decreased by the 1997 survey, constituting a major break in the level of operation of the units. Further, the percentage of enterprises selling solely in one geographical area or to one category of buyers also reduced; the enterprises were selling to more categories and in more locations in the 1997 survey compared to the 1991 survey. It is thus clear that the linkages with rural areas are weakening in favour of large cities and nearby towns.

Backward Linkages

Backward linkages were measured in terms of category and location of main input supplier in both 1991 and 1997 surveys. Table 8.30 presents the backward linkages for fast-growing enterprises in both surveys. From the table it is clear that in both years, a majority of the enterprises bought their main input exclusively from private enterprises; the percentages were 58 and 54 per cent respectively in both surveys. This reduction has been compensated by an increase in the percentage of enterprises buying from households (35 to 36 per cent) and the state sector (8 to 11 per cent). None of the units bought from collective farms, indicating low linkages between local farm and non-farm sectors.

The number of units that bought from households in the 1991 survey were equally distributed between Ha Tay and Long An. However, Ha Tay had most enterprises buying from private enterprises (93 per cent) and Long An had both the units (8 per cent) buying from the state sector. In the 1997 survey, none of the units in Long An bought from private enterprises and one unit bought from the state sector.

There were a few noticeable changes in the location of suppliers in the period between the two surveys. The linkages with the local territory increased, and the geographical reach reduced in that period. This is evidenced in the doubling of the percentage of enterprises buying from the same village or commune (15 to 34 per cent) and reduction in the percentage of enterprises buying from large cities (31 to 17 per cent) (Table 8.30). Also, the percentage of units buying from

Table 8.30: Backward linkages of main raw material in the 1991 and 1997 surveys. Rural fast growing enterprises. Percentages.

Supplier and location:	0	1–24	25–49	50–74	75–99	100	Mean
Main input supplier, 1991 survey:							
Individual	65.4	0.0	0.0	0.0	0.0	34.6	*34.6*
Private enterprises	42.3	0.0	0.0	0.0	0.0	57.7	*57.7*
State enterprises	92.3	0.0	0.0	0.0	0.0	7.7	*7.7*
Other state agency	0.0	0.0	0.0	0.0	0.0	0.0	*0.0*
Collective farms	0.0	0.0	0.0	0.0	0.0	0.0	*0.0*
Other	0.0	0.0	0.0	0.0	0.0	0.0	*0.0*
Main input supplier, 1997 survey:							
Individual	64.3	0.0	0.0	0.0	0.0	35.7	*35.7*
Private enterprises	39.3	3.6	0.0	3.6	0.0	53.6	*56.8*
State enterprises	89.3	0.0	3.6	0.0	3.6	3.6	*7.5*
Other state agency	100.0	0.0	0.0	0.0	0.0	0.0	*0.0*
Collective farms	100.0	0.0	0.0	0.0	0.0	0.0	*0.0*
Other	100.0	0.0	0.0	0.0	0.0	0.0	*0.0*
Location of main input supplier, 1991 survey:							
Same village	91.7	8.3	0.0	0.0	0.0	0.0	*1.3*
Same commune	75.0	0.0	12.5	4.2	0.0	8.3	*14.0*
Nearby town	75.0	0.0	0.0	0.0	0.0	25.0	*25.0*
Large city	66.7	0.0	0.0	4.2	0.0	29.2	*31.3*
Elsewhere	66.7	0.0	0.0	12.5	4.2	16.7	*28.5*
Location of main input supplier, 1997 survey							
Same village	92.9	0.0	0.0	3.6	0.0	3.6	*6.1*
Same commune	67.9	0.0	3.6	3.6	0.0	25.0	*27.7*
Nearby town	57.1	0.0	0.0	3.6	0.0	39.3	*41.2*
Large city	78.6	0.0	3.6	3.6	0.0	14.3	*17.1*
Elsewhere	89.3	0.0	0.0	3.6	3.6	3.6	*8.0*

other locations not listed, including imports, dropped from 29 to 8 per cent in the inter-survey period. Added to the fact that almost 86 per cent of the rural fast-growing units mentioned sufficient availability of raw materials, it is possible that the increased backward linkages with local suppliers were due to a greater availability of inputs. The main inputs, for the range of products mentioned in the previous section, included timber, cloth, paint, chemicals, fertilisers, dye powder, beverages, sugar, etc. Timber was the most common input (mainly used by carpentry and furniture units) and was obtained mainly from non-household sources.

On the whole, it appears that units were very specialised in their purchase sources; all units in the 1991 survey bought 100 per cent from one or the other source. There was some diversification by the 1997 survey; the location of suppliers also narrowed by then, indicating easier availability of inputs and closer location of suppliers, compared to the 1991 survey.

Horizontal Linkages

Horizontal linkages were measured in terms of subcontracting relationships only. As noted in the discussion on urban fast-growing enterprises, the subcontracting data are not fully comparable, since the definition used in the 1997 survey was much stricter than in the 1991 survey. Despite the narrower definition, the number of subcontracting units among rural fast-growing enterprises was greater in the 1997 survey. A total of six units (18 per cent) were engaged in subcontracting in the 1997 survey: four in Ha Tay and two in Long An. All of them had only one subcontracting partner, five with private enterprises and one with a state enterprise in the same locality. Further, only three out of the six units received any assistance from their subcontracting partner; this came in the form of procurements of raw material/fuel, obtaining credit and other support. The duration of contracts ranged from one to five months. Three of the six subcontracting units were household enterprises, two were private enterprises and one was a co-operative. It is thus clear that subcontracting was not a major feature among rural fast-growing enterprises in either the 1991 or 1997 survey.

Production Relations

Production relations were inferred from the number of annual customers and nature of the producer–client contract on advance orders. Table 8.31 presents the data for rural fast-growing as well as all surviving enterprises. Lack of data for a number of units in both years, as noted under the table, hinders exact comparability. However, the data available are enough to show that the fast-growing enterprises

Table 8.31: Production relations in the 1991 and 1997 surveys. Rural enterprises.

	% all surviving enterprises		% fast-growing enterprises	
Nature of relation	**1991^**	**1997 †**	**1991 #**	**1997 ***
No. of annual customers:				
1	0.0	6.3	0.0	3.4
2–10	50.0	32.9	51.5	37.9
Over 10	50.0	60.8	48.5	58.6
Production on advance order:				
Never	32.2	42.9	39.1	34.5
Sometimes	22.0	27.3	13.0	31.0
Always or almost always	23.7	11.7	26.1	13.8
Subcontracting	22.1	18.1	21.7	20.7

Key: ^ 28 units; † ten units; # nine units; *four units.
Note: Data on production on order not available for:

experienced similar growth to the surviving enterprises; the number of fast-growing enterprises selling to more than ten customers per year increased, as did the percentage that sometimes sold on advance order. Most enterprises in Ha Tay sold to between two and ten customers (53 per cent), while most Long An enterprises sold to more than ten customers (90 per cent).

Across ownership forms, as expected, none of the household enterprises sold to only one customer; an equal number sold to the other two categories. Private enterprises had a greater tendency to sell to more than ten customers, in both places. In 1990, too, Ha Tay had most enterprises selling to between two and ten customers (68 per cent) while most Long An enterprises (71 per cent) sold to more than ten customers per year. The pattern across ownership forms in the 1997 survey was also true of the 1991 survey.

In both the surveys, more fast-growing enterprises reported never selling on advance order. All of these were household enterprises, which implies that no private enterprise produced without an advance order, in either survey. In our sample of rural fast-growing enterprises in the 1997 survey, most private enterprises sold to more than ten customers and reported that they sometimes produced on advance order, thereby confirming our statement on the relationship between the two. Ha Tay had all the enterprises that reported they only sold on advance order. Overall, we find that the increased propensity to sell on advance order was accompanied by an increase in the number of annual customers. Both these measures are taken to reduce the risk of non-compliance on the part of the contract partner as well as to increase sales to more customers for greater revenue and profits.

Constraints

Table 8.32 presents the nature of constraints as perceived by rural fast-growing as well as all surviving enterprises in both the 1991 and 1997 surveys. Without exception, a shortage of capital heads the list of constraints for both categories in both surveys; in fact, the percentages have remained almost unchanged. However, limited demand for products was mentioned almost as frequently as capital shortage. Competition, lack of marketing, poor transport facilities and uncertain government policies were mentioned by a small minority and were less common in the 1997 survey. Wage labour affordability was not mentioned, most probably because many units used very limited wage labour. The perception of constraints was more diverse in Ha Tay than Long An. Ha Tay also saw noticeable changes in the ranking of constraints whereas it remained similar over the six-year period in Long An. An equal number of household enterprises felt constrained by capital shortage as well as limited demand. Private enterprises, although very few in number compared to household enterprises, felt the lack of capital to a greater extent.

Competition

Respondents' perceptions of the existence of competition and the nature of competitors were gathered in both the surveys. Among the fast-growing rural enterprises, a clear majority (73 per cent) felt that there were too many enterprises in their area of operations. This represents a significant increase from 36 per cent in the 1991 survey. Despite this difference in the number of enterprises acknowledging the existence of competition, the number that felt there was 'severe' competition was the same in both surveys (about 40 per cent). Also, five units had felt no competition in the 1991 survey but none was immune to this threat by the 1997 survey.

The sources of severe competition in the 1997 survey were as follows: private enterprises (27 per cent), legal imports (12 per cent) and state enterprises (9 per cent). In the 1991 survey, too, private enterprises were the dominant source of competition; 36 per cent mentioned it in addition to 9 per cent from other sources (excluding imports and state enterprises). A few enterprises felt severe competition from more than one source in both years. On the whole, the perception of increasing competition is consistent with the high degree of concern about limited demand for products.

Governmental Assistance

The relationship between rural fast-growing enterprises and the government was weak in the 1991 survey and continued to be so in the 1997 survey, with only a slight improvement. Data on government assistance were collected at two levels, one during the time of establishment and the other during the lifetime of the enterprises. At the time of establishment, only a third of the fast-growing enterprises received assistance from the government authorities, mainly with completing procedures for application (15 per cent), obtaining credits (12 per cent), tax exemptions (12 per cent) and introduction for collaboration (3 per cent). Very few units obtained assistance in multiple areas, and these were almost equally distributed between Ha Tay and Long An. Despite their larger numbers, household enterprises constituted only a third of the units that received assistance at establishment.

During the course of their operation until the 1991 survey, 85 per cent of the fast-growing enterprises did not receive any assistance, probably because a large number of them were still young at that time. Of the four units that did obtain help, two obtained assistance with financial inputs and two with marketing. By the 1997 survey, seven units obtained governmental assistance in securing credit while the remaining units did not obtain any form of government assistance. The poor linkages with government are therefore borne out very clearly by the data. Combined with the fact that very few enterprises regard governmental interference and policies as constraints, the government on the whole seems to be a passive factor *vis-à-vis* the fast-growing enterprises, without any significant positive or negative impact.

Notes

1. The last category is the latest addition to the Vietnamese private sector since the 1991 survey.

2. While this is a comparative static presentation, we must bear in mind that it is possible that units have changed forms of ownership many times in the intervening period; however, we are unable to comment on this based on the data in their present form.

3. Into five limited liability companies, two household enterprises and one partnership.

4. They included four cooperatives, one partnership and one household enterprise; two each in Hanoi, Ho Chi Minh City and Haiphong.

5. All the eight women entrepreneurs in the 1991 survey continued managing their enterprises in the 1991–97 period and one woman took over as a new owner, bringing the total number of women entrepreneurs to nine (30 per cent) in the 1997 survey.

6. Data on age and education for owners in both 1991 and 1997 surveys were available for 29 units. The remaining units had either changed ownership forms or the respondents in the 1997 survey were only managers (not owners) and so were excluded from this question.

7. See Chapter 6 for detailed discussion on how growth has occurred via increased labour productivity.

8. The higher percentage in the 1991 survey may also be attributed to the fact that data on continuity of operations were not available for 11 units. If we exclude the answers of these eleven units in the 1997 survey (nine of them operated throughout 1996), the percentage of units that operated throughout 1996 is slightly higher, at 89 per cent.

9. Asset growth rate here refers to annual average growth rate of investments (monetary) in the enterprise between the two surveys.

10. Also, there is a noticeable change in the percentage of enterprises selling exclusively to these two categories – compared to 20.4 and 12.2 per cent in the 1991 survey, these percentages changed to 21 in each category in the 1997 survey. The number of enterprises selling exclusively to individual buyers rose marginally from 20.4 to 20.8 per cent in this period.

11. The rise was from 31 to 48 per cent of its main product sales, and accounted for the highest share among the three cities.

12. A private enterprise in Ho Chi Minh City.

13. The definition used in the 1997 survey was more rigid in differentiating subcontracting from other forms of advance orders. It required a lasting buyer–seller contract based on advance orders, whereby the subcontracting

firm's product should form part of the production process of the buyer and the buyer should provide the main input or other form of substantial assistance.

14. Only one transport unit reported dealing with only one customer.

15. The unit mentioning the lack of raw material is a co-operative in Hanoi that manufactures traditional medicinal products; therefore the lack of raw materials is probably due to the highly specialised nature of raw materials.

16. Also to be noted is the apparent lack of correlation between perceptions of too many competitors and severe competition. While only 58 per cent felt that there were too many enterprises, 70 per cent experienced severe competition, implying that competition may be perceived as severe even with only a few competitors.

17. Four household enterprises became private enterprises, one became a partnership and one private enterprise transformed into a co-operative between 1991 and 1997 surveys.

18. Three units changed forms in Long An – two household enterprises became private enterprises and one private enterprise became a household enterprise.

19. The youngest enterprise in the 1997 survey was at least seven years old since one of the criteria for the survey in 1991 was that enterprises should have operated for one fiscal year.

20. A total of seven units changed ownership forms, but five of the transformations were between household and private ownership forms and so were included in entrepreneurial data in the 1997 survey, bringing about a net reduction of two units.

21. Of these, 30 per cent reported increases up to 25 per cent; another 30 per cent increases from 25–50 per cent; 25 per cent increases from 50–100 per cent; and 15 per cent report increases in excess of 100 per cent in the period between the 1991 and 1997 surveys.

22. The value of assets of the average Ha Tay firm grew from 11 to 166 million dong between the 1991 and 1997 surveys, representing a 1409 per cent growth. In Long An assets increased from 35 to 272 million dong which represented a 677 per cent growth.

23. The coefficient of correlation works out at 0.5, significant at 0.01 level.

24. This point is also confirmed in Chapter 7. One of the findings mentioned there is '[That] growth requires very high levels of capital accumulation is supported by the fact that the declining enterprises too, generally registered net increases in capital, although at much lower rates.' Also see Table 7.25 for calculations on relative and absolute capital intensity across regions and ownership forms.

25. About 61 per cent of the fast-growing enterprises reported investments in home construction in this period; hence asset growth has also come about by additions to building and land, not only machinery.

26. The fast-growing enterprises tended to use only hand tools and manually-operated machinery, and less power-driven machinery in the 1991 survey.

27. See Chapter 7, Tables 7.21, 7.23, 7.29 and 7.31, for employment performance of fast-growing enterprises by location and ownership form; also *vis-à-vis* other categories of surviving enterprises in the inter-survey period.

28. The wage employment among all surviving enterprises declined mainly due to the shedding of labour by declining enterprises. Almost 67 per cent of the declining enterprises reduced their wage labour between the 1991 and 1997 surveys; the reduction was 63 per cent, on average.

29. However, we should bear in mind that seven years were accounted for in the 1997 survey while the 1991 survey period measured only to two previous years.

9

The Non-state Manufacturing Sector in Vietnam 1991–97: An Analysis of the Closures

Bhargavi Ramamurthy

The repeat survey in June 1997 of 371 enterprises originally surveyed in 1991 in selected urban and rural areas highlighted several of the changes that these enterprises had undergone in the intervening period. Based on their performance in value addition, the enterprises were classified into five categories: closures; stagnant; declining; growing; and fast-growing (see Chapter 1 for details on surveys and definitions). Among the enterprises re-surveyed in 1997, about 65 per cent were still in operation. The rest had closed down, but the then owner/managers or their families/friends were interviewed regarding the circumstances leading to closure and the entrepreneur's present situation. By examining data relating to these closed enterprises in the 1991 survey, it is intended to present a profile of enterprises that exhibit tendencies towards closure. Wherever possible, data on the entire set of re-surveyed, surviving enterprises (excluding the closures) will be presented too, in order to give the reader a comparison of the performance of the closed firms *vis-à-vis* the survivors. Unless otherwise specified, the reference group is the enterprises that closed down, henceforth referred to as 'closures'.

Urban Enterprises

The urban surveys in 1991 and 1997 were held in the three major cities of Vietnam, namely Hanoi and Haiphong in the north and Ho

Chi Minh City in the south. Among the urban enterprises re-surveyed, about 34 per cent had closed down operations. The urban closures accounted for 57 per cent of all the closures (see Table 1.7).

Location and Organisational Structure

Among urban re-surveyed enterprises, Haiphong had the highest mortality rate[1] (48 per cent), followed by Hanoi (32 per cent) and Ho Chi Minh City (22 per cent). Across ownership forms, co-operatives had the highest mortality rate (39 per cent) and private enterprises the lowest (25 per cent); among household and partnership enterprises it was 36 and 32 per cent respectively. Hence, 27 per cent (each) of the closures were household and co-operative enterprises, followed by 21 per cent private enterprises, 16 per cent partnerships and 8 per cent state enterprises in the 1991 survey.

Co-operatives (29 per cent) and private enterprises (24 per cent) dominated the closures in Haiphong. In Hanoi, household enterprises and co-operatives each accounted for 28 per cent of the closures and in Ho Chi Minh City, more than 42 per cent of the closures were household enterprises, followed by co-operatives (24 per cent). All of the six state enterprises re-surveyed in 1997 had shut down operations in the 1991–97 period. Three of these were in Haiphong, two in Ho Chi Minh City and one in Hanoi. Overall, it appears that private enterprises fared the best, accounting for at most a fifth of the closures in all cities.

Nature of Activity

An overwhelming majority of the closures (86 per cent) were involved in manufacturing activities in the 1991 survey, in line with sample design criteria. A little over 4 per cent each were in small-scale trading and agro-processing, and about 3 per cent were repair shops. Co-operatives constituted the largest group among the closed manufacturing units (31 per cent); most of them (55 per cent) were also located in Haiphong. Next, about 57 per cent of the retail and repair shop units were also located in Haiphong in addition to 75 per cent of the state enterprises. Together, these account for the high percentage of closures in Haiphong.

Enterprise History: Years in Operation

The age of enterprises at closure is a good indicator of the long-term likelihood of firm survival. Relative to their total numbers, younger

Table 9.1: Year of establishment and age of urban enterprises at closure.

Year of establishment	% surviving enterprises	% closures	Age at closure	% closures
Before 1976	12.9	17.8	Less than 5 years	34.2
1976–80	11.4	16.4	5–10 years	24.7
1981–85	22.1	11.0	11–15 years	19.2
1986	6.4	4.1	16–20 years	8.2
1987	7.1	11.0	21–25 years	5.5
1988	6.4	12.3	Over 25 years	8.2
1989	23.6	11.0		
1990	10.0	16.4		

enterprises (less than five years old in the 1991 survey) were mainly household and private, while the older enterprises (more than ten years old) were co-operatives and partnership units. Table 9.1 presents the years of establishment of surviving enterprises and closures, and the age of the latter at the time of closure. It is very clear from the table that 34 per cent of the closures were established before 1981 and had been in operation for at least 11 years at the time of the survey in 1991.

As the second half of Table 9.1 shows, a third of the units were five years old or less at the time of closure, indicating a high degree of 'infant mortality' as well. The average age of enterprises at closure, because of this polarised pattern, was 11 years. While the proportion of 'infant mortality' is high, it must be noted that 38 per cent of the enterprises closed down within five years because of the death or retirement of the entrepreneur. A similar percentage (33) of entre-preneurs, how-ever, have continued self-employment, in a new line of business. The actions of this latter group are more significant for analysing the factors responsible for consolidation and growth of private sector enterprises.

The reasons for closure, as presented in Table 9.2, show that almost half the enterprises could not sell at profit followed by 19 per cent that closed down for personal reasons. On further investigation, almost 28 per cent of those that could not sell at profit cited too much competition or poor distribution and marketing channels as being the underlying

Table 9.2: Main reasons for closure among urban enterprises. Percentages.

Main reasons	% closures
Reasons for closure:	
Could not sell at profit	49.3
Lack of raw material	2.7
No prompt payment from customers	2.7
Interference from government officials/local authorities	1.4
Personal reasons	19.2
Other reasons	24.7
Reasons for inability to sell at profit:	
Too much competition	27.8
Low product quality	16.7
Poor distribution/marketing channels	27.8
Production costs too high	22.2
Other	5.6

reason (Table 9.2).[2] This finding underscores the importance of profits as major sources of capital accumulation, and hence firm sustenance. Household enterprises and co-operatives accounted for a third (each) of closures due to this reason. A majority of these household enterprises were less than five years old in the 1991 survey, indicating the importance of very high profit margins in the early years.

Across cities, the inability to sell at profit was more pronounced in Ho Chi Minh City, where it was mentioned by 76 per cent of the enterprises, compared to 37 and 50 per cent in Haiphong and Hanoi respectively. To the Ho Chi Minh City entrepreneurs, the low profit margins were mainly due to very high production costs (38 per cent) and competition in product markets (31 per cent); in Haiphong the reason given was poor marketing and distribution channels (43 per cent) and competition (36 per cent); while in Hanoi it was low product quality (44 per cent) followed by poor marketing channels (22 per cent). Further, the data also show that personal reasons (like retirement or the death of the owner) resulted in closure among mainly smaller units, with less than 100 million dong in initial investment, while the larger

Table 9.3: Characteristics of owner-managers in the 1991 survey. Urban enterprises.

Characteristic:	% surviving enterprises	% closures
Sex:		
Male	65.8	93.3
Female	34.2	6.7
Age:		
29 years or under	3.8	15.6
30–39 years	26.6	25.0
40–49 years	39.2	18.8
50 years or over	30.4	40.6
Mean	45.53	45.22
Education:		
Up to 4 years	15.4	0.0
5–7 years	29.5	32.3
8–10 years	35.9	41.9
Over 10 years	19.2	25.8
Experience:		
Local cadre	7.3	12.0
War veteran	7.3	4.0
State enterprise employee	36.4	48.0
Other position of responsibility	19.9	32.0
Other	29.1	4.0

units (mainly co-operatives and private enterprises) cited inability to sell at profit.

Entrepreneurial Characteristics

Entrepreneurs of closures, in the 1991 survey, were typically male, over 50 years old, with ten years' education and an employment background in a state enterprise (Table 9.3). Less than 7 per cent were women entrepreneurs. The high average age partly explains why over 32 per cent of enterprises closed down because the previous owner had retired (or, in some cases, died) by the time of the repeat survey. Close to 53 per cent of the entrepreneurs over 50 years of age were managing household enterprises, which also explains the large percentage of household enterprise closures.[3] When we compare the age of enter-

Table 9.4: Previous owner-manager's present occupation. Urban enterprises.

Occupation:	% closures
Employed for wages	8.6
Self-employed, same line of business	4.3
Self-employed, new line of business	28.6
Unemployed	11.4
Retired or dead	32.9
Other	14.3

prises and managers, we find that nearly 62 per cent of the managers over 50 were managing enterprises less than four years old at the time of the survey in 1991. These were, possibly, late entrants into the entrepreneurial scene, who had previously been employed in state enterprises, and had given up within five years of selling at sub-optimal profit levels. About 85 per cent of these entrepreneurs have subsequently retired (or died) and only 15 per cent are now unemployed.

Haiphong had a large percentage of closures with entrepreneurs over 50 (63 per cent) who have not continued in another business activity. The high average age of the entrepreneurs and the fact that a large percentage of entrepreneurs have retired (or died) points to the strong links between entrepreneur and the enterprise, with the result that the lifetime of the enterprise is limited to the lifetime of its owner.

After the enterprises closed down, as Table 9.4 shows, 33 per cent retired (or died) and 29 per cent continued self-employment in new lines of business; the latter mainly among non-household forms. Quite naturally, the majority of entrepreneurs who retired or died were mostly from the age group 50 years or older (in the 1991 survey) (74 per cent) and 40 years or older (26 per cent); all those who have changed lines of businesses belong to the age group 30–39 years. The oldest entrepreneurs have not moved to wage employment, even though 15 per cent of them report unemployment.

Primary Income Source

The lifespan of an enterprise is also determined by the presence of alternative sources of income for the entrepreneur's household. These alternative sources can either extend the lifespan by increasing the

Table 9.5: Sources of household income in the 1991 survey. Urban enterprises.

Source:	% surviving enterprises	% closures
Enterprise as sole source	52.4	33.3
Wage employment	20.7	45.5
Farming	0.7	3.0
Gifts and remittances	26.2	6.1
Scholarships	–	6.1
Pensions and transfers	–	21.2
Others	–	27.3

capability to withstand lower earnings longer; or can shorten it by making exit decisions quicker, since the household is not totally reliant on the enterprise. In our closures sample, the enterprise was the only income-yielding source of the household for more than a third of the household and private enterprises (Table 9.5)[4] in the 1991 survey. The remaining two-thirds had at least one additional income source, the most common being wage employment (46 per cent) and pensions and other transfers (21 per cent). Alternative income sources were more common among private enterprises: 70 per cent of the household enterprises were sole income sources to the owner-household. Moreover, 50 per cent of these enterprises (with no alternative source) were located in Ho Chi Minh City, followed by 30 per cent in Haiphong and only 20 per cent in Hanoi. A majority of them were also enterprises established after 1985 (91 per cent). Compared to the surviving enterprises, more closures had an additional income source (Table 9.5), which implies that a combination of small-scale household production and difficulty in selling products might have made exit decisions easier.

Since closure of the enterprise, about 53 per cent of the owner-households (of household and private enterprises only) experienced increased income, mainly in the 50–100 per cent increase range. Interestingly, nine out of ten households that experienced increased incomes had no alternative income source in the 1991 survey. We find, quite expectedly, the size of firm to be inversely proportional to the household income situation after enterprise closure; larger firms have had tougher times than smaller ones.

Table 9.6: Initial investment (at establishment) and total assets in the 1991 survey. Urban enterprises. Thousand dong.

	% surviving enterprises	% closures
Initial investment at start-up:		
Less than 1,000	2.2	1.6
1,001–10,000	31.1	20.3
10,001–50,000	28.1	25.0
50,001–100,000	5.9	10.9
100,001–500,000	25.9	34.4
Over 500,000	6.7	7.8
Total assets in the 1991 Survey:		
Less than 1,000	0.7	0.0
1,001–25,000	14.9	18.8
25,001–75,000	12.8	17.2
75,001–100,000	4.3	1.6
100,001–150,000	14.2	4.7
150,001–500,000	29.8	26.6
Over 500,000	23.4	31.3

Scale of Operations

The scale of operations is described in terms of initial investments and asset growth from establishment up to the 1991 survey. In 1996 prices, the average urban closure invested 164 million dong at start-up[5] and its assets grew to 445 million dong by the 1991 survey, at an impressive average annual rate of growth of 154 per cent. The average surviving enterprise invested 217 million dong at establishment and its assets had grown, by the 1991 survey, to 432 million dong, representing an average annual growth rate of 119 per cent. As Table 9.6 shows, while units are very heterogeneous, there is a cluster of enterprises in the categories 100,000–500,000 dong, 1–10 million dong, and 10–50 million dong (in 1996 prices).

The size of the average closure firm at establishment was largest in Haiphong (221 million dong) followed by Ho Chi Minh City (150 million dong) and Hanoi (38 million dong).[6] Haiphong, as the least advanced industrially among the three,[7] offers some indications of the non-viability of large industries (in this case co-operatives) in a market economy as yet unprepared for businesses of this size.

Table 9.7: Distribution of annual average asset growth rates by main reason for closure among urban enterprises. Percentages.

	Annual asset growth rates (%)							
	0	**1–10**	**11–20**	**21–50**	**51–75**	**76–100**	**>100**	**Total**
Could not sell at profit	37.5	25.0	50.0	100.0	33.3	100.0	42.9	*45.2*
Lack of raw materials	0.0	0.0	0.0	0.0	33.3	0.0	0.0	*2.4*
Delayed payments from customers	7.1	0.0	0.0	0.0	0.0	0.0	0.0	*2.4*
Personal reasons	21.4	37.5	0.0	0.0	33.3	0.0	14.3	*19.0*
Other	35.7	37.5	50.0	0.0	0.0	0.0	42.9	*31.0*

Household enterprises were the smallest with average initial investments of 37 million dong, while the private enterprises were the biggest, a class apart with 265 million dong. While almost 80 per cent of the household enterprises had invested less than 50 million dong, 73 per cent of the private enterprises, 50 per cent of the partnerships and 76 per cent of the co-operatives had initial investments of at least this amount.

Table 9.6 also presents the distribution of surviving enterprises and closures according to the value of their assets (in 1996 prices) in the 1991 survey. It is seen that 31 per cent of the closures had assets in excess of 500 million dong in value, which is slightly higher than the percentage among survivors. The annual average asset growth rate for closures between establishment and the 1991 survey works out to 154 per cent only, owing to one co-operative in Haiphong experiencing an abnormally high growth. If one excludes this case, the average works out to a lower 42 per cent. If we consider enterprises excluding co-operatives, we find that units set up in 1990 were the largest in the sample. They account for half the units that in the 10–50 million dong and half in the over 50 million dong categories.

Overall we find that 30 per cent of the units had not graduated from their initial investment categories since establishment, owing to zero per cent asset growth rates or the short time period between start-up and the 1991 survey.The zero per cent growth rates have occurred in private enterprises (36 per cent), co-operatives (36 per cent) and household enterprises (28 per cent). On the other hand, the highest asset

Table 9.8: Percentage distribution of investment finance at establishment by source. Urban closures.

	0	1–25	26–50	51–75	76–99	100
Own resources	10.9	1.6	12.5	10.9	12.5	51.6
Friends and family	84.4	7.8	4.7	1.6	0.0	1.6
Banks	93.8	4.7	0.0	1.6	0.0	0.0
Credit co-operatives	100.0	0.0	0.0	0.0	0.0	0.0
Local authorities	98.4	1.6	0.0	0.0	0.0	0.0
Employees	74.6	7.9	6.3	4.8	1.6	4.8
Private moneylenders	88.7	6.5	3.2	0.0	0.0	1.6
Others	95.3	3.1	0.0	1.6	0.0	0.0

growth rates (over 100 per cent) have also been found only among the co-operatives. This unique observation among co-operatives points to the extent of restructuring going on in that sector, in response to changing macro-economic circumstances. Reviewing the data on asset growth, since we have a significant representation of enterprises at both ends of the growth rate spectrum, it is unsatisfactory to regard low asset growth rates as the single determining factor. Rather, it is the combination of high investments, poor asset growth and (as Table 9.7 points out) marketing problems that gives us a more concrete picture of the enterprises heading towards closure. Close to 43 per cent of the units with more than 100 per cent growth rate in assets cited an inability to sell at profit as the main reason for closure.

Another important issue related to the scale of operation and investment is the source of finance at the time of start-up. Table 9.8 shows the extent of reliance on entrepreneurial savings vs. external credit. It is clear that more than half of the urban closures had financed all of the firm's initial investments through the owner-manager's private savings. Except for 11 per cent of the firms that used only external sources (both formal and informal), we find all other units invested a certain amount of their own resources. Among enterprises that did secure external funds, reliance on informal sources was greater than on formal sources.

Investments made since the establishment of enterprises have also displayed the same trend. Only three units secured bank loans and seven units used non-bank credit sources. The rest used their own resources. That the firms need an external source is beyond dispute. Enterprises relying on entrepreneurial savings and internally generated revenues cannot hope to survive for long and tend to collapse at the first instance of falling profits, which we suspect is what happened among the closures. It is also very disturbing to find this situation in the most developed urban areas, occurring in enterprises of all ages and sizes.

Mechanisation

Table 9.9 reveals that close to 43 per cent of the closures used both manually operated and power-driven machinery in the 1991 survey, which is a significantly lower percentage than surviving units. In conformity with the relatively higher initial investments, 54 per cent of these units were located in Haiphong, 29 per cent in Ho Chi Minh City and 28 per cent in Hanoi. Across forms of ownership, we find that the co-operatives accounted for 36 per cent of units using both manual and power-driven machinery.

Furthermore, household enterprises not only accounted for most of the units using hand tools (40 per cent), and manually operated machinery only (36 per cent), but also power-driven machinery only (41 per cent). Yet, on the whole, non-household enterprise forms had a greater propensity towards mechanisation than did household forms.

Table 9.9: Type of machinery used. 1991 survey. Urban enterprises.

Type of machinery:	% surviving enterprises	% closures
Only hand tools, no machinery	8.5	15.2
Manually operated machinery only	14.1	16.7
Power-driven machinery only	16.9	25.8
Both manually operated and power-driven machinery	60.6	42.4

Employment

The distribution of wage employees among urban closures and surviving units in the 1991 survey is clear from Table 9.10. While the average number of wage employees for the whole sample is as high

Table 9.10: Wage employment in urban enterprises. 1991 survey.

No. of wage employees	% surviving enterprises	% closures
0	22.9	21.9
1–10	34.3	29.7
11–25	25.0	23.4
26–50	16.4	15.6
51–70	0.0	9.4
Over 70	1.4	0.0

as 18 workers, as Table 9.10 shows, close to 22 per cent of the units did not use wage labour. This represents about the same proportion as found among surviving enterprises. Not surprisingly, all units without wage labour were household enterprises, which implies that all non-household enterprises had at least one wage worker. Private and partnership enterprises mainly employed between one and ten workers (with a maximum of 50), but the co-operatives kept the average up for the group, with 58 per cent employing more than 25 workers per unit. Excluding the co-operatives, the average number of wage employees halves to nine workers.

Haiphong had the highest per unit wage employment (23), followed by Hanoi (13) and Ho Chi Minh City (11). The largest employers in all three cities were the co-operatives, they were also the only units employing more than 70 wage workers. Private enterprises in Hanoi and Ho Chi Minh City did not employ more than ten wage workers. Haiphong presents a very heterogeneous picture in terms of wage employment in the 1991 survey. The private and partnership units fall into all categories of employment (except more than 70) and the households fall into all categories of less than 50 wage employees.

One important observation on employment in these units is that there is a very high correlation between the size of the initial investment and the number of wage workers, implying that capital is not necessarily displacing labour.[8] All units with more than 500 million dong in initial investment employed at least 26 wage workers and all enterprises with less than 10 million dong in initial capital employed less than 25 workers (62 per cent of the latter category did not employ any wage labour at all).

Table 9.11: Product changes and their impact. Urban enterprises. 1991 survey.

Nature of flexibility:	% surviving enterprises	% closures
Introduced new products	34.0	38.8
Made improvements to existing products	38.2	32.8
Reason for change:		
Difficult to sell current product	37.5	61.8
Increasing competition from producers	30.6	14.7
Increasing competition from imports	5.6	0.0
Requested by purchasers	19.4	20.6
Other	6.9	2.9
Degree of success:		
Unsuccessful	4.3	2.9
Not very successful	8.7	23.5
Quite successful	65.2	41.2
Very successful	21.7	11.8
Too early to tell	0.0	20.6

Another noteworthy finding is that the capital intensity[9] of the average closure in the 1991 survey was 24 million dong per worker (in 1996 prices), also significantly higher than its surviving counterpart at 10 million dong. Excluding the co-operatives, it is still higher at 28 million dong, since the co-operatives had employed more wage labour than had the others. Even though the size of the assets was larger in Haiphong, Ho Chi Minh City was the most capital-intensive region (40 million dong per worker), followed by Haiphong (24 million dong per worker) and Hanoi (11 million dong per worker).

While no unit operated without labour, about 42 per cent of the units had only wage employees, 22 per cent used only unpaid, household labour and the remaining 36 per cent used varying proportions of paid and unpaid labour, the average being 74 per cent wage labour in the 1991 survey. Further, 55 per cent of the enterprises used all of their (paid or unpaid) labour full-time and 6 per cent worked on only part-time labour. In the latter category, only one unit used unpaid labour.

Production Flexibility

One of the major advantages of small-scale production is its ability to alter production processes in response to changes in supply and demand in the input and output markets. This production flexibility is an insurance against rapidly changing markets; hence, the more flexible a firm is, the better are its chances of long-term survival. At the firm level, we measured this production flexibility as reflected in the ability of firms to introduce new products and/or make improvements in the manufacture of existing products, in terms of technology, form of output or both.

In our sample of urban closures, in a period of two years from 1989 to 1991, only about 39 per cent of the enterprises had only introduced new products, 28 per cent had introduced improvements to existing products (Table 9.11) and 33 per cent had initiated both changes – a slightly better performance than the survivors in the same period. However, it should be noted that almost 61 per cent of the enterprises that did not introduce new products or improvements were less than five years old[10] in the 1991 survey, which makes a reasonable argument that it is too early to change the product mix. Among units older than five years in the 1991 survey, there was an almost equal distribution of units that had or had not introduced any improvements. This proportion, quite understandably, was different for those established after 1985 – 19 per cent had already initiated improvements and an overwhelming 81 per cent had not.

Across ownership forms, flexibility was more dominant among non-household enterprises. Only a third of the household enterprises had introduced new products, compared to 50 per cent among the partnership and co-operative enterprises.[11] On the other hand, 35 per cent of the household enterprises made improvements to existing products, against only 27 per cent of private enterprises and 30 per cent of co-operatives. Further, much of this dynamic flexibility was concentrated in Hanoi and Haiphong.

Production flexibility (as we define here) undoubtedly reflects the strength of the enterprise, but it also indicates instability or constant changes in the output and/or input markets. By this interpretation, it appears that southern firms have faced more stable markets than their northern counterparts. This interpretation is partly brought out by the fact that close to 62 per cent of the closure firms that had introduced changes cited as the prime motivating factor a difficulty in selling the existing product, followed by requests from purchasers (21 per cent) and increasing domestic competition (15 per cent). The difficulty to sell seems to have been a stronger force for closures than for surviving enterprises (Table 9.11).

As to the success of the changes, that all the enterprises closed down by 1997 is an obvious answer. However, the immediate effects of these changes have been viewed differently. Almost 60 per cent of the closures that initiated some form of change felt it was successful (Table 9.11) to varying degrees, and a quarter of the enterprises regarded it otherwise. The Haiphong entrepreneurs were the most optimistic; they constituted half the respondents that believed their changes were successful. Another third were from Hanoi. On average, the firms that did not consider their changes successful closed down two years later, and the more optimistic ones survived for only three years after the survey in 1991. The units that felt it was too early to predict the effects also closed down within three years.

Continuity of Operations

Another indication of the good health of an enterprise is the continuity in its operations. A stable demand and supply situation in input and output markets (including supply of finance) is reflected in the enterprise's capacity to remain open and active throughout the year. Other determinants include the skills of the entrepreneur himself, in particular his strength in marketing and gathering information. In our sample we find that only a little more than half of the closures operated throughout 1990 (Table 9.12). The surviving enterprises had a larger percentage operating throughout the year. The average period of closure among the enterprises that did not operate the full year was 3.5 months among the closures and 2.4 months among the survivors.

Across ownership forms, 90 per cent of partnership enterprises, 76 per cent of the household enterprises, 73 per cent of private enterprises and only 47 per cent of co-operatives among the closures operated throughout 1990. The average of 3.5 months of closure is, thus, accounted for mainly by the co-operatives. There has been an intensive process of restructuring of the co-operatives since *doi moi* and this has also been reflected in extended periods of closure in the 1991 survey. With the co-operatives concentrated in Haiphong (55 per cent), the performance of Haiphong in terms of continuity of operations has been the poorest among the three urban areas.

Table 9.12: Continuity of operations in urban enterprises. 1991 survey.

Months operated and reasons for closure:	% surviving enterprises	% closures
Operated throughout the year*	66.9	53.4
Closed for:		
1 month	8.1	5.5
2 months	11.3	2.7
3 months	6.5	8.2
4 months	3.2	2.7
5 months	1.6	0.0
6 months	0.8	4.1
Over 6 months	1.6	1.4
Reasons for closure:		
Lack of raw material	7.9	38.9
Lack of demand	60.5	50.0
Other reasons	31.6	44.4

Key: * The 1991 survey referred to operations throughout the year 1990.
Note: Percentages for reasons for closure are based on the number of units that did not operate throughout 1990. Enterprises established in 1990 have been excluded from these calculations.

The major reasons for discontinuous operations among closures, as Table 9.12 shows, were shortage of demand, shortage of raw materials and other personal reasons. The lack of demand was felt more by household enterprises and the lack of raw materials by co-operatives. Labour was not mentioned as the reason for closure by any enterprise, mainly because close to 34 per cent of the units did not use wage labour. The instability noted in the input and output markets, while usually reflecting constraints imposed upon firms from external sources, might as well be imposed on the firms by the disadvantages of their size and/or poor linkages with the markets.

It is possible to envisage two scenarios in this regard. First, that of large firms with greater production capacity (as in Haiphong) facing as yet underdeveloped output markets, which leads to under-utilisation of capacity and discontinued operations; and second, that of small-size firms with a very limited reach (as in the household enterprises operating without wage labour) for whom tapping slightly distant, developed markets is a virtual impossibility. Next, continuity in operations also depends on the skills of the entrepreneur in marketing and production organisation. It is not realistic to isolate one reason for discontinuous operation; rather, it is a possible combination of one or more of these factors that have resulted in firm closures for extended periods of time.

Capacity Utilisation

The extent of utilisation of production capacity throws some more light on the problem of lack of demand, mentioned by enterprises that did not operate throughout the year in 1990. As Table 9.13 shows, close to 95 per cent of the enterprises did not operate at full capacity in the 1991 survey. About 28 per cent of the enterprises reported that they could more than double production if they used all their machinery and equipment.[12] This percentage is higher than among survivors. Not surprisingly, 56 per cent of the units that reported the possibility of doubling production had invested more than 50 million dong on establishment and since, up to the 1991 survey. If the capital intensity of the units is high, chronic under-utilisation of production capacity can lead to firm closure in a very short time. It is clear from the data that more than half of the units using both power-driven and manually operated machinery felt that their production could be doubled with existing capacity.

This under-utilisation of capacity might also be related to the nature of growth rate of assets noted earlier.[13] Asset growth in these enterprises comes about mainly by additions to existing capital equipment. In a situation when existing machinery is not being optimally used, incremental growth in assets is not called for. This might explain the low growth rate of assets. On the other hand, firms that have already had high growth rate of assets are the ones that suffered from severe under-utilisation of productive capacity. Attention is once again drawn to the necessity of stable product demand for generating profits as well as asset growth and optimal utilisation of existing capacity.

Across ownership forms, full capacity utilisation was found only among two private and one household enterprises. Co-operatives accounted for 44 per cent of the units that mentioned they could more than double their production. Households mainly accounted for the category that reportedly could increase production by 25 to 50 per cent.

Table 9.13: Capacity utilisation among urban enterprises. 1991 survey.

Extent of utilisation:	% surviving enterprises	% closures
Operating at full capacity	9.9	5.3
If employing all machinery and equipment, can increase production by:		
<10%	10.7	12.3
10–25%	23.7	10.5
26–50%	26.0	19.3
51–100%	16.8	0.0
Over 100%	13.0	28.1

A third of the private and partnership enterprises reported they could more than double, and increase production between 50 to 100 per cent, respectively. Across regions, Haiphong presented severe under-utilisation: not only did 36 per cent say they could increase production by 25 to 50 per cent, but among the three cities, it had half the units that could more than double production. Hanoi had a large number that could increase production by no more than 10 per cent while in Ho Chi Minh City, almost a third were working at less than half their capacity.

Forward Linkages

The nature and extent of forward linkages have important influences on the size and longevity of enterprises. The market reach in turn affects or is affected by the nature of the products. Measuring forward linkages in terms of main product sales, Table 9.14 clearly shows the distribution of sales destinations and their location. It is apparent from the table that the average firm in our sample sold mainly to the government. On average, a firm sold 44 per cent of its products to state enterprises and agencies, and directly to individual consumers (29 per cent). When we look at the nature of products sold, we find that most of the manufacturing enterprises mainly produced goods for everyday household consumption, like garments, school bags, shoes, curtains, carpets, paint, zippers, metal cookware, etc. A few also produced windows, construction materials and spare parts for machinery. Since the product range excludes capital and intermediate goods for the most part, the state agencies might be distribution centres. The agro-processing units specialising in bread-making sold a greater

Table 9.14: Forward linkages of main product among urban closures. 1991 survey. Percentages.

	0	1–24	25–49	50–74	75–99	100	Mean
Destination of sales of main product:							
Individuals	59.3	10.2	1.7	5.1	3.4	20.3	*28.6*
Private enterprises	71.2	5.1	3.4	8.5	5.1	6.8	*17.8*
State enterprises	72.9	0.0	1.7	8.5	8.5	8.5	*20.9*
Other state agency	67.8	5.1	5.1	1.7	1.7	18.6	*23.7*
Local authority	98.3	0.0	1.7	0.0	0.0	0.0	*0.4*
Tourists	98.3	0.0	1.7	0.0	0.0	0.0	*0.6*
Exports	96.6	0.0	0.0	0.0	0.0	3.4	*3.4*
Other	93.2	1.7	0.0	1.7	0.0	3.4	*4.6*
Geographical distribution of main product sales:							
Same town	7.1	3.6	7.1	10.7	8.9	62.5	*79.6*
Other rural	92.9	1.8	0.0	5.4	0.0	0.0	*3.3*
Other urban	76.8	7.1	7.1	3.6	1.8	3.6	*10.6*
Elsewhere	91.1	1.8	0.0	1.8	1.8	3.6	*6.4*

proportion to individual buyers and private enterprises (most probably, bakeries, grocery stores and the like) and on average, 26 per cent to state agencies.

Further, the greater proportion of sales to government agencies is accounted for by the co-operatives in Hanoi and Haiphong (56 per cent). In fact, the major difference between closures and surviving enterprises is in the percentage selling to state enterprises. While the closures sold 45 per cent, on average, the corresponding share among survivors was lower at 37 per cent. The number of units selling to the state sector was also higher among the closures than survivors (47 compared to 26 per cent), in addition to those selling all of their main product solely to the state sector (22 compared to 11 per cent among survivors).

An important finding from the data is that half of the units sold solely to one category of customers. As seen in Table 9.14, 27 per cent of the firms sold 100 per cent of their produce to state enterprises and agencies; 16 per cent sold to individual buyers; 5 per cent to other private enterprises and 3 per cent each solely exported or sold to tourists. With a lot of restructuring going on in the state sector since *doi moi*, we might reasonably assume that this sales specialisation caused units depending solely on state purchases to go bankrupt. These are the firms that were either unable or unwilling to adapt to the changed markets. Some of the oft-quoted strengths of flexible specialisation have probably been latent among these firms, mainly co-operatives.

Since most of the enterprises produced goods for mass consumption, the geographical location of sales was concentrated in their respective local areas. As Table 9.14 shows, the average enterprise sold close to 80 per cent of its products in the same town as its manufacture and only 11 per cent in other towns. Sales to rural areas were insignificant. This geographical limitation was more pronounced among agro-processing industries where all the units sold 100 per cent of their produce in the same town; the corresponding figure for manufacturing units was lower at 61 per cent. Overall, as the table shows, about 63 per cent sold entirely in the same town. The scenario that we obtain, considering both categories and location of buyers, is that of very strong forward linkages with the local area and limited reach with other firms and locations. The nature of products, either as cause or consequence, limited their market reach.

Backward Linkages

Backward linkages measure the relationship of the producing units with the providers of inputs. Here we measure backward linkages in terms of the location and category of sellers of the main raw material used in producing the main product. For the products mentioned earlier, the main raw materials range from iron and steel to seashells and bread flour. They include chemicals, dye, cloth, cement, sand and other construction materials. From Table 9.15 it is clear that a typical closure enterprise, in the 1991 survey, bought close to 47 per cent of its main raw material from a state enterprise or agency. Furthermore, 24 per cent of the enterprises depend solely on the state sector for their main raw material, thus indicating very strong links with the state sector.

The dependence on the state sector is greater among agro-processing units, with 66 per cent of the average firm's purchases coming from the state sector. Across cities, Ho Chi Minh City had the largest group of enterprises buying zero per cent of their raw material from the state sector (47 per cent) and Hanoi had the largest group of enterprises buying all of their main raw material from the state sector (28 per cent). The co-operatives in Hanoi and Haiphong who bought solely from the state, once again, accounted for 44 per cent. Five closure units (7 per cent), comprising three co-operatives, one private enterprise and one partnership enterprise mainly in Hanoi and Haiphong, bought and sold solely to the state sector. As with forward linkages, the main difference between closures and surviving enterprises in the 1991 survey is evidenced in the former's stronger relationship with the state: the average enterprise among closures bought 47 per cent of its main raw material from the state, compared to 32 per cent in the average survivor's purchases. The percentage of enterprises buying from the state sector was 51 among closures and 24 among survivors; the percentage buying solely from the state sector was 23 among closures and only 11 among survivors in the 1991 survey.

Backward linkages with their respective cities are stronger than forward linkages. As Table 9.15 shows, a typical closure enterprise bought 86 per cent of its main raw material from the same town in the 1991 survey. Also clear from the table is the fact that 78 per cent of the enterprises bought all of their main raw material from the same town. As with location of sales, agro-processing units bought all of their raw materials from the same town; manufacturing units bought on average 17 per cent from outside. Among the closures, five units bought all raw materials from the state sector and sold their entire main product to the state sector too. None of them had subcontracting relationships with the state or non-state sectors.

As discussed under forward linkages, this extreme dependence on the state sector might have been a major factor in closure of enterprises, in the face of growing uncertainty in the state sector restructuring in the 1990s. We may recall, at this juncture, that half the closures cited an inability to sell at profit to be the main reason for their decision to shut down. With strong local linkages, limited geographic extent of sales and excessive dependence on an unstable state sector, this inability to sell is quite a natural outcome.

On a related issue, close to 70 per cent of the enterprises mentioned that raw materials and other inputs were available in adequate quantity and quality. Among those that did experience difficulties in obtaining

Table 9.15: Backward linkages of main raw material among urban closures. 1991 survey. Percentages.

	0	1–24	25–49	50–74	75–99	100	Mean
Main input supplier:							
Individuals	64.5	4.8	3.2	6.5	1.6	19.4	*26.5*
Private enterprises	64.5	9.7	0.0	8.1	0.0	17.7	*23.9*
State enterprises	58.1	1.6	8.1	6.5	8.1	17.7	*30.7*
Other state agency	79.0	3.2	1.6	3.2	3.2	9.7	*15.8*
Collective farms	98.4	1.6	0.0	0.0	0.0	0.0	*0.3*
Other	96.8	0.0	0.0	0.0	1.6	1.6	*2.9*
Geographical location of main supplier:							
Same town	9.1	1.8	0.0	9.1	1.8	78.2	*85.6*
Other rural	94.5	0.0	0.0	0.0	1.8	3.6	*5.1*
Other urban	87.3	3.6	7.3	0.0	0.0	1.8	*4.7*
Elsewhere	94.5	0.0	0.0	1.8	0.0	3.6	*4.6*

raw materials, 40 per cent cited dependence on imports as the nature of the problem, while 25 per cent mentioned erratic supply. Most of these units were located in Haiphong (61 per cent), followed by 30 per cent in Ho Chi Minh City and the remainder in Hanoi. It was also more commonly found among household enterprises and co-operatives (30 per cent each).

Horizontal Linkages

Inter-firm linkages are very important sources of information, technology and other resource transfers, thereby influencing the survival and lifespan of firms. Horizontal linkages between firms are analysed here in terms of subcontracting arrangements only. From the data on closures, it is clear that in the 1991 survey, only 15 per cent of the firms had subcontracting relationships with other firms, mainly private enterprises (67 per cent). Enterprises subcontracting with state enterprises constituted 22 per cent and with foreign companies 11 per cent. The most common form of assistance from the parent unit took the form of procuring raw materials (60 per cent) and obtaining credit (1 per cent). The duration of contracts ranged from one to six months in the 1991 survey. Half of the subcontracting units were co-operatives. Further, subcontracting was more common in the south with 40 per cent of the subcontractors located in Ho Chi Minh City. Also, relative to the total number of enterprises, the percentage of subcontractors was highest in Ho Chi Minh City (27 per cent) compared to 19 and 9 per cent in Hanoi and Haiphong respectively.

Production Relations

Production relations refer to the client–producer contracts, analysed here by the number of customers sold to and the frequency of production on advance orders from buyers. Sales to one or more customers depend on the nature of the product and contractual agreements. In our sample, since most enterprises dealt with consumer goods, and sold a significant percentage to individual buyers, it is reasonable to assume that the number of customers will be high. As expected, most household enterprises sold to more than ten customers in the 1991 survey (90 per cent); so did 40 per cent of private firms, 64 per cent of partnership enterprises and 39 per cent of co-operatives. Sales exclusively to one customer were absent among household enterprises, but more common among co-operatives (22 per cent). The remaining units sold to between two and ten customers that year. Among the units that sold exclusively to one customer, only one unit had subcontracting relations with the buyer.

Selling to more than one customer helps the producing unit to minimise the risk of opportunism from the other party to the contract. A common way to secure payment from customers is to confirm their orders against a cash advance. This is possible only when the firm is selling to other enterprises rather than individual consumers, for the kind of products involved. We find in our data on urban closures that most of the units (53 per cent) produced almost always on advance order. The proportion of enterprises selling on advance order was highest in Haiphong (68 per cent). Considering that the average firm in Haiphong was larger than in the other two cities, it is natural that the monetary impact of non-payment or delayed payment from customers is higher and hence, too, the need for cash advances. Selling on advance order was least in Ho Chi Minh City, at 13 per cent. Across ownership forms, 73 per cent of private enterprises sold mostly on advance order; the corresponding figures being 32 per cent of household, 64 per cent of partnership and 53 per cent of co-operatives. These figures correspond well with the percentage of sales to individual consumers and other enterprises; households sold the largest proportion of their output to individual buyers, followed by partnership, private and co-operatives.

Constraints

A majority of the owners/managers (52 per cent) identified shortage of capital as the main constraint to the growth of the enterprise in the 1991 survey (Table 9.16). Competition from other enterprises (13 per cent) and limited product demand (10 per cent) followed, in that order. The shortage of capital was felt more by non-household industries; among household industries, it was too much competition from other producers (35 per cent). Among non-household industries, capital shortage was most pronounced among co-operatives with 68 per cent noting it as the main constraint; for private firms the figure was 53 per cent and for partnership enterprises, 67 per cent.

Not surprisingly, a majority of units mentioning capital shortage (41 per cent) had higher total investments, ranging from 100 million to 500 million dong. It appears that for very small units with small capital needs, the need for external capital is also limited, with the result that they do not experience capital shortage to the same extent as firms of larger size and investment. Haiphong, with its relatively larger industries, obviously had most of its units (71 per cent) complaining of capital shortage, thereby also accounting for 76 per cent of the total units in our sample registering this constraint. Unless efforts are undertaken at the macro level to expand the network of external credit sources, the survival of large industries and the growth of small industries will be greatly affected. The percentage citing capital constraints was slightly higher among closures than among survivors (Table 9.16); correspondingly, the percentage reporting limited demand was lower among the former.

Competition

Related to one of the dominant constraints mentioned above, almost 58 per cent the enterprises experienced severe competition (in the 1991 survey) from other industries in their field of manufacture, many of them from more than one category of enterprises. More than a third of the enterprises faced severe competition from other private

Table 9.16: Respondent perception of main constraint among urban enterprises. 1991 survey. Percentages.

Nature of constraint:	% surviving enterprises	% closures
Shortage of capital	42.1	52.4
Cannot afford to hire wage labour	2.9	1.6
Lack of technical know-how	2.1	1.6
Limited demand for products	15.7	9.5
Too much competition	12.9	12.7
Lack of marketing and transport facilities	5.0	7.9
Lack of modern machinery/equipment	5.7	1.6
Lack of raw materials	1.4	0.0
Lack of energy	4.3	1.6
Uncertain government policies	2.1	1.6
Inadequate premises/space	0.0	0.0
Other	5.7	9.5
No constraint	0.0	0.0

enterprises; 15 per cent from state and 11 per cent from legal imports. More than half of the enterprises that mentioned severe competition were located in Haiphong, and these were mainly private enterprises. Hanoi followed (24 per cent) and Ho Chi Minh City had the least number of units facing severe competition (21 per cent). Across ownership forms, the co-operatives accounted for 44 per cent of the units facing severe competition, mainly from private enterprises. This is indicative of the changes occurring in the traditional co-operative sector, with the advent of new private enterprises since *doi moi*.

Governmental Assistance

During establishment almost 62 per cent of the enterprises availed themselves of governmental assistance in one form or another. The most common form of assistance was with submitting relevant documents and registering units with the government departments (41 per cent), followed by procuring tax exemptions (22 per cent) and assistance with the organisation of the enterprise.

It appears that most governmental assistance was given during the establishment of the enterprises, particularly in dealing with legal or official formalities. We find that 62 per cent of the enterprises either did not approach or did not receive assistance from government officials during the lifetime of the enterprise. It may be recalled that a majority of the entrepreneurs (48 per cent) were previously state employees and an additional 44 per cent served in local or other cadres (Table 9.3). This prior relationship with the state and its attendant networks and contacts might have been helpful in obtaining assistance with managing the enterprise as well as in marketing, directly or indirectly. Added to this is the fact that closures, mainly co-operatives, had very high forward and backward linkages with the state sector, thereby accounting for greater official assistance received. The propensity to secure governmental assistance in various areas was also, not surprisingly, higher among larger firms. The same tendency is found with regard to assistance during the lifetime of the enterprise. We can reasonably argue that smaller units, by virtue of their lesser degree of formality, need less bureaucratic assistance than larger firms and so there are size-determined advantages (or disadvantages); and that governmental assistance, being mainly non-monetary in nature, is more within the purview of large firms.

Rural Enterprises

The rural survey in 1991 was held in five provinces – Ha Son Binh, Vinh Phu, Quang Ninh, Long An and Cuu Long. However, the 1997 the survey was only undertaken in Ha Tay (formerly Ha Son Binh) in the north and Long An, in the south. Therefore, in the present chapter, we shall be discussing the data on Ha Tay and Long An only. The mortality rate among rural re-surveyed enterprises was 39 per cent (Table 1.7), with 56 out of the 144 re-surveyed enterprises closing down between 1991 and 1997.

Location and Organisational Structure

Closures in the rural areas were distributed almost equally among the northern and southern sample regions. Household industry dominated, with half the enterprises belonging to this category; close to 36 per cent were private enterprises and the remaining 14 per cent belonged to other categories.[14] There were no state enterprises in the sample. Across regions, 57 per cent of household enterprises and 65 per cent of private enterprises were located in Long An. Even though Long An was host to more enterprises in each category, relatively speaking, private enterprises were less common in Ha Tay. Only 35 per cent of private enterprises were located there, against 43 per cent of household industry. Other forms of ownership, however, were more prevalent in Ha Tay (88 per cent) than in Long An (12 per cent).

Nature of Activity

The most common area of activity in the 1991 survey among the rural closures was manufacturing. Close to 50 per cent of the enterprises were involved in it, 21 per cent in agro-processing, and the remaining in various forms of commercial trading. Among survivors, the corresponding percentages were 64, 17 and 19 per cent respectively. Mortality rates among manufacturing units were lowest: 33 per cent, compared to 44 per cent among trading and 46 per cent among agro-processing units. The percentage of agro-industries on the whole, is, not surprisingly, greater among rural than urban industries. It is interesting to note that all the agro-processing units that closed down were located in Long An and that a majority of the manufacturing enterprises (88 per cent) were located in Ha Tay. This distribution probably has something to do with the extent of economic development in both these regions. In the 1991 survey Ha Tay (then known as Ha Sonh Binh) was more agrarian and had more household firms dominated by handicraft industry than Long An, which had a relatively more diversified economic base.[15]

Enterprise History: Years in Operation

The average amount of years of operation among the rural closures was approximately nine, mainly because of the 6 per cent of enterprises that had existed prior to 1976. The most striking feature relating to the age of rural enterprises is that a majority of the enterprises (59 per cent) were three years old or less at the time of the survey in 1991 (Table 9.17). This scenario stands in stark contrast to the urban enterprises, where we found more than 40 per cent of the units were 11 years old or more at the time of the survey. Infant mortality has accounted for most closures among rural enterprises, and is symptomatic of an underdeveloped economic environment for rural entrepreneurship. Table 9.17 also shows the age distribution of rural

Table 9.17: Year of establishment and age of rural enterprises at closure.

Year of establishment:	% surviving enterprises	% closures	Age at closure	% closures
Before 1976	9.6	5.6	Under 5 years	26.0
1976–80	7.2	11.1	5–10 years	52.0
1981–85	9.6	13.0	11–15 years	14.8
1986	2.4	3.7	16–20 years	1.8
1987	9.6	7.4	21–25 years	0.0
1988	19.3	18.5	Over 25 years	5.5
1989	21.7	18.5		
1990	20.5	22.2		

survivors and closures. It is clear that a high 22 per cent were only one year old in the 1991 survey and had all closed down subsequently within a maximum of six years in operation, by 1997.

Representative of the distribution of ownership forms, household enterprises accounted for more than half of the units that closed down within ten years of operation. There was no private enterprise older than 15 years in our sample; only two co-operatives and one household enterprise were established before 1976. Overall, it is apparent that most rural closures have been of a fairly recent origin and the process of consolidation has been occurring rapidly, with a large proportion of closures within ten years of operation. The reasons stated for closure (Table 9.18) will throw light on this process of consolidation.

Similar to the urban scenario, an inability to sell at profit accounted for the closure of almost 54 per cent of the rural enterprises, followed by personal reasons (retirement or death of entrepreneur) for 20 per cent of closures. Most units cited these two reasons exclusively. Almost 65 per cent of the private and 43 per cent of the household enterprises shut down as a result of low profit margins. The major reasons offered for this inability to sell at profit were: very high production costs (37 per cent), too much competition in the output market (33 per cent) and poor distribution and marketing channels (20 per cent). High production costs and competition were mentioned by Long An firms while Ha Tay firms gave poor marketing channels as the reason for low profitability. Almost 60 per cent of the units quoting low

Table 9.18: Main reasons for closing down. Rural enterprises.

Reason:	% closures
Could not sell at profit	53.6
Lack of raw material	0.0
Delayed payment from customers	0.0
Interference from government officials/local authorities	1.8
Personal reasons	19.6
Other reasons	25.0

profit margins as the reason for closure were three years old or less at the time of the survey, which highlights the importance of high profit margins and internally generated capital in the firm's early years.

Entrepreneurial Characteristics

As Table 9.19 shows, in the 1991 survey, the typical owner-manager of the (subsequent) closures was male, more than 50 years old, with a formal education of at least seven years and an employment background in a state enterprise. However, 40 per cent mention 'other' experience, which includes farming activities, thereby making it possible that many entrepreneurs have a background in farming, though the extent is not clear. The profile of this entrepreneur is not very different from that among survivors. The percentage of women entrepreneurs (almost ten) among closures is slightly higher among rural than urban areas. Similar to the urban areas, most of the entrepreneurs older than 50 years (58 per cent) were mainly managing household enterprises. While enterprises older than ten years at the time of the survey in 1991 were almost solely managed by entrepreneurs over 50 years old, they constituted only a fifth of the enterprises in this age category and the majority of 56 per cent of the entrepreneurs managed enterprises less then four years old in the 1991 survey.

Unlike the urban scenario, the average age of the enterprises itself is quite low in the rural sample and it is obvious that most entrepreneurs were managing fairly new units. The more interesting finding is that older entrepreneurs had been involved with household enterprises, whereas younger entrepreneurs (mainly under 30 years of age)

Table 9.19: Characteristics of owner-managers in the 1991 survey. Rural enterprises.

	% surviving enterprises	% closures
Sex:		
Male	83.3	90.2
Female	16.7	9.8
Age:		
29 years or less	11.9	17.6
30–39 years	23.8	29.4
40–49 years	25.0	15.7
50 years or over	39.3	37.3
Mean	44.8	43.5
Education:		
4 years or less	11.9	11.8
5–7 years	57.1	45.1
8–10 years	17.9	27.5
Over 10 years	13.1	15.7
Experience:		
Local cadre	16.1	15.2
War veteran	12.9	6.1
State enterprise employee	16.1	21.2
Other position of responsibility	6.5	3.0
Petty trader	12.9	15.2
Other	35.5	39.4

had established private enterprises. Further, it is this younger category of entrepreneurs that have had the benefits of higher education too; since most of the entrepreneurs with more than ten years of education were under 30 years of age.

Next, not surprisingly, most of the youngest entrepreneurs have had no prior work experience, while a large percentage of the other categories have been previously employed in the state sector in one form or the other. A possibly[16] disconcerting development is that 8 per cent of the managers of closures have subsequently moved into agriculture, and all in Ha Tay. Only one rural manager reported unemployment. On the whole, it appears that Long An entrepreneurs have continued self-employment in the same or other lines of business to a greater degree than in Ha Tay. Across ownership forms, subsequent movement into agriculture has been characteristic of household enterprises, while private entrepreneurs have moved into newer lines of business after the closure of enterprises.

Primary Income Source

It is apparent from the household activity data that all the closure-enterprise households were involved in some kind of agricultural activity: farming, animal husbandry, or fishery and aquaculture. All of the households recorded self-employment in agriculture throughout the year, which indicates that the enterprise was not a sole source of livelihood to any rural enterprise household (Table 9.20). This situation was slightly different among survivors, where only a quarter reported household members gainfully employed in agriculture. The most important feature is that 98 per cent of the closures had household members working (unpaid) at the family enterprise, averaging two workers other than the owner. Though not very significant, wage employment in other enterprises is also found. Other forms of self-employment were found among a fifth of the enterprises, almost all in Ha Tay. The diversity in income sources was more in Ha Tay.

Table 9.20: Sources of household income in the 1991 survey. Rural enterprises.

Source:	% surviving enterprises	% closures
Enterprise as sole source	9.1	0.0
Wage employment	5.7	8.9
Farming	25.3	100.0
Other	14.9	33.3*

Key: * Includes self-employment (20.3%) and gifts and remittances (13%).

Scale of Operations

The scale of operations, as before, is discussed in terms of initial investment and assets in the 1991 survey, in 1996 prices. The average initial investment for rural closures was 16 million dong, while the average total assets in the 1991 survey were 80 million dong. The average closure enterprise was much larger than its surviving counter-part, which had 8 million dong in initial investment and only

33 million dong in assets in the 1991 survey. However, there is a distinct difference in the scale of operations across urban and rural areas. The average urban closures unit is at least seven times larger than its rural counterpart. As shown in Table 9.21, there is a clustering of enterprises around the 1.5–5 million and 5–25 million dong (initial investment) categories among both surviving enterprises and closures, but they graduate to the 5–25 million categories and higher (in assets) by the 1991 survey. The closures with the highest initial investments (over 25 million dong) were two co-operatives, established before 1976 in Ha Tay; these are responsible for raising the average of the whole sample to 16 million dong.[17]

Across ownership forms, apart from the two largest co-operatives, household enterprises were on average a third of the size of private enterprises. The average initial investment of household enterprises was 5 million dong, with half the units investing only 3 million dong, while the average private enterprise invested 18 million dong; the median value being 14 million dong. At establishment, the average firm size in Long An was slightly smaller (14 million dong), than in Ha Tay (18 million dong), mainly because of the two co-operatives in Ha Tay, each of which had a minimum investment of 125 million dong. Excluding these two, the average Ha Tay firm is half the size of its Long An counterpart (7 million dong).

The second half of Table 9.21 shows the asset distribution in the 1991 survey among rural surviving and closures units. We find that investment on asset creation since establishment has been quite low, probably due to the fact that most units were fairly young at the time of the survey in 1991. Even though a majority of the units (61 per cent) had zero per cent growth rate of assets, the average growth rate for the sample was 13 per cent a year, mainly due to a minority (12 per cent) whose assets grew in excess of 52 per cent a year.[18] In relative terms, there is no significant difference in asset growth rates across ownership forms, since the majority were less than five years old and had zero per cent growth rates. The average asset growth rate for household enterprises is 14 per cent and the corresponding figure is 13 per cent for private enterprises. Across regions, Long An had an average rate of 14 per cent while the percentage in Ha Tay was 10. Further, the typical

Table 9.21: Initial investment (at establishment) and total assets in the 1991 survey. Rural enterprises. Thousand dong.

	% surviving enterprises	% closures
Initial investment at establishment:		
Less than 500	3.6	3.8
501–1,500	9.6	9.4
1,501–5,000	41.0	34.0
5,001–25,000	36.1	30.2
25,001–50,000	6.0	17.0
More than 50,000	3.6	5.7
Total assets in the 1991 survey		
Less than 500	0.0	3.8
501–1,500	8.0	1.9
1,501–5,000	14.9	19.2
5,001–25,000	40.2	34.6
25,001–50,000	18.4	21.2
Over 50,000	18.4	19.2

surviving enterprise grew at an annual average rate of 22 per cent while it was 13 per cent for the average closure enterprise.

On the whole, it is apparent that the rural closures have been more homogeneous, with very few outliers in terms of size and growth rates. Low asset growth is a common factor for most of the rural closures; whether it is the determining factor is hard to say at this point. We find that units that have asset growth rates in excess of 25 per cent per year mentioned an inability to sell at profit as the reason for closure of enterprises. This strengthens our hypothesis that high capital accumulation is a necessary but not sufficient condition for the healthy survival of firms.

Related to the need for capital accumulation and asset growth is the question of investment finance for rural enterprises. The reliance on own resources is much more pronounced here than among urban enterprises. Almost 66 per cent of the entrepreneurs used only their own savings for establishing the enterprise (Table 9.22). Bank financing is conspicuous by its total absence. It can be noticed that about 4 per cent of the enterprises relied on cash advances of sales to cover at least half

Table 9.22: Percentage distribution of investment finance at establishment by source. Rural closures.

	0	1–25	26–50	51–75	76–99	100
Own resources	9.4	11.32	5.7	5.7	1.9	66.0
Friends and family	88.7	3.8	5.7	0.0	0.0	1.9
Banks	100.0	0.0	0.0	0.0	0.0	0.0
Credit co-operatives	98.1	1.9	0.0	0.0	0.0	0.0
Local authorities	98.1	1.9	0.0	0.0	0.0	0.0
Employees	96.2	3.8	0.0	0.0	0.0	0.0
Private moneylenders	88.7	0.0	3.8	3.8	1.9	1.9
Advance against sales	94.3	0.0	1.9	1.9	1.9	0.0
Others	92.5	1.9	0.0	0.0	3.8	1.9

the initial investments. Since household enterprises predominate and they have the greatest propensity to use personal resources (at establishment as well as during operative years), the rural enterprises present a scenario of self-sufficient units prepared to shut down operations at any time without much cost. This trend is true even of investments financed after establishment. Only five units mention securing external finances from a non-bank source. In fact, in the 1991 survey, with more than 70 per cent of enterprises being less than five years old (see Table 9.17), it is surprising that only eight enterprises had outstanding liabilities. It is hard to overlook the high degree of uncertainty in the minds of the entrepreneurs with regard to the success of their entrepreneurial endeavours, which reflects in their weak relationships with external credit sources.

The lack of correlation between the size of enterprises and the use (not even magnitude) of external credit found among urban enterprises is even more glaring among rural enterprises. Without credit, liabilities, (usually) wage labour and a low degree of mechanisation, it is possible for entrepreneurs to start, exit or change lines of activity very easily. It seems that the firms have achieved a kind of 'organisational flexibility' that insures them against possible losses of heavy magnitude, particularly if the entrepreneurs are over 50 years old and are investing their savings in non-farm endeavours.

Mechanisation

The very distinct scale difference across urban and rural firms is well accounted for by the low degree of mechanisation among rural firms. As Table 9.23 shows, close to 70 per cent of the rural enterprises operated without power-driven machinery, with 53 per cent using only hand tools in the 1991 survey. The percentage operating without power-driven machinery was significantly greater among closures than surviving enterprises. Ha Tay had a greater percentage of units that used only hand tools (60 per cent) while Long An had the greatest number that used both manually operated and power-driven machinery. Further, according to expectations, non-household enterprises had a greater propensity to use machinery; half the household enterprises used only hand tools. Most of the agro-processing units used machinery, both manually operated and power-driven. A majority of the firms that used machinery (64 per cent) acquired it new; fewer units bought second-hand machinery (24 per cent) and the remaining 12 per cent (all in Ha Tay) constructed the machinery in-house. All the units owned the machinery they used and did not hire from external sources for temporary use.

Table 9.23: Type of machinery used among rural enterprises. 1991 survey.

Type of machinery:	% surviving enterprises	% closures
Only hand tools, no machinery	49.4	52.9
Manually operated machinery only	7.4	15.7
Power-driven machinery only	8.6	9.8
Both manually operated and power-driven machinery	34.6	21.6

Employment

The homogeneity in the scale of operations is also noted in the total employment in each of the rural enterprises. As Table 9.24 shows, close to 81 per cent of the closures employed less than ten workers, and many of these were household members, since the bottom half of the table shows that more than half of the units did not employ wage labour. The situation is similar among surviving enterprises also, though the percentage using no wage labour is slightly greater among

Table 9.24: Employment in rural enterprises. 1991 survey.

	% surviving enterprises	% closures
Total no. of employees:		
1–10	83.7	80.8
11–25	11.6	11.5
26–50	2.3	1.9
51–70	1.2	1.9
Over 70	1.2	3.8
No. of wage employees:		
0	43.7	51.9
1–10	47.1	36.5
11–25	4.6	5.8
26–50	3.4	1.9
51–70	1.1	1.9
Over 70	0.0	1.9

closures. However, the average number of employees per unit was 12 among closures and eight among surviving; the average number of wage employees per unit was seven for closures and five for surviving enterprises, because of one partnership unit in Ha Tay employing 135 wage workers.

None of the household industries used wage labour. On the other hand, all the private enterprises used some percentage of wage labour, on average the figure was 62 per cent. Only one co-operative employed 100 per cent wage workers. Ha Tay had a greater number of enterprises employing a larger percentage of wage workers; in Long An the maximum percentage of wage workers was 85. We found no significant direct correlation between the size of firms and wage employment. The co-efficient of correlation was 0.03.

In this scenario, it appears that household enterprises were mainly a source of self-employment rather than wage employment. Private enterprises, on the other hand, were more important in wage employment generation. Capital intensity (measured in terms of assets per worker) was lowest among co-operatives (4 million dong), on average, and highest among household enterprises (13 million dong) on account of their respective percentages of employment. Private enterprises were mid-way, with an average capital intensity of 7 million dong. Similarly, Ha Tay turned out to be the more capital-intensive region with 13 million dong invested, on average, in the 1991 survey compared with 7 million dong in Long An. It is highly probable that this low level of outside employment has made it easier for the firms to exit.

Production Flexibility

The importance of production flexibility has already been discussed, in the section on urban enterprises. As before, if one measures flexibility in terms of the introduction of and improvements to products and services in the period 1989–91, one might think at first glance that rural closures have not been very flexible (Table 9.25). Only 21 per cent of the rural sample introduced new products and slightly over a quarter initiated improvements to existing products and services. However close to 38 per cent of the rural enterprises were set up in 1989–90, and hence the question was not applicable to them. Moreover, an additional 30 per cent were less than five years old at the time of the 1991 survey and therefore this low degree of change is understandable.

Table 9.25: Product changes and their impact among rural enterprises. 1991 survey.

Nature of flexibility:	% surviving enterprises	% closures
Introduced new products	17.4	20.8
Made improvements to existing products	30.2	26.4
Reason for change:		
Difficult to sell current product	32.0	27.7
Increasing competition from producers	36.0	11.1
Increasing competition from imports	0.0	11.1
Purchaser requests	24.0	33.3
Other	8.3	16.7
Degree of success:		
Unsuccessful	7.7	0.0
Not very successful	23.1	12.5
Quite successful	61.5	37.5
Very successful	0.0	12.5
Too early to tell	7.7	37.5

Among those that did introduce changes, Ha Tay was more dynamic than Long An, and private enterprises were found to be slightly more flexible than household enterprises.

Regarding the immediate success of these changes, none of the respondents thought they were unsuccessful. The most important reason for this perception is that a majority of the changes were initiated upon requests from buyers (30 per cent), and not at the initiative of the producers themselves. In such cases, success is defined not as self-initiated efforts toward the development of new markets, but more as adapting to retain existing markets. The most optimistic respondents were from Ha Tay. Difficulty in selling existing products prompted another 27 per cent to alter the production mix. On the whole, production flexibility did not play a dominant role in the operations of rural enterprises.

Continuity of Operations

The implications of continuous operations throughout the year for an enterprise have already been noted. Among the rural closures, discontinuity in operations was slightly more pronounced than in urban areas – 55 per cent of the rural enterprises did not operate throughout the whole year in the 1991 survey.[19] The average period of closure (among closures) in a year was 3.3 months for those with discontinuous operations. It is clear from the data that household enterprises are more prone to close down for intermittent periods. Not only did they account for 43 per cent of the enterprises that closed down temporarily, but the average period of closure was also higher than for non-household forms. Overall, 53 per cent of the household enterprises, and 57 per cent of the private enterprises shut down operations for part of the year in the 1991 survey.[20]

It is not difficult to envisage the close relationship between agricultural and non-agricultural activities in the rural households; as Table 9.26 shows, a majority of the enterprises mentioned the agricultural peak season as the reason for closing down operations temporarily. In view of the fact that all the closures had an income from farming (Table 9.20), the percentage of 30 who cited temporary closures on account of the agricultural peak season is quite low.

Wage labour in closures is conspicuous by its near-absence and whatever household labour is used would have to be diverted to

Table 9.26: Continuity of operations in the 1991 survey. Rural enterprises.

Months operated and reasons for closure:	% surviving enterprises	% closures
Operated throughout the year*	52.9	45.2
Closed for:		
1 month	1.1	0.0
2 months	5.7	16.7
3 months	11.5	19.0
4 months	5.7	7.1
5 months	2.3	2.4
6 months	0.0	4.8
7 months	1.1	2.4
Reasons for closure:		
Agricultural peak season	52.2	30.4
Lack of raw material	17.4	0.0
Lack of demand	30.4	26.1
Other reasons	26.1	13.1

Key: * The 1991 survey refers to operations throughout the year 1990.
Note: Percentages for reasons for closure are based on the number of units that did not operate throughout 1990. All closures did not respond to this question.

agricultural operations during peak seasons and therefore, the non-agricultural enterprise would have to stop temporarily. Next, lack of demand is also mentioned by more than a quarter of the enterprises that had discontinuous operations, which reflects instability in the output markets. As explained earlier in the case of urban enterprises, it is possible that the very small size of the firms combined with low output reach create this 'lack of demand'.

Capacity Utilisation

Related to the issue of lack of demand is the extent of production capacity utilisation. Unlike the urban scenario, a greater percentage of rural enterprises (30) reported working at full capacity (See Table 9.27).[21] They were mainly agro-processing, private enterprises and all of them were located in Long An. As the table shows, close to a fifth of the closures reported that they could increase their production by more than 100 per cent if they employed all their machinery and equipment. Compared to the survivors, the closures had a greater

Table 9.27: Capacity utilisation among rural enterprises. 1991 survey.

Extent of utilisation:	**% surviving enterprises**	**% closures**
Operating at full capacity	12.2	29.6
If employing all machinery & equipment, could increase production by:		
Up to 10%	17.1	7.4
11–25%	22.0	11.1
26–50%	24.0	25.9
51–100%	14.6	7.4
Over 100%	9.8	18.5

Note: Data for 53 per cent of surviving enterprises not included due to non-availability

percentage operating at full capacity, as well as those working at less than half their capacity. Almost 19 per cent (compared to 10 among the survivors) mentioned the possibility of increasing production by more than 100 per cent.

As discussed under urban enterprises, the extent of capacity utilisation is closely related to the growth rate of assets. Apart from the fact that the rural enterprises have a greater percentage of fairly young enterprises, it is clear that half the units with zero-per-cent growth rate in assets were operating at full capacity. That most of them were household enterprises describes a scenario where we have small enterprises with low assets and growth rates usually operating at full capacity. Those at the other end of the spectrum – viz. large enterprises with high assets and growth rates – have more often been working at less than full capacity, mostly due to lack of demand. This confirms our initial statement regarding the relationship between the size of rural closures units and their capacity utilisation.

Forward Linkages

We discuss forward linkages in terms of the destination of sales of the main product of the enterprises. Table 9.28 clearly shows the percentage distribution (among closures) of sales by category and location of buyers. According to the table, rural closures sold mainly to individual buyers and private enterprises; in large cities and their own villages. Considering that Ha Tay and Long An are both closely located to Hanoi and Ho Chi Minh City respectively, it is possible

Table 9.28: Forward linkages of main product among rural closures. 1991 survey. Percentages.

	0	1–24	25–49	50–74	75–99	100	Mean
Destination of sales of main product:							
Individuals	37.8	8.1	5.4	5.4	2.7	40.5	*48.9*
Private enterprises	56.8	2.7	2.7	8.1	5.4	24.3	*35.0*
State enterprises	86.5	2.7	0.0	0.0	2.7	8.1	*10.8*
Other state agency	97.3	0.0	0.0	0.0	0.0	2.7	*2.7*
Local authority	100.0	0.0	0.0	0.0	0.0	0.0	*0.0*
Tourists	100.0	0.0	0.0	0.0	0.0	0.0	*0.0*
Exports	97.3	0.0	0.0	0.0	2.7	0.0	*2.6*
Other	100.0	0.0	0.0	0.0	0.0	0.0	*0.0*
Geographical distribution of main product sales:							
Same village	75.0	2.8	5.6	2.8	2.8	11.1	*18.3*
Same commune	75.0	5.6	2.8	5.6	0.0	11.1	*13.6*
Same rural district	77.8	5.6	0.0	2.8	0.0	13.9	*16.7*
Nearby town	91.7	0.0	2.8	0.0	0.0	5.6	*6.4*
Large city	58.3	2.8	2.8	0.0	0.0	36.1	*37.5*
Elsewhere	88.9	2.8	0.0	2.8	0.0	5.6	*7.5*

that most of these enterprises were selling relatively more to the urban population in these two cities.

It is also apparent that most closures sold exclusively to one category of buyer; 41 per cent sold solely to individual buyers, 24 per cent sold exclusively to private enterprises and so on. Also clear are the low linkages with state agencies, quite unlike the urban scenario. Around 11 per cent of the enterprises sold solely to the state; however the instability caused by a restructuring state sector does not seem to have been a reason for closure among rural enterprises, since all units selling solely to the state quoted personal reasons for enterprise closure.

On average, a firm sold close to half its main product to individual buyers, 35 per cent to private enterprises and about 14 per cent to the state sector (Table 9.28). As with the urban units, the rural products were meant for mass consumption (carpentry, construction materials, tiling, etc.), which probably accounts for the higher percentage of sales to individual buyers.

Further, there seems to be a dichotomy between those enterprises selling exclusively in the local areas (36 per cent, including same village, commune and district) and those selling exclusively in the large cities (36 per cent). This tendency was more pronounced in Ha Tay. Increasing competition in the urban centres may have led to instability in the output markets, so 60 per cent of those selling to large cities report an inability to sell at profit as the main reason for enterprise closure.

Backward Linkages

Defined in terms of source of main raw material and location, backward linkages are important determinants of industrial location and survival. As Table 9.29 shows, linkages of rural enterprises to their respective rural territories in the 1991 survey were extremely poor. This is accounted partly by the nature of the raw material; in this case the main raw material includes wood, bamboo, chemicals, fertilisers, bricks, stones etc., making it inevitable for enterprises to rely less on households and more on other private enterprises. Proximity to big cities also might have resulted in their greater reliance on out-of-town suppliers. The reliance on the state sector is slightly greater among backward than forward linkages. Close to 16 per cent of the rural enterprises bought all of their main raw material from the state sector, while only 8 per cent sold entirely to the state sector. Given the nature of the raw materials, no unit bought from collective farms, hence it is clear that interdependence between rural agricultural and non-agricultural sectors has been weaker, in this respect.

The location of input providers is a better indicator of the weak backward linkages. None of the enterprises bought their main raw material from the same village. About a fifth bought the whole quantity of main raw material solely from the same commune and large cities, while the largest number (35 per cent) bought it from nearby towns. On average, a rural enterprise bought close to 60 per cent of its main raw material from urban areas, which indicates low backward linkages with rural areas. That this trend is true of all ownership forms and spheres of activity is an important point to note, when analysing the impact of non-farm sector development on the local economy. It

Table 9.29: Backward linkages of main raw material among rural closures. 1991 survey. Percentages.

	0	1–24	25–49	50–74	75–99	100	Mean
Main input supplier:							
Households	78.1	0.0	0.0	0.0	0.0	21.9	21.9
Private enterprises	40.6	0.0	3.1	3.1	0.0	53.1	55.9
State enterprises	84.4	0.0	0.0	3.1	0.0	12.5	14.4
Other state agency	93.8	0.0	0.0	3.1	0.0	3.1	4.7
Collective farms	100.0	0.0	0.0	0.0	0.0	0.0	0.0
Other	96.9	0.0	0.0	0.0	0.0	3.1	3.1
Location of main input supplier:							
Same town	100.0	0.0	0.0	0.0	0.0	0.0	0.0
Same commune	73.0	2.7	0.0	2.7	2.7	18.9	23.5
Nearby town	56.8	0.0	2.7	5.4	0.0	35.1	38.9
Large city	70.3	2.7	5.4	0.0	2.7	18.9	23.5
Elsewhere	83.8	0.0	0.0	5.4	0.0	10.8	14.1

appears that many rural enterprises, both in Ha Tay and Long An, are located solely in rural areas, but have most of their transactions with urban areas. Geographical proximity to urban areas is the most reasonable explanation for this behaviour. Most units (70 per cent) felt that raw material availability was not a problem: the ones that felt otherwise have offered no description of the problem. Only two agro-processing units reported seasonality of supply as a problem.

Horizontal Linkages

Horizontal linkages, viewed from the point of view of subcontracting relationships, were not very prevalent among rural enterprises in the 1991 survey. Only eight enterprises (14 per cent of the sample) subcontracted; three each with private enterprises in the same town and state enterprises, and one with a private enterprise elsewhere.[22] All of the subcontracting units were in Ha Tay. The duration of contracts, however, was very short, ranging from five months to a year. Six of the eight subcontracting units mentioned receiving assistance from the parent company: four in the area of procuring raw materials, one in managerial assistance and one in training workers.

So it is clear that horizontal linkages were not a strong feature of rural enterprises either in Ha Tay or Long An.

Production Relations

Similar to the urban scenario, rural enterprises predominantly (54 per cent) sold to over ten customers in the 1991 survey. As expected, most household enterprises sold to more than ten customers, while a large number of private enterprises sold to less than ten customers. Further, a majority of enterprises selling to more than ten customers (70 per cent) a year were located in Long An, while Ha Tay accounted for more enterprises (63 per cent) selling to the category of two to ten buyers. The number of customers is determined by the nature of the product as well as the production contract. Since most of the enterprises in our sample dealt with production of goods for everyday consumption, we find that it is more common to have sales to more than ten customers.

Constraints

Data from the 1991 survey on main constraints to the enterprises, as perceived by the entrepreneurs themselves, indicate problems in both input and output markets. Specifically, as Table 9.30 points out, shortage of capital was the most frequently cited constraint (by 32 per cent of the rural enterprises), but an almost equal number (28 per cent) quoted limited demand for their products. We may recollect, at this juncture, that 54 per cent of the enterprises shut down because of an inability to sell at profit. While the percentage mentioning capital constraints is not very different from the survivors, the percentage mentioning limited demand is higher.

It is apparent that, while capital shortage can be overcome by recourse to informal sources of capital, it is harder for an enterprise to survive against limited product demand. The two possible courses of action in this situation would be to alter their product mix or shut down operations. Our earlier finding[23] shows that almost half the enterprises chose the former course, yet shut down operations. So, it is possible that a general insufficiency of demand was caused by the location of sales (in this case, mainly urban) and the attendant ills of too much competition. A significant 13 per cent of the entrepreneurs mentioned competition as a major constraint, strengthening our belief. The

Table 9.30: Respondent perception of main constraint among rural enterprises. 1991 survey. Percentages.

Nature of constraint:	% surviving enterprises	% closures
Shortage of capital	32.9	31.5
Cannot afford to hire wage labour	0.0	0.0
Lack of technical know-how	0.0	0.0
Limited demand for products	19.5	27.8
Too much competition	6.1	12.9
Lack of marketing and transport facilities	8.5	7.4
Lack of modern machinery/equipment	2.4	0.0
Lack of raw materials	1.2	1.9
Lack of energy	1.2	0.0
Interference by local officials	2.4	1.9
Uncertain government policies	3.7	3.8
Inadequate premises/space	0.0	0.0
Other	22.0	9.5
No constraint	0.0	0.0

shortage of capital was felt by an equal number of enterprises in Ha Tay and Long An, but perceptions of limited demand and competition dominated in Long An.

However, unlike the urban scenario, the shortage of capital was felt by smaller units; in fact the agro-processing units (which constitute some of largest enterprises in our sample) mentioned competition as a greater constraint than capital.[24] More manufacturing units, on the other hand, regarded capital as the main constraint (38 per cent) and limited product demand was the second most commonly cited constraint (25 per cent). Apart from capital, no other input shortage was significant; only one unit mentioned insufficiency of raw materials as a major constraint. On the whole, various factors in the product markets seemed to be the more dominant constraint. Further, not surprisingly, perceptions of limited product demand were more common among household than among non-household enterprises. Since household enterprises are generally small and more informal, their capital requirements are consequently small, and marketing can be a serious constraint, especially if the destination of products is large cities (as in our rural sample). The relatively higher incidence of the transport problem seems to be directly related to the urban destination of sales.

Competition

Competition in the product market was much more commonly felt among rural enterprises in the 1991 survey. More than a third felt that there were too many enterprises producing similar goods in the market, while 44 per cent felt that there were neither too many nor too few. This correlates with our earlier finding that only about 13 per cent regard competition as a major constraint (Table 9.30). The perception of severe competition was much more subdued among non-household forms. It was the household enterprise category that was most acutely aware of too much competition. Across regions, most of the enterprises that felt this way were located in Long An (64 per cent), while an equal number of enterprises felt there were too many enterprises in both Ha Tay and Long An. Among those that did acknowledge the existence of severe competition, the main source of competition cited was private enterprises (74 per cent), followed by legal imports (15 per cent). None of the enterprises perceived competition from state enterprises to be severe; a majority of 81 per cent of the enterprises felt that they had no competition from state enterprises.

Governmental Assistance

The data on the nature and extent of governmental assistance indicate that there were very limited relations with the government. Close to 59 per cent of the enterprises reportedly received no assistance from government authorities at the time of start-up. Among those that utilised it, assistance in completing application procedures for registration etc. was the most common form; on the whole 19 per cent of the rural enterprises used some help in this regard. The other areas where enterprises availed themselves of governmental assistance were: temporary tax exemptions (11 per cent), recommendation on line of business (4 per cent) and procuring machinery (4 per cent). An important finding is that most of the units that secured official assistance were household enterprises (64 per cent). The fact that more than a third of the rural entrepreneurs had been previously employed in the state sector and that most of them started household enterprises might explain the higher incidence of government contacts among household enterprises. It is possible that governmental linkages that had been previously established during their service have helped them in their entrepreneurial endeavours. Only five units utilised governmental assistance in more than one area.[25]

The trend is worse when we consider official assistance procured during the lifetime of the enterprises. Almost 82 per cent of the entrepreneurs did not receive (or seek) governmental assistance; among those that did, the main areas were obtaining inputs, resolving managerial issues, marketing and obtaining credit. The percentage of enterprises receiving help in any of these categories is insignificant (less than 4 per cent each). Across regions, Long An entrepreneurs showed a slightly greater propensity towards official assistance; they accounted for 57 per cent of all entrepreneurs who secured this type of support. It is thus clear that linkages with governmental authorities have been poor, and the nature of assistance has been mainly bureaucratic.

Notes

1. Excluding the state sector; there were only six state enterprises in the 1991 survey and all closed down.

2. It must be noted that half of the respondents to these questions were close friends and not the previous owners/managers themselves. Caution is therefore warranted in taking these replies at face value.

3. We may recall that most household enterprises were also less than five years old, which confirms that these older entrepreneurs started their entrepreneurial careers through establishing household enterprises.

4. The data on household income sources were collected from household and private enterprises only. The percentages calculated are, therefore, based on the number of household and private enterprises only.

5. The data on household income sources were collected from household and private enterprises only. The percentages calculated are, therefore, based on the number of household and private enterprises only.

6. Also, Haiphong had the highest proportion of enterprises set up before 1981 (56 per cent); and more than half of the Haiphong units had initial investments greater than 100 million dong.

7. At 1989 prices, the gross output of the local industry in 1990 in Haiphong was the lowest at 128 billion dong, compared to a higher 367 billion dong in Hanoi and a massive 2,180 billion dong in Ho Chi Minh City (*Statistical Year Book 1996*, (1997) General Statistical Office, Hanoi: Socialist Republic of Vietnam, Table 81, p. 130).

8. The co-efficient of correlation works out at 0.6, significant at the 1-per-cent level.

9. Capital intensity here is measured as investment on assets per worker not necessarily a wage employee.

10. Capital intensity here is measured as investment on assets per worker not necessarily a wage employee.

11. Only the private enterprises fared worse than household enterprises on this count, since only 25 per cent of private enterprises introduced new products.

12. Of these, 43 per cent were co-operatives, 25 per cent were private enterprises, 19 per cent were partnerships and 13 per cent were household enterprises.

13. Of these, 43 per cent were co-operatives, 25 per cent were private enterprises, 19 per cent were partnerships and 13 per cent were household enterprises.

14. The other categories included five partnerships and two co-operative enterprises.

15. See the Introduction in *Employment Generation through Private Entrepreneurship in Vietnam* by Per Ronnås (1992), (SIDA/ILO-ARTEP, pp. 17–19) for a discussion of economic characteristics of the provinces in 1991.

16. We know from Table 9.19 that close to 40 per cent of entrepreneurs had previous experience in 'other' areas, but we do not know the specifications therein. It is not unreasonable to assume that this category might include agriculture; but we do not know how many entrepreneurs had actually moved from agriculture to industry in the first place. As a result, we cannot say it is disconcerting for sure. After trying industry for a while, this 8 per cent might have gone back to agriculture, in which case it is not as disturbing as if they entered agriculture as a forced alternative.

17. Excluding the two co-operatives, the average for the group is 11 million dong.

18. They were three household enterprises (two in Ha Tay and one in Long An) and two private enterprises (in Long An).

19. We have excluded 14 industries (25 per cent of our rural closures sample) which started operations in 1990, from this calculation.

20. Relative to their respective numbers, the percentage among household enterprises is lower, since their absolute number is higher; but relative to other ownership forms, the household enterprises account for a larger percentage of discontinuously operative enterprises.

21. This percentage is based on the number of respondents to this question, which was low, at 48 per cent. The remaining respondents did not reply.

22. Data on the subcontracting partner are not available for the eighth unit.

23. See the section on Rural Production Flexibility.

24. In fact, only one agro-processing unit mentioned capital shortage as a constraint.

25. These include organisation of the enterprise, obtaining credit and introduction for collaborative ventures.

10

Summary and Conclusions

Per Ronnås and Bhargavi Ramamurthy

The economic structure of the Republic of Vietnam has been undergoing fundamental transformation since the initiation of *doi moi*, the winds of change, which heralded a new era of market economy in the late 1980s. In the framework of the reforms, a major role has been assigned to the infant non-state industrial sector in generating employment, income and growth for the whole nation. Development of the non-state manufacturing sector, particularly small-scale industries, was imperative since the state industries were deemed both inefficient and ill-equipped to assume the role of growth engines, and for the modernisation of the economy as a whole.

Statistics relating to the performance of the non-state sector outside agriculture, however, reveal mixed results, and on the whole describe a sector that has not met the high expectations of the reforms, in its role as a growth engine. However, the performance of the non-state manufacturing sector has been impressive in both numbers as well as the extent of transformation at the micro level. Based on two comprehensive surveys in 1991 and 1997, the present study provides an in-depth study of the transformation of the non-state and small-scale manufacturing sector in the 1990s.

The survey results, due to the methodology followed, is more representative of the urban scenario than the rural one. Since the surveys were held in the three major cities of Vietnam – Hanoi, Ho Chi

Minh City and Haiphong – the results provide us with a fairly representative picture of urban Vietnam. However, for the rural sample, close proximity to urban centres might have had a lot of influence on the behaviour of enterprises in Ha Tay and Long An. This influence is particularly seen in the linkages of rural enterprises to large cities. We cannot, therefore, conclusively assert that our rural results are very representative of rural Vietnam. A similar endeavour in more remote rural locations might present a totally different picture. However, the pressure to grow and succeed has, no doubt, been common to all parts of Vietnam, the rural scene being no exception.

General Characteristics

Generally speaking, small-scale enterprises in Vietnam were considerably larger and more robust in the 1997 survey than they had been six years earlier. Income, capital and assets have all grown, among the urban as well as the rural enterprises. Furthermore, higher levels of value added per worker unveil growth not only in size, but also in efficiency. The increases in labour productivity are universal and in many instances remarkable. In Hanoi it increased by as much as 70 per cent. This growth has been linked to a general increase in the capital intensity of the enterprises. Workers today have much more machinery and equipment at hand than six years ago. However, there are exceptions to the trend towards both larger and more efficient enterprises. In Haiphong enterprises today use less capital and labour and have lower levels of income than they did six years ago, although the value added produced per worker has increased. This suggests that restructuring in Haiphong has resulted in smaller as well as more efficient enterprises.

Most urban enterprises are located in premises that are fully owned by the owner(s) of the enterprise, yet separate from the living quarters of the owner family. In rural areas, particularly in Ha Tay, it is more common for the enterprise to be located in the same premises as the owner household resides in. Virtually all urban enterprises have access to power, tap water and telephone. The provision of such facilities has also improved vastly in the rural enterprises since the 1991 survey, but it still falls short of the levels attained in the urban areas. It is particularly encouraging to note that the share of rural enterprises with electricity has increased from less than half in the 1991 survey to almost 100 per cent in the 1997 survey.

The enterprises generally provide the main source of income to the owner families. Only in Hanoi do about a quarter of the owner households derive most of their income from other sources. The proportion of owner households which claim to have suffered a decline in income in the past two years is also much higher in Hanoi than in the other two cities. In the rural areas, the incomes of the owner households have generally had a more positive development in Ha Tay than in Long An.

A majority of the enterprises state that they could increase production by 10 to 50 per cent without any additional capital investment. Only in Ho Chi Minh City do most enterprises operate at the maximum capacity level. Intense competition is the most frequently stated constraint to growth of enterprises in Ho Chi Minh City, while lack of demand is more of a problem in Hanoi and Ha Tay. In Haiphong and Long An, shortage of capital is more commonly seen as the main constraint to growth.

Origin

It appears that a majority of 'new' urban enterprises surveyed in 1997 had been set up since the initiation of *doi moi.* The diversity of ownership forms has been greater than was the case among the enterprises surveyed in 1991. The typical entrepreneur is a middle-aged male with at least ten years of education and prior experience in similar fields in a position of responsibility. This prior experience, in fact, has been a major motivating factor for undertaking independent entrepreneurial activity. On establishment, the most severe difficulties faced by them have mainly been lack of capital and marketing outlets. Government regulations and bureaucratic procedures are not mentioned as major constraints. On the contrary, a large majority of enterprises obtained official assistance during the start-up period. There is a significant lack of external capital in start-up investments of the firms and this is indicative of weak financial institutions and a still insecure economic environment for investments with high risk and volume. In our sample, Hanoi has the largest percentage of household enterprises and hence, the size of investments is small, in relation to the other cities. Enterprises established after 1990 have a greater propensity to secure external credit and official assistance. These factors describe an economic environment that is becoming increasingly favourable for private entrepreneurial growth and sustainability; yet a lot remains to be done to stabilise this growth.

The origin and development history of rural Vietnamese enterprises are, in many ways, similar to the those of urban enterprises. Since national macro-economic conditions have been the same, and private sector industry is of a fairly recent origin, we find that entrepreneurial responses and perceptions have been similar, though rural Vietnam is less diverse than urban Vietnam. Household and private enterprises dominate the scene. The typical rural entrepreneur is a middle-aged male, with at least seven years of education and previous experience in a position of responsibility. Local traditions have been major motivating factors, apart from this previous experience in establishing enterprises. Lack of capital and marketing outlets are the most frequently cited 'severe' constraints at the time of establishment, and many enterprises did not receive any official assistance at that time. The scale of enterprise operations is limited mainly to the entrepreneur's own savings, with little reliance on external capital. Furthermore, the enterprises in the north are much larger than those in the south, and manufacturing units are larger than agro-processing units. Overall, it appears that there is a healthy environment developing for rural private entrepreneurship and formal institutions are the most urgent need of the hour in determining their future success and growth.

Linkages

Regarding forward linkages, non-state enterprises are the biggest clients for enterprises in Hanoi and Ho Chi Minh City, and sales here are geographically more dispersed today than they were in the 1991 survey. By contrast, the establishments in Haiphong are more local today, and they have a higher share of individual persons as clients than the average firm in the other cities. State agencies, which accounted for more than 10 per cent of urban sales six years ago, have completely disappeared from the scene, but the number of clients has still increased. Production exclusively on advance order is not as common today as it used to be, nor is subcontracting.

Perceptions of severe competition are more widespread in Hanoi and Ho Chi Minh City than in Haiphong, but regardless of the city, non-state enterprises pose the worst threat. Only in Hanoi is the share of enterprises that perceives severe non-state competition smaller in the 1997 than in the 1991 survey. Competition from state enterprises is considered less of a threat today, except in Haiphong. In Haiphong and Ho Chi Minh City the percentage feeling there are too many enterprises on the market is higher today than in the 1991 survey, however fewer have accumulated unsold goods today. The markets are oversupplied according to most enterprises, regardless of location, much more so today than in the 1991 survey, but sales channels are on the other hand less of an obstacle than they used to be.

Individual buyers are the most important customers for rural enterprises, in particular in Long An and to a larger extent than in the 1991 survey. The enterprises in Long An, accordingly, sell more locally and have more customers than those in Ha Tay, though the average number of clients is higher today than in the 1991 survey in the rural areas in general. As much as 70 per cent of the firms in Long An firms never produce on order, while 75 per cent of those in Ha Tay do so at least occasionally. In rural, as in urban areas, production exclusively on advance order is less common today, but subcontracting has, in contrast to the case of the urban enterprises, become more common, especially in Ha Tay. The partner is usually a non-state enterprise, which in many cases also provides assistance with raw material and credits. A somewhat higher share of rural household enterprises than rural private firms is engaged in subcontracting.

A higher share of the enterprises in Ha Tay than in Long An experience severe competition. Irrespective of area, non-state enterprises pose the worst threat, more in the 1997 than in the 1991 survey. The percentage mentioning state competitors has increased as well, but from very low levels. The perception that there are too many enterprises in the market is also more common in Ha Tay than in Long An. As a consequence, a higher share of enterprises in Ha Tay than in Long An have accumulated unsold goods. The reasons are oversupplied markets in both areas, but more enterprises refer to this in Long An than in Ha Tay, and this problem is more severe in both areas today than it was in the 1991 survey.

As for backward linkages, non-state enterprises are the major raw material suppliers to the enterprises covered by the survey, in rural as well as urban areas. Households are more important suppliers to agro-processing enterprises than they are to manufacturing ones, while the roles of collective farms and state agencies are marginal in general. For urban businesses, about 90 per cent of the inputs are bought locally, while there is a difference in the countryside between undertakings in Long An, securing more from large cities, and Ha Tay, using sources in nearby towns. Price is still the most important criterion, in urban as well as rural areas, when selecting suppliers, but at least in urban areas, quality aspects are mentioned more often than they were in the 1991 survey. The methods used when selecting suppliers differ even within the respective areas; the enterprises in Hanoi and Ha Tay use existing personal contacts more while those in Haiphong and Long An undertake their own search efforts.

The number of enterprises with difficulties in locating sufficient quantities of inputs was lower in the 1997 than in the 1991 survey, both in the cities and in the countryside. The share with quality problems has decreased as well in the urban areas, but increased in the rural ones, especially in Ha Tay. The urban establishments with insufficient quantities buy somewhat more from state enterprises and less from households, use personal contacts more often, but do not search for suppliers very much on their own. The rural firms in the same position also use personal contacts to a greater extent, and concern themselves more about continuity in supply.

Taxes and Fees

An overwhelming majority of the enterprises pay taxes and the share of enterprises not paying any taxes at all would seem to have gone down somewhat in the 1990s. By and large the tax burden does not appear to be very heavy, the enterprises covered by the survey paid on average the equivalent of about 4 per cent of their turnover in tax. As might be expected, household enterprises are more lightly taxed than other, usually, larger enterprises. Similarly, enterprises in urban areas, not least in Ho Chi Minh City, tend to pay more than those in rural areas. Sales taxes account for between half and three-quarters of all taxes paid, followed by profit tax at 20 per cent. Most taxes are paid to the district authorities, while virtually nothing is paid to the national authorities. Contrary to popular belief, 'informal fees' do not appear to impose a very heavy burden on most of the enterprises. About 70 per cent of the enterprises stated that they had paid such fees in the past year, but the amounts paid were usually rather small; averaging 4 per cent of total turnover.

Generally speaking, the larger enterprises pay relatively more in such 'fees' than the smaller enterprises. Thus, payments by household enterprises were on the whole quite small, but for the other larger types of enterprises these fees typically amounted to more than 3 per cent of their turnover and 8–15 per cent of their value added. In a number of instances the payments were very high indeed. There was no correlation between the payment of taxes on the one hand and the payment of 'informal fees' on the other, which suggests that such fees are not paid as a means to avoid paying formal taxes. Indeed, it is difficult to discern any clear-cut pattern in the payment of 'informal fees', indicating that these fees are levied in a rather haphazard manner.

Labour and Employment

By the 1997 survey, the private manufacturing sector in Vietnam had clearly become a source of wage employment rather than self-employment. Wage workers engaged on a regular and usually full-time basis make up the core of the enterprises' workforce in both urban and rural areas. A vast majority of the workers are recruited from outside the owner household. In the urban areas this is the case with over 90 per cent of the workforce, except in the household enterprises, where the figure reaches 75 per cent. In the rural enterprises, too, an overwhelming majority of labourers originate from outside the household. The survey thus confirms the importance of the non-state manufacturing sector as a source of wage employment creation. A comparison with the results of the survey in 1991 shows that full-time, remunerated and non-household labour has become more important in all types of enterprises, both in urban and rural areas.

The average worker is male, between 20 and 40 years old, and has nine years of formal education. Women make up approximately a third of the workforce. The educational differences between the north and the south of the country noted in the 1991 survey had diminished by the 1997 survey, but the educational level of the workforce remains lower in the rural than in the urban areas. It should be noted that the private manufacturing sector provides employment opportunities also for those with primary but not secondary education, a group that is largely excluded from state employment. In the north of the country at least half of the workers have prior experience as production workers, suggesting that many of them were once employees in state enterprises. Even among rural enterprises, prior experience as a production worker tends to be more common than a background exclusively in agriculture. By contrast, a background exclusively in agriculture is rather uncommon, in both regions. On the positive side, this suggests that labour is not pushed into non-farm activities by an inability to make ends meet in agriculture. On the negative side, it should be noted that the evidently poor employment linkages between agriculture and rural industries imply a lack of dynamism and occupational flexibility in the rural labour market.

An examination of the wage structure yields a more or less expected pattern. Wages tend to be higher in the south than in the north and higher in urban than in rural areas. The wage differences between the various ownership forms of enterprises are rather small. In the urban areas, male wages are on average 12 per cent higher than those paid to women, while in the rural areas the wage gap is considerably larger. A comparison of the wage data from the 1991 survey and from the 1997 survey results in two important conclusions. First, there has been a substantial increase in real wages. Second, there has been a remarkable equalisation of wages. In the 1991 survey there was a large differential in wages between the north and the south, between rural and urban, as well as between men and women. By the 1997 survey these differences had diminished greatly, except for the rural–urban differences. Wage differentials have decreased not only across locations, ownership forms and gender, but also within each sub-category. Thus, there is strong evidence of a broad equalisation of wages within the non-state manufacturing sector. Compared to the situation in the 1991 survey, the proportion of enterprises granting social benefits to their workers has increased substantially. However, the picture is not uniform. Social benefits are more frequently granted by enterprises in Ho Chi Minh City than by those in the two northern cities and they remain primarily an urban phenomenon. In the rural areas, social benefits are the exception rather than the rule.

Friends and relatives play a large part in the recruitment of workers, primarily through personal recommendations or providing contacts. The role of labour exchanges or other formal means of labour mediation remains insignificant. Still, few enterprises complain of difficulties in finding skilled labour. Labour mobility appears on the whole to be rather low. However, the enterprises in Ho Chi Minh City and the private enterprises in general provide an exception to this rule as they register much higher rates of labour turnover. Job security, too, appears to be reasonably good. Few enterprises stated that any workers had been fired during the previous year.

Transformation in the Intersurvey Period

A comparison of the enterprises surveyed in 1991 and in 1997 reveals that the non-state manufacturing sector registered considerable growth and consolidation in terms of size, capital base, capital intensity and labour productivity in the 1990s and that this process has been accompanied by a sharp reduction in the regional differences in these regards. Since both surveys were stratified by ownership forms, it rules this factor out as the determinant. Besides, the transformation has been seen in all ownership forms. While the increased level of indebtedness might explain the higher asset base, the fact that this indebtedness is still of a relatively low order implies that this growth has been supported largely through own capital.

It is clear that the transformation of the non-state manufacturing sector has taken place through two parallel processes. First, through the appearance of new enterprises that are larger, more capital-intensive and with a higher labour productivity than existing enterprises. The second process has been the growth and transformation of existing enterprises.

In order to examine the first of these processes, the enterprises surveyed in 1997 were divided into two age groups: those established prior to 1991 and those established in 1991 or after. A comparison of these two groups shows that the newer enterprises generally are much larger than the older ones. The large difference in average size was found in all locations covered by the survey. In Hanoi, in particular, the newer enterprises were also found to be much more capital-intensive and to have a much higher labour productivity. The establishment of increasingly large enterprises has clearly been a main factor behind the general increase in the size of firms.

The increasing size of the newly established firms has been accompanied by a sharp increase in the share of private enterprises, shareholding and limited liability companies and a decrease in the share of co-operatives and partnership firms among the new establishments. However, this change in the ownership structure of new firms can only partly explain the increase in size. Among both household and private enterprises, the newer firms tend to be larger than the older ones, particularly in the urban areas. The newer household enterprises also tend to be considerably more capital-intensive than the older ones, suggesting that the difference between household enterprises and other types of enterprises in this regard is diminishing. The incidence of debts is higher among the younger firms than among the older, no doubt reflecting an increase in the availability of credit at the time of establishment. While this is a positive development, the rather small magnitude suggests that it can hardly have been a major factor behind the increased size of new enterprises.

There has been a pronounced shift in the type of people who set up enterprises. Whereas in the past most managers were recruited from the ranks of blue-collar workers, in the majority of firms that have appeared since 1991 the managers have previous experience in managerial, professional or administrative positions. The shift has been most pronounced in Hanoi, where two-thirds of the managers in the enterprises established since 1991 have come from the ranks of white-collar workers, as against only 21 per cent prior to 1991. This demonstrates that the transformation of the non-state manufacturing sector in the 1990s has not only been towards larger enterprises, but has also entailed a qualitative change, requiring managerial skills beyond those obtained at the shop floor.

An examination of the performance in the 1990s of the enterprises surveyed in 1991 shows that the vast majority of the enterprises fall into two distinct categories: those that have grown at a very rapid pace and those that have closed down or suffered a pronounced decline. Between a quarter and a third of the enterprises have grown in terms of value added by more than 10 per cent per year, while some 45-65 per cent of the enterprises have either closed down or declined by more than 2.5 per cent per year. Less than 15 per cent of the enterprises fall in between these two categories, having stagnated or registered only modest growth.

This distinct polarisation of enterprises into successes and failures is consistent with the impression that the 1990s was a decade of dramatic structural change amid growth. This environment offered great possibilities of growth for those astute and adaptable enough to exploit these opportunities, while it was merciless on the enterprises that failed to adapt and change with the times.

An examination of the development of enterprises by location supports the impression that these changes were more dramatic in the north than in the south. Thus, Hanoi had a higher proportion of fast-growing enterprises as well as a higher mortality rate than Ho Chi Minh City. On the whole, the enterprises in Hanoi stand out as much more dynamic than those in Ho Chi Minh City. The average annual growth rate among the enterprises in Hanoi was 12.5 per cent per year, compared to only 4.6 per cent for those in Ho Chi Minh City.

The highest proportion of fast-growing enterprises was found among the household enterprises, both in rural and in urban areas. This is an important and encouraging finding. The small household enterprises are often neglected in the statistics and in policy discussions. Yet, they make up the overwhelming majority of the non-state enterprises. This study shows conclusively that they are not only numerous, but also dynamic. A large number of them grow at such a rapid pace that the nature of their operations inevitably changes from being household-based to becoming dependent on hired labour. In view of the large number of such enterprises, it is clear that they constitute a main source of employment and income generation as well as of growth of production.

Another interesting finding is that quite a few of the co-operatives, particularly in the urban areas, have been successful. Thus, a fair share of the co-operatives, which as a group are often perceived to be moribund, have apparently managed to adapt to the more market-oriented environment and have prospered.

It is primarily the ability to accumulate capital at a very rapid pace that determines the survival and growth of the small-scale manufacturing enterprises. While this link may seem trivial at first, the nature of the link and its implications are not. First, the threshold in terms of capital accumulation for an enterprise to achieve fairly rapid and substantial growth is very high. In urban areas, even the enterprises growing by a modest 2.5 to 10 per cent per year had an average rate of capital accumulation of 23 per cent, while for the fast-growing enterprises the rate was a staggering 38 per cent. Second, as the alternative to rapid growth in most instances is decline and, sooner or later, closure, the ability to achieve very high rates of capital accumulation is a precondition not only for growth, but also for the long-term viability of the enterprise. Third, in the virtual absence of access to credits, accumulation of capital has to be self-generated and is therefore tantamount to very high profit margins. In other words, just making ends meet or achieving modest profits is not enough to ensure long-term viability of the enter-prise. The option of just muddling along does not exist for most enterprises.

The need for high rates of capital accumulation to achieve growth and to survive has been strongest in the north and in the rural areas, that is in the relatively less developed areas. It is in these areas that the rates of capital accumulation among the expanding enterprises as well as the mortality rates have been highest. Similarly, the rate of accumulation needed for growth has been higher for the household enterprises than for other types of enterprises. This pattern is in line with the conclusion that the rapid changes in the overall economic environment exercise strong pressure on existing enterprises to develop or succumb to market forces and that, as a consequence of increasing market integration, the pressure to restructure and improve efficiency and productivity has clearly been strongest in the less developed areas. In places like Hanoi and Ha Tay this pressure has resulted in a dramatic transformation of the surviving enterprises.

The picture of rapid change combined with a marked reduction in the differences in size, capital intensity, labour productivity and wages between enterprises of different types and in different areas, which emerged from the 1991 and 1997 enterprise surveys, is also reflected in the development of the cohort of enterprises surveyed in 1991. Thus, the very large differences in size, capital intensity and labour productivity revealed in 1991 had, among the surviving enterprises, been substantially reduced by 1997.

In view of the very high rates of capital accumulation among the growing enterprises, it comes as no surprise that growth has been capital- rather than labour-intensive and that growth has mainly been achieved through increased labour productivity rather than through increased employment. While the low employment elasticity of growth may be lamented from the point of view of employment generation, it would be wrong to see this as a failure in the development of the non-state manufacturing sector. It should be seen in the light of the fact that most enterprises in the 1991 survey, particularly in the north and in the rural areas, were very weak in respect to capital endowment, technology and productivity, and that severe doubts were raised about their ability to survive in an increasingly competitive environment. Restructuring, consolidation and increased efficiency and productivity remain the *sine qua non* for the survival and growth of these enterprises. While this results in improved labour productivity and wages, this approach is not compatible with highly labour-intensive growth.

Analysis of the Winners

The most important outcome of the study of the fast-growing enterprises is that there is no prototype of a successful enterprise. The fast-growing enterprises constitute a very broad range of units in terms of size and mode of operations. These enterprises have demonstrated an enormous amount of adjustment and change, reflecting their flexibility and adaptability in the period between the two surveys. Growth in value added has not only been accompanied by greater quantities of assets, employment, etc.; more importantly, it has occurred along with changes in the entire mode and level of functioning of the enterprises. Specifically, this changing (or changed) face of rural enterprises is a huge milestone in the transformation of rural industry in Vietnam. The performances of household and co-operative enterprises have not fallen short of other non-state forms. There is ample evidence that urban–rural, intra-rural, intra-urban and north–south differences have been narrowed down, although not eliminated, not only in terms of assets, investment and employment; but also in qualitative terms like mechanisation, production flexibility and so on. On the whole, the six years between 1991 and 1997 have seen major changes in the character of fast-growing enterprises.

In the period between the two surveys, enterprises have changed ownership forms, lines of activity and location, more noticeably among urban units. The importance of the enterprise to the owner-households has increased enormously, particularly among rural units. Annual average asset growth rates have stood at 56 per cent for rural and 38 per cent for urban units; about 66 per cent of the rural units shifted from use of hand tools to power driven machinery. Wage employment, production flexibility, continuity of operations and capacity utilisation have all increased, for both urban and rural units. The adaptability is seen best among forward linkages of urban enterprises, in terms of both categories and location of buyers. Ha Tay in the rural sample has seen a major transformation as well. High asset growth rates and reliance on firm-generated revenue stand out as the most common features among fast-growing enterprises. Entrepreneurial skill has, no doubt, been a very decisive factor behind all these changes. These entrepreneurs are behind the survival and growth of the fittest enterprises in the private sector in Vietnam.

Analysis of the Closures

Mortality rates among resurveyed enterprises have been highest in Haiphong, followed by Hanoi and Ho Chi Minh City. Inability to sell at profit was the most common reason for closure and most entrepreneurs have continued self-employment in other lines of business after the closure of the unit. Entrepreneurs over the age of 50 were the prevalent category and they mainly owned household and private enterprises started in the late 1980s, in both regions. The lifespan of the enterprises seems to be limited to the lifespan of the owner. There were distinct scale differences between urban and rural units, but rural units were more homogeneous. A serious factor common to both locations was the near absence of external credit usage, both at start-up and during operative years. In terms of linkages, urban and rural units behaved similarly in 1990, with very strong linkages to urban and very weak linkages to rural areas. Since co-operatives formed a major percentage, the urban closure sample had very strong links to the state sector.

There is an overall distinction between two sets of closures (excluding co-operatives) in both urban and rural areas in the 1991 survey: the first set comprises of small household enterprises, with little or no labour, who work close to full capacity and cater largely to a local market. The other set is of larger enterprises, mainly non-household forms, with a slightly larger geographical reach and better modes of operation. In the rural areas, it appears that the small household enterprises have been basically supplemental income sources; hence, with the advent of greater competition, these entrepreneurs (mainly older than 50 years) have ceased trading.

Irrespective of size, location and type of enterprise, firms have had to depend on high rates of internally generated capital, which in turn emphasised the need for strong output markets. With the relative ease of entry and exit into the entrepreneurial sector and a passive government, there have been too many entrepreneurs investing their savings on mainly household consumption goods, trying to sell in cities, with the result that too much competition has driven away a lot of them, irrespective of size. This volatility, which is unfortunately not uncommon to transition economies like Vietnam, is inevitable to maintain the presence of only the most efficient enterprises.

Policy Implications

The methodology of the two surveys offers some unique perspectives for the study of non-state manufacturing enterprises in Vietnam. The six years between the two surveys have seen a whole range of dramatic changes, that could only be captured by the re-survey of enterprises in 1997 in addition to repeating the survey for a second set of enterprises. From among the whole series of findings and analyses, certain themes emerge, which form a basis for formulating policies aimed at fostering a healthy, non-state manufacturing sector in the future.

Some of the main themes may be described as follows. First, the 1990s have seen a rapid development towards market integration in Vietnam, with the result that the differences between north and south Vietnam, urban and rural areas and intra-urban and intra-rural areas have narrowed down considerably with regard to enterprise size, efficiency and wages. Second, there continues to be an unparalleled reliance on own capital and a near lack of external capital sources both for establishment as well as operation of the enterprises. This tendency is clearly borne out by the 1991 survey, the 1997 survey of 'new' enterprises, as well as the analyses of winners and closures. The need for capital accumulation, on the one hand, has been very high and the reliance on own capital on the other hand, has been equally high. This has been common to all enterprises, irrespective of ownership form or location. Next, all the studies clearly show that dynamism and flexibility have been widespread, the household and co-operative enterprises being no exception. This is, perhaps, one of the most important outcomes from the repeat survey. The small household enterprises are often neglected in the statistics and policy discussions, as a minor periphery of the non-state sector. However, we have seen that the highest proportion of fast-growing enterprises was found among household enterprises, both in rural and in urban areas, and they also provide a major source of wage employment. Which leads to the conclusion that ownership forms *per se* do not determine survival and growth. In the light of the above, a few basic policy conclusions may be drawn from all the studies, most of which concern in one way or another the need to promote flexibility.

Policies to encourage new start-ups and facilitate closures of less successful firms

The studies clearly document that the establishment of new enterprises and the closure of the less successful existing enterprises are key components in the overall development and transformation of the non-state manufacturing sector. The establishment of new enterprises has been a main factor behind the growth in size and strength of the enterprises as well as the most important source of employment creation. The passivity of the government sector stands out clearly in the analyses of winners and closures. A main policy conclusion must therefore be to remove, as far as possible, bureaucratic, administrative or other obstacles to the establishment of new enterprises, as well as to provide a legal and administrative framework for an orderly closure of enterprises. Apart from reviewing and revising existing legislation, it is also very important that authorities concerned in the field assume a truly facilitating rather than obstructive or indifferent attitude to the local establishment of enterprises.

Facilitate endogenous growth and graduation into new ownership forms

Endogenous growth of enterprises plays a vital role in the development of the sector as a whole. The growth of the, initially small, household enterprises stands out as particularly important and noteworthy. It is important that such growth is as far as possible facilitated and not obstructed by administrative barriers. It is very clear from the winners that enterprises have used various means to stay in operation and grow, with changes in ownership forms, location and nature of activity. In this context, there would seem to be a need to review the relevance of the present division of enterprises into different ownership forms and the criteria used for this division, and, in particular, to ensure that enterprises can change from one ownership form to another with a minimum of bureaucratic hassle. The most urgent issue would seem to be to facilitate household enterprises to change into 'more advanced' ownership forms. However, it is also important to ensure that the procedures for transforming private and co-operative enterprises into limited liability companies are made as easy as possible. The fiscal legislation and policies also need to be reviewed and streamlined to ensure that they do not discriminate against certain types of enterprises or provide disincentives to change the ownership form of an enterprise.

Government support for flexibility

There is also scope for the government and local authorities to play a proactive role in promoting flexibility. There is an increasing need for well-functioning and efficient labour market institutions, capable of playing an effective role in the mediation of labour as well as in providing short-term training and re-training of workers. There is also likely to be a need to offer training in rudimentary business administration and entrepreneurship to managers and owners of household enterprises in order to facilitate the growth and development of these enterprises, as the knowledge needed to run a 'larger' enterprise in many ways differs from that needed to run a small household enterprise. A case can also be made for providing consultancy and other services to small-scale enterprises locally, particularly in the field of marketing information and more general business intelligence.

Taxation policies

The very high rates of capital accumulation needed to ensure not only growth, but also the long-term viability of an enterprise, have implications for the taxation of the enterprises. An obvious conclusion is that profits should not be taxed as long as they are reinvested in the enterprise, but should only be taxed once they withdrawn from the enterprise.

Promote efficient financial sector

The studies show that credits play an increasing and positive, but still limited role for this sector. While there is clearly still a great need to expand and improve the credit facilities for the non-state manufacturing enterprises, there is a danger in regarding credits as a panacea. As a policy instrument, increased availability of credit has its limits and is only effective as part of a more comprehensive policy package. Accumulated own capital is likely to remain the main source of funding both for the start-up and expansion of businesses. First, the high mortality rate among new firms implies that lending to new small enterprises will inevitably be a high-risk business and demand premium interest rates. Second, the very high rates of capital accumulation needed for growth cannot be secured on a sustainable basis primarily through credits, but can best be achieved through a judicious mix of own capital and loans. Rather than devising schemes for subsidised credits to small-scale enterprises, the best long-term service to this sector would no doubt be the promotion of the development of an efficient and comprehensive financial sector, accessible to small-scale enterprises and offering credit on a strictly non-discriminatory and commercial basis. Removal of all government guarantees for loans taken by state enterprises would, by itself, be a major step in this direction.

Do not try to pick winners

The present study as well as more in-depth studies on successful enterprises and on enterprises that have closed down, based on the cohort of enterprises surveyed in 1991 and in 1997, reveal the extreme difficulty of identifying individual determinants for the success or failure of an enterprise. A main conclusion must be that it would be both futile and counter-productive to try to pick 'winners' in advance, either with regard to branches of industry, ownership forms or individual enterprises on the basis of predetermined criteria. This is a strong argument to counter discriminatory policies which target preselected types of enterprises and, instead, to focus on universally applied policies and measures.

Regional policies

However, a case can be made for one type of non-universal policies, namely regional policies. The marked reduction in the regional differences in enterprise characteristics and performance – with regard to capital intensity, efficiency, productivity, etc. – which has accompanied the overall transformation of the non-state manufacturing sector in the 1990s, is obviously a most welcome development. However, it puts the enterprises in the less developed and rural areas under an enormous pressure to restructure and increase their efficiency. The case of Ha Tay clearly shows both the difficulties as well as the potential benefits of this process. However, while Ha Tay today stands out as something of a success story, there are obviously many other areas, not covered by the survey, which are in a more disadvantaged position and where the prospects for successful development are far from certain. A strong case can therefore be made for policy measures designed to facilitate the restructuring, strengthening and overall development of the small-scale manufacturing sector in less developed, primarily rural areas, particularly as such policies would work in tandem with an ongoing spontaneous overall development of market integration. While it is beyond the scope of the present study to provide a blueprint for such policies, any plan needs to focus on such issues as: improved physical infrastructure, particularly electrification; improved credit facilities and credits earmarked for specific regions, but not for specific branches or types of enterprises; fiscal incentives; assistance with marketing information and provision of other extension services; and incentives to local authorities to facilitate the development of local enterprises.

Index of Figures and Tables

Note that all references are to figure and table numbers, not to page numbers. Generally, further discussion on data found in a figure or table is located in the adjacent text. (F = Figure, T = Table)